Evidence Law
in the Trial Process

The West Legal Studies Series

Your options keep growing with West Legal Studies

Each year our list continues to offer you more options for every area of the law to meet your course or on-the-job reference requirements. We now have over 140 titles from which to choose in the following areas:

Administrative Law	Family Law
Alternative Dispute Resolution	Federal Taxation
Bankruptcy	Intellectual Property
Business Organizations/Corporations	Introduction to Law
Civil Litigation and Procedure	Introduction to Paralegalism
CLA Exam Preparation	Law Office Management
Client Accounting	Law Office Procedures
Computer in the Law Office	Legal Research, Writing, and Analysis
Constitutional Law	Legal Terminology
Contract Law	Paralegal Employment
Criminal Law and Procedure	Real Estate Law
Document Preparation	Reference Materials
Environmental Law	Torts and Personal Injury Law
Ethics	Will, Trusts, and Estate Administration

You will find unparalleled, practical support

Each text is augmented by instructor and student supplements to ensure the best learning experience possible. We also offer custom publishing and other benefits such as West's Student Achievement Award. In addition, our sales representatives are ready to provide you with dependable service.

We want to hear from you

Our best contributions for improving the quality of our books and instructional materials is feedback from the people who use them. If you have a question, concern, or observation about any of our materials, or you have a product proposal or manuscript, we want to hear from you. Please contact your local representative or write us at the following address:

West Legal Studies, 3 Columbia Circle, P.O. Box 15015, Albany, NY 12212-5015

For additional information point your browser at
www.westlegalstudies.com

West Legal Studies

an imprint of Delmar Publishers

an International Thomson Publishing company I(T)P®

Evidence Law
in the Trial Process

Margaret T. Stopp, J.D.

University of West Florida

WEST LEGAL STUDIES

an International Thomson Publishing company I T P ®

Albany • Bonn • Boston • Cincinnati • Detroit • London • Madrid
Melbourne • Mexico City • Minneapolis/St. Paul • New York • Pacific Grove
Paris • San Francisco • Singapore • Tokyo • Toronto • Washington

Delmar Staff

Publisher: Susan Simpfenderfer
Acquisitions Editor: Joan Gill
Developmental Editor: Rhonda Dearborn

Production Manager: Wendy Troeger
Production Editor: Laurie A. Boyce
Marketing Manager: Katherine Hans

COPYRIGHT © 1999 Delmar. West Legal Studies is an imprint of Delmar, a division of Thomson Learning. The Thomson Learning™ is a registered trademark used herein under license.

Printed in the United States of America
6 7 8 9 10 XXX 06 05 04

For more information, contact Delmar, 3 Columbia Circle, PO Box 15015, Albany, NY 12212-0515; or find us on the World Wide Web at http://www.westlegalstudies.com

International Division List

Asia
Thomson Learning
60 Albert Street, #15-01
Albert Complex
Singapore 189969
Tel: 65 336 6411
Fax: 65 336 7411

Australia/New Zealand:
Nelson/Thomson Learning
102 Dodds Street
South Melbourne, Victoria 3205
Australia
Tel: 61 39 685 4111
Fax: 61 39 685 4199

Latin America:
Thomson Learning
Seneca, 53
Colonia Polanco
11560 Mexico D.F. Mexico
Tel: 525-281-2906
Fax: 525-281-2656

Spain:
Thomson Learning
Calle Magallanes, 25
28015-MADRID
ESPANA
Tel: 34 91 446 33 50
Fax: 34 91 445 62 18

Japan:
Thomson Learning
Palaceside Building 5F
1-1-1 Hitotsubashi, Chiyoda-ku
Tokyo 100 0003 Japan
Tel: 813 5218 6544
Fax: 813 5218 6551

UK/Europe/Middle East
Thomson Learning
Berkshire House
168-173 High Holborn
London
WC1V 7AA United Kingdom
Tel: 44 171 497 1422
Fax: 44 171 497 1426

Canada:
Nelson/Thomson Learning
1120 Birchmount Road
Scarborough, Ontario
Canada M1K 5G4
Tel: 416-752-9100
Fax: 416-752-8102

Library of Congress Cataloging-in-Publication Data
Stopp, Margaret T.
    Evidence law in the trial process / Margaret T. Stopp.
        p.   cm.
    Includes bibliographical references and index.
    ISBN 0-314-12909-X
    1. Evidence (Law)—United States. 2. Trial practice—United States.
3. Legal assistants—United States—Handbooks, manuals, etc.
I. Title.
KF8935.Z9S75   1999   98-42163
347.73'6—dc21   CIP

CONTENTS

PREFACE

A NOTE TO INSTRUCTORS

This book is a product of the author's experience in the classroom—teaching evidence law to undergraduate paralegal, criminal justice, and prelaw majors for ten years—and in the practice of law.

Evidence law cannot be taught in a theoretical vacuum. The entire trial process must be understood. That process begins with the event that is the origin of the dispute, whether it is contract negotiations or a criminal act. The investigation of the case starts there.

Students can gain a better understanding of evidence law by attending one or more jury trials in the local community and preparing a report related to evidentiary matters covered in the trial. This exercise allows students to correlate what was observed in the courtroom with what is discussed in the classroom. The experience could prove invaluable.

While studying the differences between the Federal Rules of Evidence and state rules, the students should have a copy of the state rules where they are attending school. Or the instructor may choose to provide the students with copies of only the state rules that differ from the federal rules. The major differences are integrated into the discussions in this text in a way that should raise the awareness of the students regarding the differences between state and federal practices.

The "Illustration" features in the book are based on case law. These descriptions of true cases are more effective than hypothetical illustrations that may or may not demonstrate how the evidence rules actually operate.

Throughout the book, excerpts of cases are presented in the "Applications," followed by questions to help the student focus on the evidentiary issues explored by the courts. Thus students can see how real evidentiary issues were resolved. The questions also serve as a springboard to class discussions.

The "Exercises" give students the opportunity to apply the Federal Rules of Evidence and state rules to fact patterns. They also highlight areas of differences between federal and state rules.

In order to facilitate the learning process, terms are defined in the margins where they are discussed and in a glossary. Rules discussed in a chapter are listed at the end of the chapter as well as being displayed in the text at the point of discussion. Each chapter ends with a summary, then a list of "Checkpoints" that outline the content of the chapter.

The *Instructor's Manual* that accompanies the text suggests the answers to the Class Discussion Questions and the Exercises. It also contains a sample syllabus and sample examination questions.

A NOTE TO STUDENTS

Issues related to evidence law may first appear at trial, but those issues have their origins at the time the evidence was created. In other words, the trial process actually begins with the event that led to the trial. It is when the dispute arises that evidence, or proof, first emerges. The investigator gathers that evidence, and the paralegal helps the attorney prepare for trial by marshalling the evidence and dealing with issues related to its admissibility. This text emphasizes the importance of the investigation stage in both civil and criminal cases.

Read about trials in your local community, as well as those that receive national attention. Apply what you learn in the classroom to interpreting what you read about actual court cases. Putting classroom information together with news reports of current cases will help in your understanding of the rules of evidence.

Work through the Applications and Exercises assigned by your instructor to test your understanding of the application of evidence law. When preparing for examinations, revisit the chapter summaries and Checkpoints. These features of the book are meant to assist you in the learning process. The glossary is useful when you come across a word previously defined in the margin of another chapter and you need to refresh your memory as to its meaning.

INTERNET LEARNING RESOURCES

To learn more about the cases that have captured national attention, visit Internet sites that provide details of the trials. Court TV Online is one site. It often follows current trials as well as maintaining files on older cases. The Internet address is **www.courttv.com/**.

Oral arguments before the United States Supreme Court are available on the Oyez cite. The Internet address is **http://oyez.nwu.edu/**. State high courts also may have Web sites where oral arguments before the state's highest court are available. One example is Florida and the JOSHUA site. The Internet address is **http://justice.courts.state.fl.us/**.

Surf the Internet for other sites related to trials and evidentiary issues. However, always determine the creator of the site so you can evaluate the credibility of the information you find online.

The Internet offers the legal professional a rich source of information about companies and products that might be useful in preparing for trial, including where to obtain expert witnesses. Take advantage of this fast-growing resource.

The evidence rules are important to civil and criminal trials. With an understanding of the rules, you will be a better prepared paralegal, law enforcement officer, or law school student.

ACKNOWLEDGMENTS

I must first acknowledge my husband Harry and my daughter Victoria, since they have so graciously put up with my writing effort. Not far behind them are my friends and family, who have patiently listened to my frustrations and triumphs related to the writing of the book. My colleagues and students at the University of West Florida have supported me throughout the creative process. I thank them as well.

My first editors at West Publishing, Elizabeth Hannan and Patty Bryant, encouraged me to write the book and got me through the early chapter reviews. Rhonda Dearborn, the editor from Delmar who took over the project, was helpful throughout the final revision and publication stage. Maggie Jarpey gets my thanks for her work as the copyeditor.

I also want to express my deep appreciation to the following paralegal educators whose detailed and careful reviews were invaluable to me in revising the first draft of the book:

C. Suzanne Bailey
Auburn University at Montgomery

Paula Hardiman
Community College of Rhode Island

Melinda G. Hess, J.D.
College of St. Mary

David C. Jarratt, M.A., J.D.
Concordia University, Wisconsin

Yvon J.R.J. Le Blanc
Arlington Court Reporting College

Lynn B. Mares
University of Oklahoma
Legal Assistant Education

Joy O'Donnell
Pima Country Community College

Debbie Steele
Central Piedmont Community College

Margaret T. Stopp

TABLE OF CASES

Overview of the Trial Process

UNDERSTANDING THE MODERN TRIAL PROCESS

In order to understand the modern trial process, it is helpful to understand its historical and theoretical underpinnings. In the United States, the **trial process** includes both the trial and preparation for trial and is part of an **adversarial system** that has developed over the centuries.

History

When William the Conqueror invaded England in 1066, he grafted his way of settling disputes onto the system already in place. That system was based on the use of **ordeals**, which required the survival of physical exposure to fire or water, according to divine will. William introduced confined combat, in which men who had a dispute would fight each other according to preordained rules. This was a contest where the men were tested and the physical winner then exacted compensation or demanded punishment of the losing party. God was no longer the primary determinant in settling disputes; men were.

trial process The actions taken to prepare for trial, and the trial itself, for the purpose of determining and enforcing legal rights of the opposing parties.

adversarial system The system of resolving legal conflicts where each party is represented by an attorney who argues the client's position by presenting evidence with the intent to establish the legal rights of the client.

The Modern Trial

Over time this form of physical combat became symbolic, and parties were represented by advocates who argued to judges and juries on their behalf. However, the underlying concept remained the same—confined combat according to preordained rules. This idea is still the heart of the adversarial system today. Each party is represented by an attorney who argues the client's position. It is not a truth-finding system, but one of advocacy for the client and "may the best-represented party win."

The modern trial, then, involves parties represented by attorneys whose role it is to present the best possible case on behalf of their clients to the **trier of fact**, which is usually a jury. The goal is not a literal search for truth, but a presentation of evidence by opposing parties through their attorneys. The **evidence** utilized is that which best serves the interests and goals of the individual party. Evidence includes the testimony of witnesses as well as the presentation of tangible items, the purpose of which is to prove a party's contention. The evidence offered by each of the parties is challenged directly by the opposing party through impeachment, with the intent of discrediting the facts offered by the opponent. The skill and degree of preparedness of each party's attorney thus has a tremendous impact on the picture painted for the jury. Consequently, the ability and competence of paralegals and investigators become a critical factor in helping the trial attorney present the strongest possible case, which includes capitalizing on the weaknesses of the opponent's case.

The judge makes decisions with regard to **matters of law**, sometimes referred to as *questions of law,* which are the disputed legal contentions raised by the parties to the litigation. For example, one matter of law settled by the judge is what evidence the jury will be allowed to hear and see at trial. The judge is guided in determining matters of law by the rules of procedure, the rules of evidence, and prior decided cases.

The jury decides **matters of fact**, sometimes referred to as *questions of fact,* which are the issues related to whether and how the disputed event occurred. The judge determines what the jury will hear and see with regard to the disputed event (as a matter of law), and the jury decides what happened based on this information (matters of fact). The jury is the trier of fact, unless a jury is not used in a case. Then the judge determines matters of law, and the judge is also the trier of fact.

For the purposes of this book, the assumption is that the cases are tried with a jury, so the "trier of fact" refers to the jury unless otherwise stated. The respective roles of judge and jury are covered in more detail in Chapter 3.

PROCEDURAL RULES AND RULES OF EVIDENCE

Rules of procedure and rules of evidence, in both federal and state courts, supply the methods and form for carrying on a lawsuit.

Rules of Procedure

The civil, criminal, and appellate procedure rules govern the way in which the trial process moves forward, from the point where a complaint is filed or a

ordeal A ritual where disputes were settled with a person being subjected to some peril as a test, with the outcome regarded as the consequence of divine intervention.

trier of fact In a trial, the person or group of persons with the responsibility of deciding which party should prevail; the jury in a jury trial and the judge in a nonjury trial.

evidence Various forms of proof submitted to a trier of fact in court in order to support a party's claims or defenses in a lawsuit.

matters of law Also called *questions of law,* these are the disputed legal contentions raised by the parties during the litigation process, as determined by the judge.

matters of fact Also called *questions of fact,* these are the occurrence or non-occurrence of an event, as determined by a trier of fact.

criminal defendant enters the legal system, through the procedure for appealing a judgment entered at the conclusion of a trial. Once an action is initiated, **discovery** takes place, where each side learns more about the opponent's evidence. Then the **pretrial conference** is held, where the parties define what is actually in dispute and therefore will be the focus of the evidence at trial.

Motions in limine are utilized by parties to challenge evidence that the opponent may want to offer during trial. The paralegal can help in the preparation of motions or in contesting the opponent's motions by researching the law and marshaling the necessary evidence relevant to the subject of the motion. A motion in limine is a request by a party to the judge for a determination of whether certain contested evidence will be admissible at trial. The judge's **order** is the decision by the judge as to whether the moving party should prevail on the motion. The judge's decision is reached after a hearing and, in federal court, after submission of a memorandum of law supporting or opposing the motion.

Rules of Evidence

The rules of evidence are similar in federal courts and state courts, and they share the same purpose, which is to offer a framework for conducting the trial process (Figure 1-1).

Helpful reference books containing the court rules applying to federal and state court actions are the West publications of *Federal Civil Judicial Procedure and Rules* and the state rules of court for both federal courts and state courts. These books are published regularly as revisions are made in the rules. Attorneys often have an ongoing subscription to receive the books as they are updated.

The rules of court have the power of law. Attorneys, paralegals, and investigators must be familiar with all of the pertinent rules of court in order to

discovery The pretrial process where the parties to litigation learn about information held by the opponent, which includes disclosure of facts, documents, and related matters. Discovery is governed by rules of procedure.

pretrial conference A meeting with the trial judge and the parties to a lawsuit before the trial begins. Its purpose is to define the matters at issue and in need of resolution at trial.

motion in limine A request for a court order, often before trial, to exclude reference at trial to anticipated evidence because the evidence allegedly violates a rule of law or a rule of evidence or procedure.

order A direction or command issued by a judge on a matter related to a lawsuit.

FIGURE 1-1

Court rules provide a framework for conducting the trial process.

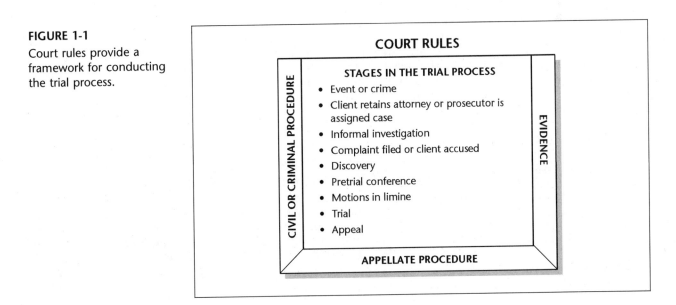

COURT RULES

CIVIL OR CRIMINAL PROCEDURE

STAGES IN THE TRIAL PROCESS

- Event or crime
- Client retains attorney or prosecutor is assigned case
- Informal investigation
- Complaint filed or client accused
- Discovery
- Pretrial conference
- Motions in limine
- Trial
- Appeal

EVIDENCE

APPELLATE PROCEDURE

effectively represent clients. As an example, the Federal Rules of Civil Procedure govern the procedural progress of a lawsuit from the filing of a complaint, through discovery, pretrial motions, pretrial conferences, and through the trial itself.

Similarly, in a criminal case, the Federal Rules of Criminal Procedure govern the prosecution of a defendant by the government, supplying the manner of proceeding to the defense attorney and prosecutor from preliminary matters, to the trial, and through the verdict.

The Federal Rules of Appellate Procedure usually apply after the trial has concluded and the party who lost at trial, the **appellant**, decides to take the case to the appropriate appellate court, and possibly to the United States Supreme Court. The **appellee** is the party that wins at the trial court and opposes the appellant in the appeal.

At common law, the appellant was referred to as the *plaintiff in error* and the appellee as the *defendant in error.* These two terms often are used in older cases that may be helpful precedents when researching a current legal problem. When research is done to determine the applicability of a rule to a current problem, it must be remembered the American legal system follows the traditions of a **common law** system, and the rules of court must be read in conjunction with case law. The American common law system has its origins in the English system, in which judicial decisions form the basis for law. However, in America today, law is found both in statutes and in case law, so the two sources of law are essential to the legal system.

For learning more about the applicability of the procedural rules in a particular situation, annotated compilations of the rules are useful, as are *American Jurisprudence* and state encyclopedias, practice books from various publishers, and continuing legal education materials. These sources incorporate the text of the rules and relevant case law.

The civil and criminal procedural rules are not the subject of this book. However, they need to be kept in mind in the trial process because the rules of evidence do not operate in a vacuum. The evidence rules are only one set of rules that govern the trial process. The trial process is like a piece of fabric woven with the threads of all of the rules of court, the evidence presented for each case, and the relevant rules of law that apply. Other threads in this fabric include the social setting of the case and the personalities of the participants, as well as the culture of the American people and, in particular, of the members of the community where the trial takes place.

appellant The party who brings the matter to the reviewing court. At common law, the appellant was known as the *plaintiff in error.*

appellee The party who argues to the reviewing court against setting aside a judgment. At common law, the appellee was known as the *defendant in error.*

common law A system of law that originated in England and was adopted in America, based on the decisions of judges, which generally are followed in settling subsequent similar disputes.

THE TRIAL PROCESS

For a coherent understanding of the rules of evidence, they must be placed in the framework of the trial process. The trial process is not a sterile environment of rules dispassionately applied. Rather, the trial process remains confined combat, in which the goal is to defeat the opponent using every available means, including the rules of court and the social baggage that the participants bring to the contest. The evidence rules are a mechanism in this trial process that allow the coherent presentation of the needs and desires of the parties to the jury.

The legal professionals involved in the trial process, the attorneys with their paralegals and investigators, and the judge who is the overseer of the process, must be familiar with all of the rules of court. This text concentrates on the rules of evidence as only one thread in the fabric of the trial process, a thread that can mean the difference between winning and losing a case. A trial attorney, whether in a civil or criminal case, can utilize the talents of paralegals and investigators in weaving threads of evidence into a fabric strong enough to stand the slashing by opponents at trial. The fibers forming the threads of evidence are created long before the actual trial begins, in the investigation and preparation stages where paralegals and investigators play an important role.

With this in mind, the paralegal can better understand the importance of matters preliminary to the trial itself, and how critical it is to properly prepare evidence for presentation to the jury. The trial actually begins when the client comes to see the attorney for advice on a civil or criminal matter, the underlying events often having already occurred. For the prosecutor, the trial process actually begins with the commission of the crime and the initial investigation by law enforcement.

The paralegal and investigator can assist the attorney in preparing for trial by understanding that the trial process begins with the initial event or crime. It is from this point that the fiber for the threads of evidence is spun into the fabric of a coherent tale that will be presented to the jury and to the judge at trial.

Even though fewer than 5 percent of the 90 million cases filed in state courts reach the trial stage, 4.5 million cases is a significant number of cases.[1] And regardless of the trial statistics, the settlement of civil cases and effective plea agreements in criminal cases occur where there has been attention to detail and careful preparation of a case.

ELEMENTS OF CIVIL AND CRIMINAL ACTIONS

The manner in which the threads are best woven for the most compelling story for the jury and the judge is determined by the loom on which the threads are attached. The two possible looms are the frameworks for either a civil action or a criminal action (Figure 1-2).

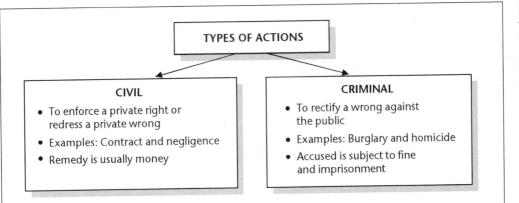

FIGURE 1-2
The framework for the trial process may be of the civil or the criminal type.

civil action Cases involving persons or entities who desire to enforce a private right or to redress a private wrong.

plaintiff The person or entity initiating a civil action.

defendant In a civil case, the person or entity disputing the action initiated by a plaintiff. In a criminal case, it is the party who is the accused.

remedy In a civil action, that which redresses a wrong or enforces a right.

verdict The opinion of the trier of fact as to who should prevail at trial.

judgment A judicial determination of the rights of the parties before the court.

contract An agreement between parties where the law recognizes a duty and gives a remedy for a breach of duty.

consideration In contract law, something of value given in return for a performance or promise to perform.

Civil Actions

A **civil action** involves persons or entities who become involved in a dispute where there is a desire to enforce a private right or to redress a private wrong. The parties are called **plaintiff** and **defendant**. The **remedy** sought may be money or injunctive relief or the severing of a legal relationship. The jury renders a **verdict**, which is followed by a **judgment** entered by the trial court judge. The judgment confers liability, or fault, on one of the parties and declares the remedy for the prevailing party.

Two types of civil actions that will be the basis for most of the examples used throughout this text are based on contract law and tort law, especially personal injury cases. The basic elements of those types of civil actions are reviewed here so that the relationship between the law and the presentation of the evidence is clear.

Contract Law

Contract law generally involves enforcement by the courts of promises between parties, who may be individuals or entities, when the elements for a legally binding contract are established. Lawsuits based on a contract were 18 percent of the caseload of state courts of general jurisdiction in 1993, when 20 million civil and domestic relations cases were filed.[2] That percentage translates into approximately 3.6 million cases, meaning that a significant number of attorneys have clients with lawsuits based on contract law.

The *Restatement of Contracts, 2d.* defines a **contract** as a promise or a set of promises for the breach of which the law gives a remedy, or the performance of which the law in some way recognizes as a duty.[3] To prove a contract meets the requirements of this definition and is legally enforceable, a party must provide evidence that the elements of a binding contract exist (Figure 1-3). There must be an agreement between competent parties for which there is consideration. The agreement consists of the *offer* and the *acceptance* (which will be defined shortly), showing that the parties had a meeting of the minds on the nature of the agreement. **Consideration** is something of value given in return for performance or a promise of performance, indicating bargaining between the parties.

FIGURE 1-3

To be legally enforceable, certain elements of a contract must be proven.

ELEMENTS OF AN ACTION BASED ON CONTRACT

- Agreement: offer and acceptance
- Capacity
- Consideration
- Breach
- Damages

A plaintiff who claims the existence of a legal relationship that rises to the level of a contract must first establish that there was an agreement. The agreement is broken down into offer and acceptance. The **offer** is a proposal by one party to another. The **acceptance** is when the other party assents to the proposal. In other words, there is bargaining between the parties, with the result that there is a meeting of the minds. This agreement may be oral or written, and can involve an uncomplicated transaction or a complex array of transactions. Contracts may be (1) expressly stated by the parties or (2) implied from the circumstances surrounding the bargaining.

Contracts underlie a variety of relationships, such as employment, buying and selling of goods, rental of equipment and vehicles, sale and leasing of property, and lending of money. Sometimes the contract rules governing these relationships are refined and codified in statutes such as the Uniform Commercial Code. Even then, the general common law principles of contract law can remain relevant.

There are rules as to who can enter into contracts. Parties to contracts may be persons or entities, such as corporations and partnerships. But they must have the **capacity** to enter into an agreement—that is, the ability to understand and carry out the terms of the agreement, not impaired by age or mental ability.

A defendant who is being sued based on an alleged contract can raise certain defenses. Someone who has not attained the age of legal majority or who is mentally incompetent is protected by the law; contracts entered into by such parties may be set aside. And if the defendant can provide facts showing that the parties never had an agreement because of fraud, mistake, misrepresentation, duress, or undue influence, the plaintiff's claim fails.

A lawsuit based on a breach of contract is traced to the time the alleged agreement is negotiated between the parties. The attorney must review the facts surrounding the initiation of the contract between the parties, as well as the occurrences after that time in order to adequately represent the client in the matter. The investigation of the facts and circumstances must be made with the legal requirements for a valid and binding contract in mind.

Assuming the subject matter of the contract is legal, the elements of a contract include an agreement (offer and acceptance), consideration, and capacity. The elements form a single unit, but the individual parts must be supported by a minimum of evidence. If the plaintiff cannot present a minimum of evidence to support each element of a contract, the plaintiff has not established a *prima facie* case, and the defendant is not required to disprove anything that the plaintiff has presented. The plaintiff's lawsuit may be dismissed before the defendant presents any evidence to disprove the plaintiff's case. A ***prima facie* case** is one where a party presents enough evidence to meet the legal requirements of a cause of action, so the party will prevail if the opposing party fails to contradict the evidence or present a cogent defense.

Assuming that the plaintiff establishes a *prima facie* case, the defendant then must present evidence to contradict the evidence offered by the plaintiff or present evidence which constitutes a defense to contract formation. Some defenses are lack of capacity, mistake, fraud, misrepresentation, duress, undue influence, and illegality. The defenses must be supported by evidence. An

offer In contract law, where a party manifests a willingness to enter into a bargain with the intent of securing the assent of another party.

acceptance In contract law, the consent to the terms of an offer.

capacity In contract law, the mental ability to enter into a contract.

***prima facie* case** A party presents enough evidence to meet the legal requirements of a cause of action, so the party can prevail unless the opposing party contradicts the evidence or presents a cogent defense.

example would be testimony that the defendant is only 15 years old as evidence to support the defense of lack of capacity.

The defendant may also offer evidence that contradicts the evidence relied on by the plaintiff to support any element of the contract. Thus the plaintiff's case will be destroyed if the defendant's evidence is accepted by the jury instead. By **impeaching** the testimony of the plaintiff's witnesses, the defendant's evidence can make the plaintiff's witnesses look like liars or people who for some other reason should not be believed.

Tort Law

Tort law encompasses actions based on a civil wrong committed by one party against another. A party can be a person or an entity. Although tort law includes intentional acts, negligence, and strict liability, the emphasis here is on negligence, because litigation often is the result of a negligent act. The most common acts of negligence involve automobile accidents. Lawsuits as a result of automobile accidents constituted 60 percent of all tort filings in state courts in 1993. Premise liability cases followed, at 17 percent, malpractice at 7 percent, product liability at 4 percent, and miscellaneous tort actions at 14 percent.[4]

In order for a plaintiff to recover from a defendant based on a claim of **negligence**, the plaintiff must present evidence supporting four legal elements (Figure 1-4):

1. *Duty,* which requires that a party conform to a defined standard of care.
2. *Breach* of that duty, meaning the party fails to conform to the standard of care.
3. *Causation,* that is, a direct connection between the conduct of the defendant and the injury to the plaintiff.
4. *Damages,* which compensate a party for an actual loss due to injuries, and usually take the form of money.

impeach Demonstrate a witness is not telling the truth.

negligence Failure to exercise the degree of care that a reasonable person would exercise under the same circumstances.

If a plaintiff cannot provide at least one piece of evidence to support each one of these elements, the plaintiff's claim against the defendant fails. The plaintiff has not established a *prima facie* case.

If the plaintiff does establish a *prima facie* case, the defendant must present evidence to contradict the evidence presented by the plaintiff. The defendant may also decide to raise a defense, which must be proven with evidence.

FIGURE 1-4

Negligence is proven by four legal elements.

ELEMENTS OF AN ACTION BASED ON NEGLIGENCE
• Duty
• Breach of duty
• Proximate cause
• Injury/Damages

Defenses can include, depending on relevant state law, comparative negligence, assumption of the risk, contributory negligence, and last clear chance.

Criminal Actions

Criminal law deals with conduct prohibited by the government and sets forth the punishment to be imposed for violation of federal or state criminal statutes. Crimes are against public order and are defined in the criminal statutes of state or federal governments, as passed by a state legislature or by Congress. State courts handled 13 million criminal cases in 1993, far more than the cases handled in federal courts.[5] This larger number is understandable since most federal crimes are a violation of state statutes as well.

Criminal law also includes the defenses that can be raised by a person accused of a crime, such as insanity, alibi, intoxication, heat of passion, self-defense, and entrapment. Another defense is to assert that someone else committed the crime. Still another is to claim that the government's witnesses are not telling the truth.

The parties are the government and the defendant. The state or the United States is a named party, depending on whether the crime is a violation of state or federal criminal statutes. Prosecutors can be called *district attorneys, state attorneys, county attorneys,* or *United States attorneys.* The defendant is found guilty or not guilty of violating the law. With a guilty verdict, the punishment that the defendant receives can be a fine, imprisonment, or both.

The elements of a crime that must be proven by the prosecution in order to convict a defendant are found in statutes and are often explained in cases. Inherent in almost all crimes are two requirements (Figure 1-5). First, the defendant must have had the requisite state of mind, referred to as a "guilty mind," or **mens rea**. Second, the defendant must have physically committed the act, which is called **actus reus**.

It is imperative that the paralegal and the investigator have a clear understanding of the elements of the particular crime that the accused allegedly committed. With theoretical knowledge of the elements that the government must prove in order to convict a defendant, the paralegal or investigator can concentrate on (1) the evidence that could prove the commission of a crime or (2) a valid defense to the accusation of criminal conduct.

Burglary is a crime involving property and is defined in most state statutes as an unlawful entry (actus reus) coupled with the person's intent (mens rea) to commit a specific crime once inside the structure or vehicle. The prosecutor must present evidence that supports the contention that a defendant entered a structure or vehicle without permission, and that the defendant had the intent to commit a crime once inside.

mens rea The mental state necessary to the commission of a crime.

actus reus The criminal act.

burglary An unlawful entry coupled with the intent to commit a specific crime once inside the structure or vehicle.

ELEMENTS OF CRIMINAL ACTIONS

- Mens rea ("guilty mind")
- Actus reus (criminal act)

FIGURE 1-5

Two elements are necessary for an action to become a crime.

Criminal homicide is a category of crimes against persons. Specifically, it includes all homicides where (1) the accused intentionally killed someone without legal justification or (2) accidentally killed someone as a consequence of reckless or grossly negligent conduct. An example is murder in the first degree. The prosecutor must present evidence that the defendant killed a human being with premeditation and that the defendant acted willfully and deliberately in order to prove murder in the first degree.

A defendant may raise certain affirmative defenses to the accusation of murder that, if the jury believes them, will excuse the defendant from criminal conviction. Each element of these defenses, such as insanity and self-defense, must be supported by evidence presented by the defendant at trial.

On the other hand, if a defendant simply relies on the defense of "I didn't do it," then the defendant's attorney will attempt to attack the evidence presented by the prosecution to show the jury that the state's case is not believable.

ROLE OF PARALEGALS AND INVESTIGATORS

In the trial process, paralegals and investigators are legal professionals who work under the supervision of an attorney. The place of employment can range from a sole practitioner's office, to corporate headquarters, to the prosecutor's office or public defender's office.

Duties can include client or victim contact and investigation of the circumstances involved in the case. The investigation may encompass visiting and examining the site of the disputed action, taking pictures, finding and interviewing witnesses, and locating expert witnesses. Particularly, the paralegal is often responsible for seeing that the material related to the case is organized properly and that exhibits needed for trial are prepared and meet the legal requirements that make them admissible as evidence.

If the paralegal or investigator works in a prosecutor's office, duties might include similar activities, with a view toward ensuring the integrity of evidence gathered and processed by law enforcement agencies.

The paralegal's and investigator's focus, regardless of the type of case, must be on a possible trial in the future. This is where the importance of knowledge of the trial process and the rules of evidence is critical. What the paralegal and investigator must understand is that the basis for the story that is going to unfold before the jury at trial starts with the early investigation of the case and the careful gathering of evidence long before the trial begins. What is going to be presented to the jury is evidence, and evidence means testimony and tangible objects presented to the jury by the parties.

If certain testimony or an object is essential to a case, it is important for the paralegal and investigator to be sure the evidence is admissible, so it will be heard or seen by the jury. The role of the investigator is to ensure the integrity of the evidence gathered during the investigation. If there is any question as to admissibility, the paralegal can prepare before trial to meet possible challenges from the opposing party by a thorough review of the rules of evidence and the applicable case law. Will testimony be subject to a claim of privilege? Is the testimony hearsay? How can the relevance of the evidence be established or attacked? These are some of the questions that will be addressed in the following chapters.

criminal homicide The intentional killing of a person without legal justification, or the accidental killing of a person as a consequence of reckless or grossly negligent conduct.

ETHICAL ISSUES

As legal professionals, paralegals and investigators have a duty to participate in the trial process according to all of the rules, including those regulating the actions of their supervising attorneys. Paralegals and investigators must become familiar with the parameters of legal representation, particularly the duties owed to the parties involved and to the legal profession in general.

Confidentiality is a cornerstone of legal representation. Paralegals and investigators must be vigilant in maintaining the confidences of clients, even in the face of pressure from friends and family who might show an interest in the details of the paralegal's or investigator's job. If the case is one that is of interest to members of the community, pressures for disclosure might be still more intense.

During investigations, paralegals and investigators must be careful to represent themselves in their respective capacities, not as attorneys. This is also true with regard to client or victim contact, where the client or victim might ask the paralegal or investigator for an opinion on the chances of prevailing in the case. Advice with regard to the law and how it will affect the case is for the supervising attorney to discuss with a client or victim.

Finally, the roles of paralegals and investigators may be to do the investigation and background work, but it is up to the supervising attorney to delegate duties and guide their activities. It is the attorney who has the legal education and experience that results in the effective use of the abilities of auxiliary personnel in the trial process. A client is best served where the attorney works in tandem with the paralegal and investigator so that they pool their respective talents, with the attorney always maintaining the appropriate level of supervision. As a team, each with defined roles, the attorney, the paralegal, and the investigator can be formidable in the adversarial setting in representing the interests of a client or the government in the litigation process.

SUMMARY

The trial process has deep historical roots. It is part of an adversarial system where parties are represented by attorneys who advocate on behalf of their clients. At trial, evidence supporting each party is offered. The judge determines matters of law and the jury determines matters of fact, all within the context of procedural rules and evidence rules.

The legal professionals in the trial process are the attorneys, their paralegals and investigators, and the judges. In order to effectively represent a client, the attorneys, paralegals, and investigators need to understand the evidence rules. The evidence presented at trial is a product of investigation and preparation that begins when the client retains an attorney or when the crime is investigated. The judge decides what testimony and tangible objects the party's attorneys will be allowed to present to the jury. All of this is in the framework of the rules of evidence.

There are two types of actions, civil and criminal. Two examples of civil actions are contracts and torts. Two examples of criminal actions are burglary and criminal homicide. Each of these actions has elements that must be proven in order for the plaintiff or prosecutor to prevail. Defenses to the actions exist, which must be supported by evidence.

It is the attorney who delegates tasks and supervises the paralegal and investigator, who, in turn, must avoid misrepresenting their roles in the trial process. The attorney, paralegal, and investigator can form a formidable team in representing the interests of a client.

✓ CHECKPOINTS

❏ Two types of actions:
   1. Civil: private interests (e.g.) contract and negligence.
   2. Criminal: public interest (e.g.) burglary and criminal homicide.

❏ Trial process:
   1. Begins with the event or criminal act.
   2. Evidence is in the form of testimony and tangible objects discovered or prepared prior to trial.

3. Adversarial process, in which each party's attorney marshals evidence to present the strongest possible case at trial.

4. Paralegals and investigators work under the supervision of an attorney and are part of the team working for the client.

5. Judge decides matters of law.

6. Jury decides matters of fact.

7. Rules of procedure and evidence govern the trial process.

⚖ APPLICATIONS

Application 1-1

The following case is an appeal from a decision of the Alaska Workers' Compensation Board (Board) to the Alaska Supreme Court. Donald Childs applied to the Board for workers' compensation benefits, alleging that he was injured when he was employed by the Kalgin Island Lodge (Lodge). The Lodge argued to the Board that Childs was not an employee of the Lodge when the injury occurred because there was no employment contract between Childs and the Lodge. There was no contract, the Lodge argued, because the formal hiring process was not complete at the time Childs was injured. Workers' compensation benefits could be awarded only if Childs were an employee of the Lodge. The Board agreed with the Lodge, and Childs appealed the decision because it resulted in a loss of benefits to him. Note that the trier of fact is the Board, not a jury. Although application of evidence rules may be somewhat relaxed in an administrative hearing such as the one conducted here, the case demonstrates the evidence needed to prove the existence of an employment relationship before workers' compensation could be collected.

Childs v. Kalgin Island Lodge
779 P.2d 310 (Alaska 1989)

I. FACTS AND PROCEEDINGS

In July 1986, Childs, a professional pilot, sought employment with the Lodge as a pilot and guide. In order to obtain employment, Childs contacted Charles Tulin (Tulin), who interviews and recommends pilots to be employed by the Lodge. Even though Tulin was not the owner of the business which operated the Lodge, he apparently owned certain Lodge facilities and was the co-owner of the real property, improvements and equipment used by the Lodge, including all airplanes.

The Board found that the final hiring decisions normally rested with the Lodge's corporate president and board of directors. It is unclear, however, whether Tulin also had authority, actual or apparent, to hire Childs without their prior approval. However, it is clear from the record that Tulin's recommendations to the Lodge regarding hiring were given at least great weight and would be seriously considered. The corporate president and owner of the business was Tulin's son, Don Tulin.

On or about June 30, 1986, Tulin requested that Childs come to Tulin's law office for an interview. Following the interview, Tulin asked Childs to call him after the July 4th weekend. Childs called as instructed and was invited to lunch on July 7, 1986.

Childs testified that at lunch, Tulin offered to employ him for $3,500 per month, which he accepted. Tulin testified that no such offer was made. Tulin instructed Childs to report to his office the next day. Childs did so. At this time, Tulin informed the insurance agent for the Lodge, both by mail and by phone, that Childs should be added to the Lodge's insurance coverage. Tulin directed Childs to hand-carry the insurance agent's letter to the post office to insure prompt delivery and response, which Childs did.

Later that day, at Tulin's request, Childs drove to Lake Hood, where Tulin introduced Childs to various Lodge employees. While there, Childs assisted in loading a plane for a flight to the Lodge, pumped the plane's floats and filled it with 25 gallons of fuel. He then signed for the fuel on behalf of the Lodge. Childs testified that on this occasion, he was instructed to inspect the Lodge's planes and begin making a list of the repairs that needed to be completed for the upcoming winter. He further testified that he was instructed to begin setting up maintenance schedules for the Lodge's planes and programs for pilot selection and training. Later that day, Childs gassed and changed the oil on another of the Lodge's airplanes. He paid for the gas and oil with a Lodge check, given him by Tulin's wife.

Childs was informed by Tulin that he would accompany Tulin out to the Lodge on either July 10 or July 11. Childs prepared gear and readied himself for the trip to the Lodge. He was told the trip would be the following day.

On July 11, 1986, Tulin introduced Childs to Don Tulin. Childs testified that he was instructed by both men to use Tulin's law office facilities to work on a marketing program for the Lodge. At this time, Childs made several phone calls in furtherance of marketing for the Lodge.

At about 4 p.m., Childs either volunteered or was asked by Tulin to go to a sporting goods store to pick up two fishing rods. The rods were to be bought with a personal check from Tulin. On the way to the store, while driving Tulin's car, Childs was involved in an auto accident and was injured. He filed a worker's compensation claim after submitting his Notice of Occupational Injury to Tulin.

After depositions and hearings, the Board denied Childs' claim. The Board based its decision on its conclusion that no express contract existed between the Lodge and Childs, because not all of the formal hiring process had been completed at the time of the accident. The Board further concluded that because no emergency situation existed during the time in question, Childs was not an emergency employee and therefore could not receive the benefits of the Act. One member of the Board dissented on the ground that Childs was in a "tryout" period and the Act's coverage should apply under the emergency exception.

Childs appealed to the superior court, which affirmed the Board's decision. The court concluded that the Board applied the correct law and that there was substantial evidence to support its findings of fact. Thus, because no emergency existed and no express contract was made, no relationship existed between the parties which would entitle Childs to coverage under the Act. Therefore the superior court concluded that worker's compensation benefits were properly denied, and the Board's decision was affirmed.

II. DISCUSSION

To determine the issue presented before this court, we need only consider whether the Board applied the proper legal test to reach its conclusions. [FOOTNOTE 2: Even though the facts were disputed before the Board, at oral argument counsel for the Lodge conceded that Childs performed all the work he alleged. No factual dispute remains before the court.] This court has consistently maintained that it will not vacate findings of the Board when supported by substantial evidence. However, if the Board's decision rests on a an incorrect legal foundation, review is not so limited. In such cases, independent review of the law is proper.

The Act provides that an employee is a person employed by an employer, and an employer is, in part, "a person employing one or more persons in connection with a business or industry."

The Board correctly recognized that before an employee/employer relationship exists under the Act, an express or implied contract of employment must exist. The Board also correctly recognized that employment generally begins after a meeting of the minds has been reached between the employee and the employer, for it is at that point that a contract is formed. Furthermore the Board correctly noted that volunteer work, standing alone, does not necessarily establish an employee/employer relationship for the purposes of the Act.

However, in applying the above law the Board incorrectly concluded that employee/employer relationships exist only when an express contract for hire is finalized by completion of the hiring process, or an implied contract is formed based on emergency circumstances. The superior court followed the same analysis.

Situations arise in which employee/employer relationships exist without either an express contract or an emergency situation. This court has never declared that express contracts are formed only after the formal hiring process is complete, nor have we adopted the view that only emergency situations may sustain implied contracts for hire. Because the Board failed to apply the correct legal analysis under which an employee/employer relationship can be created, we must remand the case to the Board for consideration in light of the following.

A. EXPRESS CONTRACT

As noted in *Fjeldahl v. Homer Co-op. Ass'n,* 11 Alaska 112, 135 (D.Alaska 1946), "to employ" means to make use of the services of another. "To be employed in anything means not only the act of doing it, but also to be engaged to do it; to be under contract or orders to do it." We agree with the holding of the New Mexico Supreme Court that mere formalization of a contract for hire is not the controlling factor in determining whether an employment contract exists.

The formation of an express contract requires an offer encompassing its essential terms, an unequivocal acceptance of the terms by the offeree, consideration and an intent to be bound.

The Board failed to determine whether Tulin had authority to hire Childs. If so, the Board failed to determine whether Tulin offered Childs a pilot/guide position for $3,500 a month and whether Childs accepted Tulin's offer. The Board also failed to consider the possibility that Childs offered to work for Tulin or the Lodge at $3,500 a month, and Tulin accepted. The Board's failure to determine whether an offer and acceptance was made, regardless of whether the formal hiring process was complete, leads us to conclude that the correct express contract analysis was not considered.

B. IMPLIED CONTRACT

An implied employment contract is formed by a relation resulting from "the manifestation of consent by one party to another that the other shall act on his behalf and subject to his control, and consent by the other so to act." The Board should make its determination whether an implied contract was formed by considering all the factors in light of the surrounding circumstances. This court has adopted the position that "ordinarily no single feature of the relation is determinative ... and each case must depend upon its own facts." Furthermore, words and acts of the parties should be given such meaning as reasonable persons would give them under all the facts and circumstances present at the time in question.

There is sufficient evidence here from which it may be found that the Lodge employed Childs, even though no express contract is found. By utilizing his services and by controlling the time, manner and location his work, the Lodge knowingly allowed Childs to act on its behalf, performing many of the job-related skills for which he was being considered. [FOOTNOTE 5: Even though Childs was being considered for a pilot/guide position and he never flew a Lodge plane, he did various other tasks associated with that position including: unloading a car and loading a Lodge airplane; pumping an airplane float; fueling an airplane and signing for the fuel as a Lodge representative; change the oil on another airplane and paying for the oil with a Lodge check; making marketing phone calls for the Lodge; and taking Tulin's car to locate fishing rods for Tulin.] The Board erred when it failed to consider these factors and their implications under the circumstances. Thus, the correct implied contract analysis was also not considered.

III. CONCLUSION

The decision of the superior court is REVERSED and the case is REMANDED to the superior court with directions to remand it to the Board for further proceedings consistent with this opinion.

Class Discussion Questions

1. In order for Childs to recover under the Workers' Compensation Act, he had to establish that he had an employment contract with the Lodge. What was the evidence offered by Childs to prove that there was a meeting of the minds, that is, there was an offer by the Lodge for employment and acceptance by Childs?

2. The Lodge contended that there was no evidence of an express employment contract. The Lodge contended that there was no contract because the offer was not complete. What did the Lodge contend was needed for completion of the hiring process and therefore formation of an employment contract?

3. How did the drama unfold for the Board (the trier of fact in this case)? That is, who were the main characters to testify so that the Board could learn the facts about the dispute between the Lodge and Childs?

4. What does it mean to Childs that the case was reversed and remanded?

Application 1-2

In the following negligence action, a child is injured when a playmate swings a golf club and hits her in the face. The injured playmate sued the father of the swinging playmate, on the theory that the father was negligent because he knew the club was in the yard and he did not remove it.

Lubitz v. Wells
19 Conn. Supp. 322, 113 A.2d 147 (1955)

The complaint alleges that James Wells was the owner of a golf club and that he left it for some time lying on the ground in the backyard of his home. That thereafter his son, the defendant James Wells, Jr., aged eleven years, while playing in the yard with the plaintiff, Judith Lubitz, aged nine years, picked up the golf club and proceeded to swing at a stone lying on the ground. In swinging the golf club, James Wells, Jr., caused the club to strike the plaintiff about the jaw and chin.

Negligence alleged against the young Wells boy is that he failed to warn his little playmate of his intention to swing the club and that he did swing the club when he knew she was in a position of danger.

In an attempt to hold the boy's father, James Wells, liable for this son's action, it is alleged that James Wells was negligent because although he knew the golf club was on the ground in his backyard and that his children would play with it, and that although he knew or 'should have known' that the negligent use of the golf club by children would cause injury to a child, he neglected to remove the golf club from the backyard or to caution James Wells, Jr., against the use of the same.

The demurrer challenges the sufficiency of the allegations of the complaint to state a cause of action or to support a judgment against the father, James Wells.

It would hardly be good sense to hold that this golf club is so obviously and intrinsically dangerous that it is negligence to leave it lying on the ground in the yard. The father cannot be held liable on the allegations of this complaint.

The demurrer is sustained.

Class Discussion Questions

1. Whether a demurrer will be sustained is decided by the trial court judge before trial begins. Consult a dictionary of legal terms, and explain the purpose and basis for a demurrer, as well as the modern name of the motion in many courts today.

2. In this case, the plaintiff/child alleged that the father of her playmate was negligent for leaving the golf club in the yard and for not telling his son to leave it alone. What type of evidence might the plaintiff have offered at trial to prove this allegation?

3. Did this court believe that the father's leaving the golf club in the yard was a negligent act? Explain the reasoning of the court.

4. Recall the elements of a negligent tort: duty, breach of duty, causation, and damages. List at least one piece of evidence that supports each element, noting any unsupported elements. Include in your answer the nature of the duty Mr. Wells owed to Judith Lubitz.

5. List at least one piece of evidence that supports each element of a negligent tort as between James Wells, Jr., and Judith Lubitz. Include in your answer the nature of the duty Junior owed to Judith Wells.

Application 1-3

In the following case, the defendant was convicted of breaking and entering a building with the intent to commit a felony. One of the elements of the crime that the state had to prove was the intent of the defendant to commit grand larceny, which was a felony.

West v. State
289 So. 2d 758 (Fla. 3d DCA 1974)

Appellant, defendant in the trial court, seeks review of a judgment and sentence of two years incarceration for breaking and entering a building with intent to commit a felony, to wit: grand larceny.

The evidence at trial revealed that appellant broke into the Buccaneer Lodge, where he recently had been employed, on June 8, 1972. Two police officers observed appellant enter an office area of the building, and they waited approximately forty minutes for him to leave, when they arrested him. Police searched the appellant and discovered only two keys to the building in his possession. Further testimony indicated damage within the office to a desk drawer and to the door lock, and that a supply cabinet had been rifled. However, items of personal property in the office including a watch, typewriters and an adding machine in excess of $100 in value had not been disturbed.

Based upon this evidence, the jury returned a verdict of guilty. Appellant argues that the trial judge should have directed a verdict of acquittal at the close of the state's case because the evidence failed to prove an element of the crime, intent of the appellant to commit grand larceny.

Appellant concedes that the state satisfactorily proved a breaking and entering, and he is not guiltless. Therefore, we do not find error in the court's denial of a directed verdict of acquittal.

However, there is merit to appellant's contention that the state failed to prove he intended to commit grand larceny. It is clearly the law that the element of intent in Fla.Stat. § 810.02 F.S.A., under which appellant was convicted, may be proven by circumstantial evidence.

However, the Florida Supreme Court in *Jalbert v. State,* Fla.1957, 95 So. 2d 589, stated, "In the absence of other evidence or circumstances, the best evidence of what he (the defendant) intended to steal is what he did steal." This court has held that where the state's only evidence of an intent to commit grand larceny in a case of this nature is that a dwelling house contained property valued in excess of $100, such evidence is not sufficient to prove intent. In the instant case, the evidence shows that appellant was caught with two keys to the Buccaneer Lodge in his possession. We have determined from the record that the evidence was sufficient to prove only a breaking and entering with intent to commit a misdemeanor, to-wit: petit larceny.

[T]he judgment and sentence appealed is reversed and the cause is remanded with directions to the trial court to enter a judgment against the appellant for breaking and entering with intent to commit a misdemeanor, to-wit: petit larceny, and to impose a new sentence.

Reversed and remanded, with directions.

Class Discussion Questions

1. The prosecutor used the testimony of the police officers to prove that the defendant broke into the Buccaneer Lodge. What facts related in the testimony could lead to the inference that the defendant did not have permission to be in the Lodge?

2. Who else probably testified on behalf of the state with regard to permission to be in the Lodge?

3. The court stated that the defendant's intent to commit grand larceny could be proven by circumstantial evidence. In this case, what evidence, if available to the prosecution, would have been proof of the defendant's intent to commit grand larceny?

4. The testimony of the police officers established that the defendant had two keys to the building in his possession when he was arrested. The court found that this was circumstantial evidence that the defendant committed what crime?

EXERCISES

1. Review the rules of civil and criminal procedure that apply in your state court system. Are memoranda of law supporting motions in limine required before a hearing is set by the judge?

2. Locate the rule books published by West that compile the state rules of court for federal courts in your state and also the rules governing the procedure in your state.

3. For your state, locate the annotated rules of civil and criminal procedure.

4. Look up the civil procedure and evidence rules in your state encyclopedia to see how they are treated.

5. What is the style of a criminal case in your state?

6. What is the title of the party representing the government in a criminal case in your state?

7. On the Internet, locate sites for your state court system. For example, the site maintained by the Florida Supreme Court can be located by typing in "Florida courts" for the search. List the information available at your state court web site, including links.

NOTES

[1] *Examining the Work of State Courts, 1993.* Report by the National Center for State Courts, the Conference of State Court Administrators, and the State Justice Institute.

[2] *State Courts, 1993.*

[3] *Restatement of Contracts, 2d.*

[4] *State Courts, 1993.*

[5] *State Courts, 1993.*

Evidence Rules at Trial

HISTORY OF THE FEDERAL RULES OF EVIDENCE ———————

Prior to the codification of evidence law, the various rules that governed the regulation of proof at trial were contained in case law. Decisions in state courts and in the federal court system were not always in accord. The result was a lack of uniformity and a need for legal professionals to be familiar with the holdings of multiple cases.

Creation of the Federal Rules of Evidence

The National Conference of Commissioners on Uniform State Laws promulgated the Uniform Rules of Evidence in 1953. Although the Uniform Rules were not adopted by many jurisdictions, they were influential in the development of the Federal Rules of Evidence, as was the California Evidence Code, adopted in the state of California in 1965.

The Federal Rules of Evidence were compiled by a panel of lawyers, judges, and legal scholars. These individuals chose what they considered the better reasoned cases on which to base the rules of evidence. The Uniform Rules of Evidence and the California Evidence Code provided a framework within which to work.

After being submitted to Congress by the Supreme Court, the Federal Rules of Evidence became effective on July 1, 1975.[1] Case law continues to be important because the rules of evidence are construed by the courts on a regular basis. However, with the codification of evidence law, the process for change to the rules is more systematic; periodic amendments to the Federal Rules of Evidence are processed according to 28 U.S.C. § 2072 *et seq.*

Rule 1103. Title

These rules may be known and cited as the Federal Rules of Evidence.

Relationship to State Evidence Rules

The Federal Rules of Evidence have served as a model for codification of evidence law in a majority of the states. There are a great number of similarities between state and federal laws, so understanding the Federal Rules of Evidence is a basis for understanding state rules. However, even the states that have essentially adopted the Federal Rules of Evidence have some significant differences from them. Some of the more common differences will be noted throughout the text.

APPLICATION OF THE RULES ———————————————

The Federal Rules of Evidence apply to several different areas of federal litigation.

Federal Courts

Essentially, the federal rules apply in the federal court system, which includes the trial courts (district courts), bankruptcy courts, and actions before magistrate judges. The rules are applicable in both civil cases and criminal cases.

Rule 1101. Applicability of Rules

(a) **Courts and judges.** These rules apply to the United States district courts, the District Court of Guam, the District Court of the Virgin Islands, the District Court for the Northern Mariana Islands, the United States courts of appeals, the United States Claims Court, and to United States bankruptcy judges and United States magistrate judges, in the actions, cases, and proceedings and to the extent hereinafter set forth. The terms "judge" and "court" in these rules include United States bankruptcy judges and United States magistrate judges.

(b) **Proceedings generally.** These rules apply generally to civil actions and proceedings, including admiralty and maritime cases, to criminal cases and proceedings, to contempt proceedings except those in which the court may act summarily, and to proceedings and cases under title 11, United States Code.

Privileged Matters

Under the Federal Rules of Evidence, privileged matters are protected at all stages of both civil and criminal proceedings. A **privilege** exists when certain protected relationships are involved, such as attorney-client, clergy member–penitent, and husband-wife. If it is found by the judge that a protected relationship existed and that the communication was made in a confidential setting, the judge will not require disclosure of the communication. Privileges are covered in detail in Chapter 12.

Rule 1101. Applicability of Rules

(c) **Rule of privilege.** The rule with respect to privileges applies at all stages of all actions, cases, and proceedings.

Other Proceedings

The Rules of Evidence are not used in **grand jury** proceedings. A grand jury proceeding is one in which a prosecutor presents evidence for consideration by the grand jury with regard to investigation of criminal wrongdoing. The grand jury is allowed to hear testimony of witnesses that would not be allowed in a trial court. An example of this type of evidence is hearsay, which is covered in Chapters 10 and 11. Rule 1101 allows a grand jury to consider hearsay evidence and to listen to a witness relate what someone else said to the witness about a matter related to the alleged criminal activity. The role of the grand jury is to determine whether there is enough evidence of criminal wrongdoing to bring a person to trial. The grand jury does not determine guilt. That is the role of the trial court jury, sometimes referred to as the **petit jury**.

The trial jury determines matters of fact from the evidence presented by the parties at trial, and renders a verdict in the case. The trial jury is made up of six to twelve jurors, who listen to the evidence presented at trial, receive instructions on the applicable law from the judge, and deliberate in order to agree on a verdict.

Rule 1101 also lists several other areas where the Rules of Evidence do not apply, including criminal proceedings such as sentencing, probation, issuance of warrants, and release on bail. The judge can thus make a determination of how to best handle these specific procedures related to a criminal defendant based on all available evidence without the constraints of the Rules of Evidence, since the guilt of the defendant is not an issue.

privilege A right enjoyed by a party when a communication is within a relationship that is recognized by the law as confidential, allowing the speaker to shield the communication from disclosure.

grand jury A group of people selected according to law to investigate and inform on crimes committed within its jurisdiction. The grand jury has the power to accuse persons of crimes (indict) when there is sufficient evidence to warrant holding a person for trial.

petit jury Trial jury, which determines matters of fact in civil and criminal cases and renders a verdict.

Rule 1101. Applicability of Rules

(d) **Rules inapplicable.** The rules (other than with respect to privileges) do not apply in the following situations:

(1) Preliminary questions of fact. The determination of questions of fact preliminary to admissibility of evidence when the issue is to be determined by the court under rule 104.

(2) Grand jury. Proceedings before grand juries.

(3) Miscellaneous proceedings. Proceedings for extradition or rendition; preliminary examinations in criminal cases; sentencing, or granting or revoking probation; issuance of warrants for arrest, criminal summonses, and search warrants; and proceedings with respect to release on bail or otherwise.

Partial Application

Section (e) of Rule 1101 details those proceedings where the Rules of Evidence apply only to the extent that other rules or statutory authority do not govern. The full text of the rule can be found in the appendix.

Rule 1101. Applicability of Rules

(e) Rules applicable in part.   ...

OVERVIEW OF A TRIAL

The Rules of Evidence are fundamental to the trial process. They regulate the information that can be heard by the trier of fact, which is in most cases the jury. The rules are the theoretical framework used by the parties to argue to the judge why certain testimony should be allowed or why a document should be shown to the jury. Think of the trial as a serious game where the goal is to achieve justice, and the Rules of Evidence as the directions dictating how the game will be played.

Rule 102. Purpose and Construction

These rules shall be construed to secure fairness in administration, elimination of unjustifiable expense and delay, and promotion of growth and development of the law of evidence to the end that the truth may be ascertained and proceedings justly determined.

The trial is the culmination of the investigation and discovery done by the parties, in preparation for the trial, through their attorneys and their paralegal and investigative staff. The trial itself begins with jury selection and continues through opening statements and presentation of the plaintiff's case in a civil matter or the prosecutor's case on behalf of the government in a criminal case. If the plaintiff or the prosecutor establishes a *prima facie* case and survives a motion for a directed verdict, then the defendant has the opportunity to present a case.

Motions

Generally, a **motion** is an application to a judge requesting an order or ruling in favor of the moving party. Motions may be made orally or in writing, supported by a memorandum of law that argues the legal basis for the request. Motions often relate to legal issues that the moving party wants the judge to decide before the case proceeds.

In a **motion for directed verdict**, a party requests that the judge find for the moving party and end the trial because the opponent failed to present (1) evidence to support all the elements needed for the civil or criminal action or (2) the necessary defense to that action. The argument is that the opponent failed to present a *prima facie* case or to properly present evidence to support the necessary defense to the action. The motion is considered by the judge in the light most favorable to the nonmoving party.

In criminal cases in some jurisdictions, the defendant asks the judge to grant a **motion for judgment of acquittal**, rather than moving for a directed verdict. A motion for a judgment of acquittal is available only to the defendant in a criminal case and not to the prosecutor, since the United States Constitution affords the defendant the right to have a jury determine guilt.

In a personal injury case, a successful motion for directed verdict means that the plaintiff did not prove that the defendant had a duty to the plaintiff. In a criminal case, the defendant might argue that the government did not present evidence to support each element of the crime. For instance, in an action involving a charge of burglary, the defendant might argue that the government failed to present testimony proving the defendant lacked permission to enter the building where the alleged burglary occurred.

If the judge denies the motion for directed verdict or judgment of acquittal, the trial proceeds. After closing arguments are presented by each side, the judge instructs the jury on the law, and the jury deliberates and returns a verdict. Closure of the trial phase in a civil case comes with a judgment that conforms with the jury verdict and is signed by the judge and entered on the record. In a criminal case, sentencing brings closure to the trial process.

The parties in a civil case, and a losing defendant in a criminal case, may file post-verdict motions and take the case on appeal. But for the purposes of the Rules of Evidence, the trial process has concluded. However, an evidentiary issue may be the basis for the appeal, in which case the Rules of Evidence remain pertinent.

The Trial as Drama

This discussion so far has been a clinical explanation of the trial process. However, the drama of the trial process must be considered for a real understanding of what happens in the courtroom. The trial process is like a play staged for a critical audience seated in the jury box. Each of the participants has a defined role in the unfolding of the drama. The jurors come to the courtroom with little or no knowledge of the facts related to the dispute that they are to settle. Theoretically, the jury is like a clean slate, ready for the parties to create a picture with evidence of what happened between the parties.

It is the role of the attorneys for the opposing sides to present the evidence, with the goal that the jury will interpret the drama in a way that is favorable to

motion A request by a party to the judge for a ruling in favor of the moving party.

motion for directed verdict A request to the court for a verdict without consideration by a jury because the plaintiff fails to present a *prima facie* case or the defendant fails to present a necessary defense.

motion for judgment of acquittal A request by a defendant in a criminal case for the court to direct a verdict of not guilty without consideration by the jury, based on the failure of the prosecutor to prove every element of the charge.

them. The judge's role is that of a director, overseeing the trial process and making determinations on the admissibility of evidence. The judge, using the evidence rules, filters the evidence that the opposing attorneys attempt to use to fill in the details of the drama. The roles of the judge, jury, and the attorneys in this process are covered in Chapters 3 and 4.

TYPES OF EVIDENCE

Evidence is what the jury will use as the basis for its deliberation regarding who should prevail in a case. Evidence is the proof that each side believes supports its legal position, the information that shows to the jury who the winner should be at the conclusion of the drama.

Classified as either *direct* or *circumstantial,* evidence comes in the form of testimony of witnesses, documents, and physical objects.

Direct Evidence

If the testimony of witnesses or the presentation of physical objects or documents is **direct evidence**, the jury can conclude from the testimony, object, or document that a fact has been established. The only qualifier is whether the jurors believe the testimony, document, or object is what the proponent says it is. Direct evidence directly proves a fact in issue.

Testimony that is direct evidence results from first-hand perceptions by the witness. For example, in response to a question from the plaintiff's attorney asking what the witness saw on June 22 at the intersection of Davis Highway and Brent Lane, the witness might state, "I saw the Lincoln barrel through the intersection when the light was red for it." The testimony proves the Lincoln ran the red light, if the jurors believe what the witness said.

In a murder trial where the victim was shot, the prosecutor calls the investigating detective to the stand. The prosecutor shows the detective a gun. In response to a question from the prosecutor, the detective states that she found it next to the murder victim. Again, the only issue for the jury is whether to believe the detective. If the jurors believe the detective, then the testimony is direct evidence that the object, the gun presented by the prosecutor at trial, is the gun found at the murder scene.

Direct evidence is based on first-hand knowledge that is a product of the testifying witness's sensual perception. The witness saw, heard, smelled, or felt something. If the jury believes the witness, then a fact is established: the Lincoln ran the red light; the gun was found at the murder scene.

Circumstantial Evidence

Circumstantial evidence, unlike direct evidence, necessarily involves inference. The witness testifies, and from that testimony the jury can infer what the party calling the witness wants to prove. A verdict can be based on proof that is established by inference this way, but not on mere speculation or conjecture.

In the personal injury action involving the driver of the Lincoln, the plaintiff must establish that the driver breached a duty of care, in this case by

direct evidence Testimony or physical objects offered by a party that allow a jury to conclude that a fact has been established without having to use inference.

circumstantial evidence Testimony or other evidence that requires the trier of fact to draw an inference in order to establish a fact.

running a red light. The best way to establish such a breach is by direct evidence, with the testimony of the witness who saw the Lincoln run the red light. If the party does not have the benefit of direct evidence, it must rely on circumstantial evidence to establish the breach of the duty of care. Plaintiff's witness, in response to a question, might say, "From where I was standing, I noticed that the left arrow light was green for the Pinto when it started to make a left at the intersection. I didn't see what happened next because I turned into the furniture store parking lot." The inference here is that the light was red for the Lincoln when the Lincoln entered the intersection and struck the Pinto, which supports the plaintiff's contention that the driver of the Lincoln breached a duty of care. See Illustration 2-1.

Illustration 2-1 _____

In a lawsuit by surviving parents of a flight attendant who was killed in an airplane crash, the plaintiffs wanted to recover for the post-impact pain and suffering of their daughter. To recover, they had to prove she was at least briefly conscious following injury.

They presented evidence she was not dismembered, but severely burned and found in the braced position flight attendants are trained to assume prior to a crash. Witnesses also testified that the impact and disintegration of the airplane took several seconds.

The jury could infer from this circumstantial evidence that the victim was conscious after impact and before her death, and she suffered during that time either from impact injuries or the massive burns. *Pregeant v. Pan American World Airways, Inc.,* 762 F.2d 1245, 1249–1250 (5th Cir. 1985).

With circumstantial evidence, there are two issues for the jury:

1. Believability of the evidence.
2. The conclusion to be drawn from the evidence.

With direct evidence, believability of the evidence is the only issue. Figure 2-1 compares the two types of evidence.

With regard to the gun found by the detective, her testimony established only that the gun was found at the murder scene. However, this testimony is also circumstantial evidence that the gun was the murder weapon. The detective did not see the killer pull the trigger of the gun, but the fact that the gun was found at the murder scene leads to the inference that the gun was the murder weapon used by the killer. Note that a single piece of evidence can be direct evidence of one fact and circumstantial evidence of another fact.

The evidence presented in these examples, whether direct or circumstantial, is not enough proof to establish that the driver of the Pinto should recover money from the driver of the Lincoln, or that the defendant in the murder trial is guilty. In each case, we have only one small piece of the story. It takes many pieces of evidence for a plaintiff's attorney or a prosecutor to win the minds of the jurors—in other words, to put together a complete story. It is important to remember that "a brick is not a wall."[2] One piece of evidence is one brick. In order to prove all the elements of a cause of action, or "build a wall," multiple bricks are needed.

FIGURE 2-1
Evidence may be direct or
circumstantial.

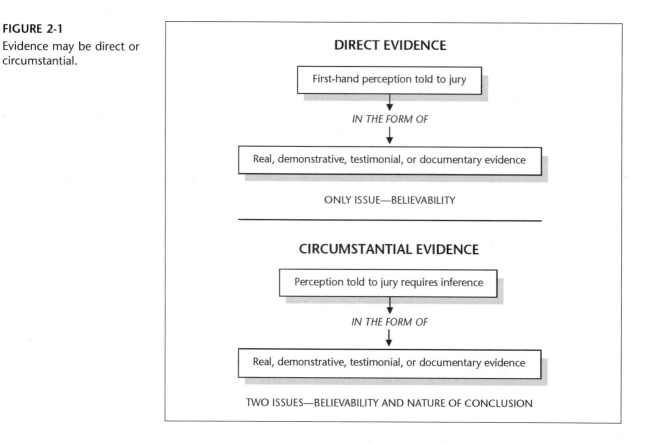

DIRECT EVIDENCE

First-hand perception told to jury

IN THE FORM OF

Real, demonstrative, testimonial, or documentary evidence

ONLY ISSUE—BELIEVABILITY

CIRCUMSTANTIAL EVIDENCE

Perception told to jury requires inference

IN THE FORM OF

Real, demonstrative, testimonial, or documentary evidence

TWO ISSUES—BELIEVABILITY AND NATURE OF CONCLUSION

Parties prefer direct evidence, because no inference is required with direct evidence, but few cases that go to trial have an abundance of direct evidence. Most parties must rely on circumstantial evidence to convince a jury. If there is overwhelming direct evidence by credible witnesses, a civil case will be settled and a criminal case will end in a plea agreement before trial. But generally the situation is more like this: the witness did not see someone walk across the sandy beach; the witness saw only the footprints in the sand that leads to the inference that someone walked across the beach.

Real, Demonstrative, Testimonial, and Documentary Evidence

Another distinction is made with regard to the physical objects that may be used at trial. Physical objects may be direct or circumstantial evidence and are further classified as either real or demonstrative evidence. **Real evidence** is an object that was a direct part of the incident, such as the gun in the murder case. Real evidence allows jurors to draw a first-hand conclusion based on the evidence of their senses.

Demonstrative evidence is an aid used by a witness to assist the jury in understanding the witness's testimony. In the murder case, the detective could use a drawing of the scene of the murder to show the placement of the body and the location of the gun in order to help the jurors understand what she is

real evidence An object produced at trial for inspection by the jury.

demonstrative evidence An object or thing that assists the jury's understanding of testimony.

trying to convey to them as an illustration of her testimony. Demonstrative evidence also can be a model or map. Demonstrative evidence illustrates and clarifies, and it is not a direct part of the incident.

With enhanced technical capabilities, the use of demonstrative evidence in civil and criminal trials is playing an increasingly important role in impressing jurors, particularly in complex cases. Demonstrative evidence is explored in detail in Chapter 7.

Testimonial evidence is the most common form of evidence. It includes the oral evidence given by a witness at trial while under oath. **Documentary evidence** is a document, like a written contract. In a later chapter, we will find that documentary evidence is often introduced through a witness who can also testify to the document's *authenticity,* that is, the document is what its proponent says it is. Thus, testimonial evidence and documentary evidence are often intertwined. Either form of evidence may be direct or circumstantial evidence in a case.

RELATIONSHIP BETWEEN TRIAL AND APPELLATE PROCESSES

Although the use of the Rules of Evidence essentially ends with the conclusion of the trial, the rulings by a judge on evidentiary matters are in the shadow of the appellate process. The loser at trial needs a legal basis on which to appeal the jury's verdict to a higher court. The loser, called the *appellant* or *plaintiff in error,* needs a reason based on a mistake made by the judge on a matter of law, such as a decision on the admissibility of evidence. The winner at trial, the *appellee* or the *defendant in error,* will argue on appeal that the trial judge's decision was legally correct at the same time that the appellant is arguing that the judge made an egregious error that cost the appellant the verdict.

Objections

The appellate court usually will not consider a trial court judge's determination on admissibility of evidence unless the opponent at trial challenged the evidence by objecting to it at the time the evidence was offered. Generally, when the court admits evidence, an **objection** to it must state the reason for the objection, unless the reason is obvious from the context of the interchange in the courtroom.

The attorney at trial sometimes interrupts the testimony of a witness by saying, "Objection, Your Honor," and then stating the reason for the objection. Opposing counsel may respond, and then the judge rules on the objection, either *sustaining* (upholding) the objection or *overruling* (rejecting) the objection. Often, during trial preparation, objections can be predicted, and the paralegal can research the underlying legal issue so the attorney can effectively argue why the judge should sustain or overrule an objection.

Once the judge rules, the parties must proceed accordingly. Either the jury will get to hear the evidence or not hear the evidence, depending on the judge's ruling. Figure 2-2 gives an example of an objection.

testimonial evidence Statements by witnesses under oath at a legal proceeding.

documentary evidence A document that has legal effect and is offered at a legal proceeding.

objection A procedure where a party asserts that the opponent's evidence is improper and that the judge should not allow the jury to have the evidence.

FIGURE 2-2

An objection may be overruled or sustained.

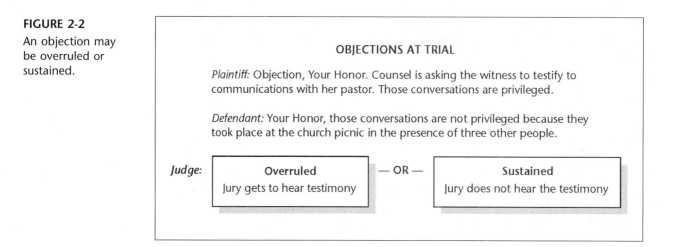

OBJECTIONS AT TRIAL

Plaintiff: Objection, Your Honor. Counsel is asking the witness to testify to communications with her pastor. Those conversations are privileged.

Defendant: Your Honor, those conversations are not privileged because they took place at the church picnic in the presence of three other people.

Judge:

Overruled	— OR —	Sustained
Jury gets to hear testimony		Jury does not hear the testimony

Offers of Proof

When the judge refuses to allow a party to introduce evidence for the jury to hear, the aggrieved party must make an offer of proof to preserve the objection for a possible appeal. An **offer of proof** is where the party who is a proponent of the evidence states what a witness will say, or shows the court the object and tells the court what the witness will say about the object. The offer of proof may entail calling the witness to the stand to testify without the jury being present. The judge sends the jury from the courtroom before the offer of proof is made. In this way, the judge acts as a filter. The judge hears the evidence, and the record is made for the appeal. The jury is called back into the courtroom by the judge, and the trial resumes without the jury's having heard the evidence because the judge determined that the proffered evidence was not admissible.

Rule 103.   Rulings on Evidence

   (a) Effect of erroneous ruling.   Error may not be predicated upon a ruling which admits or excludes evidence unless a substantial right of the party is affected, and
      (1) Objection.   In case the ruling is one admitting evidence, a timely objection or motion to strike appears of record, stating the specific ground of objection, if the specific ground was not apparent from the context; or
      (2) Offer of proof.   In case the ruling is one excluding evidence, the substance of the evidence was made known to the court by offer or was apparent from the context within which questions were asked.

The Record

A stenographic record of the trial is made so that if the proponent of the evidence decides to appeal the verdict (assuming the proponent loses the case), a **transcript** of the trial is available as a writtten record of the evidentiary issue. The appellate court knows nothing about the trial except what is contained

offer of proof A procedure where evidence is presented at trial outside the hearing of the jury in order to establish for the record the nature of the evidence the judge has ruled as inadmissible.

transcript An official written copy of legal proceedings, usually prepared by a court reporter.

in the written record, or transcript, that was prepared originally by a court reporter during the trial.

Also, it is from the transcript of the trial that the attorneys prepare their briefs for the appellate court. **Briefs** provide an outline of the case, with sections stating the facts of the case as presented at trial in support of the verdict, legal arguments in support of the positions taken by the parties, and generally an argument to the court as to why the verdict should or should not stand based on the alleged mistake made by the trial court judge.

The Appeal

The mistake of the trial court judge that is alleged on appeal by the appellant must be one that affected a substantial right of the appealing party. In other words, the appellant says to the appellate court that the reason the jury did not find for the appellant was that the judge made a mistake in filtering specific evidence. That is, as a matter of law, the judge made a mistake in allowing the jury to hear, or not allowing the jury to hear, specific evidence. And the appeal alleges that the mistake was not harmless, because the outcome of the trial would have been different but for this mistake by the judge. If the appellate court agrees, the mistake at trial is called **reversible error.**

Rule 103. Rulings on Evidence

(b) Record of offer and ruling. The court may add any other or further statement which shows the character of the evidence, the form in which it was offered, the objection made, and the ruling thereon. It may direct the making of an offer in question and answer form.

(c) Hearing of jury. In jury cases, proceedings shall be conducted, to the extent practicable, so as to prevent inadmissible evidence from being suggested to the jury by any means, such as making statements or offers of proof or asking questions in the hearing of the jury.

If the appellate court agrees with the appellant that the judge made a mistake that affected the outcome of the trial, the case is then **remanded**, or sent back, to the trial court for a new trial, where the judge must take into account the decision by the appellate court on the admissibility of the evidence. The second time the case is tried, the trial court judge filters the contested piece of evidence in accordance with the directions of the appellate court.

In the previous example of the murder trial, assume that it is established at trial that the gun found at the murder scene belongs to the defendant. The detective testifies that the gun was found at the murder scene. The defense objects to the detective's testimony because a "chain of custody" was not established by the prosecutor in questioning the detective. A proper **chain of custody** in this case would include a written record of who had the gun when, and for what purpose. The chain begins at the time the evidence is taken into the custody of law enforcement or investigator, and it continues through the trial.

In our hypothetical case, the defense shows that the gun from the murder scene was taken from the police evidence room before trial without being

briefs Written arguments prepared for an appeal, outlining the facts and legal arguments that are the basis for the appeal.

reversible error A mistake made by a judge as to a matter of law that substantially affects the rights of one of the parties during trial.

remand To send a case back to the court below for action consistent with the appellate court's opinion.

chain of custody The written record that establishes the location of physical evidence from the time it is collected until the time it is offered as evidence at trial.

signed out properly. The police records do not show who signed the gun out or for what purpose, only that it was checked out and returned a day later. Before the gun was checked out of the evidence room, the police had not had the opportunity to take down the serial number to check for ownership.

The defense can argue to the trial court judge, outside the hearing of the jury, that the gun in the courtroom is not in fact the one found at the murder scene and does not belong to the defendant. The judge can rule against the defendant and allow the jury to hear the detective testify about the gun. The defendant can attempt to impeach the testimony of the detective based on the break in the chain of custody.

Harmless Error

Assume the gun is the strongest circumstantial evidence against the defendant at the trial, where no direct evidence links the defendant to the murder.

The defendant can argue to the appellate court that but for the gun evidence and the detective's testimony regarding it, the jury would have found in favor of the defendant. If the appellate court agrees with this contention and finds that the mistake by the judge in admitting the evidence was not harmless, the appellate court could find for the defendant and remand the case for a new trial where the detective could not testify about the gun found at the scene.

Generally, the mistakes of law alleged by an appellant are not adequate for the appellate court to change the outcome of the trial. The trial court decision would then stand, and the appellant would remain the loser, because the trial court judge committed **harmless error**. It was an error, but not one that the appellate court thinks substantially affected the appealing party's rights or the outcome of the case (Figure 2-3).

More than likely, the appellate court will find that there was enough other evidence to support the verdict regardless of the evidentiary mistake alleged on appeal. In other words, it was not a close case, and the evidence as a whole overwhelmingly supported the verdict.

harmless error A mistake as to a matter of law made by the judge at trial but that did not sufficiently prejudice the appellant to warrant a modification of the court's decision.

FIGURE 2-3

A judge's mistake that has no substantial effect on the trial is a harmless error.

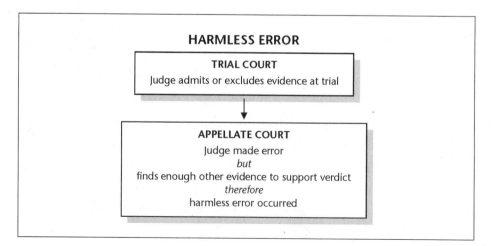

HARMLESS ERROR

TRIAL COURT
Judge admits or excludes evidence at trial

APPELLATE COURT
Judge made error
but
finds enough other evidence to support verdict
therefore
harmless error occurred

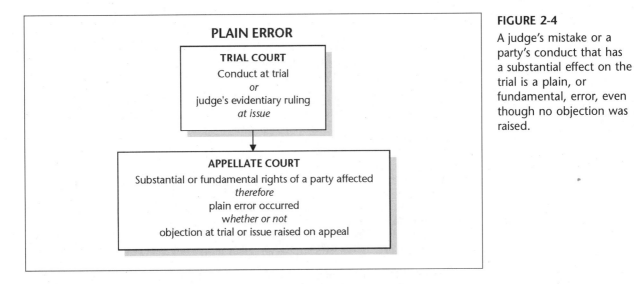

FIGURE 2-4
A judge's mistake or a party's conduct that has a substantial effect on the trial is a plain, or fundamental, error, even though no objection was raised.

Plain Error

Sometimes the appellate court reviews the record of a trial and finds that an action by a party or a ruling by the judge substantially affected the rights of another party. The opposing party does not have to object at trial for this kind of error to be raised on appeal. The appellate court can find that there was **plain error** because the conduct or judicial mistake was so egregious that even though there was no objection at trial and the issue was not raised on appeal, the conduct or mistake resulted in an adverse verdict (Figure 2-4). If the court finds plain error, the case is then remanded for a new trial in light of the ruling by the appellate court and its view of the offensive conduct or mistake.

Appellate courts do not find plain error very often. Ordinarily, the burden is on the parties at trial to raise timely and appropriate objections and to argue the grounds for the appeal to the appellate court. But plain error involves conduct so wrong that a new trial is deemed necessary. Plain error is referred to as *fundamental error* in some states because of case law predating the federal rules. For instance, when the Florida Evidence Code was adopted, Florida appellate decisions had been consistently using the phrase *fundamental error*. To avoid confusion, the Florida Evidence Code conformed to the practice of using this phrase instead of *plain error,* as is used in the federal rules.

Both terms (plain and fundamental) imply that the error goes to the foundation of the case, that it is a part of the very essence of the case. The conduct of a party or the mistake of the trial court judge is so overt, it does not require a party to raise it on appeal, and the appellate court can recognize it on its own. See Illustration 2-2.

Rule 103.   Rulings on Evidence

(d) Plain error. Nothing in this rule precludes taking notice of plain errors affecting substantial rights although they were not brought to the attention of the court.

---

plain error A mistake as to a matter of law by the trial court judge that substantially affects the rights of the appellant and, even though it was not objected to at trial, warrants a reversal of a verdict; also called *fundamental error.*

Illustration 2-2 _____

In a nuisance action, plaintiffs were homeowners who sued the owner of a sod transfer and pine straw baling operation, alleging the defendant engaged in an illegal use of his property, interfering with the plaintiffs' quiet enjoyment of their property.

The closing argument by the attorney for the plaintiffs appealed to the juror's passions, asking them to "envision themselves pulling rats out of their pools, bales of pine straw starting fires in their yards, and thousands of mosquitoes and other vermin flying in their neighborhood." Plaintiffs won.

The closing argument resulted in a finding of fundamental error (plain error) by the appellate court.

Where the closing argument is pervasive, inflammatory, and prejudicial, precluding the jury's rational consideration of a case even after corrected by proper instruction from the judge, fundamental error has occurred. Fairness of the trial is damaged to the point that the public's interest in the justice system is compromised. The juror's consideration of the evidence in the case was overwhelmed by the inflammatory and prejudicial comments made in the closing argument.

The trial court judge had granted the defendant's motion for a new trial because the judge did not think his instruction cured the effects of the closing argument. The **pro se** defendant did not raise the issue on appeal. *Tremblay v. Santa Rosa County,* 688 So. 2d 985, 987–988 (Fla. 1st D.C.A. 1997).

_____

The Courtroom

When a trial is without a jury, the judge decides issues of fact as well as law, and evidence rules are not applied strictly. The judge acts as his or her own filter, without having to be concerned that the "trier of fact" will be unduly prejudiced by what the trier of fact hears. The reasoning is that the trier of fact is the judge, a person with sophisticated knowledge of the law, unlike a jury, made up of laypersons and thus more likely to be prejudiced by evidence.

Furthermore, the uninitiated observer in the courtroom should not be shocked when the judge errs in an evidentiary ruling. A judge may not be as knowledgeable about the rules of evidence as the attorneys would like the judge to be. And the mistake may be judged a harmless error on appeal. At most trials, enough evidence is offered to keep the mistake from making a difference in the outcome.

SUMMARY _____

The Federal Rules of Evidence are codified and periodically amended in a process outlined by federal statute. The courts continue to interpret and explain the rules as controversies are litigated.

Most states have adopted evidence rules modeled after the federal rules. Nevertheless, there can be significant differences.

The federal rules apply to a variety of proceedings in the federal court system, but they do not apply to grand jury proceedings and enumerated criminal proceedings where guilt is not an issue.

pro se A person handles the person's own case in court without an attorney.

The trial is a drama unfolding before the jury, with the judge directing the action. The parties make requests to the judge in the form of motions, the results of which determine the direction a case may take.

Two types of evidence can be presented to the jury: direct evidence and circumstantial evidence. Direct evidence proves a fact in issue without relying on inference. Circumstantial evidence necessarily involves inference, or proof of a fact in issue by presenting indirect evidence.

Most evidence is in the form of testimony, but evidence can also include real evidence (physical objects), documents, or demonstrative evidence that illustrates the testimony of a witness.

During the trial, parties must object to the exclusion of any evidence they think should be admitted so that the issue will be preserved in the written record for an appeal. An offer of proof is made outside the hearing of the jury in order to make the record but not prejudice the proceeding when the judge has ruled the evidence inadmissible.

After considering the appeal, the appellate court can find reversible error and remand the case for proceedings consistent with the ruling of the appellate court. On the other hand, the appellate court may agree with the appellant that the trial court judge erred with regard to an evidentiary ruling, but the appellate court may decide the error was harmless because there was enough other evidence to support the verdict.

A well-prepared attorney who is knowledgeable about the evidence rules often can influence the judge with persuasive arguments on evidentiary issues. Preparation comes from the hard work and professionalism of the legal team. In criminal cases, law enforcement personnel whose job it is to gather and analyze evidence in a prescribed manner work with the prosecutor, who may also have an investigator and a paralegal. In civil cases, the legal team includes paralegals and investigators.

With a broad understanding of the context of the trial as taking place in the shadow of the appellate court, it is apparent why the parties should prepare for trial with a thorough understanding of the Federal Rules of Evidence. The purpose is twofold: to get enough evidence to the jury through the judge and to keep the opponent from getting contrary evidence to the jury. The Rules of Evidence and the case law are the framework within which this process occurs. The judge and the attorneys must have a working understanding of the Federal Rules of Evidence in order for the drama to sensibly unfold before the jury. All must be aware of the appellate court waiting in the wings, ready to critique the performance if asked.

✔ CHECKPOINTS

❑ Federal Rules of Evidence
  1. Codified.
  2. Case law interprets.
  3. Many state rules similar.
❑ Application of Federal Rules of Evidence
  1. Federal court system, generally.

  2. Privileged confidential communications inadmissible.

  3. Not used in the following:
    ▪ Grand jury proceedings.
    ▪ Criminal proceedings where guilt is not an issue.

❑ Overview of the trial
  1. Motions request judge decide an issue: oral or written.
  2. Motion for directed verdict and motion for judgment of acquittal request an end to the proceeding because the opponent failed to make a *prima facie* case.
❑ Types of evidence
  1. Direct: no inference.
  2. Circumstantial: inference.
  3. Real: object or thing.
  4. Demonstrative: explains testimony.
  5. Documentary: documents.
❑ Trial and appeal
  1. Objections at trial preserve dispute for appeal.

  2. Offers of proof: written or oral evidence presented at a hearing outside presence of jury so evidentiary issue is preserved for appeal.
  3. Appeal: transcript and briefs supplied to the appellate court.
  4. Reversible error: mistake warrants further action by lower court.
  5. Remand: sent back to trial court.
  6. Harmless error: mistake not a problem because overwhelming evidence supports verdict.
  7. Plain error: fundamental error affects rights of party and necessitates reversal of verdict.

APPLICATIONS

Application 2-1

During the murder trial of O. J. Simpson in California in 1995, the team of defense attorneys attempted to establish that the police investigation of the murder scene was flawed and that there were numerous opportunities for the police to tamper with evidence implicating Mr. Simpson. The prosecution called witnesses to testify about blood samples and other physical evidence it hoped would implicate Mr. Simpson in the eyes of the jury.

FROM THE ASSOCIATED PRESS
by Linda Deutsch
February 23, 1995

LOS ANGELES—One of the detectives in charge of the O. J. Simpson case conceded Wednesday that the investigation was flawed by failures to collect blood from a gate, preserve the contents of Nicole Brown Simpson's stomach and test blood splattered on her back.

Detective Tom Lange, on the stand for a third day, said some of the holes in the case were the fault of evidence technicians and the coroner.

But the detective stoutly defended other decisions that were his own. And the normally placid witness bristled when defense attorney Johnnie Cochran Jr. pressed him on why no test was performed to determine if Nicole Brown Simpson had been raped.

"In my observation and my experience, sex was the last thing on the mind of this attacker. It was an overkill, a brutal overkill. There was no evidence of rape," Lange said, abandoning his usual dispassionate police lingo.

Cochran seemed taken aback and frantically tried to stop the detective's statement with an objection in mid-sentence, but failed. Court was recessed for the day moments later.

Cochran's questioning of the taciturn Lange was part of a long-range attempt to portray the police investigation of Nicole Brown Simpson and Ronald Goldman was so sloppy that the blood and other forensic evidence cannot be trusted.

Cochran showed the jury a photo of the woman's bare back splattered with blood—blood that was washed off by the coroner's office without being tested.

Asked if he believed that evidence could be useful, Lange said, "I felt it might be important, yes."

"It would be a key factor if that were the perpetrator's blood, isn't that correct?" Cochran asked.

"It may or may not be," Lange said, "but I would liked to have had that blood."

Lange also acknowledged that he asked criminalist Dennis Fung on June 13 to collect blood from a rear gate of the condo and found out that it was not done until July 3—three weeks after the police crime-scene tape had come down.

Class Discussion Questions

1. The forensic evidence that was the subject of Detective Lange's testimony included blood samples taken (or not taken) from the crime scene or Nicole Brown Simpson's body. Are the blood samples direct or circumstantial evidence of Mr. Simpson's guilt?

2. What is an example of evidence that the prosecutor might present as direct evidence of Mr. Simpson's guilt?

3. In a case where there is no direct evidence of a defendant's guilt, why and how is the police investigation even more important to the prosecutor?

Application 2-2

In the case that follows, Mr. Smith appealed his conviction for first-degree murder. He alleged on appeal that the state failed to offer any evidence of premeditation, an element of first-degree murder that the state had to prove.

Smith v. State
568 So. 2d 965 (Fla. 1st D.C.A. 1990)

WOLF, Judge.

The appellant, Donald Lewis Smith, was previously married to the victim, Judy Smith. Although they had divorced, they were living together at the time of Judy's disappearance on March 17, 1988. The victim was last seen alive at a party with the appellant where they had been seen holding hands.

On March 18, the victim was supposed to have picked up the couple's two children from her father who was baby-sitting. She never appeared. The appellant told a number of inconsistent stories concerning his wife's disappearance. Donald went to the victim's father's house after the disappearance and told him that Judy had left because she was tired of being a wife and mother. He later told the victim's supervisor at work that his wife had disappeared, he didn't know where she went, and she would be back in about two weeks. The appellant told the next-door neighbor that he and Judy had a fight and that she had voluntarily left. Several days after the disappearance, however, the next-door neighbor noticed that all of the victim's personal items, including eyeglasses and contacts, were still at the trailer.

On Tuesday, the 22nd, a neighbor urged the appellant to report to the police that Judy was missing. The appellant agreed but, in fact, never called the police.

There is evidence that both the appellant and the victim were involved in affairs with other persons. The appellant told the victim's supervisor that at the party on the 17th he discovered that the victim was having an affair with a co-worker. About three or four days after the disappearance, the next-door neighbor observed the appellant and another woman with their arms around each other.

The police found the body of Judy Smith floating in Tampa Bay on March 27, 1988. The body was wrapped in chains and had a blue bedspread taped around it.

An autopsy was performed and the medical examiner reported that the body had been in the water for six to eight days. He could not find any evidence of trauma or a wound, but stated that such evidence could have been obscured by decomposition. The medical examiner concluded that the victim died of asphyxiation due to strangulation or drowning. He could not tell, however, whether the victim had been strangled and killed prior to being placed in the water.

The police later searched the appellant's trailer. Among the items seized was the trunk lining from the appellant's car. A chain, similar to the one found on the body that had previously been seen by several neighbors, was not found on the property. In addition, a bedspread was found which matched the bedspread wrapped around the victim's body.

At trial, an FBI agent testified as an expert on forensic chemistry that he examined that pieces of black tape and the bedspread wrapped around the victim's body and noted pink fibers adhering to both exhibits. These fibers were synthetic plastic. The expert testified that he found identical pink fibers on the trunk liner and insulation from the appellant's car. He also compared the tape from the bedspread with tape which had been seized from the defendant's workplace and testified that it was the same type of tape. Appellant was arrested for first degree murder.

Following deliberations, the jury found the defendant guilty of first degree murder.

Premeditation is the essential element which distinguishes first degree murder from second degree murder.

> Premeditation is more than a mere intent to kill; it is a fully formed conscious purpose to kill. This purpose to kill may be formed a moment before the act but must exist for a sufficient length of time to permit reflection as to the nature of the act to be committed and the probable result of that act.

Premeditation may be proven by circumstantial evidence. *Cochran v. State*, 547 So. 2d 928 (Fla. 1989). Whether the evidence fails to exclude a reasonable hypothesis of innocence is generally a jury question. If there is substantial, competent evidence to support it, the jury verdict will not be reversed. *Id.* at 930. However, *Cochran* also says, "Where the element of premeditation is sought to be established by circumstantial evidence, the evidence relied upon by the state must be inconsistent with every other reasonable inference." *Id.*

Where the state's proof fails to exclude a reasonable hypothesis that the homicide occurred other than by premeditated design, a verdict of first degree murder cannot be sustained. Some of the evidence from which a jury may infer premeditation is the nature of the weapon, presence or absence of adequate provocation, previous difficulties between the parties, the manner in which the homicide is committed, the nature and manner of the wound, and the accused's actions before and after the homicide.

In the instant case, however, the state was unable to prove the manner in which the homicide was committed, what occurred immediately prior to the homicide, the nature of the weapon, or the nature of any wounds. In addition, there was no evidence of the presence or absence of provocation and very little evidence of previous difficulties between the appellant and the victim.

Even taking the evidence presented in the light most favorable to the state, as we are required to do by *Cochran,* the state merely established the following: the parties were divorced but were still living together; the appellant was having an affair which continued immediately after the death of the victim; on the night the victim disappeared, the appellant may have discovered that the victim was having an affair; the appellant took a number of steps to cover up the crime, including not immediately reporting to the police that the victim was missing and lying about the fact that the victim voluntarily left the trailer. The strongest evidence against the defendant concerned his efforts to conceal the homicide.

While all of these factors are consistent with a homicide, none of them is inconsistent with a killing which may have occurred in the heat of passion or without premeditation. Because the evidence is not inconsistent with every reasonable hypothesis of innocence, we must vacate the judgment for first degree murder and instruct the court to enter a judgment for second degree murder.

Class Discussion Questions

1. In Florida, can the state use circumstantial evidence to prove premeditation?
2. The court states that a jury may infer premeditation from different evidence, including
   a. The nature of the weapon.
   b. Presence or absence of adequate provocation.
   c. Previous difficulties between the parties.
   d. The manner in which the homicide was committed.
   e. The nature of the wound.
   f. The defendant's actions before and after the death of the victim.

Review the summary of the testimony, and fill in a fact that either supports or fails to support each of these categories of evidence.

3. What circumstantial evidence led the jury to convict the defendant of Judy Smith's murder? That is, what were the bricks that made the wall, or picture, for the jury?
4. Who was the witness who connected the black tape and bedspread found around the victim's body to the defendant?

Application 2-3

The following excerpt is from a case that was an action based on products liability against the manufacturer of automobile batteries. The plaintiff was a 16-year-old boy permanently blinded in one eye when a car battery exploded. Mr. McKnight alleged that a negligent design or manufacturing defect caused the explosion that resulted in his injury. The jury found for Mr. McKnight and awarded him $1.2 million in compensatory damages. The defendant appealed, alleging that the judge erred by admitting certain testimony of the plaintiff's expert witness, Dr. Jacobson. He performed experiments with car batteries and testified with regard to the issue of the cause of the explosion of the battery at issue in this case. The court found that the trial court erred in admitting evidence of one of the battery tests (the "leak" test), but not another (the "coordinate" test). Note the references to the trial transcript.

McKnight v. Johnson Controls, Inc.
36 F.3d 1396 (8th Cir. 1994)

HANSEN, Circuit Judge.

On August 10, 1988, Randy C. McKnight, a 16-year-old Missouri resident, was permanently blinded in one eye when an automobile battery designed and manufactured by JCI, a Wisconsin company, exploded. On the day of the accident, McKnight borrowed a friend's car and drove it to his residence. He shut off the ignition for a few minutes while he went inside. When he returned to the car, it would not start. He popped the hood and twisted the battery cable on the negative terminal attempting to get a better connection. He tried the car again, and it still would not start. He again attempted to get a better connection by twisting the battery cable and repeated this procedure two or three times. When he twisted the battery cable on the last attempt, the battery exploded. The battery had been purchased at a local store six to eight months earlier.

McKnight filed this products liability action against JCI. The case eventually went to trial on McKnight's claims of strict product liability and negligent design or manufacturing defect. The parties agreed that the explosion occurred when a spark from the battery ignited hydrogen gas escaping from the battery. The issue for trial was whether the hydrogen explosion occurred as a result of a defect in the battery before it was shipped by JCI or from damage to the battery's vent caps caused by improper care for or use of the battery after it was purchased.

The case was tried the first time in March 1992. The jury could not reach a verdict, and a mistrial was declared. On retrial in September 1992, McKnight prevailed, and the jury awarded him $1.2 million in compensatory damages. The district court denied JCI's motion for judgment as a matter of law and its alternative motion for new trial. JCI appeals.

The key question is whether a new trial should have been granted to avoid a miscarriage of justice. ("The district court can only disturb a jury verdict to prevent a miscarriage of justice.")

JCI's argument for judgment as a matter of law focuses on the testimony of Dr. Jacobson, McKnight's expert witness. JCI argues the district court should have excluded his testimony on a number of grounds and that when the testimony is properly excluded from the record, this court must enter judgment as a matter of law because there is no evidence to support the jury verdict. Alternatively, JCI argues that the errors in admitting Jacobson's testimony or any of a number of other errors the district court committed, at a minimum, entitles JCI to a new trial.

Not all errors in admitting evidence, however, are grounds for reversal. Reversal is not required when the erroneous admission of evidence is harmless. "For there to be harmless error, the improperly admitted evidence cannot have had a 'substantial influence' on the jury's verdict." Stated another way, the error is harmless only if "the error did not influence or had only a slight influence on the verdict."

After careful study, we cannot say that the improperly admitted leak test evidence had a "substantial influence" on the jury's verdict. The harmful effect of the improperly admitted evidence is reduced where there is substantial evidence in the record beyond the evidence improperly admitted to support the jury's decision. Here, the coordinate test, which we have concluded was properly admitted, provides substantial evidence to support the jury's decision. The coordinate test indicated that there were gaps in the fit of the caps to the battery wells which were large enough to allow significant amounts of hydrogen gas to escape the battery. The coordinate test alone supports Jacobson's theory of the cause of the explosion.

Moreover, in closing argument, McKnight relied on Jacobson's theory of the explosion with very little reference to the experimental leak test he used to reach those conclusions. We find only two brief references to the leak test in McKnight's entire closing argument. (Tr. Vol. V. at 144, 146–147.) In making those references, McKnight never argued that the leak test reconstructed the accident or otherwise demonstrated how the accident happened. McKnight focused his closing argument instead on the results from the coordinate test and on the other evidence he introduced. McKnight argued to the jury that the coordinate test established that there was a gap in the fit between the battery wells and the gap was large enough to cause the explosion, (Tr. Vol. V. at 144–45, 173–174); that JCI's own earlier tests had established the explosion theory that Jacobson advocated in this case, (id. at 142–143); that JCI never did any testing for leaks at the factory in spite of their knowledge of the possibility of explosions, (id. at 143); and that JCI's experts' testimony about the "interference fit" of the vent caps on the wells could not be believed, (id. at 145–46, 174–75).

We cannot find that the improperly introduced evidence from the leak test was a focal point or a substantial portion of McKnight's case. Because of the testimony from the plaintiff's expert which admitted the differing conditions, and the strong countervailing evidence from JCI which pointed out the probable resulting effects of the differences between the accident and the leak test experiment conditions, we cannot say with confidence that the trial court's error affected JCI's substantial rights. Accordingly ... , we conclude that the trial court's error in admitting the leak test evidence was harmless and, therefore, not a basis for reversal in this case.

... JCI failed to object to Jacobson's testimony on the basis that he was not qualified as an expert or that he lacked a scientific basis for his opinions. "Without an objection and a proper request for relief, the matter is waived and will receive no consideration on appeal absent plain error." JCI argues strenuously that it did object to Jacobson's qualifications as an expert and the scientific basis for his opinions. The record does not support JCI's assertions.

JCI argues that it objected to both Jacobson's qualifications and the scientific basis for his opinions in the following statement:

> If the Court please, the objection to this testing and the opinions concerning this testing goes to the foundation for the testimony. The witness has said that the two batteries are substantially similar. And I submit to the Court that when the witness is attempting to prove what he's attempting to prove with these tests, and that is the exact fit of plugs and caps in the holes, that the foundation must be more than that. What he's trying to do here is to use a test on a battery, for which a foundation hasn't been laid sufficiently, to prove the ultimate issue in this case, and that is a defect that gaps exist between the plugs and the walls. And I submit to the Court that a sufficient foundation to use this battery in that way has not been laid in this case. (Tr. Vol. III at 73).

This objection fails to raise any question about the scientific validity of the principles and methodology underlying his testimony. Likewise, this objection fails to raise any question about whether his tests were the type relied upon by experts in the field to indicate JCI was objecting to his testimony under Rule 703. An objection on one ground does not allow a party to argue on appeal that the evidence should have been excluded on different grounds.

To the extent that JCI is arguing that the district court was required to exercise its gatekeeping authority over expert testimony without an objection, we disagree.

The only remaining question is whether the district court committed plain error in allowing this evidence into the record. JCI has not argued for, nor do we find, plain error.

JCI next argues that the trial court impermissibly allowed Jacobson to offer speculative testimony that there was a manufacturing defect in the battery. JCI asserts that Jacobson testified that "[t]here could very well be a manufacturing defect," (Tr. Vol. III at 107), and that it was merely possible that a manufacturing defect occurred and that such testimony should not have been allowed, (id. at 156). McKnight claims again that JCI failed to object to this testimony and has thus waived the argument. JCI argues that it did object to the testimony when it moved to strike his testimony and its conclusion and when it made a motion for a new trial or judgment as a matter of law and asserted these issues.

The testimony that JCI claims is unduly speculative came in both during Jacobson's direct examination (id. at 107), and during JCI's cross-examination of him, (id. at 156). We first point out that the only objection JCI points to as preserving the error for appeal came at the close of Jacobson's direct testimony, before the alleged speculative testimony on cross-examination came into the record. (Id. at 146–48.) Moreover, a review of JCI's objection shows that JCI never even addressed the speculative nature of the testimony. This objection clearly and simply addressed only the causal connection between his testimony and the ultimate issue McKnight needed to prove. (Id.)

Moreover, JCI's argument essentially concedes that JCI made no contemporaneous objection. Federal Rule of Evidence 103(a)(1) requires objections to evidence to be "timely." "The rule is well settled in this circuit that for an objection to be timely it must be made at the earliest possible opportunity after the ground of objection becomes apparent, or it will be considered waived." If the ground for the objection becomes apparent while the witness is testifying, a subsequent motion to strike the testimony after the witness finishes does not preserve the issue for appeal. We find that the grounds asserted for objecting to Jacobson's "speculative" testimony on direct examination were apparent at the time Jacobson provided the testimony and, thus, the motion to strike was not a timely objection, and no error can be predicated on the court's determination of it.

Having considered all of the assignments of alleged error, the judgment of the district court is affirmed.

Class Discussion Questions

1. The appellate court found the trial court judge erred in allowing in testimony by Dr. Jacobson on the leak test that he conducted. However, the appellate court did not order a new trial for the defendant. Explain why the defendant did not get the relief requested.

2. JCI contended an objection was raised at trial to Dr. Jacobson's qualifications as an expert and to the scientific basis for his opinions. In fact, what was the nature of JCI's objections, as quoted by the court from volume III of the transcript, at page 73?

3. The court found the objection at trial was to the foundation issue, and on appeal, JCI said the objection was to qualifications as an expert and to the scientific basis of the experiment. Why would the court not allow the foundation objection to cover the two issues raised on appeal?

4. Does a motion to strike after a witness testifies at trial satisfy the requirements of timely objection?

EXERCISES

1. Does your state refer to plain error as fundamental error? Locate the specific rule in your state evidence rules.

2. In your state, is a motion for directed verdict in a criminal case referred to as a motion for judgment of acquittal?

3. The witness testifies, "I saw the defendant flee from the room where the victim was found murdered."
   a. The statement is direct evidence of what?
   b. The statement is circumstantial evidence of what?

4. In a personal injury case, is the mutilated hand of the plaintiff direct or circumstantial evidence of the permanent injury that is alleged?

5. In a personal injury case, is a skeletal model that is a reproduction used for explanatory purposes demonstrative evidence or real evidence?

6. Is a jury viewing of a scene where the incident at issue occurred, and where no commentary is allowed, an example of demonstrative evidence or real evidence?

RULES REFERENCED IN THIS CHAPTER

Rule 1103. Title

Rule 1101. Applicability of Rules

Rule 102. Purpose and Construction

Rule 103. Rulings on Evidence

NOTES

[1] The general rulemaking power of the United States Supreme Court and the procedures followed in exercise of this power are found in 28 U.S.C.A. §§ 2072–2074 (West 1995). The rulemaking power is subject to public and congressional review.

[2] Edward W. Cleary. *McCormick's Handbook of the Law of Evidence*. St. Paul: West Publishing Co., 1984.

Role of the Judge and Jury at Trial

ROLE OF THE JUDGE

The roles of the judge and the jury in the federal court system developed over time along distinct lines. Generally, the judge decides matters of law, such as the admissibility of evidence. The jury determines the facts, after hearing the evidence, deciding what happened between the parties. In a majority of states, the judge and jury have similar roles as in the federal court system. The judge sees that the trial runs smoothly, without wasting the time of the participants.

Rule 611. Mode and Order of Interrogation and Presentation

(a) **Control by court.** The court shall exercise reasonable control over the mode and order of interrogating witnesses and presenting evidence so as to (1) make the interrogation and presentation effective for the ascertainment of the truth, (2) avoid needless consumption of time, and (3) protect witnesses from harassment or undue embarrassment.

Recall the discussion in Chapter 2 of the jury as a clean slate, without knowledge of the details of the dispute to be tried before it. The case unfolds before the jury through evidence presented by the two opposing parties. The role of the judge is to see that the adversarial process is confined within defined limits and the trial is conducted appropriately. Part of the judge's role is to filter what evidence the parties will be allowed to present to the jury. The Rules of Evidence and related case law set the parameters within which the judge determines what the jury can see and hear, deciding evidentiary issues as a matter of law. In enforcing the Rules of Evidence, the judge assures that each party will receive a fair opportunity to present a case. The judge keeps the jury from hearing matters that might prejudice its consideration of the case.

Rule 103. Rulings on Evidence

(c) **Hearing of jury.** In jury cases, proceedings shall be conducted, to the extent practicable, so as to prevent inadmissible evidence from being suggested to the jury by any means, such as making statements or offers of proof or asking questions in the hearing of the jury.

The trial court judge is obligated to rule promptly on evidentiary objections. The judge may call witnesses on the judge's own initiative and can question those who testify so long as there is no hint of partisanship. Based on precedent, the trial court judge may even comment on the weight of the evidence and the credibility of witnesses. However, this practice is not allowed in every state. See Illustration 3-1 for an example of a state rule contrary to federal practice.

Illustration 3-1

A judge may not sum up the evidence or comment to the jury upon the weight of the evidence, the credibility of the witnesses, or the guilt of the accused. § 90.106 of the Florida Evidence Code.

Matters Outside the Judge's Control

Impressions on the clean slate of the jury's collective mind are controlled to some degree by the judge, because the judge serves as a filter for what evidence will be presented. However, the analogy of the clean slate should not be carried too far. Jurors come to the courthouse with their own biases, beliefs, and worldviews. During the trial, they are allowed to see not only certain evidence but, at the same time, observe the demeanor of the lawyers, the judge, and the witnesses.

Furthermore, every fact that may play a role in the decision of the jury does not require proof. For instance, if the case involves a train, every juror assumes certain unproven facts, that a train is big, heavy, runs on tracks, and is moved by at least one car that has an engine for locomotion. Evidence presented by the parties, as well as unproven facts, taken together, result in the verdict. The unproven facts may also be in the form of personal beliefs held by individual jurors. Although the attorneys attempt to regulate who sits on a jury through questioning of the citizens called to the courthouse by a summons, all the jurors chosen are nevertheless human beings who are products of their upbringing, and their cultural baggage underlies the clean slate on which the evidence will be placed. So, in fact, the clean slate is a mosaic rather than an unpatterned board.

Although jury selection is not a part of this text, it must be remembered that the jury is the critical audience for whom the courtroom drama is played. In preparing for the presentation of evidence, whether through an expert witness or demonstrative evidence, one should never forget the potential audience of jurors and judge.

Keep in mind that although the trial court judge determines matters of law and the jury decides what evidence it will accept as the facts in the case, it is the attorneys who provide the evidence and make objections to the opponent's evidence. Since the trial is part of the adversarial system, it is the responsibility of the attorneys to object to evidence at the time it is offered during the trial. Generally, if an attorney does not make a timely objection, as was discussed in Chapter 2, the objection is waived and cannot be raised on appeal, unless the admission or exclusion of evidence is plain error. When a party does not raise an objection at trial, the jury is allowed to rely on the evidence and use it to support its verdict, even though the judge might not have allowed the evidence in if a timely objection had been made.

On the other hand, attorneys should not necessarily object to all the evidence that arguably may violate a rule of evidence. Tactically, attorneys must carefully choose where to object, because the jury wants to hear the evidence and may suspect an attorney who constantly raises objections of trying to hide something. Experienced attorneys frame objections with the jury in mind. For instance, consider this objection: "Objection, Your Honor. This is not the original document, so it is not reliable." Here the attorney states the reason for the objection, creating a record in the event of a subsequent appeal while also providing information to the jury.

PRELIMINARY QUESTIONS DETERMINED BY THE JUDGE ————

The judge acts as a filter of the evidence that the parties want to present at trial for the jury's consideration. Rule 104 deals with the judge's role as a filter—that is, the manner in which the judge must proceed in deciding whether contested evidence should be heard by the jury. The judge gets to hear evidence that does not comply with the Rules of Evidence, but only to determine if the jury should hear certain other evidence that a party is offering.

Competency of Witnesses

preliminary questions
Matters that must be determined before certain evidence is admissible.

competent witness A person legally qualified to testify at trial.

The judge, then, often decides **preliminary questions**, which are based on underlying facts. For example, when a party wants to put a child on the stand to testify, it is up to the judge to decide whether the child is a **competent witness**. Rule 601 offers some guidance to the judge as to who can testify at trial.

Rule 601.   General Rule of Competency

Every person is competent to be a witness except as otherwise provided in these rules. However, in civil actions and proceedings, with respect to an element of a claim or defense as to which State law supplies the rule of decision, the competency of a witness shall be determined in accordance with State law.

If a child's testimony is offered, the child is presumed to be a competent witness, a person who can testify at trial. If the opposing party challenges the competency of the child to testify, alleging the child does not understand what telling the truth means, the judge must look to underlying facts, such as the age of the child and the child's understanding of the concept of telling the truth. The judge can get this information by interviewing the child or allowing opposing counsel to question the child, or both. The process takes place with the jury out of the courtroom.

After considering the underlying facts related to the child's understanding of telling the truth, the judge then decides the preliminary question. If the preliminary question here is answered by the judge ruling the child as a competent witness, the jury is brought back into the courtroom to hear the testimony of the child. The preliminary question was answered in favor of the proponent of the child's testimony, so the jury hears the testimony. The judge clearly is acting as a filter of the evidence in this instance. If the jury were privy to the preliminary process, and the judge decided that the child could not be a witness, it would be unlikely that the jury could be effectively instructed to ignore all that it heard about the child. The information heard by the judge was the basis for answering the question of whether the child could testify. The jurors' interest is only in the substance of the child's testimony and whether they believe what the child has to say.

The jury determines credibility and believability of the witness once the judge decides if the child meets the requirements of the evidence rule. The judicial determination of preliminary questions by considering underlying facts to determine whether evidence will be heard by the jury is often referred to as a **Rule 104(a) determination**.

Rule 104.   Preliminary Questions

(a) **Questions of admissibility generally.**   Preliminary questions concerning the qualifications of a person to be a witness, the existence of a privilege, or the admissibility of evidence shall be determined by the court, subject to the provisions of subdivision (b). In making its determination it is not bound by the rules of evidence except those with respect to privileges.

There are other circumstances in which a Rule 104(a) determination is necessary. A party may want someone to testify as an expert. The judge decides if the witness qualifies as an expert.

Rule 104(a) determination
The deciding by a judge of preliminary questions using underlying facts to decide whether evidence will be heard by the jury.

Rule 702. Testimony of Experts

If scientific, technical, or other specialized knowledge will assist the trier of fact to understand the evidence or to determine a fact in issue, a witness qualified as an expert by knowledge, skill, experience, training, or education, may testify thereto in the form of an opinion or otherwise.

The judge determines the preliminary question of whether the underlying facts—the potential witness's knowledge, skill, experience, training, or education—establish him or her as an expert.

Exclusion of Evidence

A party may ask the judge to exclude the testimony of a witness, claiming the way in which the potential witness learned of certain matters was through confidential, privileged communications. It is the judge's role to determine whether the relationship and circumstances needed for a privilege to apply existed at the time of the communication—that is, whether the parties were married, or whether the person sought legal advice from someone the person believed to be an attorney. The underlying facts considered by the judge must establish that a special relationship existed between the witness and the other person and that the communication was confidential. Then the judge issues a ruling, excluding the testimony if the underlying facts establish the existence of a privilege. Evidentiary issues related to witnesses and privileges are covered in more detail in the chapters that follow.

Another evidence rule that can result in the exclusion of evidence is the **hearsay** rule. The hearsay rule is used when a witness attempts to testify as to what another person said outside the courtroom, in order to prove the truth of the matter that is the subject of the statement made outside the courtroom. Like the examples already discussed, the hearsay rule requires a preliminary determination by the judge as to whether the proposed testimony is in fact hearsay, and then whether an exception to the rule applies. This rule is subject to numerous exceptions. If the judge decides an exception applies, the jury will get the opportunity to hear evidence that otherwise would be excluded as hearsay.

For example, suppose the judge listens to the hearsay statement and the circumstances under which it was made and decides the statement was an "excited utterance," one of the exceptions to the hearsay rule. This hearsay statement makes it through the filter, and the jury has the opportunity to digest the testimony that was uttered by someone in a state of excitement and apply that information to the determination of who should prevail in the case. The hearsay rule and its exceptions provide many opportunities for the judge to act as a filter by determining preliminary questions, as will be seen in later chapters.

hearsay A statement by a witness of what someone else said out of court, offered as evidence of the truth of the statement.

Criminal Cases

The judge also determines whether the rights of a defendant in a criminal trial have been violated. Where the defendant alleges such a violation, the judge hears facts about the alleged violation and determines whether the jury will hear, for example, the confession made to the police. If the judge decides that the confession was obtained in violation of the defendant's constitutional rights, the jury will not hear the confession. Rule 104(c) explicitly requires that hearings with regard to admissibility of confessions be conducted outside the presence of the jury. Whether the police violated the constitutional rights of an accused is a preliminary question that the judge can answer only after hearing all the facts surrounding the confession, without the jury present. This process safeguards the defendant's right to a fair trial.

Rule 104. Preliminary Questions

(c) Hearing of jury. Hearings on the admissibility of confessions shall in all cases be conducted out of the hearing of the jury. Hearings on other preliminary matters shall be so conducted when the interests of justice require, or when an accused is a witness and so requests.

(d) Testimony by accused. The accused does not, by testifying upon a preliminary matter, become subject to cross-examination as to other issues in the case.

Sidebars

Other than issues related to criminal confessions, hearings that serve as a basis for Rule 104(a) determinations may be held without the jury present if "the interests of justice require, or when an accused is a witness" so long as the defendant asks the court for a hearing without the jury present. If it is possible that the jury might be exposed to information while the preliminary determination is argued that would prejudice its deliberations, then the attorney should be sure arguments are made outside the hearing of the jury.

Sometimes evidence may be presented to the judge at **sidebar**, which suffices to keep the matter outside the presence of the jury without making the jury leave the courtroom. The attorneys approach the bench and speak to the judge in lowered voices while the court reporter records the sidebar just as other parts of the trial are recorded, so that the conferences are a part of the trial transcript and available in the event of an appeal. Illustration 3-2 explains sidebars that were conducted in the O. J. Simpson criminal trial.

Illustration 3-2 _____

This article was published February 26, 1995.

Step up to Sidebar for Blistering Earful
Associated Press. Los Angeles—"Talk About Your Bar Brawls,"
Pensacola News Journal, February 26, 1995.

"Baloney!" says defense attorney Johnnie Cochran Jr. one day.

"Is he wearing the robe in this courtroom today?" prosecutor Christopher Darden sniffs toward Cochran another day.

"All right, children, please," Superior Court Judge Lance Ito implores more than once.

sidebar A conference at the bench with a court reporter present, with the parties arguing an evidentiary matter outside the hearing of the jury.

It's life at the O. J. Simpson sidebar, where everyone knows your name—usually "mud"—and folks don't have to worry about impressing or alienating anybody but each other and the judge since the jury can't hear.

Several times a court session the lawyers can be seen huddling with Ito at the bench—known in legal circles as a sidebar conference—and transcripts show that the conversations are usually more interesting, and revelatory, than what goes on in open court.

When the lawyers aren't taking digs at each other, they're outright insulting their learned colleagues. Even the judge takes his share of abuse. Humor, though, also is in plentiful supply. Informality is the norm.

The topics range from the arcane—many discussions center on such legal matters as hearsay objections—to what Denise Brown told a detective upon hearing her sister had been killed. ("He did it!" she said, referring to Simpson).

It also was revealed in a sidebar that Nicole Brown Simpson's family won't let either the prosecution or defense interview her children about what the kids may have told police the night of the murders.

Often the sidebars yield news, but few reporters ever know about the news until much later. The transcripts rarely are made available the day of the conferences, and only then at a stiff same-day fee of $8.33 a page.

The sidebar is useful during trial. Before trial, the parties might choose to file a **motion in limine** and set a hearing with the judge in order to settle an evidentiary issue before the trial begins. This procedural avenue is useful when an evidentiary question is particularly important in a case. If the issue that is the subject of the motion in limine comes up again at trial, the opposing party must object at trial, because motions in limine may not be conclusive for purposes of appeal.

At the hearing, where a court reporter usually is present, each party has the opportunity to submit evidence and argue the admissibility of the evidence in issue, such as an alleged coerced confession. The jury is not present when the judge hears each party's underlying facts and legal arguments. The judge's decision often is rendered in a written **order**. The issue can be settled before trial, and the parties must present their cases at trial accordingly. If the judge withholds a decision until trial, the hearing serves as an early opportunity to educate the judge on the issue. When the evidence is presented at trial, a sidebar conference may be the setting in which the issue is finally settled.

Figure 3-1 summarizes some of the aspects of a Rule 104(a) determination. Illustration 3-3 provides common examples of Rule 104(a) situations.

motion in limine A request for a court order, often before trial, to exclude reference at trial to anticipated evidence because the evidence allegedly violates a rule of law or a rule of evidence or procedure.

order A direction or command issued by a judge on a matter related to a lawsuit.

Illustration 3-3 _____

Examples of 104(a) situations

1.   TESTIMONY—FOUNDATION
     PRELIMINARY QUESTION: Has the party laid a proper foundation for testimony of the witness?
     Rule 403, Chapter 5

2. DOCUMENTS—ORIGINALS
   PRELIMINARY QUESTION: Is the original document available?
   Rule 1002, Chapter 7

3. DOCUMENTS—AUTHENTICITY
   PRELIMINARY QUESTION: Is the document what it appears to be?
   Rule 901, Chapter 7

4. WITNESSES—COMPETENCE TO TESTIFY
   PRELIMINARY QUESTION: Does the witness understand what it means to tell the truth, and does the witness have the capacity to relate the truth?
   Rule 601, Chapter 8

5. WITNESSES—EXPERTS
   PRELIMINARY QUESTION: Does the witness have the requisite qualifications?
   Rule 702, Chapter 9

6. PRIVILEGES—LAWYER/CLIENT, HUSBAND/WIFE, CLERGY/PENITENT
   PRELIMINARY QUESTION: Does a special relationship exist, and is the communication confidential?
   Rule 501, Chapter 12

7. FAIR TRIAL ISSUES—CONFESSIONS
   PRELIMINARY QUESTION: Was the confession voluntary?

8. FAIR TRIAL ISSUES—SEARCH AND SEIZURE
   PRELIMINARY QUESTION: Was the acquisition of evidence by law enforcement constitutional?

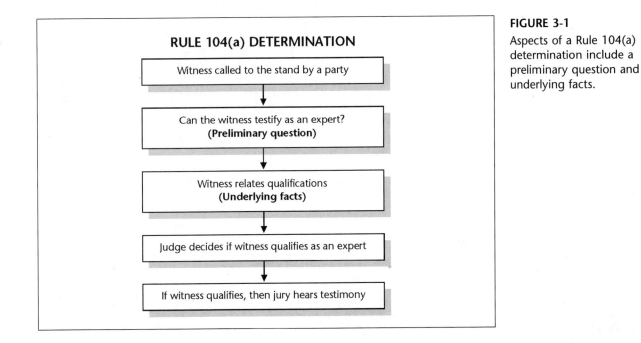

RULE 104(a) DETERMINATION

Witness called to the stand by a party

↓

Can the witness testify as an expert?
(Preliminary question)

↓

Witness relates qualifications
(Underlying facts)

↓

Judge decides if witness qualifies as an expert

↓

If witness qualifies, then jury hears testimony

FIGURE 3-1
Aspects of a Rule 104(a) determination include a preliminary question and underlying facts.

THE JURY AND PRELIMINARY QUESTIONS

The judge normally hears underlying facts to determine preliminary questions. However, there are circumstances where the jury will determine preliminary questions by hearing underlying facts as to that issue. Rule 104(b) is practical and necessary to the flow of a trial, allowing the jury to sometimes determine preliminary questions. The jury gets to hear the underlying facts and then it decides the preliminary question.

Rule 104. Preliminary Questions

(b) Relevancy conditioned on fact. When the relevancy of evidence depends upon the fulfillment of a condition of fact, the court shall admit it upon, or subject to, the introduction of evidence sufficient to support a finding of the fulfillment of the condition.

Preliminary Questions Determined by the Jury

Parties call witnesses in the order that makes their cases most understandable and persuasive to the jury. This practice may result in testimony that is not entirely relevant at the time offered because other evidence is needed to show how this evidence relates to the issue a party must prove.

For instance, where notice of a defect is an element that must be proven in a products liability case, a witness is called to testify that the defendant knew about the defect because the witness wrote to the defendant about the defect. However, the witness may not be able to testify whether the defendant received the note, receipt being required before proof of notice is complete. The attorney can assure the judge that another witness will testify that the defendant received the note. The judge can then conditionally admit the testimony of the witness on the stand. The condition that must be fulfilled for the evidence of notice (testimony the note was written) to be admitted is the testimony of the second witness promised by the attorney.

If the second witness is never produced, the judge can later exclude the testimony regarding the note, ordering the jury not to use the testimony about the note in determining the outcome of the case. The party who must prove notice will have failed to do so since it was not proven that the defendant had notice of the defect.

If the jury had heard evidence of the note and its receipt by the defendant, then the jury could have decided there was notice, thus answering the preliminary question on notice. But because the plaintiff failed to provide all the facts necessary to the determination of the notice question, the jury would be instructed to ignore the testimony of the witness who wrote the note.

Conditional Admission of Evidence

conditionally admit The judge decides to allow evidence to be used by the jury, subject to later evidence confirming its relevance.

In the determination by the judge of whether to **conditionally admit** evidence, the judge need only find *prima facie* evidence exists. This is a very low threshold of proof in which, in the case of the note being received by the defendant in our previous example, it appears to the judge from the argument of the attorney that the note was not only sent, but that a later witness will testify that the note was read by the defendant.

If the judge allows the evidence to be conditionally admitted, the jury gets to hear the underlying facts—in this example, having to do with notice—before a final determination on admissibility is made. If the judge does not believe that a witness will later testify that the note was sent, the jury will not hear the testimony of the witness who allegedly sent the note. But if the judge allows the testimony of the first witness, and then the second witness testifies, the jury decides whether the evidence proves the defendant had notice.

Preliminary questions determined by the jury along with the conditional admission of evidence mean, for all practical purposes, that the evidence each party presents to the jury can be offered in a logical order. It often takes the testimony of multiple witnesses to create a compelling picture for the jury. The picture is like a puzzle, with the evidence serving as pieces to form a picture of the party's case for the jury. Rule 104(b) is necessary at trial so that the trial can proceed, with each party forming its picture efficiently and logically, one piece at a time.

Weight of the Evidence

Both the judge and the jury hear evidence, with the judge making Rule 104(a) decisions on admissibility and the jury deciding whether to believe the evidence it hears. The jury considers preliminary facts for conditional evidence and ultimate facts to determine whether a party should win or lose a case. Then the jury decides the **weight of the evidence** after hearing it and seeing it in court. It is the jury that sorts out the pieces of evidence to come up with the facts that best represent the underlying event leading to the lawsuit. The jurors weigh the evidence for believability and persuasiveness.

Rule 104.   Preliminary Questions
(e) Weight and credibility.   This rule does not limit the right of a party to introduce before the jury evidence relevant to weight or credibility.

When the jury deliberates on the fate of the parties, their biases, beliefs, and worldviews will come into play. How well the attorneys presented their cases often is reflected in the jury's determination. The jurors heard and watched the witnesses, saw evidence, and observed the lawyers and the judge. But it is through their own filters as a collective group of citizens that they determine the outcome of the case. The jurors' filters often color the pieces of evidence presented by the parties. The pieces of evidence may take on an unintended hue in passing through the individual juror's filter. The picture that emerges may not be quite what either party intended.

The jury decides what weight to give the evidence. For instance, the party's expert witness may be a terrific scientist, but jurors may also perceive a hesitancy in the testimony leading them to disregard much of the testimony, thus diminishing the value of the piece of evidence in its place in the final picture. Another witness, called by the opposing party, with a self-confident presentation,

weight of the evidence
The more convincing evidence offered at trial, as determined by the jury.

may sway the jury to give this expert witness's testimony greater weight. The effect of this witness's testimony thus increases the impact of this evidence on the final picture.

Consider the words of Jerome Frank, a respected American jurist, in order to understand the importance of how evidence is presented in court:

> What the trial court thinks happened may, however, be hopelessly incorrect. But that does not matter—legally speaking. For court purposes, what the court thinks about the facts is all that matters. The actual events, the real objective acts and words ... , happened in the past. They do not walk into court. The court usually learns about these real, objective, past facts only through the oral testimony of fallible witnesses. Accordingly, the court, from hearing the testimony, must guess at the actual, past facts. Judicially, the facts consist of the reaction of the judge or jury to the testimony.[1]

JUDICIAL NOTICE

Certain facts are so well known or so easy to verify using a reliable source that proof of them is not required. No evidence must be introduced at trial to prove that a fact is true if the judge takes **judicial notice** of the fact.

In a civil case, the fact judicially noticed is presented to the jury as an undisputed fact. The jury must accept the fact as true, and the opposing party is barred from offering evidence to the contrary. However, in a criminal case, because of constitutional considerations, judicial notice cannot be used if the fact judicially noticed could result in a conviction. The prosecutor must prove all elements of an offense to satisfy the Sixth Amendment. The following discussion relates more to civil cases.

Notorious and Manifest Facts

judicial notice The judge recognizes the existence of a fact without a party offering evidence to prove the fact, based on common knowledge or by reference to an indisputable source.

notorious facts Facts that are common knowledge in the community where a court sits.

manifest facts Facts that can be easily verified in an indisputable source.

adjudicative facts Facts related to proving a cause of action.

Under Rule 201(b), judicial notice may be taken under two circumstances. The first circumstance is without an offer of proof because the fact is so well known in the community where the court sits. This fact is known as a **notorious fact**. The second circumstance is by providing the court with a source that easily verifies the proffered fact. This fact is known as a **manifest fact**.

Under either circumstance, the fact must be an **adjudicative fact**, one related to the "who, what, when, where, or why" of the case being tried. Adjudicative facts are ones related to an issue in the case and that otherwise would have to be proven by a party to a jury. If the time that the sun set on a particular day is a fact related to an issue in a case, it can be readily determined by consulting an almanac. If the fact that numbered streets in the city in which the court sits run east and west is relevant to the case being tried, it can be judicially noticed so long as this is something commonly known in that community.

Rule 201. Judicial Notice of Adjudicative Facts

(a) Scope of rule. This rule governs only judicial notice of adjudicative facts.

(b) Kinds of facts. A judicially noticed fact must be one not subject to reasonable dispute in that it is either (1) generally known within the territorial jurisdiction of the trial court or (2) capable of accurate and ready determination by resort to sources whose accuracy cannot reasonably be questioned.

For an example of what facts should not be judicially noticed, see Illustration 3-4.

Illustration 3-4 _____

In a products liability case, the trial court judge took judicial notice "of the fact that the government conducts numerous crash-worthiness tests, and the well-known rollover problems of vehicles having a higher center of gravity."

The appellate court said these matters were not beyond dispute. The quantity and nature of the government tests are not common knowledge, and the tests cannot be readily proven through a source of unquestionable accuracy. Neither is the rollover propensity of vehicles with high centers of gravity well known. "Most people probably know little if anything about how high centers of gravity cause vehicular accidents." *Carley v. Wheeled Coach,* 991 F.2d 1117, 1126 (3rd Cir. 1993).

As the Federal Rules of Evidence do not list the specific matters appropriate for judicial notice, it is necessary to refer to federal case law for guidance. In some states, such as California and Florida, matters that may be judicially noticed are specifically enumerated in the state's rules of evidence.

Judicial notice may be taken at any time, which means before trial, at trial, or on appeal. With regard to the appeal, judicial notice can be taken by the appellate court whether or not a party requests judicial notice in the appeal. If a party requests judicial notice of a fact, the court must consider the appropriateness of that request.

Before a request is made, the paralegal should prepare by reviewing relevant case law and necessary data or sources supporting the fact, since the adverse party will have an opportunity to argue the impropriety of taking judicial notice. If a trial court judge properly notices a fact, the appellate court must accept that fact as established in considering the appeal.

Rule 201. Judicial Notice of Adjudicative Facts

(c) When discretionary. A court may take judicial notice, whether requested or not.

(d) When mandatory. A court shall take judicial notice if requested by a party and supplied with the necessary information.

(e) Opportunity to be heard. A party is entitled upon timely request to an opportunity to be heard as to the propriety of taking judicial notice and the tenor of the matter noticed. In the absence of prior notification, the request may be made after judicial notice has been taken.

(f) Time of taking notice. Judicial notice may be taken at any stage of the proceeding.

Judicial notice of a fact is simply an evidentiary shortcut, a way by which a party can present a fact to the jury without offering extended proof of that fact. Where the time of sunset is an issue, the party who wants the time into evidence would typically call an astronomer or meteorologist to prove the time. Instead of calling a witness, simply supplying the judge with the entry in an almanac is enough; the jury is supplied the time without needless testimony.

Finally, a judge's personal knowledge cannot be judicially noticed if the knowledge cannot be verified or if it is not commonly known in the community. Figure 3-2 summarizes the types of facts involved in judicial notice.

FIGURE 3-2

Facts appropriate for judicial notice must be adjudicated facts of either the notorious or the manifest type.

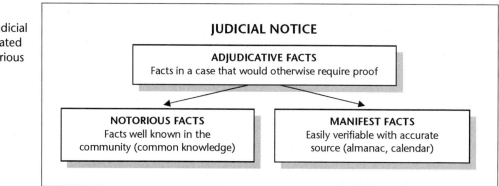

Legislative Facts

Rule 201 does not apply to legislative facts. **Legislative facts** apply universally and are not developed as part of a particular case. These are policy facts relating to legal reasoning and the lawmaking process. They include assumptions made by judges used as a basis for application of a rule of law to the case. For example, in *Brown v. Board of Education,* 347 U.S. 483 (1954), the Supreme Court of the United States held that separate schools for different races violated the constitutional rights of Negro children. The court based its ruling on the assumption that segregated education had a detrimental effect on Negro children. This assumption, a legislative fact, relates to issues of public policy and human behavior.

The distinction between adjudicative facts and legislative facts is not always clear. If a court wants a certain result, it may characterize the judicially noticed fact as either adjudicative or legislative in order to meet the immediate circumstances and desired outcome.

legislative facts Facts that are related to policy and legal reasoning and have wider application than to the proof of a particular cause of action.

Since Rule 201 does not apply to legislative facts, Rule 201(g) requires a trial court judge to instruct the jury that a judicially noticed fact is conclusive and not subject to argument if it is an adjudicative fact. If a judicially noticed fact is a legislative fact, there is no requirement that the judge instruct the jury that the legislative fact is conclusive. If a judge does not instruct the jury pursuant to Rule 201(g), and that failure is raised on appeal, the appellate court can hold that the fact was a legislative fact, not an adjudicative fact, and reject the appeal.

Rule 201. Judicial Notice of Adjudicative Facts

(g) Instructing jury. In a civil action or proceeding, the court shall instruct the jury to accept as conclusive any fact judicially noticed. In a criminal case, the court shall instruct the jury that it may, but is not required to, accept as conclusive any fact judicially noticed.

Because the analysis for determining whether a judicially noticed fact is legislative or adjudicative is not always clear, it is important to read and analyze the case law, paying particular attention to the relationship between the outcome of the appeal and the fact in question and relating the facts of the case at hand to the facts contained in the relevant precedent.

SUMMARY

Before a case goes to trial, the paralegal and investigator need to have a clear understanding of the elements of the cause of action that require proof. That proof will be in the evidence marshaled by the paralegal and investigator. If a piece of evidence is critical to proving an element of the case, and its admissibility is questionable, the paralegal should anticipate any problems by research into the admissibility of the evidence. The investigator must take care to protect the physical integrity of evidence, paying particular attention to chain of custody.

If evidence is subject to an objection based on the hearsay rule, a privilege, a constitutional challenge, or some other challenge, the paralegal should provide the attorney with a memorandum outlining the anticipated objection, along with the legal research to meet the challenge. If judicial notice will be requested at trial, the paralegal should prepare for that request by obtaining any books or documents that may be needed to establish the appropriateness of judicial notice.

An attorney who appears well prepared in court better serves the client. Orderly presentation of evidence and the appearance of being well-prepared have a positive impact on the jury. The jury may be a clean slate as far as the case at hand is concerned, but the jurors are nevertheless members of the community who are alert to the human dynamics of the lawsuit. The jurors, and the judge, are the audience to whom the drama is played. Be sure they see a well-prepared script where all the pieces of evidence fall into place.

✓ CHECKPOINTS

❑ Role of the judge
   1. Decides admissibility of evidence.
   2. Conducts trial in an orderly fashion.
❑ Preliminary questions determined by the judge
   1. Hears underlying facts.

2. Decides preliminary question that determines whether jury will hear disputed evidence.
3. Examples:
   a. Competency of a witness.
   b. Qualifications of a witness.

c. Privileged matters.

d. Hearsay.

e. Constitutional rights of a defendant in a criminal case.

4. Procedure:

a. Motion in limine.

b. Sidebars.

❑ Preliminary questions determined by jury

1. Conditional admission of evidence for orderly presentation of case.

2. Once a question determined, considers weight of evidence.

❑ Judicial notice

1. Adjudicative facts: proof related to issue in the case.

2. Notorious facts: common knowledge in the community.

3. Manifest facts: easily verifiable in unimpeachable source.

4. Legislative facts: apply universally and relate to legal reasoning.

5. Adjudicative versus legislative facts on appeal:

a. Distinction may not be clear between the two.

b. Judge must instruct jury on adjudicative facts, not legislative facts.

c. If there is no instruction, on appeal the court may characterize it as legislative, so no error results.

✎ APPLICATIONS

Application 3-1

The following excerpt is a case involving a wrongful death action filed in federal court in Massachusetts. Normally this type of case is filed in state court, but here the person who died (Garbincius) was a resident of New York, and the defendants (Boston Edison Company and Charles Contracting Co., Inc.) were from Massachusetts, so there was diversity of citizenship. When citizens of different states are involved in a lawsuit where alleged damages meet a statutory minimum, the lawsuit can be heard in federal court instead of a state court.

One defendant had a contract with the other to do excavation of streets in Boston. Paul Garbincius drove his automobile into an excavation on a street in Boston and died as a result of injuries received in the crash. Peter Garbincius, the father, was appointed administrator of his son's estate, and filed the lawsuit. The jury found for the plaintiff and both defendants appealed. One of the issues on appeal was whether there was reversible error because the trial court judge admitted certain testimony of one of plaintiff's expert witnesses.

Garbincius v. Boston Edison Co.
621 F. 2d 1171 (1st Cir. 1980)

The Admission of Testimony and Evidence

Both defendants claim that it was error for the court to allow George Kent to testify as an expert and give an opinion as to highway construction safety. In a diversity jurisdiction case, the Federal Rules of Evidence with respect to expert witnesses control. Under Fed.R.Evid. 104, preliminary questions concerning the qualification of a potential witness are determined by the court. Fed.R.Evid. 702 provides:

If scientific, technical, or other specialized knowledge will assist the trier of fact to understand the evidence or to determine a fact in issue, a witness qualified as an expert by knowledge, skill, experience, training, or education, may testify thereto in the form of an opinion or otherwise.

Our standard of review of the trial court's determination of admissibility of expert opinion is the clearly erroneous test.

Kent was a graduate civil engineer who had worked for the Interborough Rapid Transit Company in New York form 1929 to 1943, one and one-half years of which were spent investigating claims and accidents. His safety work had to do with controlling automotive traffic when supports for the elevated railway were being removed from streets. He was also responsible for safety procedures to be followed when street excavations for repairing underground sewer lines and cables were dug. After that, he had extensive experience with Stone and Webster relative to the construction and operation of power plants. Prior to trial, Kent had studied publications on traffic safety procedures to be used during highway construction. He familiarized himself with photographs of the scene of the accident, the accident reports filed, and the depositions of investigating officials. We find that it was not clearly erroneous for the district court to have allowed Kent to give his opinion about the adequacy of the number and placement of the devices used for warning motorists of the excavation. While his work experience in traffic safety procedures during highway construction stopped in 1943, we think this background plus his engineering training and focused study preparatory to trial made him, but just barely, a qualified witness whose testimony could assist the jury.

Affirmed.

Class Discussion Questions

1. In a diversity case involving wrongful death, do state evidence rules or the Federal Rules of Evidence apply with respect to qualification of expert witnesses?

2. The qualification of an expert witness is governed by which rule and subsection? Under this rule, who decides whether a witness is an expert?

3. What were the underlying facts that the appellate court reviewed in determining whether George Kent was qualified as an expert witness? Explain the significance of the underlying facts.

4. What was the preliminary question that the trial judge had to answer with regard to George Kent? Did the appellate court agree with the trial court judge with regard to George Kent's status as a witness?

Application 3-2

The order in which evidence is presented to the jury is left to the parties to decide. However, if testimony of a witness is offered, and the other party objects because certain other necessary evidence has not been presented at trial, the attorney who is the proponent of the evidence can assure the court that the evidence will be connected later in the case.

In the following case, the defendant, Roger Cote, was indicted along with two others for violation of, and conspiring to violate, federal firearms laws. Prior to trial the two codefendants (Estabrook and Giles) entered into agreements with the government in which they benefited by agreeing to testify against Cote.

At trial, the first witness called by the prosecution was Estabrook. She testified that she had lived with Giles and that her cousin, Cote, had proposed to Giles that they break into houses and steal items, including jewelry, silver, and weapons for resale. In two months' time, she saw at least eight guns brought into the apartment that she shared with Giles.

The government then called four persons to the stand whose homes had been burglarized in order for them to testify as to what was stolen and also to identify any weapons that were recovered. The defense objected to the testimony of two of the witnesses because the defendant was not charged in the indictment with burglary of their homes.

At sidebar, the prosecutor stated that these two burglaries were an overt act in the conspiracy. The judge allowed the testimony of the two witnesses but instructed the jury that the government still had the burden of proving that Cote conspired with Giles in planning the burglaries of these two homes.

Other witnesses were called who testified that they purchased guns from Giles. These were the same guns that the four homeowners said were stolen from them. None of these witnesses connected Cote with the sale of the weapons.

Giles was then called by the prosecution. He testified that Cote originally approached him about committing break-ins. He said that Cote burglarized two homes with him, but not the two others. Even though these two burglaries fell within the time period of the conspiracy count of the indictment, the judge struck all evidence concerning these two burglaries because Cote was not involved in the planning or execution of these crimes and had not received any of the guns. The judge gave a curative instruction to the jury, telling them to disregard the testimony of two of the four homeowners.

The government rested its case. The defense presented alibi witnesses for the dates of the two burglaries listed in the indictment.

Cote was found guilty on all three counts of the indictment.

United States v. Cote
744 F.2d 913 (2d Cir. 1984)

DISCUSSION

The government concedes that the evidence of two burglaries and several sales of weapons, consisting of the testimony of five witnesses and of six firearms admitted as exhibits, was irrelevant. The exposure of the jury to this evidence occurred because of a tactical decision by the government as to the order of its proof. Giles, the witness who was to connect Cote to the Antos and Blymiller burglaries, could have testified first, and the evidence in question would have been self-evidently irrelevant. Instead, the prosecutor chose to save Giles for last ... The result was thus to expose the jury to the irrelevant evidence described above.

We appreciate the need for leeway so counsel may select the most persuasive order of proof. We also recognize that this goal, or a desire to expedite, the pace of the trial by putting all of a witness's testimony on at once, may require that evidence be admitted provisionally with a view to connecting it up by later evidence, as is expressly contemplated by Fed.R.Evid. 104(b). However, representations, express or implied, that otherwise irrelevant evidence will be tied to a defendant by subsequent testimony should not be made without a good faith and objectively reasonable belief that the missing links will in fact be supplied.

No reason has been offered in the instant case for the failure to connect this evidence to the defendant. Giles had pled to one count and was cooperating with the government. The prosecutor thus either knew or should have known of the content of his testimony when she offered the evidence relating to the Antos and Blymiller burglaries. If doubt existed, such evidence, which was cumulative even if connected to Cote by Giles, should not have been offered until after Giles testified.

We turn now to the question of whether the jury's exposure to the evidence in question calls for reversal notwithstanding the striking of that evidence and the giving of cautionary instructions by the district judge. We believe the inference of prejudice here is irresistible.

The stricken evidence included six firearms and the testimony of two crime victims, and of three other people who purchased stolen weapons. This testimony and the physical exhibition of firearms to the jury enhanced the chances of a conviction even though it was irrelevant.

Cote was portrayed as having suggested the break-ins to Giles, and the jury's verdict may well have been influenced by a lingering belief that Cote was morally responsible for all of Giles' conduct, notwithstanding the cautionary instructions as to his legal liability. This taints the entire verdict.

We also note that the evidence against Cote was not overwhelming. No disinterested witness linked Cote to any burglary or sale of stolen weapons, and no weapons were ever found in his possession. The witnesses who implicate Cote were co-defendants who testified against him in the hope of lenient treatment. Moreover, Estabrook's testimony was vague and confused and did not link specific crimes to specific dates. She could say only that Giles and Cote had conspired to commit burglaries, and that she had seen Cote bring weapons into her house. Giles' testimony was more damaging but hardly irresistible, a fact underlined in three previous state burglary prosecutions that resulted in acquittals of Cote despite Giles' testimony against him. Cote, on the other hand, offered alibi evidence for the remaining two burglaries, including a neutral witness whose testimony tended to undermine Giles' version of the Tedona burglary.

Considering both the cause of the error, the nature of the evidence involved, and the closeness of the case, we believe that cautionary instructions could not adequately protect the defendant's right to consideration of his guilt by a jury uninfluenced by extraneous matters. We therefore reverse.

Class Discussion Questions

1. Why did the appellate court expect the government to know what the contents of Giles's testimony would be at trial?

2. What was the significance of Giles's testimony with regard to the four victims whose homes were burglarized?

3. What would have happened at trial if Giles had been called before Antos and Blymiller?

4. Why do you think that the prosecution called Giles as its last witness?

Application 3-3

Government of the Canal Zone v. Burjan V.
596 F.2d 690 (5th Cir. 1979)

Mauricio Burjan V. (Villarreta) was convicted on June 20, 1977 on two counts of grand larceny from the person in violation of 6 C.Z.C Sec. 1342(2) in a nonjury trial before the United States District Court for the Canal Zone. He was sentenced on August 15, 1975 to serve two concurrent five-year sentences.

III. JURISDICTION

The final and more troublesome challenge to the convictions is Burjan's contention that the government failed to establish that the trial court had jurisdiction because it did not show that the charged offenses were committed in the Canal Zone. It is unimportant, of course, that this point is raised for the first time on appeal, as an attack on the subject matter jurisdiction of the trial court may be raised at any stage. F.R.Cr.P. 12.

There is direct evidence of the place of the thefts. There is, however, no direct evidence in the record that these places were in the Canal Zone. Nor did the trial judge take judicial notice that the places where the offenses occurred were in the Canal Zone. But it has long been the rule in this circuit that "[p]roof of venue as a jurisdictional fact may be shown by circumstantial evidence as well as by direct evidence.... In addition, this court has consistently adhered to the rule that venue as a jurisdictional fact is a proper subject for judicial notice. The question, then, is whether there was evidence at trial from which the trial court could have decided that the places of the offense were in the Canal Zone, or, alternatively, whether there are sufficient facts disclosed by the record that would enable this court by taking judicial notice of Canal Zone boundaries to conclude that the disputed places of the offenses were within the Canal Zone.

Before considering those questions, several preliminary points must be made. First, this court may take judicial notice of governmental boundaries under the Federal Rules of Evidence. Rule 201 permits a court to take judicial notice of an adjudicative fact that is "not subject to reasonable dispute in that it is either (1) generally known within the territorial jurisdiction of the trial court or (2) capable of accurate and ready determination by resort to sources whose accuracy cannot reasonably be questioned."

This court has been furnished with maps of the boundary between the Canal Zone and the Republic of Panama, including the location of boundary markers, in the general area where the offenses involved here occurred. The maps were furnished and their accuracy certified by the Chief of Surveys Branch of the Panama Canal Company. They are "sources whose accuracy cannot reasonably be questioned," by resort to which the boundaries of the Canal Zone may be accurately and readily determined. [FOOTNOTE 6: We take judicial notice of maps numbered ...]

This court has on several occasions taken judicial notice, or has approved a trial court's taking judicial notice of geographical locations and boundaries. And while there exists no comprehensive authoritative list of the types of sources "whose accuracy cannot reasonably be questioned" and which, therefore, may be judicially noticed, official government maps have long been held proper subjects of judicial notice.

It is also important to note that the boundaries of the Canal Zone may be judicially noticed by this court, even though notice was not taken by the trial court. Rule 201(f) of the Federal Rules of Evidence provides that "[j]udicial notice may be taken at any stage of the proceeding," and the Advisory Committee's note to this provision explains that it permits the taking of judicial notice at any state, "whether in the trial court or on appeal." Moreover, subsection (g) of the Rule does not preclude the taking of judicial notice in this case. That subsection provides that in criminal cases a jury must be allowed to disregard facts judicially noticed. The Sixth Circuit ... has read this provision as precluding the taking of judicial notice of an element of a crime by an appellate court in a criminal jury case. Without intimating our view as to the correctness of that decision, we note that the considerations that led the Sixth Circuit to its conclusion ... are not applicable when, as here, the right to jury trial has been waived. Rule 201(g) is, by its terms, inapplicable in a nonjury case. For the same reason it is unnecessary to decide where to what extent, if any, the sixth amendment right to trial by jury limits the power of an appellate court to take judicial notice in a criminal jury case. Finally, the taking of judicial notice of adjudicative facts by an appellate court does not offend the sixth amendment's guarantee of the right to confront witnesses at least where, as here, the facts judicially noticed—the location of geographical boundaries—are indisputable. We conclude, then, that we may take judicial notice of the boundaries of the Canal Zone and, consequently, whether the trial court had jurisdiction over the offenses.

The final point that must be made before examination of the record is that, while "[i]t is axiomatic that the prosecution must always prove territorial jurisdiction over a crime in order to sustain a conviction therefor," "the standard of proof [on this element] is more relaxed than for other elements of a criminal prosecution. It is necessary only that the location of criminal activity be established by a preponderance of the evidence ... ."

Applying these principles, we conclude that there was insufficient record evidence of the relative locations of the places of the thefts and the Canal Zone boundaries. The trial court did not take judicial notice or otherwise hear direct evidence of Canal Zone boundary locations. Yet the record indisputably locates where the theft charged in count I occurred. That fix permits this court to determine, by taking judicial notice of its boundaries, that the offense charged in count I took place within the Canal Zone.

The victim of the first offense, Isabel Caballero, and her cousin, Ada Ponce, who were together at the time of the offense, both testified that when the offense occurred they were walking on the Canal Zone side of the street past the Bridge of the Americas on the way from Amador to Panama City. The maps show that the street upon which they were traveling is either Thatcher Highway or Fourth of July Avenue (a continuation of Thatcher Highway) and that the Canal Zone side of the street is within the boundaries of the Canal Zone. We conclude, then, that the first offense took place within the Canal Zone and that, consequently, the trial court had jurisdiction over this offense. Thus each of the appellant's arguments with regard to count I (the first offense) have been rejected, and the conviction under that count is AFFIRMED.

This same reasoning, however, does not permit affirmance of the conviction under count II. The record does not reveal the location of the offense charged in count II with sufficient accuracy to enable this court to take judicial notice that the location of the offense was within the boundaries of the Canal Zone. The victim of the second offense, Mark Soleday, testified that when the offense occurred he was walking on the Panama side of Fourth of July Avenue "down across the street from the bus stop as you come out of Balboa." Whether Soleday was in the Canal Zone or not depends upon how far down Fourth of July Avenue he had proceeded since coming out of Balboa Road. That cannot be determined from the record, and, consequently, the location of the offense cannot be fixed with sufficient accuracy as to permit this court to take judicial notice that the offense took place within the Canal Zone. Thus, as it cannot be determined that the trial court had jurisdiction over the offense charged in count II, the conviction under that count is REVERSED.

AFFIRMED IN PART AND REVERSED IN PART.

Class Discussion Questions

1. Did the court characterize the boundaries of the Canal Zone as an adjudicative fact or a legislative fact?

2. Explain why Rule 201(g) did not apply to this case.

3. Which court can take judicial notice?

4. This is a criminal case, but the court said Rule 201(g) was not applicable. What was the court's reasoning?

5. Why did the court affirm the defendant's conviction on count I and reverse the conviction on count II? Correlate your answer with the judicial notice of the boundaries of the Canal Zone.

EXERCISES

1. Review the rules of evidence for your state. Is a trial court judge allowed to sum up the evidence and comment to the jury on the weight of the evidence? Cite the appropriate rule.

2. The following fact patterns relate to judicial notice of adjudicative facts and legislative facts.

a. The defendant mother was charged with cruelty to a child in violation of a Georgia child abuse statute, as it applied to a federal reservation through a federal statute. The alleged act occurred at her residence located at Fort Benning, Georgia, where the child died.

Autopsy results disclosed bruises all over the two-and-one-half-year-old victim's body, as well as a fractured skull and a broken collarbone. There was also a tear in the liver and a lacerated heart, which was the immediate cause of death.

On appeal, the defendant alleged reversible error because the judge took judicial notice that Fort Benning, Georgia, was on land belonging to the United States and was under the jurisdiction of the United States. The defendant asserted that the judge committed reversible error because the judge did not inform the jurors that they were not bound to accept this fact, citing Federal Rule of Evidence 201(g).

The issue is whether the judicially noticed fact is an adjudicative fact or a legislative fact.

- Make an argument for each position. Then state how you think the appellate court ruled and the probable reasoning for the result.

b. A street musician challenged a city ordinance regulating use of public property in Old Town, Alexandria, Virginia, including public sidewalks and walkways. He was precluded from playing and lecturing about his bagpipes in Old Town. He argued that the city ordinance and its restrictions were a violation of his First Amendment right to free expression of speech in public places.

The trial court judge for the Eastern District of Virginia in Alexandria was a longtime resident of Alexandria. He took judicial notice of the character of Old Town pursuant to Federal Rule of Evidence 201(b) as facts generally known within the jurisdiction of the court. However, he did not include in the record any details as to the character of Old Town, particularly its physical layout and pedestrian and vehicular traffic patterns.

The rule of law that was applied in this case centered on the manner of expression and whether it was basically incompatible with normal activity of a particular place at a particular time. The ordinance had to be the least restrictive alternative for achieving the purpose of providing a safe environment in Old Town.

- Argue that the character of Old Town is a fact appropriate for judicial notice.
- Explain what is needed for the trial record, and why it is needed, if judicial notice is taken of the character of Old Town.
- Argue that it is not appropriate to take judicial notice of the character of Old Town.
- Assuming that judicial notice of the character of Old Town is not appropriate, explain how the parties can get this information into the record.

RULES REFERENCED IN THIS CHAPTER

Rule 611. Mode and Order of Interrogation and Presentation

Rule 103. Rulings on Evidence

Rule 104. Preliminary Questions

Rule 601. General Rule of Competency

Rule 702. Testimony of Experts

Rule 201. Judicial Notice of Adjudicative Facts

NOTES

[1] Jerome Frank. *Courts on Trial: Myth and Reality in American Justice.* (Princeton, NJ: Princeton University Press, 1949), pp. 15–16.

Burdens of Proof and Presumptions at Trial

SETTING THE SCENE

Investigations are complete, the case prepared, and now it is time for trial. The scene is set, and the drama is about to begin. The plaintiff or the prosecutor is "on stage," sitting at a table usually nearest to the jury. The defendant sits at another table, while the judge presides in a commanding position that is physically higher than the tables of the other court participants. When a representative from the clerk of court's office attends trial, the representative usually sits near the bench. The court reporter often sits in front of the judge's elevated area. The witness box is on the side of the judge closest to the jury.

The jury can number between six and twelve citizens, summoned to the courthouse before the trial for questioning. The number of jurors needed for trial depends on federal law or state statutes. The jury is the group of individuals chosen by the parties from a larger panel after **voir dire**, which is the questioning of prospective jurors to determine whether they are qualified to sit on the jury. In federal court, the trial court judge often does most of the questioning, while in state courts, the attorneys often do the questioning. The voir dire examination is completed as a preliminary matter to the trial itself.

voir dire The questioning of prospective jurors to determine if they are suitable to decide a case.

The plaintiff, the party who filed the lawsuit, makes the first opening statement to the jury. The **opening statement** is an overview of the case, outlining the evidence that will be presented to the jury. The defendant's attorney then has the opportunity to make an opening statement. The opening statements do not argue the case. At the end of the trial, the parties get an opportunity to present closing arguments. In its **closing argument** each side argues to the jury why it should prevail, based on the evidence offered at trial and the applicable law.

In a criminal case, the prosecution presents its opening statement to the jury first. In a civil case, the plaintiff goes first. The reason for their going first is that they are the ones who started the process of bringing the dispute to the court. Thus, they open "Act I" with this presentation to the jury.

After the defense follows with its opening statement, the plaintiff (in a civil case) or the prosecutor (in a criminal case) proceeds to present evidence to the jury as part of "Act II." When the plaintiff rests its case, the defendant generally concludes Act II with a presentation of evidence. Act II gives the parties the opportunity to present witnesses, physical evidence, and exhibits to the jury for its consideration. This is the time when the majority of the impressions are made on the jury, which by now is not so clean a slate.

The reason that Acts I and II proceed in this order is because a plaintiff and a prosecutor have the duty of proving facts that support the cause of action. These parties must prove the existence of evidence supporting their theory of the case. If it is a personal injury case, the plaintiff must prove to the jury elements of a negligent tort, that the defendant had a duty to the plaintiff, that the defendant breached the duty, that the breach by the defendant caused the injury to the plaintiff, and that the plaintiff incurred injuries as a result. If it is a criminal case, the prosecutor must prove that the defendant did the unlawful act as defined in the statutes. Chapter 1 covered these matters in more detail.

opening statement Explanation by attorneys, usually at the beginning of a trial, based on evidence that will be offered, of their version of what happened between the parties and how they think the law should be applied to the case.

closing arguments After both sides have completed their cases, each side summarizes the evidence presented at trial and argues to the jury why the party should prevail based on the evidence and applicable law.

burden of proof Includes the requirement that a party present evidence to support allegations or defenses (*burden of production*) as well as the need to provide enough evidence to convince the jury one party should prevail over the other (*burden of persuasion*).

burden of production Requirement that a party offer evidence to support a claim or defense.

BURDEN OF PROOF

The order of presentation of evidence evolved as a part of the trial process over time. Generally, this order of presentation of evidence is characterized as the allocation of the **burden of proof**. Each party has a defined responsibility in meeting its burden of proof, as well as an order in which this must be accomplished. Each party must present evidence to the jury in a specified order and of minimal quality in order to meet its burden of proof.

The use of the phrase "burden of proof" can be confusing, because two different types of burdens are encompassed in the one phrase: the burden of production and the burden of persuasion. Although the burdens are similar, important distinctions do exist.

Burden of Production

In most cases, the plaintiff and the prosecutor initially bear the **burden of production**. If they do not proceed with the initial presentation of evidence supporting the action against the defendant, the case will not move forward, and the judge has authority to end the proceedings instead of allowing it to languish with no action. If the plaintiff or prosecutor do not offer evidence to support their allegations, the defendant will submit a *motion for a directed verdict* (discussed shortly) to the judge, asking the judge to end the case with a verdict in its favor because the party with the burden of production failed to meet its burden. If the judge grants the motion, the jury is dismissed and will have no further opportunity to hear evidence related to the case.

Of course, this is not the normal situation. The plaintiff or prosecutor at trial does present evidence to the jury in an effort to meet the burden of production. The burden of production is met by putting witnesses on the stand to testify about events related to the dispute and by introducing physical evidence and using exhibits. The burden of production often includes the **burden of going forward with the evidence**. Once the plaintiff, who has the burden in a civil case, meets the burden of production by presenting adequate evidence to satisfy the judge as a matter of law, the plaintiff will rest its case.

Once the plaintiff rests its case, the defendant has the opportunity to present evidence. In a civil case, the burden of production has now shifted to the defendant. If the defendant does not offer evidence to support its theory of the case as to why the defendant should not be held accountable to the plaintiff, the judge may, upon motion by the plaintiff, enter a **directed verdict** for the plaintiff. Where the evidence presented by the plaintiff begs for rebuttal to the point that no reasonable person could decide in any way but for the plaintiff, it is incumbent upon the defendant to meet its burden of production and present **rebuttal evidence**. If the defendant chooses not to do so after the plaintiff rests its case, the plaintiff can ask the judge to rule in the plaintiff's favor. The case will end if the judge decides as a matter of law that no other conclusion is possible except that the plaintiff should prevail.

Where a defendant has **defenses** to raise that rebut the plaintiff's allegations, the defendant has the burden of production—to produce evidence that supports the defense. For example, in a negligence case, the defendant may raise the defense of **assumption of risk**. Then the defendant must offer evidence that the plaintiff knowingly and purposefully put himself or herself in harm's way and thus assumed the risk of harm.

In a civil case, the burden of production may shift back and forth between parties any number of times during the case. Each party initially presents its evidence to the jury, and then rebuttal opportunities are possible so that each party has the chance to contradict evidence offered by the opponent. As long as the parties present minimal evidence to support either the cause of action or the defense to the cause of action, each has met its burden of production.

Whether the parties have met their respective burdens of production is a decision for the judge to make, not the jury. If the judge believes the burden of production has been met, then the judge lets the case continue so that the jury will have an opportunity to decide which party should prevail.

A criminal case does not operate in quite the same manner as a civil case. Constitutional requirements demand that the government present proof that the defendant committed a crime according to statutory definitions. The burden of production never shifts to the defendant on this requirement of proof. It is not within the power of the prosecutor to ask the judge at the close of its **case-in-chief** to find the defendant guilty as a matter of law, even if the

burden of going forward with the evidence Requirement that a party produce evidence on an issue or risk losing on that issue.

directed verdict The judge tells the jury how to decide a case, or the judge makes the decision for the jury because a party has not met the burden of production.

rebuttal evidence Proof offered by a party to contradict evidence offered by the opposing party.

defenses Issues raised by a defendant that, if proven, preclude the plaintiff in a civil case from recovery, or the government in a criminal case from obtaining a conviction.

assumption of risk Knowingly and purposefully exposing oneself to harm; a defense to allegations of negligence.

case-in-chief The main body of evidence offered by a party; does not include rebuttal evidence.

defendant chooses to offer no evidence. In a criminal case with a jury, the judge cannot find the defendant guilty; this can only be done by the jury. The jurors make the determination of whether the government has produced enough evidence to meet the statutory requirements of what is required to convict a defendant. However, a judge can grant a **judgment of acquittal** at the close of the government's case if the defendant convinces the judge that the prosecutor did not present a *prima facie* case.

The burden of production in a criminal case can shift to the defendant when the defendant raises a defense that requires proof, such as insanity or alibi. In this case, after the prosecutor offers evidence to prove the case-in-chief, a defense is raised to excuse or disprove the alleged conduct, and the burden of production thus shifts.

Burden of Persuasion

The **burden of persuasion**, the second type of burden of proof, requires evidence that will convince a jury that a party should prevail. Once the judge decides the parties have met their burdens of production in a civil case, it is up to the jury to weigh everything that has been heard and seen at trial and decide who should win. It is up to each party to persuade the jurors to accept its view of what happened between the contestants. Essentially, parties can meet their burdens of production, but there must be a winner and a loser in the litigation process. Determination of the winner and loser is left to the jury, with the onus on each of the parties to convince the jury of who should win. It is the jury that determines the quality of all of the evidence provided in the case by both parties, that is, who has met the burden of persuasion.

James W. McElhaney, a law professor and regular contributor to the *ABA Journal,* explains what it means to meet the burden of persuasion.

> The theory of the case is not just the set of legal elements that establishes a cause of action or a defense. The law tells you almost nothing about how to try the case. The law only tells you the bare minimum facts you need to keep from being thrown out of court.
>
> Look at it this way: If the legal elements of a case were a plan for building a house, they might tell you to have at least three walls, a fireplace and two windows—and leave the rest up to you. But don't expect your entry to win the home show if all you put up is three walls, a fireplace and two windows.
>
> Every part of your case has to be measured against the way the judge and jury look at the world. Winning is as much the product of the images you present and the impressions they create as it is the facts you prove.[1]

McElhaney's words show the importance of correlating the theme of a case with its proof. The attorney, with the legal assistant's help, can organize the evidence in a case using a common theme. For instance, in a criminal case, the defense might center on the theme that the defendant was not at the scene of the crime and took no part in the crime's commission. In a civil case, a theme might incorporate evidence emphasizing long-term knowledge of harm caused by a product and its continued marketing by the corporation in spite of the knowledge.

judgment of acquittal In a criminal case, the term sometimes used to describe a directed verdict when the government fails to present enough evidence to support its case against a defendant.

burden of persuasion Requirement that a party offer enough evidence to convince a jury the party should prevail.

Standards of Proof

Utilizing a theme assists the jury in determining which party meets the burden of persuasion. The jury must measure the facts that it finds from the evidence using one of three **standards of proof**:

1. Preponderance of the evidence.
2. Clear and convincing evidence.
3. Evidence beyond a reasonable doubt.

It is the jury's province to determine who should prevail, but the judge provides the standard of proof that the jurors are required to use during their deliberations to measure the evidence presented by the parties. The judge explicitly instructs the jury on the level of proof required for a party to prevail in a case.

In most civil cases, jurors are required to use the standard of proof called **preponderance of the evidence**. The jurors are instructed by the judge to view the evidence within a framework where the facts establish that one party's side is more likely to be true than the other party's side. This standard does not require a high degree of quality and quantity of evidence in favor of one party over the other. Some commentators put this standard of proof in terms of a 51 percent probability that one party should prevail over the other. The preponderance of the evidence is the amount of evidence that takes the parties from being even in their proof of their cases to just tipping the balance in the judgment of the jury as to who should win. In other words, preponderance of the evidence is enough evidence to tip the scales of justice.

In some states, preponderance of the evidence is put in terms of **greater weight of the evidence**. The judge instructs the jurors before deliberation thus:

> "Greater weight of the evidence" means the more persuasive and convincing force and effect of the entire evidence in the case.[2]

Clear and convincing evidence involves a higher standard of proof and is used in some civil cases. It is not as prevalent a standard as preponderance of the evidence. The standard is usually used to measure evidence related to special issues in a case, such as a dispute about whether a contract to make a will is valid. It is also the standard used in a civil proceeding to determine whether someone should be committed to a psychiatric facility or whether parental rights should be terminated. The quality of proof must be better and more convincing than that required in a routine civil trial. This higher standard of proof is often a matter of public policy, acknowledging that the outcomes of some court actions are more consequential than others.

The standard of clear and convincing evidence can be put in terms of probability; it is very probable that a fact is true and that this and other facts make it very probable as to which party should prevail. It takes better evidence, whether in quantity or quality, to meet this measure of proof, which is a higher standard than preponderance of the evidence, but not as high a standard as evidence beyond a reasonable doubt.

As an example, if the jury hears the evidence in a dispute over whether there was a valid contract to make a will, the jurors must measure that evidence

standard of proof The measure of proof required to prevail in a case.

preponderance of the evidence Standard of proof in most civil cases that requires enough evidence to tip the scales in favor of one of the parties.

greater weight of the evidence Phrase used in some states instead of *preponderance of the evidence* to mean the same thing.

clear and convincing evidence Standard of proof in some civil cases where the outcome involves social policy issues; requires a higher degree of quality evidence than *preponderance of the evidence*.

against the standard of clear and convincing evidence. The evidence has to be enough to more than just tip the scales in favor of a person alleging a contract to make a will. The evidence must be such that it appears very probable that the person entered into a contract to make a will.

The third standard is evidence **beyond a reasonable doubt**, used in criminal cases only. As previously mentioned, the government bears the burden of production in a criminal case, which is not shifted to the defendant. At the same time that the government is meeting its burden of production, the government must also persuade the jury that the defendant should be convicted. The level of evidence to meet the standard of proof is very high. The government must provide the jury with evidence that is of sufficient quantity and quality that it demonstrates a very high probability of guilt. This standard of proof is sometimes put in terms of the jurors being 90 percent sure that the evidence points to guilt, although this numerical measure may not be utilized in the courtroom. The jury must be fully satisfied that the defendant is guilty, based on the evidence presented by the government.

Juries in California are given the following instruction by the judge as an explanation of evidence beyond a reasonable doubt before deliberations begin.

> A defendant in a criminal action is presumed to be innocent until the contrary is proved, and in the case of a reasonable doubt whether his guilt is satisfactorily shown he is entitled to a verdict of not guilty. This presumption places upon the state the burden of proving him guilty beyond a reasonable doubt. Reasonable doubt is defined as follows: It is not a mere possible doubt because everything relating to human affairs, and depending on moral evidence is open to some possible or imaginary doubt. It is that state of the case which, after the entire comparison and consideration of all the evidence, leaves the minds of the jurors in that condition that they cannot say they feel an abiding conviction to a moral certainty of the truth of the charge.[3]

In closing arguments, the prosecution and the defense elaborate on this standard of proof, sometimes using charts with phrases explaining what "beyond a reasonable doubt" means. This practice is allowed by the judge so long as the phrases fall within legally acceptable meanings, as determined by prior decided cases and the judge's instructions.

In a criminal case, the burden of persuasion, like the burden of production, is not shifted to the defendant on the issue of innocence. Constitutional requirements put both the burden of production and the burden of persuasion on the government. Again, the consequences of criminal proceedings against a citizen are viewed as the worst possible ones since those consequences can include incarceration. This is the logic behind making the standard of proof the highest in criminal cases.

beyond a reasonable doubt Standard of proof in criminal cases that requires a high degree of quantity and quality of evidence to support a conviction.

Summary of Burdens of Proof

In a trial, each party is allocated burdens of proof. These burdens of proof are divided into the burden of production and the burden of persuasion (Figure 4-1). The judge determines whether a party has met its burden of production, whereas the jury determines which party meets the burden of persuasion. Jurors are told to utilize one of three standards of proof in measuring to what

FIGURE 4-1

The burdens of proof include burdens of production and persuasion.

BURDENS OF PROOF

(1) BURDEN OF PRODUCTION

Judge decides if met by plaintiff or prosecutor (*prima facie* case)

Civil Case

Burden shifts to defendant to rebut
Defendant has burden of production for any defenses raised

Criminal Case

Burden does not shift to defendant on issue of innocence
Defendant has burden of production for defenses

(2) BURDEN OF PERSUASION

Jury decides which party should prevail

Standards of proof to measure the evidence must be used

Civil Case

Preponderance of evidence
Clear and convincing evidence

Criminal Case

Beyond a reasonable doubt

---

degree they are persuaded. If a party fails to meet the burden of persuasion, it means that the party did not offer evidence of such quantity and quality that the jurors were persuaded to the degree necessary to find for that party.

PRESUMPTIONS

The allocation of the burden of proof in a trial allows an orderly presentation of evidence to the judge and to the jury. Evidence that might support a party's position in a case must be proven to the jury, and the evidence as a whole must meet one of the standards of proof. The evidence is conveyed to the jury through testimony, physical evidence, and exhibits.

Civil Cases

The quantity of evidence needed to prove that a fact is true is sometimes governed by **presumptions**. A presumption allows a party to prove an ultimate fact (the presumed fact) by proving a basic fact first. The proof of the basic fact results in the automatic proof of the ultimate fact. In other words, the plaintiff can automatically prove B by proving the existence of A. The proof of A allows the jury to presume the existence of B. The use of presumptions to prove certain facts is an evidentiary shortcut that relates to both the burden of production and the burden of persuasion.

presumption An allowable conclusion based on proof of underlying facts.

Rule 301. Presumptions in General in Civil Actions and Proceedings

In all civil actions and proceedings not otherwise provided for by Act of Congress or by these rules, a presumption imposes on the party against whom it is directed the burden of going forward with evidence to rebut or meet the presumption, but does not shift to such party the burden of proof in the sense of the risk of nonpersuasion, which remains throughout the trial upon the party on whom it was originally cast.

Rule 301 applies to civil actions and proceedings, not to criminal cases.

As an example, there is a presumption recognized in many states against suicide. If a person dies, and evidence is offered in the form of a death certificate, the presumption is allowed that the person did not die as a result of suicide. In a case in which a beneficiary is suing a life insurance company for nonpayment on the policy, the presumption against suicide makes it easier for the beneficiary to prove the insured did not commit suicide. This point is critical where the insurance policy states that there will be no death benefits paid to the beneficiary if the insured committed suicide. All the beneficiary has to do at trial is prove that the insured died. The insurance company then has to prove that the death was a result of suicide, thus shifting the burden of production of evidence on the issue of suicide to the insurance company and away from the beneficiary.

It is important to note that the beneficiary maintains the burden of persuasion. The plaintiff continues to have the burden of persuading the jury that its position is the best one. If the defendant insurance company produces evidence that the death was a result of suicide, the plaintiff needs to rebut that evidence or risk that the jury will find the insurance company's evidence more persuasive. If the insurance company's evidence of suicide is weak, the presumption is not rebutted, and the proof of the death of the insured remains enough to persuade the jury that the death was not a result of suicide.

Many states govern the use of presumptions at trial in their own rules of evidence and in statutes. Federal courts apply state law on presumptions when the cause of action involves substantive state law. Otherwise, in cases in federal court based on a federal cause of action, federal treatment of presumptions applies.

Rule 302. Applicability of State Law in Civil Actions and Proceedings

In civil actions and proceedings, the effect of a presumption respecting a fact which is an element of a claim or defense as to which State law supplies the rule of decision is determined in accordance with State law.

For the paralegal, this confusion is resolved by first deciding which law applies to the rule on presumptions—either federal law or state law. With this decision made, the paralegal can proceed to research the law related to presumptions in the appropriate jurisdiction. Although it is beyond the scope of this text to engage in a detailed discussion of presumptions, a number of common presumptions are commonly recognized as affecting the burden of producing evidence. The common presumptions listed in Illustration 4-1 operate until the opposing party offers proof that the presumed (ultimate) fact does not exist. If contradictory proof is offered, the proponent of the ultimate fact must offer more proof that the ultimate fact exists in order to rebut the opponent's evidence.

Illustration 4-1 _____

COMMON PRESUMPTIONS

Proof of the BASIC FACT proves the ULTIMATE FACT.

1. A properly addressed and mailed letter is presumed to have been received by the addressee.
   ultimate/presumed fact: letter received by addressee
   basic fact: letter properly addressed and mailed

2. A person absent for seven years is presumed dead.
   ultimate/presumed fact: person is dead
   basic fact: person's unexplained absence for seven years

3. An attorney has the authority to act on behalf of the attorney's client.
   ultimate/presumed fact: attorney acts on behalf of client
   basic fact: attorney states that the attorney has the authority to act on behalf of the client

4. The driver of a vehicle that crashes into the rear of another vehicle is negligent.
   ultimate/presumed fact: driver is negligent
   basic fact: driver crashes into the rear of another vehicle

5. A will once in the possession of the testator is not found after the death of the testator and is revoked.
   ultimate/presumed fact: will revoked
   basic fact: will cannot be found after testator's death

Criminal Cases

Presumptions in criminal cases differ significantly from those in civil cases. Because of constitutional requirements of due process and fair trial, the government always has the burden of proving every element of a crime beyond a reasonable doubt. However, federal case law provides that some presumptions are allowed, though not required, in criminal cases. Again, the paralegal needs to research federal case law related to presumptions in criminal cases to determine what is and is not constitutionally valid (see Illustration 4-2).

Illustration 4-2 _____

Federal criminal statutes may include presumptions that allow juries to infer certain knowledge on the part of the defendant. That knowledge is an element of the crime the prosecution is excused from proving so long as the basic fact is proven. Statutory presumptions that lessen the government's requirement of presenting evidence on certain elements of the crime run into constitutional problems based on due process issues.

In *Leary v. United States,* 395 U.S. 6 (1969), the statute under which Dr. Timothy Leary was convicted included a provision he had to have knowledge that the marijuana in his possession had been illegally imported. The court held that proof of the basic fact—possession—could not support the ultimate fact—knowledge the marijuana was illegally imported.

The court did not believe someone in possession of marijuana would necessarily know the marijuana was illegally imported. The court noted not all marijuana is foreign-grown, and consumers of the product generally do not even think about where it was grown. Therefore, it would be unfair and would serve to deny Dr. Leary due process of law, to infer that he knew the marijuana was illegally imported. Such an inference would make the job of the prosecution too easy in its role of proving guilt of the defendant. See also *Barnes v. United States,* 412 U.S. 837 (1973); *Turner v. United States,* 396 U.S. 398 (1970); *United States v. Romano,* 382 U.S. 136 (1965); *United States v. Gainey,* 380 U.S. 63 (1965); and *Tot v. United States,* 319 U.S. 463 (1943).

SUMMARY

When the trial is ready to begin, prospective jurors are questioned to determine whether they can be fair in hearing the evidence of the parties. Once the jury is in place, the parties present their opening statements to the jury, summarizing the evidence to be presented and how the parties think the law should be applied.

To facilitate an orderly and fair presentation of the evidence, burdens of proof must be met in a specific order and manner. There are two burdens of proof: burden of production and burden of persuasion. The burden of production requires the party who instigated the case—that is, the plaintiff or the prosecutor—to present evidence of a *prima facie* case. If the plaintiff or prosecutor fails to meet the burden of production, a directed verdict or judgment of acquittal may be entered by the court.

If the plaintiff meets the burden of production, the defendant presents rebuttal evidence and also has the burden of producing evidence with regard to defenses that are claimed. In a criminal case, the defendant does not have to produce evidence to prove innocence, but the defendant has the burden of producing evidence on claimed defenses.

The burden of persuasion, the second category of burden of proof, requires the parties to present the necessary quantity and quality of evidence to convince the jury the party should prevail. The judge instructs the jury on the standard of proof appropriate for the type of case. In most civil cases, the measure of proof is preponderance of the evidence, where one of the parties must offer enough evidence to tip the scales in the party's favor. Clear and convincing evidence is the measure of proof in a limited number of civil cases. Here, more and better evidence must be offered to meet this standard. Finally, criminal cases require the most and best evidence in order to convict a defendant. The government must offer enough evidence to convince a jury of a defendant's guilt beyond a reasonable doubt.

How much proof and the type of proof a party must offer to prove a fact is sometimes governed by presumptions. If a presumption is recognized as a matter of law, there is a decreased need for the quantity of evidence necessary to prove something. State and federal law recognizes various presumptions that allow a party to prove a basic fact that in turn proves an ultimate fact. The jury is allowed to come to a conclusion once basic facts are offered into evidence without further need of proof by the proponent.

Since the proponent still must persuade the jury in its favor, if the opponent offers rebuttal evidence, the proponent may need to present a greater quantity of evidence than initially required to trigger the presumption.

Presumptions are treated differently in civil and criminal cases, with a greater latitude of use in civil cases because liberty of the defendant is not an issue.

The paralegal must understand the law as it relates to presumptions so that the presumptions can be used effectively. Also, in the event the opponent offers rebuttal evidence, the case must be prepared so that other evidence can be offered to persuade the jury on the matter in issue.

✔ CHECKPOINTS

❑ Setting the scene
1. Voir dire: picking the jury.
2. Opening statements: preview of the case.

❑ Burden of proof
1. Two types:
   a. Burden of production: the party instigating the action or presenting a defense offers evidence.
   b. Burden of persuasion: offering sufficient quantity and quality of evidence to convince the jury.
2. Burden of persuasion and standards of proof
   a. Preponderance of the evidence: required in most civil cases; must tip the scales.
   b. Clear and convincing evidence: required in some civil cases involving special issues; must provide more and better proof than in preponderance of the evidence.
   c. Beyond a reasonable doubt: required in all criminal cases; must provide more and better proof than in clear and convincing evidence.

❑ Presumptions
1. Defined: proof of a basic fact leads to an allowable conclusion without more evidence.
2. Civil cases:
   a. Common presumptions allow evidentiary shortcut.
   b. State and federal courts may allow different presumptions.
   c. If rebutted, more proof is necessary to meet burden of persuasion.
   d. Common presumptions:
      - Properly addressed and mailed letter received.
      - If unexplained absence of seven years, a person is dead.
      - Attorney can act on behalf of client.
      - Driver who crashes into back of another vehicle is negligent.
      - A will was revoked if cannot be found.

APPLICATIONS

Application 4-1

Dick v. New York Life Insurance Co.
359 U.S. 437 (1959)

MR. CHIEF JUSTICE WARREN delivered the opinion of the Court.

The question in this case is whether the Court of Appeals for the Eighth Circuit, under the applicable principles hereinafter discussed, properly held that it was error to submit to a jury's determination whether an insured died as a result of suicide or accident.

Petitioner is the beneficiary of two policies issued by respondent in 1944 and 1949 insuring the life of her now-deceased husband, William Dick. Each policy contained a clause which provided that double indemnity would be payable upon receipt of proof that the death of the insured "resulted directly, and independently of all other causes, from bodily injury effected solely through external violent and accidental means," but that the double indemnity would not be payable if the insured's death resulted from "self-destruction, whether sane or insane."

Mr. Dick met his death while alone in the silage shed of his farm. The death resulted from two wounds caused by the discharge of his shotgun. [FOOTNOTE 1: The gun was a Stevens, 12 gauge, double barreled shotgun with two triggers placed one behind the other. It weighed approximately seven pounds. It had an over-all length of 46 inches and measured 32 inches from muzzle to triggers.] Petitioner filed proofs of death but respondent rejected her claim for double indemnity payments on the ground that Mr. Dick had committed suicide. Petitioner then filed suit in the North Dakota courts. Her complaint set forth the policies in issue, the facts surrounding her husband's death, an allegation that the death was accidental, and a demand for payment. Respondent removed the case to the United States District Court for the District of North Dakota on the grounds of diversity of citizenship and jurisdictional amount. It then filed an answer to the complaint in which it set up suicide as an affirmative defense to the demand for double indemnity payments. Respondent admitted liability for face amounts of the policies ($7,500) and no issue is presented concerning those amounts.

Trial proceeded before the district judge and jury. The evidence showed that the Dicks, who had been happily married since 1926, lived on a farm near Lisbon, North Dakota, where they raised sheep, cattle and field crops. Five of the six quarter sections of the farm were unmortgaged and Mr. Dick, who was not known to have any financial problems, had nearly $1,000 in the bank. He was known as a "husky," "strong," "jolly" man who was seldom moody. "If he had anything on his chest, he would get it off and forget about it." Dick got along well with his neighbors and was well liked in the community. He was 47 at the time of his death. He was five feet seven inches tall, weighed approximately 165 pounds, and was generally healthy. The coroner, who was also Dick's personal doctor, testified that Dick was a mature, muscular, physically able workman who, three weeks before his death, was bright and cheerful. About a year and a half before his death, Mr. Dick visited the doctor and complained that he felt tired and pepless. His condition was diagnosed as mild to moderate non-specific prostatitis for which he received sulfa treatments and hormone shots. But the record is devoid of evidence that the condition was serious or particularly painful or that Mr. Dick was especially concerned with it. The Dicks reared five children. One daughter still lived with them and attended high school in nearby Elliott. Dick got along well with his whole family.

The evening before he died, the family returned from Elliott and ate ice cream and watched television together. Mr. Dick helped his daughter with a school problem in general science explaining to her the intricacies of a transformer. He slept soundly that night. He intended to help his cousin—a neighbor—make sausage the following day. He arose the next morning, milked the cows, ate a hearty breakfast, and spoke with his wife about their plans for the day. He said nothing to indicate that he contemplated doing anything out of the ordinary. About 8:30 a.m., Mrs. Dick drove their daughter to school. Mr. Dick backed the car out of the garage for his wife and said goodbye in a normal way. He was then in the process of feeding milk to the pigs and silage to the cattle.

Mrs. Dick returned in about a half hour and proceeded to work in the house. Later, when she thought it was time to leave for the cousin's house, she went to locate Mr. Dick. She walked to the barn and called for him but there was no answer. She then went to the little 8 foot by 12 foot silage shed adjacent to the barn and saw Mr. Dick lying on the floor. He was fully clothed for the zero weather Lisbon was then experiencing and he wore bulky gloves and a heavy jacket which was fully zipped up. Near him lay his shotgun. A good part of his head appeared blown off and she knew from his appearance that he was dead. She hurriedly returned to the house and called Mr. Dick's brother who lived nearby. He came immediately and at Mrs. Dick's direction went to the silage shed. There he saw Mr. Dick lying with his head to the northwest and his feet to the southeast of the shed. The body was along the south wall with the feet near the corner. Later, when he examined the shed more closely, he found a concentration of shotgun pellets high in the northwest corner of the shed and other pellets four to five feet from the floor in the southeast corner. He also noticed a sprinkle of frozen silage on the floor of the shed and on the steps leading to the door from the shed.

James Dick, the deceased's nephew, also responded to Mrs. Dick's call. He stated that upon arriving at the Dicks' house, he saw a tub newly filled with ground corn in the silage yard and that normally his uncle fed silage with a topping of ground corn to the cattle. He also stated that the cattle were just then finishing the silage presumably laid out by Mr. Dick before his death.

At about 11 a.m., the sheriff arrived. Mr. Dick was still lying where he had died. The sheriff examined Mr. Dick's shotgun and found two discharged shells in its chamber. The gun was dry and clean and there were no bloodstains on it or on the gloves which Dick was still wearing. The sheriff also noticed some of the shot patterns found by Dick's brother and saw some brain tissue splattered on the southeast corner. He found a screwdriver lying on the floor about a foot from the gun. The Dicks used the screwdriver to open and close the door to the silage shed because the doorknob was missing.

Soon thereafter the coroner arrived. He testified that Mr. Dick's body contained a shotgun wound on the left side and one on the head. The body wound was mortal, but not immediately fatal. It consisted of a gouged out wound on the left lateral chest wall which removed skin, fat, rib muscles and portions of rib from the body. In addition, other ribs were fractured and Dick's left lung was collapsed. In the coroner's opinion, it was the type of wound which would have had to result in immense pain, although it probably would not have made it impossible for Dick again to discharge the gun. The wound to the head caused immediate death. According to the testimony of the sheriff and a member of the Fargo police department, both wounds were received from the front. In the sheriff's opinion, the chest wound was received from an upward shot into Dick's body, but this testimony conflicted with another statement of the sheriff indicating that the wound was received from a downward shot.

It was clear from the testimony that Mr. Dick was an experienced hunter. Petitioner testified that he kept the shotgun in the barn because of attacks on his sheep by vicious dogs during the preceding year. A number of the sheep had been killed in this manner. In addition, Dick had mentioned seeing foxes near the barn. Mrs. Dick testified that when her husband went hunting, he sometimes borrowed his father's gun because he didn't trust his own. She was with him once when the gun wouldn't fire and had been told that occasionally it fired accidentally. In addition, Dick's brother testified that while hunting with Dick he heard a shot at an unexpected time which Dick explained as an accidental discharge that occurred "once in a while." The gun was over 26 years old.

The sheriff testified that after the death he tested Dick's gun by cocking and dropping it a number of times. The triggers did not release on any of these occasions. The sheriff also explained that the gun had a safety and could not discharge with the safety on. The safety was off during each of his tests. Finally, the sheriff stated that each trigger had approximately a seven-pound trigger pull.

No suicide notes were found. Mr. Dick had said nothing to his relatives or friends concerning suicide. He left no will.

At the conclusion of the evidence, respondent unsuccessfully moved for a directed verdict. The court charged the jury that under state law accidental death should be presumed and that respondent had the burden to show by a fair preponderance of the evidence that Dick committed suicide. The jury returned a verdict of $7,500 for petitioner. Respondent's motions for judgment not-withstanding the verdict and for new trial were denied.

In this Court and before the Court of Appeals, both parties assumed that the propriety of the District Court's refusal to grant respondent's motions was a matter of North Dakota law. Under that law, it is clear that under the circumstances present in this case a presumption arises, which has the weight of affirmative evidence, that death was accidental. Proof of coverage and of death by gunshot wound shifts the burden to the insurer to establish that the death of the insured was due to his suicide. Under North Dakota law, this presumption does not disappear once the insurer presents any evidence of suicide. Rather, the presumed fact (accidental death) continues and a plaintiff is entitled to affirmative instructions to the jury concerning its existence and weight. This is not to say that under North Dakota law the presumption of accidental death may not be overcome by so much evidence that the insurer is entitled to a directed verdict. For it is clear that where "there is no evidence in the record that can be said to be inconsistent with the conclusion of death by suicide," or "the facts and circumstances surrounding the death [can] not be reconciled with any reasonable theory of accidental or nonintentional injury," the state court may direct a verdict for the insurer even though the insurer is charged with the burden of providing that death was caused by suicide. These state rules determine when the evidence in a "suicide" case is sufficient to go to a jury. They are not directed at determining when the presumption of accidental death is rebutted, and thus excised from the case, because, as stated above, the presumed fact of accidental death continues throughout the trial and has the weight of affirmative evidence.

The Court of Appeals, in its opinion, reviewed the evidence in detail and resolved at least one disputed point in respondent's favor. It found, as "definitely established by the evidence," that "neither barrel [of the shotgun] could have been fired unless someone or something either pulled or pushed one of the triggers." It stated that "[o]ne can believe that even an experienced hunter might accidentally shoot himself once, but the asserted theory that he could accidentally shoot himself first with one barrel and then with the other stretches credulity beyond the breaking point." [FOOTNOTE 6: The court of Appeals admitted the improbability of Dick's being able to pull the triggers with bulky gloves on but believed that this was offset by the probability that he used the screwdriver to push the triggers. This resolution of the facts seems strained indeed. The presence of the screwdriver was accounted for by testimony indicating that it was used to open the silage shed door. And the jury could reject as improbable the court's implicit theory that a man mortally wounded in the chest and bulkily clothed could hold a heavy shotgun at arm's length and shoot off his head particularly when he was wearing heavy gloves that could only be inserted in the trigger guard with difficulty.] And it concluded that the facts and circumstances could not "be reconciled with any reasonable theory of accident, and that, under the evidence, the question whether the death was accidental was not a question of fact for the jury." Judgment was reversed with directions to dismiss the complaint. 252 F.2d 43. We granted certiorari, 357 U.S. 925.

In our view, the Court of Appeals improperly reversed the judgment of the District Court. It committed its basic error in resolving a factual dispute in favor of respondent that the shotgun would not fire unless someone or something pulled the triggers. Petitioner's evidence on this score, despite the "tests" performed by the sheriff, could support a jury conclusion that the gun might have fired accidentally from other causes. Once an accidental discharge is possible, a jury could rationally conceive of a number of explanations of accidental death which were consistent with evidence which the jury might well have believed showed the overwhelming improbability of suicide. The record indisputably shows lack of motive—in fact there is affirmative evidence from which the jury could infer that Dick was a most unlikely suicide prospect. He was relatively healthy, financially secure, happily married, well liked, and apparently emotionally stable. He left nothing behind to indicate that he had committed suicide and nothing in his conduct before death indicated an intention to destroy himself. The timing of the death, while in the midst of normal chores and immediately preceding a planned appointment with neighbors, militates against such a conclusion. Dick's presence in the shed and the accessibility of the gun are explicable in view of the fact that dogs had previously attacked his sheep and the fact the door in the shed provided a convenient exit to the adjoining fields. And a jury could well believe it improbable that a man would not even bother to remove his bulky gloves, or thick jacket, when he intended to commit suicide even though those articles of clothing made it difficult to turn the gun on himself.

In a case like this one, North Dakota presumes that death was accidental and places on the insurer the burden of proving that death resulted from suicide. Under the *Erie* rule, presumptions (and their effects) and burden of proof are "substantive" and hence respondent was required to shoulder the burden during the instant trial. After all the evidence was in, the district judge, who was intimately concerned with the trial and who has a firsthand knowledge of the applicable state principles, believed that the case would go to the jury. Under all the circumstances, we believe that he was correct and that reasonable men could conclude that the respondent failed to satisfy its burden of showing that death resulted from suicide.

Reversed.

Class Discussion Questions

1. What was the presumption in North Dakota with regard to cause of death?

2. Which party had the burden of producing evidence that Mr. Dick committed suicide?

3. What facts did Mrs. Dick have to show in order to get the benefit of the presumption so that she could receive the life insurance proceeds under the double indemnity clause?

4. Did the court believe that New York Life produced enough evidence to lead to the conclusion that Mr. Dick could have died only by suicide?

5. Did the court find that it was reasonable for a jury to conclude that the death was accidental?

6. Under North Dakota law, did Mrs. Dick lose the benefit of the presumption when New York Life offered evidence of suicide?

7. What was the advantage of the presumption of accidental death to Mrs. Dick's case?

Application 4-2

Carvalho v. Raybestos-Manhattan, Inc.
794 F.2d 454 (9th Cir. 1986)

CYNTHIA HOLCOMB HALL, Circuit Judge:

Plaintiff-appellant Moana Carvalho (plaintiff or Carvalho), appeals from the decision of the district court finding her cause of action barred by Hawaii's two-year statute of limitations for tort claims, Hawaii Rev.Stat. § 657-7. We vacate the decision of the district court and remand for a new trial on the statute of limitations issue.

I.

Plaintiff, acting as administratrix of her husband's estate, filed this action against defendant-appellee Raybestos-Manhattan (Raybestos) and other producers and distributors of asbestos-related products on July 28, 1980, seeking damages for the death of her husband Manuel Carvalho (Manuel). Manuel worked at the Pearl Harbor Naval Shipyards from 1941 through 1971, and died of asbestosis and asbestos-related lung cancer on September 4, 1978. The jury awarded $213,046.62 in compensatory damages against twelve manufacturers, and $500,000 in punitive damages against Raybestos.

At trial there was conflicting evidence regarding when the cause of action accrued. The district court instructed the jury that plaintiff had to prove each element of the cause of action by a preponderance of the evidence. The court also posed two special interrogatories to the jury on the question of accrual, asking the jury to specify the date on which Carvalho was informed or should have known (1) that he was suffering from asbestos-related cancer and asbestosis, and (2) that these diseases were the result of Raybestos' negligence or Raybestos' defective products. The district court denied Carvalho's request to inform the jury of the reason for the interrogatories. The court also declined to instruct the jury that Raybestos had the burden of establishing the date on which plaintiff's cause of action accrued, even though both parties had proposed such instructions.

In answer to the special interrogatories the jury found that Carvalho knew or should have known that his illness was asbestos related and that his illness was attributable to the defendants' negligence or defendants' defective products on July 5, 1978. Accordingly, the district court concluded that the cause of action was barred by the two-year statute of limitations in section 657-7, and set aside the award.

Plaintiff petitioned for a new trial arguing that the jury's findings regarding Carvalho's knowledge on July 5, 1978 were not supported by substantial evidence, and that the district court committed error by not informing the jury of the significance of the interrogatories or instructing the jury that Raybestos had the burden of proof regarding accrual. The district court denied the motion, finding sufficient evidence to support the verdict and concluding that any error in failing to instruct on the burden of proof for accrual was harmless. Plaintiff filed this timely appeal. 28 U.S.C. § 1291.

II.

Taken as a whole the instructions and interrogatories must fairly present the issues to the jury. If the issues are fairly presented, the district court has broad discretion regarding the precise wording of the instructions and interrogatories.

Although Hawaii has not addressed the issue, other jurisdictions have consistently recognized that placing the burden of proof on the wrong party in a civil action generally constitutes reversible error. These courts have emphasized that the burden of proof affects all aspects of the jury's verdict and that it is impossible to determine whether the erroneous burden of proof was outcome determinative.

Courts have also concluded that the failure to give any burden of proof instruction may constitute reversible error under circumstances similar to this case. *Lewis v. Washington Metropolitan Area Transit Authority,* 463 A.2d 666, 672–73 (D.C.App. 1983). In *Lewis* certain building owners sued the Washington Area Transit Authority (WATA) and Dravo Corporation, which was building a subway for WATA, for damages to their building allegedly caused by negligent construction of the subway. The building had been leased to another company and operated as a shoe store by Gilbert Tebeleff. After finding cracks in the building Tebeleff accepted a payment from defendants and signed a release. The cost of repairs later turned out to be much greater than the amount defendants paid to Tebeleff. The owners sued defendants, and defendants argued that the release by Tebeleff was binding on the owners because Tebeleff was acting as the owners' agent. Defendants had the burden of proof regarding agency because agency was part of the affirmative defense. *Lewis,* 463 A.2d at 672. The trial court instructed the jury that the owners had the burden of proving their case, but declined to instruct that defendants had the burden of establishing agency. *Id.* at 672–73. The appellate court reversed finding that the failure to instruct on the defendants' burden to prove agency was error. *Id.* at 673. The court concluded that the error was not harmless because of the potentially misleading general burden of proof instruction, and the closeness of the agency issue. *Id. See also Olivarez,* 694 S.W.2d at 93–94 (finding interrogatories which failed to provide the jury any indication that the plaintiff had the burden of proof regarding the duration of incapacity in workmen's compensation action reversible error).

III.

We conclude that the Hawaii courts would follow the above authorities and find that the district court committed reversible error by instructing the jury that plaintiff had the burden of proof on all elements of the cause of action without instructing that Raybestos had the burden of proving accrual.

Under Hawaii law the defendant has the burden of proof on all affirmative defenses, including the statute of limitations. This includes the burden of proving facts which are essential to the asserted defense. A cause of action accrues under Hawaii law when the plaintiff knows, or through the exercise of reasonable diligence should know, of his injury, the defendant's negligence (or violation of a duty), and the causal connection between the two. *Jacoby v. Kaiser Foundation Hospital,* 1 Hawaii App. 519, 622 P.2d 613, 617 (1981). Thus, under Hawaii law, Raybestos had to establish that Carvalho knew, or should have known, the elements which trigger accrual under *Jacoby* before July 28, 1978.

The district court erred because the instructions and interrogatories did not fairly inform the jury that Raybestos had this burden. As in *Lewis, supra,* the general burden of proof instruction given by the district court was misleading. A juror will not understand that the questions regarding accrual are not elements of the plaintiff's cause of action unless the instructions or interrogatories specify the distinction. The district court's failure to give any instruction on the burden of proof for accrual had the effect of placing the burden on Carvalho because the general burden of proof instruction that was given.

This error was not harmless. Under Hawaii law "'[e]rroneous instructions are presumptively harmful and are a ground for reversal unless it affirmatively appears from the record as a whole that the error was not prejudicial.'" The evidence regarding when Manuel knew or should have known that his illness was asbestos related and that he had a cause of action against Raybestos is conflicting. On the record before us, we cannot say that the erroneous burden of proof did not affect the jury's determination of the date of accrual.

IV.

The decision of the district court is VACATED and this action is REMANDED to the district court for a retrial of the statute of limitations issue. Should the retrial result in a determination that Carvalho's claim is not time barred, the previous jury award should be reinstated.

Class Discussion Questions

1. What affirmative defense was raised by Raybestos to the plaintiff's claim that, in the view of the district court, barred recovery from Raybestos?

2. The date on which the cause of action accrued is the date the two-year statute of limitations began to run. According to the appellate court, which party should have had the burden of proof on this issue at trial, and why?

3. In order to prove the date of accrual, what must the defendant establish that the plaintiff knew?

4. Why did the appellate court find that not allocating the burden of proof to the defendant was reversible error in this case?

5. What do you think the appellate court meant by burden of proof? Did the court mean burden of production, burden of persuasion, or both? Explain your answer.

Application 4-3

Wilson v. United States
232 U.S. 563 (1914)

MR. JUSTICE PITNEY delivered the opinion of the court.

This case comes here upon two separate writs of error allowed upon the same record, to review judgments of the District Court imposing fine and imprisonment upon each of the plaintiffs in error, upon their conviction on an indictment founded upon the act of Congress of June 25, 1910, commonly known as the White-Slave Act (236 Stat. 825, c.395).

The case was brought directly to this court, because the constitutionality of the statute was drawn in question. This question has since been settled adversely to plaintiffs in error. Nevertheless, we must retain jurisdiction for the purpose of passing upon the other questions in the record.

There were numerous counts in the indictment, and a general verdict of guilty. The substance of the charge was that defendants caused and procured two girls to be transported in interstate commerce from Milwaukee, Wisconsin, to Chicago, Illinois, for the purpose of prostitution. There was also a count charging a conspiracy to commit the same offense. The theory of the Government, sufficiently stated in the indictment and supported by evidence at trial, was that in pursuance of an understanding between defendants and a man named Corder, they gave him eleven dollars in money, with instructions to proceed from Chicago to Milwaukee, induce one or both of the girls to return with him to Chicago, paying their transportation and other expenses out of the eleven dollars, and bring them to a house of prostitution in the latter city kept by the defendants; and that Corder carried out these instructions to the letter, bringing both girls over an interstate electric railway line and escorting them to defendants' house for the purpose of prostitution.

Of the questions of law that are raised, only the following seem to require mention:

1. ..... 4. .....

5.   Error is assigned upon the instructions of the trial court to the jury respecting the presumption of innocence, and the definition of reasonable doubt. Counsel for defendants preferred no request upon the subject previous to the delivery of the charge. The court instructed the jury in substance that the arrest of defendants, their indictment by the grand jury and their arraignment, were no evidence whatever of their guilt; that the presumption of innocence meant that at the beginning of the trial they were as innocent of the charges as any man in the jury-box; that this presumption continued to abide with the defendants as a complete protection, unless and until it gave way because inconsistent with the existence of a situation proved by the evidence in the case beyond all reasonable doubt; that by that [reasonable doubt] was meant, not the frame of mind of a man endeavoring to find a way out for somebody accused of crime, not a mere capricious doubt, not a frame of mind suggested by something occurring in the trial of the case or in the argument of counsel not based on evidence in the case; but that "reasonable doubt is that frame of mind which forbids you to say, all evidence considered and weighed, 'I have an abiding conviction of the defendant's guilt,' or as it has been expressed, 'I am convinced of the defendants' guilt to a moral certainty.' If you can say that you have such a conviction, then you have no reasonable doubt, and your verdict should be guilty. On the contrary, if that is your frame of mind, if you are in the frame of mind where if it was a matter of importance to you in your own affairs, away from here, you would pause and hesitate, before acting, then you have a reasonable doubt." At the conclusion of the charge counsel for defendants said: "I should like that the court say a little more on the reasonable doubt, as I believe it was limited only to a moral certainty. That is the only sentence I heard about that." The argument here is that the instruction as given is faulty, because the court did not tell the jury that the Government must prove its case against defendants beyond a reasonable doubt. As we read the charge, it meant nothing less than that, and was sufficiently favorable to defendants.

We find no error in the record.

Judgments affirmed.

Class Discussion Questions

1. Outline and explain how the jury instruction used at this trial demonstrates that the prosecution has the burden of production and the burden of persuasion.

2. How does the court explain "evidence beyond a reasonable doubt"?

3. Did the Supreme Court find that the jury instruction was sufficient?

EXERCISES

1. In your state trial courts, do the attorneys for the parties examine prospective jurors, or do the judges conduct voir dire?

2. In your state, in a criminal case, is it appropriate to use the term *directed verdict* or *judgment of acquittal*?

3. What are the standards of proof in your state called? Is one of the standards defined in the jury instructions called *preponderance of the evidence* or *greater weight of the evidence*?

4. What presumptions are recognized in your state?

RULES REFERENCED IN THIS CHAPTER

Rule 302 Applicability of State Law in Civil Actions and Proceedings

NOTES

[1] James W. McElhaney. "Litigating in Theory." *ABA Journal,* June 1995, p. 97. Copyright (1995) by James W. McElhaney of Case Western Reserve University School of Law, Cleveland, Ohio. Reprinted with permission of the copyright holder.

[2] *Florida Standard Jury Instructions in Civil Cases,* 3.9 Greater Weight (Preponderance) of Evidence Defined (1997).

[3] *California Jury Instructions Criminal,* Presumption of Innocence—Reasonable Doubt—Burden of Proof 2.90 (5th ed. 1997).

Relevant Evidence

OUTLINE

RELEVANCE

The preceding chapters set the stage with an introduction to the trial itself. Roles of the participants in the trial were explained, as were the rules of evidence that help define those roles. Terminology was presented that will be used throughout the text and is fundamental to an understanding of the application of the rules of evidence at trial. To this foundation, new elements in the trial can be added.

Our attention will now turn to the rules that relate to the administration of evidence at trial. Will the evidence make it through the judge acting as a filter for the jury? The answer to this question lies in the rules the judge must follow in determining the admissibility of evidence. In this chapter, the rules related to relevance will be explored.

To be admissible, relevant evidence must be (1) logically relevant and (2) legally relevant. If the evidence is not logically relevant, there is no need to continue the analysis of whether the evidence is legally relevant. The evidence is not admissible because it is irrelevant.

Logical Relevance

Evidence that has **logical relevance** is proof a party wants to offer at trial that relates to the issues in the case and tends to prove the party's contentions. When determining whether certain testimony should be admitted when an

logical relevance Evidence that relates to proving a cause of action and tends to prove an issue in a case.

objection is raised by the opponent, the judge first considers whether the proof relates to the proponent's case. Does the evidence have a bearing on the case-in-chief of the plaintiff or prosecutor or on a defense raised by the defendant? Then the judge considers whether the testimony tends to prove the party's evidentiary point.

Simply requiring evidence to relate to the issues in the case allows a broad spectrum of evidence. To somewhat narrow the spectrum of acceptable evidence, the judge determines if the evidence also appears to demonstrate that the party's contentions are true.

Rule 401. Definition of "Relevant Evidence"

"Relevant evidence" means evidence having any tendency to make the existence of any fact that is of consequence to the determination of the action more probable or less probable than it would be without the evidence.

The test for relevance, then, is a two-prong test:

1. Does the evidence *relate* to the issues that must be proven at trial? That is, does the evidence help the jury determine what the outcome of the trial should be?

2. Does the evidence *tend to prove* the fact for which it is offered? That is, does the evidence provide the jury with information that makes the existence of a fact more probable?

If every bit of information that related to a case were admissible, the jury would suffer an information overload. The judge, as the filter for evidence offered by the parties, lightens the information overload by determining if the proffered evidence does more than just relate to the dispute. The evidence must tend to prove an element of the cause of action or defense. Even if the evidence has a bearing on the case, if it does not in any way tend to prove an issue in the case, the judge will not allow the evidence to be presented to the jury because it is not relevant.

For instance, parties may be in litigation because of a contract dispute where the defendant maintains that the contract was discharged by performance. The plaintiff does not agree, and she alleges a breach of the contract. The plaintiff offers into evidence a letter written by the plaintiff to her cousin, complaining about defendant's lack of performance on the contract. The letter relates to the issue of breach of contract, and it tends to prove the defendant did not do what the defendant promised under the terms of the contract. Using the test for relevance, the letter would be admissible at the trial for the jury to consider on the issue of breach. The letter is logically relevant because it relates to the dispute between the parties and it tends to make the breach of contract more probable than if the jury were not allowed to see the letter as evidence.

On the other hand, where a defendant is tried for sexual assault, evidence that the defendant purchased stolen goods the week before the alleged assault is not logically relevant to proving the defendant sexually assaulted the victim.

There is no logical relationship between what the prosecutor has to prove in a sexual assault case and the defendant's purchase of stolen goods.

Relevant evidence is simply a question of logic based on experience and accepted assumptions concerning human behavior, rather than a question of law.

Relevance questions emerge frequently at trial because the parties rely primarily on circumstantial evidence to persuade the jury. **Circumstantial evidence** relies on inference; that is, evidence is presented to the jury as a springboard to a conclusion. In a personal injury trial involving an automobile struck by a freight train at a crossing with a roadway, the plaintiff might offer the testimony of another driver who states the lights were not flashing when the automobile crossed the tracks. From this testimony, the jury can infer the signals malfunctioned. Assuming it was the duty of the railroad to maintain the signals, this is indirect, or circumstantial, evidence of the railroad's breach of its duty to motorists who cross its tracks. The witness's testimony that the signals did not work is a springboard to the conclusion that the railroad did not properly maintain the signals.

The plaintiff must prove a breach of duty by the railroad. The item of evidence, the testimony of the witness with regard to the signals, relates to the issue of whether the railroad company breached its duty to the plaintiff. It also tends to prove the breach of duty. The conclusion that a jury would draw from the testimony of the witness is logical and draws on the common sense and experience of the jurors.

Keep in mind the relevant evidence relating to the breach of the railroad's duty to maintain the signals is only one brick in the wall that will create the whole picture for the jury. It takes many bricks to create a compelling picture for the jury, convincing jurors of why and how the accident occurred. The evidence will make it through the judge's filter as admissible evidence for the jury to consider, but alone it is not sufficient to make the plaintiff's case. The issue of relevance applies to all the evidence a party wants the jury to digest, including evidence not in dispute. Background information may not be in dispute, but it helps parties to present a clear picture to the jury. So does a variety of real and demonstrative evidence. Thus, charts, computer graphics, photographs, weapons, and injuries may be relevant even though they mainly illustrate testimony.

Legal Relevance

In determining the admissibility of logically relevant evidence, the judge must also consider whether the evidence has **legal relevance** as a matter of law. Even though evidence may be logically relevant, it may be kept from the jury because it is not legally relevant. Rule 402 states that all relevant evidence is admissible unless certain exceptions apply. For example, relevant evidence is not admissible if there is a provision of the Constitution of the United States, an act of Congress, other rules of evidence, or other Supreme Court rules that override relevance. As a matter of law, the evidence would not be admissible if there is another legal authority that would disallow the evidence, in spite of

circumstantial evidence Testimony or other evidence that requires the trier of fact to draw an inference in order to establish a fact.

legal relevance Relevant evidence that does not violate a specific rule or law.

the fact it was relevant. Rule 401 defines relevant evidence in broad terms, while Rule 402 begins to set parameters on admissibility.

Rule 402.   Relevant Evidence Generally Admissible; Irrelevant Evidence Inadmissible

All relevant evidence is admissible, except as otherwise provided by the Constitution of the United States, by Act of Congress, by these rules, or by other rules prescribed by the Supreme Court pursuant to statutory authority. Evidence which is not relevant is not admissible.

Other rules of evidence that might form a basis for arguing against relevant evidence being heard by the jury include the hearsay rule, the best evidence rule, and the rule related to privileges. Other rules promulgated by the Supreme Court that could keep relevant evidence from being heard at trial are the Rules of Criminal Procedure and the Rules of Civil Procedure.

Another impediment to the admissibility of relevant evidence can be statutes enacted by Congress or by state legislatures. For example, intercepted radio communications cannot be divulged unless authorized by the sender.[1] In other words, a witness cannot testify to what the witness heard on a radio communication unless one of the exceptions in that statute applies. This is a matter of public policy embodied in a federal statute because lawmakers decided it is more important to protect radio communications from eavesdroppers than to give information to a jury for its consideration in a dispute.

Constitutional considerations also have an impact on whether the judge will allow the jury to hear relevant evidence. A confession to murder certainly is relevant to a prosecutor's case, but if the police obtained the confession by questioning a suspect in spite of repeated requests for an attorney, the confession will not be allowed into evidence by the judge, and the jury will not hear it or even know that it exists. Figure 5-1 summarizes the considerations the judge might consider in determining the admissibility of relevant evidence.

Rule 403—More Prejudicial than Probative

Finally, logically relevant evidence also must survive a challenge to its admission under Rule 403. Although the evidence is logically relevant, it may not be legally relevant because there is a danger of unfair prejudice, confusion of the issues, misleading the jury, undue delay, waste of time, or it may be cumulative evidence.

Rule 403.   Exclusion of Relevant Evidence on Grounds of Prejudice, Confusion, or Waste of Time

Although relevant, evidence may be excluded if its probative value is substantially outweighed by the danger of unfair prejudice, confusion of the issues, or misleading the jury, or by considerations of undue delay, waste of time, or needless presentation of cumulative evidence.

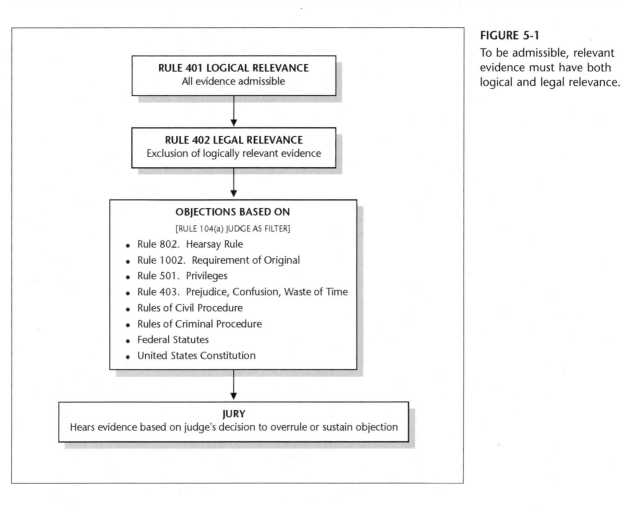

Rule 403 is the basis for an important means of excluding relevant evidence. The rule supplies the **Rule 403 balancing test** for use by the judge in filtering out evidence (Figure 5-2). The judge considers the value of the evidence in establishing a claim (probative value) against other risks (unfair prejudice, confusion of issues, misleading the jury, undue delay, waste of time).

If the risks are great enough, the judge will not let the jurors hear or see the evidence even though it would otherwise be helpful in their determination of who should prevail in the case. The risk of unfair prejudice means that a jury will be swayed more by emotion than reason in determining which party should prevail. If the evidence might lead jurors to decide a case because of sympathy or hatred, or because the jurors would be horrified by what they were shown, then their ability to use reason would be impaired, and the evidence should be excluded. It is the judge who weighs these factors as a matter of law. The judge's decision on whether to admit or exclude the evidence may be a basis for an appeal if the opposing party makes a timely objection and can argue on appeal an "abuse of discretion" by the judge. Illustration 5-1 gives an example of an abuse of discretion.

Rule 403 balancing test Is the evidence more prejudicial than probative— that is, more unfair than helpful to the jury in its determination of a case?

FIGURE 5-2

The Rule 403
balancing test
weighs probative
value against
certain risks.

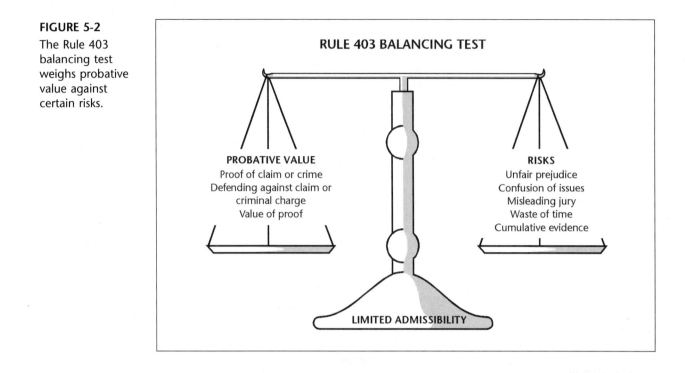

FIGURE 5-2

The Rule 403 balancing test weighs probative value against certain risks.

Illustration 5-1 _____

A defendant convicted of manslaughter got a new trial because the prosecutor was allowed to use a tape recording of the victim's deathbed statement to police. The victim's statement was taped while he was on an emergency room table dying. Screaming in agony as medical personnel inserted an expander inside his chest cavity and a tube to draw blood from his swollen chest, the victim responded to a police officer's questions, saying "a dude named Mike" stabbed him.

There was no doubt that the victim knew he was dying as the officer continued to ask questions. The victim began to moan loudly and he screamed, "Oh, please, please, please." He then lapsed into unconsciousness and the tape ended. He died soon after.

The case was remanded for a new trial where the officer could testify as to what the victim said without the use of the tape. The tape was unfairly prejudicial, and it was an abuse of discretion on the part of the trial court judge to allow the jury to hear it. *Johnson v. State,* 534 So. 2d 1212 (Fla. 4th D.C.A. 1989).

_____

In a prosecution for murder where the medical examiner is a witness, the prosecution may attempt to use a large number of graphic photographs from the autopsy of the victim, and the defense would probably object to admitting any of them. The judge likely would meet the defendant's objection by approving only a few of the photographs, provided the photographs demonstrated the testimony of the medical examiner or had some other probative value that would not be outweighed by their prejudicial effect. If the judge thinks the jurors might decide against a defendant simply because the graphic pictures create in their minds the need to convict anyone in the defendant's seat, then the probative value is outweighed by the prejudicial effect of the autopsy pictures.

Evidence can be admissible for different purposes, that is, to prove one fact but not another. The photographs might not be admissible because they are pictures of a child's lacerated heart that would horrify the jury and influence jurors to find a defendant guilty based on emotion or undue emphasis rather than reason (as was proposed in Illustration 5-2). However, if the defendant is charged with murder, and the prosecutor must prove as a matter of law that the defendant used cruel and excessive force, the pictures might be admissible to demonstrate the force used. They would be inadmissible to illustrate the medical examiner's testimony, because their probative value would not outweigh their prejudicial effect.

Where the statute puts the burden on the prosecutor to prove cruel and excessive force, the pictures help the prosecution meet the burden. But the defendant can argue that the testimony without the pictures serves the same purpose. The judge would then decide whether the jury should see the pictures.

Illustration 5-2 _____

In *United States v. Bowers,* 660 F.2d 527, 529–530 (5th Cir. 1981) the court said in part: "Appellant argues that the jury was unduly prejudiced by the government's introduction in evidence of a color photograph of the child's lacerated heart. The photograph was clearly relevant. Under Fed.R.Evid. 403, however, the court may have been required to exclude the evidence "if its probative value [was] substantially outweighed by the danger of unfair prejudice." … To be sure, the photograph had the potential to inflame the jury, but we consider it no more inflammatory than photographs that portray the sort of death suffered by the victim in this or any other case where the circumstances surrounding death are at issue. The photograph, here, was essential to the government's case if it was to meet its burden of showing that appellant brought cruel and excessive physical force to bear on her child. We cannot say that the prejudice inherent in the photograph substantially outweighed its probative value."

Rule 403 also gives the judge the latitude to exclude cumulative evidence. If a party wants to call five witnesses who will testify to the same thing, an objection based on Rule 403 likely would prevail. The judge has a responsibility to see that the trial proceeds efficiently, without repetitive presentation of evidence.

Limiting Instruction

In deciding whether to admit evidence that might be unfairly prejudicial, the judge must consider the availability of a limiting instruction. A **limiting instruction** is given by the judge to the jury in order to direct the jury on how it should use specific evidence when deciding a case. Rule 105 requires the objecting attorney to request a limiting instruction, but the instruction's

limiting instruction Direction by the judge to the jury on how it should use evidence in deciding a case.

availability alone can weigh in favor of letting the jury hear evidence that otherwise could have been excluded because it was unfairly prejudicial.

Rule 105. Limited Admissibility

When evidence which is admissible as to one party or for one purpose but not admissible as to another party or for another purpose is admitted, the court, upon request, shall restrict the evidence to its proper scope and instruct the jury accordingly.

Regarding the photographs of the lacerated heart, the jurors could be told that the photographs should be considered by them only as they tend to prove or not prove the level of force used in the murder. This limiting instruction might further state the photographs were not meant to overcome a rational consideration of all of the evidence against the defendant as the jurors decide whether the state proved its case beyond a reasonable doubt.

The result is the jury gets to see some of the photographs because the Rule 403 objection was enough to cut down on the number of photographs but not to exclude all of them. At the same time, the judge will grant the request for a limiting instruction on the purpose of the photographs, so the jury is directed on the purpose of the photographs as they consider all of the proof against the defendant.

Rule 403 is a gold mine of opportunity for exclusion of relevant evidence. It should be used for all that it is worth. And where Rule 403 fails to keep evidence out, Rule 105 might be helpful with a limiting instruction, or there might be other, more specific rules that will keep the evidence from reaching the jury. If an objection is based on a procedural rule, statute, or constitutional consideration, and the argument fails, Rule 403 is there to use as a fall-back argument.

Detrimental Evidence

Finally, there is a difference between unfairly prejudicial evidence and detrimental evidence. Unfairly prejudicial evidence gives an advantage to one party that is outside the bounds of fair play. It is some form of evidence that leads jurors to a decision based on emotion or undue emphasis rather than a reasonable consideration of all of the evidence presented by the parties. **Detrimental evidence** is harmful to the position taken by a party in litigation—that is, it may hurt a party's case—but it is within the bounds of fairness and generally is admissible.

Jurors see and hear evidence that is the basis for their verdict in a case. In the adversarial system, the attorneys advocate for their respective positions and try to discredit the opponent's position with detrimental evidence. However, if the evidence goes beyond the bounds of fair play, and rises to the level of being unfairly prejudicial, the rules offer relief to the objecting party.

The attorneys write the script for the drama, but the judge, utilizing the rules, determines what parts of that script the jury will see and hear. If dialog in the script is outside the established rules, and the other party objects to it on that basis, the drama will go on without that portion of the script if the judge so decides.

detrimental evidence
Proof in a case that harms the opponent's position.

LAYING A FOUNDATION

As a practical matter, how an attorney presents evidence to the jury can also be a factor in its admissibility. Rule 401 interfaces with Rule 602, which requires that a witness have personal knowledge of the matter that is the subject of the witness's testimony.

Rule 602. Lack of Personal Knowledge

A witness may not testify to a matter unless evidence is introduced sufficient to support a finding that the witness has personal knowledge of the matter. Evidence to prove personal knowledge may, but need not, consist of the witness' own testimony. This rule is subject to the provisions of rule 703, relating to opinion testimony by expert witnesses.

Personal knowledge is demonstrated by a process of **authentication**, which is achieved through recognition testimony. The attorney asks the witness on the stand background questions to show the witness has a basis for the witness's testimony. Asking these preliminary questions is called **laying a foundation**.

The foundation is built with questions to demonstrate the reliability and accuracy of the story the witness relates on the stand. When a paralegal investigates a case by interviewing potential witnesses, the paralegal should determine from the potential witnesses the basis for their statements. The crucial testimony might be, "I saw the black Mercedes swerve across the center line right before the collision with the school bus." Before the attorney elicits this testimony on the stand, background questions need to be asked and answered. These questions might include where the witness was on the day of the collision and how the witness had the opportunity to observe the collision. The foundational questions should demonstrate the witness has first-hand knowledge of the matters that are the subject of the witness's testimony.

"Objection, no foundation," is commonly heard at trial. The objection is often appropriate, because the attorney questioning the witness knows the story in detail but forgets that the jury and the judge need to be filled in on the background related to how the witness knows what was seen or heard. This objection can be avoided, and the continuity of the presentation of the evidence to the jury preserved, by laying a proper foundation when eliciting testimony from the witness.

Chain of Custody

When a party wants the jury to see an object or hear about the results of a test based on samples, the attorney must establish a **chain of custody** in order to lay the foundation for testimony about the object or the testimony. The chain of custody is especially important when the evidence might be confused with other objects, or when there is a possibility of someone having tampered with evidence.

A foundation is laid by asking the witness preliminary questions to trace the origin and path of the evidence. If the evidence is an object, testimony

authentication The introduction of evidence that proves a document or object is what it appears to be.

laying a foundation Presenting preliminary evidence needed to make other, more important evidence, relevant.

chain of custody The written record that establishes the location of physical evidence from the time it is collected until the time it is offered as evidence at trial.

must establish that it is the same object originally described by the witness. In a criminal case, foundation questions might relate to the identification of the object. For example, when a witness removes a knife from the sealed evidence bag at trial, that witness might testify that he or she put that knife in the bag after finding it next to the body of the victim. If the knife was removed from the evidence room before trial for testing of blood on the knife, the witness can testify that notes on the bag establish when and why the knife was removed and when it was returned. The chain of custody is established by questions that lay a foundation for the witness's testimony that the knife is the same knife found next to the victim and hence is the murder weapon.

SUMMARY

As the paralegal or investigator conducts an investigation or prepares evidence for trial, background information supporting a witness's claim of personal knowledge must be included. The background information serves as the basis for questions that lay a foundation for the witness's critical testimony related to the proof of or defense against a claim.

Because of the subjective nature of the Rule 403 balancing test, attorneys need to be prepared to argue for admissibility or exclusion of evidence. It is within the judge's discretion to admit or exclude evidence. If the admission or exclusion of the evidence becomes the basis for an appeal, the appellate court likely will find that even if the judge made a mistake, it was harmless error. The appellate court will reason that when evidence wrongly passed through the filter, it was harmless error because there was enough other evidence to justify the jury's verdict. If the judge excludes the evidence over the objection of counsel, the appellate court will find harmless error, reasoning that the excluded evidence would not have affected the jury's verdict. Because of the discretion afforded to trial court judges by appellate courts, it is imperative that the attorney be knowledgeable about the effective use of Rule 403 during trial.

All evidence is important in establishing the validity or invalidity of a claim or the guilty or not guilty verdict for an accused criminal. The paralegal and investigator should identify evidence that might be subject to a relevance objection at trial. Evidence may meet the test for logical relevance yet not be admissible because it is not legally relevant.

The paralegal and investigator should identify any other rules of evidence, statutes, or constitutional considerations that might exclude logically relevant evidence. Pertinent case law should be researched to determine how the appellate courts have dealt with specific issues, such as the number and nature of photographs admissible at trial. A limiting instruction may overcome a Rule 403 objection, so the jury will get to consider the "almost" unfairly prejudicial evidence.

Admission of detrimental evidence is important in a case because it is evidence that discredits the opponent and supports the proponent's case. Detrimental evidence is fair, so it is not subject to a Rule 403 objection as unfairly prejudicial.

The paralegal and investigator who are familiar with the legal elements of a cause of action can discover evidence that supports the case and do the research necessary to meet admissibility objections that might be raised, either before trial by motions in limine or during trial when the evidence is presented. Background information is important to allow the establishment of a proper foundation for when witnesses testify. It is especially important to present the evidence to the jury clearly in order to create a compelling picture of the case.

 CHECKPOINTS

❑ Relevance
  1. Logical relevance: whether evidence relates to the cause of action, and whether the evidence tends to prove the issues.
  2. Legal relevance: whether a constitutional provision, statute, or other rule excludes evidence that is logically relevant.

❑ Rule 403
  1. Balancing test: whether the evidence is more prejudicial than probative.
  2. Whether the evidence will confuse the issues, mislead the jury, unduly delay the proceeding, waste time, or be cumulative.

❑ Limiting instruction
  1. Evidence admissible to prove one issue, but not another.

  2. Judge directs jury to use evidence for only the issue it may prove.

❑ Detrimental evidence
  1. Causes harm to an opponent's case.
  2. Goal of adversary is to introduce as much as possible.
  3. Not necessarily unfairly prejudicial.

❑ Laying a foundation
  1. Asking background questions in order to establish that the witness has first-hand knowledge.
  2. Chain of custody: foundation for identification of objects related to the case.

APPLICATIONS

Application 5-1

In this case, Whitney Allen sued Seacoast Products, Inc., along with the company's insurers. Mr. Allen sought recovery under the Jones Act, 46 U.S.C.A. § 688, as well as under the general maritime law of unseaworthiness of the vessel, *Louisiana*. The trial court granted Mr. Allen's motion for directed verdict. The jury heard evidence related only to the issue of the amount of damages that should be awarded to Mr. Allen. By general verdict, the jury awarded $240,000 to Mr. Allen.

The *Louisiana* was a ship designed to net and store up to 1,100,000 pounds of Menhaden fish for transfer to a Seacoast fish-meal processing plant. However, the ship went after the fish only when spotter aircraft radioed the location of schools of Menhaden.

In June of 1977 the aircraft notified the *Louisiana* that there was a partially sunken vessel nearby the *Louisiana*'s location. The captain of the *Louisiana* decided to investigate the salvage possibilities of what turned out to be a 45-foot shrimper. The appellate court noted that maritime law encourages salvage, allowing rewards to the owner of the salving vessel, its captain, and crew.

The appellate court went on to detail the facts found at trial.

Allen v. Seacoast Products, Inc.
623 F.2d 355 (5th Cir. 1980)

Acting on this impulse so encouraged by the admiralty, Captain Dixon attempted to salvage. He decided to attach the lifting cables of the davits used for the 36-foot boats and then pull the shrimper into shallow waters. There, the partially sunken vessel could be dragged ashore by land-based winches. But all of this depended on bringing the *Louisiana* alongside and on there being some flotation remaining in the shrimper (since the *Louisiana*'s lifting cables were not capable of raising such a large, partially sunken vessel out of the water). So to test the shrimper's buoyancy and then to bring the *Louisiana* close enough to attach the lifting cables, Captain Dixon took out one of the 36-foot boats and strung two 50-foot mooring lines between the stern of the shrimper and the bow of the *Louisiana*. The lines were strung in a separated configuration, from the side of one vessel to the side of the other, and were not "doubled up." The lines used were one and a quarter inch diameter nylon lines, normally used in doubled up manner for tying the *Louisiana* to a dock. Captain Dixon then returned to the bridge of the *Louisiana*. Allen noticed that the captain had cut his legs when coming back aboard and followed him to the bridge.

Captain Dixon then had the pilot back the *Louisiana* away from the shrimper, pulling on the lines, "to see if the shrimp boat was still ... partially floating." Nothing happened until the captain decided to stop backing the *Louisiana*. At that point the sea surged and one of the already taut lines parted. Like a rubber band, the line flew back and hit Allen as he stood on the bridge, causing the eventual loss of his eye.

At the close of the essentially undisputed evidence, the Trial Judge granted Allen's motion for a directed verdict on liability, stating that "there's no way that a jury composed of reasonable people could reach a different conclusion on the facts of this case ..."

[Based on the facts, the trial judge went on to find the *Louisiana* unseaworthy, the captain negligent, and that negligence imputed to Seacoast.]

The Damage Award

We finally come to Seacoast's claim that the jury verdict of $240,000 was excessive and proceed to the particular facts of this case.

[FOOTNOTE 23: The jury was properly instructed that the damage award may include compensation for impairment of future earning capacity, lost wages, medical expenses, and pain and suffering. The jury was also cautioned that the award:

cannot be governed by sympathy, or prejudice, or any motive whatsoever except a fair and impartial consideration of that evidence, and you must not allow any sympathy that you may have for either party to influence you in any degree whatever in arriving at your verdict.

Seacoast argues that the allegedly excessive verdict resulted from Allen's demonstration of the removal and replacement of his artificial eye in front of the jury. As for Allen's demonstration, the Trial Judge did not abuse his discretion in determining that the demonstration's probative value (in showing the daily regimen which Allen must endure) outweighed its prejudicial effect. F.R.Evid. 403; *Rozier v. Ford Motor Co.,* 573 F.2d 1332, 1347 (5th Cir. 1978). We find no error of any substance. Moreover, considering the record as a whole, it appears that any prejudice was too slight to influence the jury's verdict.]

As of the date of the trial it is essentially undisputed that Allen had lost some $30,000 in wages in the two years since his injury. Unpaid medical expenses of approximately $5,000 were additionally anticipated. Impairment of future earning capacity was, however, a much disputed item. There was evidence that tearing problems in Allen's good left eye made it impossible for him to work in dusty environments. Allen had recovered very little depth perception at the time of trial, though there was some evidence that after a time he might recover up to 75 percent. His peripheral vision was obviously affected, and there was very substantial evidence that this limitation combined with the impairment of his depth perception would prevent Allen from ever returning to his former job. There was testimony from both sides concerning the willingness of employers to hire one-eyed persons. It was also asserted that Allen should not take any job posing any substantial risk to his remaining eye. Assuming that Allen's loss of an eye was a total disability, expert testimony established that the present value of Allen's future earnings over a remaining working life of thirty years amounted to between $155,000 and $304,000. Seacoast contested those estimates and now argues that Allen is immediately employable at his previous wages, so that the special damages component of the jury verdict could have been at most $35,000.

Compensation for pain and suffering, the general damages component, was also a much disputed item. Allen was in excruciating agony for a short period after his accident, perhaps as long as a month afterwards. While he is now essentially free of physical pain, there is ample evidence of his humiliation and emotional suffering from being disfigured for life. The evidence also shows that Allen will experience a number of problems in everyday life, including impairment of recreational activities.

Because the jury's general verdict does not distinguish between the various types of damages, we are at a disadvantage in reviewing the award. We believe it is fair to say that the jury could conclude that Allen's future earning capacity was impaired, though not totally. And the pain and suffering component of the award should have been substantial. It seems reasonably clear that those two items together must have constituted approximately $200,000 of the jury's $240,000 verdict. But we reject Seacoast's contention that the entire amount was attributable to pain and suffering alone. Considering the extent of Allen's (past and future) pain and suffering and the probability of substantial impairment of future earning capacity, we conclude that the award is very generous but not shocking to our conscience. Nor could we direct that it be for a lesser sum than found. Accordingly, we hold that the verdict was not excessive.

AFFIRMED.

Class Discussion Questions

1. On what issue did the jury hear evidence? Explain by describing what led to the injury.

2. Why did the trial judge grant Allen's motion for a directed verdict on the issue of liability?

3. Special damages and general damages are types of compensatory damages. Special damages, sometimes called consequential damages, include compensation for losses that are peculiar to a plaintiff as a result of someone else's fault. General damages generally result from the defendant's kind of conduct.
   a. What were the types of special damages that Allen had to prove at trial in order to recover money from Seacoast?
   b. Speculate on how Allen presented evidence to the jury to prove general damages.
   c. What was the basis for the trial judge's allowing the demonstration of the removal and replacement of Allen's artificial eye?
   d. The appellate court conceded that the damages award was "very generous." Explain the practical importance of getting into evidence the artificial eye demonstration, in spite of the trial court's instruction to the jury.

Application 5-2

Haney v. Mizell Memorial Hospital
744 F.2d 1467 (11th Cir. 1984)

FAY, Circuit Judge:

This diversity medical malpractice action was brought against Dr. John Meigs and Mizell Memorial Hospital asserting negligence in the diagnosis and treatment of plaintiff Rickey E. Haney, who now is a quadriplegic. The jury which heard this case returned a verdict in favor of the defendants, ... Haney assigns as reversible error several evidentiary rulings by the district court, ... we affirm.

Haney and a friend began drinking beer and whiskey shortly after noon on December 4, 1981, and continued doing so until early the next morning, when they retired for the day. They greeted the following morning with more beer and whiskey in Haney's home, and then visited a few local taverns. The merriment of that Saturday afternoon, however, came to an abrupt halt when the car Haney and two of his companions were occupying ran off a country road and overturned several times.

Haney's friends managed to crawl out of the car, which had come to rest on its right side. Haney, who was hanging out of the driver's door, was lowered by them to the ground. At this time, Haney complained of back pain. His friends rolled him over on the ground to discover the source of the blood they noticed on him.

The emergency medical technician who arrived with the rescue squad strapped Haney to a hard backboard and attempted to immobilize his neck with a technique called "sandbagging." During transport to Mizell Memorial Hospital, Haney cursed, struggled to free himself of the straps to the backboard, and tried to sit up, despite warnings that any movement could be dangerous. The technician described Haney as uncooperative and noticed that he smelled of alcohol.

In the emergency room, Haney showered profanities on the medical personnel. He also lifted himself off the backboard and looked around, in defiance of orders to the contrary. The nurses who initially examined him believed he was extremely drunk. Their examination of him revealed no neurological problems. In fact, Haney exhibited full range of motion with his arms and legs. Because of his unruliness and apparent inability or unwillingness to communicate to them exactly where he was in pain, the nurses were unable to localize the source of Haney's discomfort.

Dr. Meigs, the emergency room physician on duty, next examined Haney. Haney's obstreperousness impeded the doctor's efforts to give him a thorough neurological examination. When asked where he hurt, Haney complained of pain in the neck, then upon further questioning would deny pain there and identify another part of his body, and so on. After extensive interrogation, Dr. Meigs concluded that the source of Haney's pain was an abrasion on the shoulder blade, which was promptly treated. Dr. Meigs also sutured the laceration to Haney's head. Since the doctor was concerned about Haney's level of intoxication and the possibility of a head injury, he admitted Haney for overnight observation. No x-rays were ordered.

[The court went on to describe how Haney's condition deteriorated during the night and that it became apparent that there was neurological damage to the spinal cord from two fractured cervical vertebrae.]

Haney brought suit against Dr. Meigs and Mizell Memorial Hospital essentially alleging negligent diagnosis and treatment of him. A jury trial lasted nearly three weeks.

At trial, Haney contended that while the fracture probably occurred during the car accident, the actions of the defendants caused a subluxation of the damaged vertebrae resulting in permanent paralysis. Haney introduced evidence that proper medical procedure would have included prompt x-rays of his neck. Expert witnesses called on his behalf testified that x-rays would have prompted concern over a possible fracture thereby resulting in immobilization of the neck. His experts further testified that immobilization would have diminished the likelihood of permanent paralysis.

The defendants, on the other hand, presented evidence that because of Haney's intoxication, combativeness, and unwillingness to cooperate with medical personnel, it was nearly impossible to properly diagnose him. The defendants' experts also opined that Haney's own movements could have caused the ultimate injury. These witnesses further testified that irrespective of defendants' conduct, the spinal cord damage more likely than not occurred during the car accident, and it was only a question of time before this damage manifested itself in permanent paralysis. The jury returned a verdict for the defendants, and judgment was entered by the district court.

HANEY'S USE OF ALCOHOL AND DRUGS

Haney also argues that the district court erred in admitting evidence of Haney's use of alcohol and drugs. He basically asserts, albeit inartfully, that: (1) evidence of his alcohol and drug use was irrelevant; (2) even if relevant, the probative value of this evidence was substantially outweighed by the danger of unfair prejudice; and (3) in any event, defendants improperly were allowed to introduce into evidence privileged communications. We address these assertions seriatim.

Relevant evidence is "evidence having any tendency to make the existence of any fact that is of consequence to the determination of the action more probable or less probable than it would be without the evidence." Fed.R.Evid. 401. With this broad definition of relevance in mind, we conclude that evidence of Haney's alcohol and drug use was highly relevant to many issues in this case, several of which were raised by Haney himself.

Initially, there is no doubt that Haney's level of intoxication when treated was relevant to his ability to communicate with medical personnel and their ability to restrain and obtain cooperation from him. Additionally, an examination of Haney's complaint reveals the relevance of his history of alcohol and drug use. Haney prayed therein for damages to cover future mental anguish, rehabilitation care, and loss of earnings. As the deposition testimony of Dr. Lawrence J. Gilgun, the clinical psychologist who treated Haney after the accident, reveals, Haney's ability to face his alcohol and drug problem would play a crucial role in his ability to adjust emotionally to his infirmity and become more fully rehabilitated. Dr. Gilgun also opined that Haney's vocational outlook would be much brighter if he did not indulge in alcohol and drugs. Moreover, the district court found that the challenged testimony was admissible, and, perforce, relevant, to rebut testimony offered by Haney pertaining to his lifestyle and quality of life before that accident. We will not disturb that finding.

Haney alternatively claims, relying on Fed.R.Evid. 403, that the district court should have excluded this evidence since whatever probative value it might have had was substantially outweighed by its danger of unfair prejudice. The district court, however, expressly found to the contrary. A trial court has broad discretion in balancing the probative value of evidence against its potential prejudicial effect, and we will not upset the balance struck unless there has been a clear abuse of discretion. We find no such abuse in this case.

Haney also would have us reverse in this case because the district court allowed into evidence Dr. Gilgun's deposition. As already noted, this deposition contained certain references to Haney's alcohol and drug problem. Haney contends its admission was barred by Florida privilege law.

The parties agree that Florida law provides the rule of decision on the privilege issue. See Fed.R.Evid. 501. Florida, by statute, recognizes a psychotherapist-patient privilege. See Fla.Stat. § 90.503 (1983). Haney, however, apparently ignores that part of the statute which provides that no privilege exists "[f]or communications relevant to an issue of the mental or emotional condition of the patient in any proceeding in which he relies upon the condition as an element of his claim or defense." Id. § 90.503(4)(c). As we have seen, Haney explicitly prayed for damages to compensate him for mental anguish, rehabilitation care, and loss of future earnings. Obviously, his discussion with Dr. Gilgun about his alcohol and drug use was not only relevant to these claims, but was inextricably bound to them. Hence, Haney may not invoke the privilege he effectively waived by bringing this action.

… we AFFIRM.

Class Discussion Questions

The appellate court extensively covers the facts related to Mr. Haney's intoxication. Mr. Haney, the appellant, makes a twofold argument that evidence offered by the defendants of his use of alcohol and drugs should not have been heard by the jury.

1. To what issues did the court find the evidence of intoxication relevant? Note that this is an action based on an allegation of medical malpractice.

2. How did the appellate court deal with Mr. Haney's argument that the probative value of the evidence was outweighed by its prejudicial effect?

3. Mr. Haney claimed the psychotherapist-patient privilege with regard to the conversations he had with Dr. Gilgun, the clinical psychologist who treated him after the accident. Since the psychotherapist-patient relationship is favored under applicable Florida law, on what basis did the court affirm the admission of Dr. Gilgun's testimony?

EXERCISES

1. Assume that you are a paralegal for the Assistant United States Attorney in Miami. The office is prosecuting two employees of a corporation for knowingly misleading United States government export officials about zirconium shipments the corporation sent to a Chilean arms maker. The zirconium ended up as fiery pellets in $150 million worth of jet-mounted cluster bombs the arms maker allegedly sold to Iraqi leader Saddam Hussein during the Iran-Iraq war in the 1980s.

   The paperwork provided to the government export officials stated that the zirconium was for individual use, such as mining. The prosecutor wants to offer into evidence one of the 8-foot-long cluster bombs that has been defused. It was found in an Iraqi desert bunker after the Gulf War. The defendants oppose admission of the bomb and have filed a motion in limine to suppress admission of the cluster bomb.

   a. Outline the arguments that support the prosecutor's contention that the bomb is relevant, using the test for relevancy.

   b. In order to lay a foundation, what kinds of questions should be asked of what kind of witness?

   c. Outline the defendants' arguments that admission of the bomb would be prejudicial, using the Rule 403 balancing test.

   d. Speculate as to how the court will rule on the motion in limine.

2. Obtain an evidence container or bag from your local police department or prosecutor's office. What information is requested on the container?

3. Contact a paralegal in your community who does investigations. Ask what methods are used to collect and preserve evidence for use at trial.

RULES REFERENCED IN THIS CHAPTER

Rule 401. Definition of "Relevant Evidence"

Rule 402. Relevant Evidence Generally Admissible; Irrelevant Evidence Inadmissible

Rule 403. Exclusion of Relevant Evidence on Grounds of Prejudice, Confusion, or Waste of Time

Rule 105. Limited Admissibility

Rule 602. Lack of Personal Knowledge

NOTES

[1] 47 U.S.C.A. § 605 (West 1991 and West Supp. 1996) Unauthorized publication or use of communications.

C H A P T E R

6

Limits on Relevant Evidence

OUTLINE

INTRODUCTION

All relevant evidence is admissible under Rule 401, unless other rules set limits on admissibility. The limits in Rules 402 (irrelevant evidence inadmissible) and 403 (unfairly prejudicial evidence inadmissible) were discussed earlier. This chapter discusses further limitations on the admission of relevant evidence as contained in Rules 404 through 415. These rules set the parameters for admission or exclusion of categories of evidence, including evidence of character, habit or routine practice, subsequent remedial measures, compromises and offers to compromise, payment of medical expenses, pleas and plea discussions, liability insurance, sexual disposition of a victim, sex offenses, sexual assaults, and child molestation. Figure 6-1 presents a summary of these limits on the admissibility of relevant evidence.

FIGURE 6-1

All relevant evidence is admissible under Rule 401 except as limits in Rules 402 through 415 apply.

RULE 401
ALL LOGICALLY RELEVANT EVIDENCE ADMISSIBLE

Specific Relevance Issues

Rule 406 Habit and routine practice admissible *to prove* action in conformity

Rule 413 Other sexual assaults by defendant admissible *to prove* action in conformity

Rule 414 Other child molestations by defendant admissible *to prove* action in conformity

Rule 415 Other child molestations and sexual assaults by defendant admissible *to prove* action in conformity

RULE 402 AND RULE 403
RESTRICTIONS ON ADMISSIBILITY OF RELEVANT EVIDENCE

Specific Relevance Issues

Rule 404 Character evidence *not admissible unless* exception applies

Rule 405 Methods of proving character evidence if exception applies

Rule 407 Subsequent remedial measures *not admissible to prove* negligence

Rule 408 Compromise and offers to compromise *not admissible to prove* liability or invalidity of a claim

Rule 409 Payment of medical expenses *not admissible to prove* liability

Rule 410 Pleas and pleas discussions *not admissible*

Rule 411 Insurance against liability, or lack of insurance, *not admissible to prove* negligence

Rule 412 Past sexual behavior or sexual predisposition of victim *not admissible unless* exception applies

---

Rules 404 through 412, with the exception of Rule 406, outline limitations on the admissibility of categories of evidence. Rules 406 and 413 through 415 define specific categories of relevant evidence that are admissible.

The rules that limit the use of relevant evidence are not absolute bars to admissibility, because the evidence may not be admissible to prove one matter yet be admissible to prove another matter. With this set of rules, it is very important to think in terms of alternatives. For example, evidence of liability insurance is not admissible to prove negligence, but it may be admissible to prove ownership of property where ownership is denied. When the jury hears evidence of a defendant having liability insurance, the jury must not use that evidence as a basis for its determination of negligence and how much to award the plaintiff. The evidence of insurance must be used by the jurors only to determine if the defendant owned the property where the plaintiff alleges the injury took place.

CHARACTER EVIDENCE

Before there can be a discussion of admissibility of character evidence, there must be a definition of what is meant by character. **Character** is a collection of features and traits that make up the individual's disposition, or nature. It is evidenced by a consistent pattern of behavior. Character traits include such things as honesty, courage, integrity, peacefulness, temperance and carefulness, as well as their opposites, dishonesty, cowardice, lack of integrity, violence, intemperance and recklessness. The character traits can be construed as moral qualities, ethical standards, and principles governing behavior.

Rule 404. Character Evidence Not Admissible to Prove Conduct; Exceptions; Other Crimes

---

   (a) Character evidence generally. Evidence of a person's character or a trait of character is not admissible for the purpose of proving action in conformity therewith on a particular occasion, except:
      (1) Character of accused. Evidence of a pertinent trait of character offered by an accused, or by the prosecution to rebut the same;
      (2) Character of victim. Evidence of a pertinent trait of character of the victim of the crime offered by an accused, or by the prosecution to rebut the same, or evidence of a character trait of peacefulness of the victim offered by the prosecution in a homicide case to rebut evidence that the victim was the first aggressor;
      (3) Character of witness. Evidence of the character of a witness, as provided in rules 607, 608, and 609.
   (b) Other crimes, wrongs, or acts. Evidence of other crimes, wrongs, or acts is not admissible to prove the character of a person in order to show action in conformity therewith. It may, however, be admissible for other purposes, such as proof of motive, opportunity, intent, preparation, plan, knowledge, identity, or absence of mistake or accident, provided that upon request by the accused, the prosecution in a criminal case shall provide reasonable notice in advance of trial, or during trial if the court excuses pretrial notice on good cause shown, of the general nature of any such evidence it intends to introduce at trial.

Acting in Conformity with a Character Trait: Inadmissible Evidence

Rule 404 establishes that, in general, the judge must not allow character evidence to be heard by the jury when the proponent wants to use it to prove someone acted in conformity with the character trait. It is debatable whether a person's behavior or action in one instance has anything to do with character traits. The underlying issue in this rule seems to be a mistrust of human nature; people do not always act in conformity with established character traits. Human behavior is not necessarily that predictable; therefore, evidence of a character trait offered to prove a person acted in conformity with the trait raises questions of relevance. Does the character trait relate to the cause of action, and does it tend to prove the cause of action? The prohibited chain involving character and action is shown in Figure 6-2.

character Consistent behavior that reflects a person's disposition or nature.

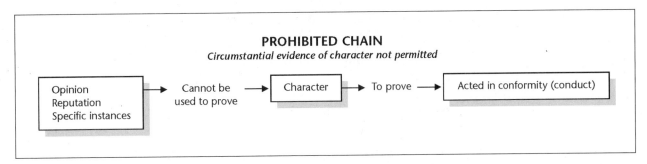

FIGURE 6-2 Character evidence cannot be used to prove actions based on conformity with character.

For example, in a trial in which the plaintiff is suing the defendant in a personal injury action because the defendant allegedly ran over the plaintiff when the defendant was impaired by alcohol consumption, the plaintiff might try to introduce evidence establishing the defendant as a "drunk." Since intemperance is a character trait, it cannot be introduced to prove the defendant acted in conformity with the character trait.

When Character Is an Issue

Evidence of character is relevant when character is (1) an element of a claim in a civil case, (2) an element of a crime that the prosecutor must prove in order to carry the burden of proving a defendant guilty, or (3) an element of a defense. Civil causes of action where character is an element of the claim include defamation, negligent entrustment or retention, and custody. Where character is an element of a claim, defense, or a crime, evidence of a character trait is relevant and can be used to prove action in conformity with that trait. Rule 404 does not bar admissibility in these circumstances, because the character evidence is relevant when character is an issue. Illustration 6-1 gives three examples.

Illustration 6-1 _____

Examples of three causes of action where character is an issue:

1. *Defamation:* Plaintiff sues defendant because defendant called plaintiff a thief; defendant pleads affirmative defense of truth; plaintiff's character is in issue because thieves are dishonest, and honesty (or lack of it) is a character trait.

2. *Negligent retention:* Bartender slams bottle over patron's head in fit of anger; patron sues bar owner for negligently retaining employee with a violent disposition; violent character of employee in issue and violence is a character trait.

3. *Custody:* who is better guardian of child in issue; evidence of good character of potential guardians is in issue.

Rule 404 is meant to keep jurors from considering evidence of a character trait when character is not a part of the claim, defense, or crime. Illustration 6-2 gives three examples. Character evidence may be admissible to test the credibility of a witness by impeachment, a topic that will be covered more thoroughly in Chapter 8.

Illustration 6-2 _____

Examples Using Rule 404(b)

1. Defendant is on trial for shooting his wife, but he claims the gun accidently discharged while he was cleaning it. The prosecution can introduce evidence the defendant tried to stab his wife six months before the shooting, and at that time he was convicted of assault. The evidence of bad character (violent disposition) is offered to prove "absence of mistake or accident," not action in conformity with bad character.

2. The prosecution can offer evidence the defendant on trial for burglary stole burglar tools shortly before the burglary at issue occurred. The evidence is offered to prove "preparation," not that the defendant is a thief.

3. Where the crime charged is passing counterfeit money, and the defendant denies knowing the money was counterfeit, the prosecution can offer evidence the defendant passed counterfeit money in the past to prove "knowledge" regarding counterfeit money, not that the defendant has the propensity to commit this crime.

_____

Acting in Conformity with a Character Trait: Admissible Evidence

Rule 404 does not prevent admission of all evidence of a character trait. There are exceptions to the general rule of inadmissibility outlined in the rule. Under Rule 404(a)(1), a defendant in a criminal case can offer evidence of good character, but this gives the prosecution the opportunity to rebut the evidence of good character with evidence of bad character. If a defendant chooses to introduce character evidence, it must relate to the trait involved in the crime charged. For example, a defendant charged with embezzlement could introduce evidence of past honesty. From this evidence, the defendant would like the jury to infer that the defendant does not possess the character trait necessary to the crime of embezzlement, that is, dishonesty. However, the prosecution can rebut the evidence of honesty with a witness who could testify to specific instances of defendant's dishonesty, reputation for dishonesty, or the witness's opinion of the dishonesty of the defendant.

In criminal actions under Rule 404(a)(2), evidence of the character of a victim can be offered by the defendant to support a defense, such as self-defense when the charge is homicide. Violence as a character trait of the victim can be offered by the defendant to support a theory of self-defense to excuse the defendant's action. Again, the defendant risks the prosecution's offer of rebuttal evidence.

Subsection 3 of Rule 404 applies to both criminal and civil cases. The character of any witness can be explored as long as the character evidence relates to credibility as a witness. Rules 607, 608, and 609 must be read in conjunction with Rule 404(a)(3), because the three rules outline who can attack credibility of a witness and how it can be done through impeachment of a witness, which is covered in Chapter 8.

Rule 404(b) is the gateway to admissibility of character evidence. Generally, evidence of other crimes, wrongs, or acts cannot be used to prove that a defendant has bad character traits and acted in conformity with those character traits. However, in criminal cases, prosecutors freely use the exceptions in Rule 404(b) to build cases against defendants. Judges have broad discretion in determining admissibility of evidence of character for the purposes enumerated in Rule 404(b). Evidence of crimes, wrongs, or acts can be used to prove something other than the bad character of a defendant. The evidence can be used to prove: motive, opportunity, intent, preparation, plan, knowledge, identity, or absence of mistake or accident. This exception creates abundant opportunity for admission of evidence of bad acts of the defendant.

The use of character evidence to prove any of the eight exceptions to the general rule against admissibility of character evidence can be used by the jury as substantive evidence of the defendant's guilt. In other words, character evidence here is used to prove the defendant in fact committed the crime. In a recent 5-4 decision, the United States Supreme Court set limits on the admissibility of a prior conviction when the prior felony conviction has nothing to do with the current criminal charge. The Court requires a **Rule 403 balancing test** when the name and nature of the earlier crime may result in unfair prejudice. Illustration 6-3 presents an example.

Illustration 6-3 _____

Johnny Lynn Old Chief was arrested after an argument where a gunshot was fired. He was charged with assault with a dangerous weapon and using a firearm in a crime of violence. Furthermore, he was charged for violation of a statute that made it unlawful for a convicted felon to possess a firearm. The earlier felony conviction was for assault causing serious bodily injury.

Because Old Chief believed that revealing the name and nature of the earlier crime would unfairly prejudice the jury, he wanted to stipulate and request the trial court judge to instruct the jury he had been convicted of a crime punishable by imprisonment exceeding one year. The prosecution objected, and the trial court judge allowed the prosecution to use the name and nature of the earlier crime. Old Chief was convicted on all counts.

The United States Supreme Court reversed the conviction and remanded the case for a new trial without reference to the name and nature of the earlier crime. The Court reasoned Rule 404(b) does not allow evidence of an earlier crime to prove a person has the propensity to commit the current crime. The prosecution does not have unbridled discretion to use details of a prior conviction where the details result in unfair prejudice, that is, implying the defendant was of bad character and acted in conformity with his bad character.

The Court said the trial court judge should have weighed the prejudicial effect of using the name and nature of the earlier crime (Rule 403 analysis) against just telling the jury of the earlier conviction for a felony. This bare statement was enough for the jury to have what it needed to convict under the statute making it unlawful for a convicted felon to possess a firearm, but not so much as to unfairly prejudice the jury against the defendant on the remaining charges related to using a firearm. *Old Chief v. United States,* ____ U.S. ____, 65 U.S.L.W. 4049 (1997).

Rule 403 balancing test Is the evidence more prejudicial than probative—that is, more unfair than helpful to the jury in its determination of a case?

Because the Rule 404(b) exceptions are widely used by prosecutors against defendants, there is a notice requirement in the rule. The prosecutor must tell the defendant before crimes, wrongs, or acts are going to be used against the defendant, whether in the case-in-chief, as possible rebuttal evidence, or for impeachment purposes. The rule is not specific with regard to the timing and form of the notice, leaving adequacy of notice within the discretion of the judge. If the judge decides that the notice is adequate, an objection based on unfair prejudice, confusion of issues, or waste of time can still be argued (Rule 403).

However, the notice requirement has no bearing on character evidence where character is an element of the crime charged. Elements of a crime are defined by statute, so the defendant is on notice by virtue of the specific charge that character is an issue and is relevant. No further notice is needed on the prosecutor's intent to use evidence of character at trial for any relevant purpose.

How to Prove Character

Once it is established that character evidence is an element of a claim, defense, or crime, or that the character evidence falls under one of the enumerated exceptions in Rule 404, then Rule 405 must be consulted with regard to the acceptable methods for proving character.

Rule 405. Methods of Proving Character

(a) Reputation or opinion.   In all cases in which evidence of character or a trait of character of a person is admissible, proof may be made by testimony as to reputation or by testimony in the form of an opinion. On cross-examination, inquiry is allowable into relevant specific instances of conduct.

(b) Specific instances of conduct.   In cases in which character or a trait of character of a person is an essential element of a charge, claim, or defense, proof may also be made of specific instances of that person's conduct.

Character is usually proven by (1) a witness who can testify as to the reputation of the person whose character trait is in issue or (2) opinion testimony of the witness as to the person's pertinent character trait. Testimony with regard to specific instances of conduct (the third method in Rule 405) is limited to cases where the character trait is an essential element of the charge, claim, or defense. Reputation and opinion testimony are also available methods of proving character where the character trait is an essential element of the charge, claim, or defense (Figure 6-3).

Before a character witness can testify on direct examination as to the **reputation** of the person whose character is in issue, a foundation must be laid. Questions must be asked to establish the witness's familiarity with the community's view of the person's character trait. The purpose of these questions is to establish that the witness has heard other members of the community discuss the person's character. Thus, the person's reputation in the community can be established through this witness's testimony. The community might be the person's employment community, social circle, or the community at large.

reputation What people in a community think about a person.

FIGURE 6-3
When character evidence is admissible, it can be proven by reputation, opinion testimony, or specific instances of conduct.

CIRCUMSTANTIAL EVIDENCE OF CHARACTER

FORM OF PROOF
Reputation
Opinion

ON CROSS-EXAMINATION
Specific instances of conduct to impeach

CHARACTER EVIDENCE AN ELEMENT OF CHARGE, CLAIM, OR DEFENSE

FORM OF PROOF
Reputation
Opinion
Specific instances of conduct

ON CROSS-EXAMINATION
Specific instances of conduct to impeach

FIGURE 6-3
When character evidence is admissible, it can be proven by reputation, opinion testimony, or specific instances of conduct.

Before the witness can give an **opinion** on the character of the person whose character trait is at issue, questioning must establish that the witness has a basis for the opinion. The witness must first testify that the witness knows the person's character. Once this foundation is laid, the opinion can be elicited.

On cross-examination, the party who wants to challenge the reputation or opinion testimony can do so by asking questions about specific instances of conduct that imply the witness does not have complete information about the person's character. Of course, this kind of questioning should be used only when the opposing party has a good-faith basis for believing in the existence of specific instances of conduct that do not conform to the witness's picture of the person's reputation or the witness's opinion of the person's character.

Where the character of a person is an essential element of the charge, claim, or defense, specific instances of conduct that demonstrate a character trait are admissible through direct examination of the witness. Character would be an essential element, for instance, in a defamation claim based on the defendant telling other clients of a broker that the broker is a crook. The character of the broker is at issue, so specific instances demonstrating the broker's honesty or dishonesty can be asked of a witness.

It is important to note that not all states follow the federal model for establishing character evidence through character witnesses. Some states, such as Florida, continue the older tradition that opinion testimony is unreliable. Again, logic does not always prevail in the law. Reputation, which is rumor and gossip related by the witness, seems less reliable than personal opinion based on acquaintance with the person whose character trait is at issue. Logic aside, the paralegal needs to know how character evidence can be proven when a case is tried in state court.

opinion What a witness thinks about a person, based on the witness's knowledge of the person's character.

SIMILAR ACTS OR OCCURRENCES

Certain types of evidence have been dealt with by the courts to the extent that general rules regarding admissibility have developed. This evidence includes similar acts or occurrences, and similar accidents or injuries.

In determining the relevance of similar evidence, the first step is to determine the similarity between the past acts or occurrences, accidents or injuries, and the one that is in issue in the current litigation. The reason that a party would want to present similar evidence to the jury is for the inference that since it happened before, it probably happened this time. In most cases, this inference is not valid. Even if evidence is found relevant because it is similar evidence, risk of confusion and unfair prejudice often outweigh the helpfulness of the evidence.

Generally, previous tort claims are not admissible to prove the invalidity of a present claim. But if a plaintiff claims injury to a part of the body that was the subject of a previous claim, the evidence of the previous claim might be admissible to prove the present claim is false or exaggerated.

If a defendant denies the existence of a dangerous condition that caused the plaintiff's injury, prior claims are admissible to prove the defendant's prior knowledge of the dangerous condition. Prior claims are not admissible, however, to prove that because there were other similar claims, this present claim is valid.

Absence of similar accidents might be admissible to prove a lack of knowledge of the danger, though not absence of negligence.

Where the issue of intent is an element of the cause of action, it may be proven by similar acts in the past. For instance, the intent to discriminate may be proven by similar instances of not hiring a member of a protected class. The evidence cannot be offered for the inference that a defendant did not hire women in the past and so did not hire the plaintiff. But it can be offered to prove the defendant's intent to discriminate against women applicants.

The framing of the argument to the judge when an objection is made is critical to the determination of admissibility that will be made by the judge on the spot. The question to keep in mind is the purpose for which the evidence is offered. Although invalid for one purpose, the evidence might be admissible for another purpose. When a valid purpose is articulated by the proponent of the evidence, opposing counsel cannot keep it out because it is detrimental to the case. Often the only objection left is a Rule 403 argument, that any probative value is outweighed by unfair prejudice.

HABIT AND ROUTINE PRACTICE

The distinction between character and **habit** lies in the idea that habit is more reliable than character. Character is evidenced by a consistent behavior that by implication defines a person's disposition or nature. The Federal Rules of Evidence gives this explanation of habit:

habit A person's regular response to a repeated specific situation.

> "Habit," in modern usage, both lay and psychological, is more specific. It describes one's regular response to a repeated specific situation ... A habit ... is the person's regular practice of meeting a particular kind of situation

with a specific type of condition, such as the habit of going down a particular stairway two steps at a time, or of giving the hand-signal for a left turn, or of alighting from railway cars while they are moving. The doing of habitual acts may become semi-automatic.[1]

People have habits; organizations have **routine practices**, which are equivalent to habits. Because habit and routine practice are essentially automatic, they are considered as "highly persuasive proof of conduct on a particular occasion."[2] The relevance of habit and routine practice lies with their repetition. As a practical matter it is easier to establish the existence of routine practice than of habit.

Rule 406. Habit; Routine Practice

Evidence of habit of a person or of the routine practice of an organization, whether corroborated or not and regardless of the presence of eyewitnesses, is relevant to prove that the conduct of the person or organization on a particular occasion was in conformity with the habit or routine.

Unlike character evidence, which has restrictions on admissibility, evidence of habit or routine practice is admissible in both civil and criminal cases. It can be shown by reputation, opinion, and specific instances, so long as the proper foundation is laid. It must be clear that there have been a sufficient number of instances of behavior to constitute the action as habit or routine practice.

Evidence of habit or routine practice is admissible to prove action in conformity with the habit or routine practice. For instance, a witness can testify to the mailing routine in a business, which proves a particular letter was mailed. The jury can then decide whether the letter was mailed based on the weight of the evidence, that is, how credible the testimony of the witness is regarding the mail routine.

Not all states follow the federal model. Florida, for instance, makes no mention in its code of habit, only routine practice. Admissibility of habit is left to the discretion of the trial court judge, with a reliance on case law as a guide. Habit is admissible if it corroborates other evidence of the occurrence of an event. Again, the paralegal needs to be aware of the differences between federal and state evidence rules. Illustration 6-4 gives an example of a state evidence rule.

Illustration 6-4

The defendant was charged with manslaughter by an intoxicated motorist. The state had to prove the defendant was intoxicated at the time of the accident, and that the defendant's intoxication indirectly caused the death of the victim by being the cause of the accident. The Florida Supreme Court held that alcoholism is not a character trait but rather is a habit. Testimony leading to the inference that the defendant was an alcoholic corroborated other evidence of intoxication at the time of the accident. Evidence of habit is admissible as corroborating evidence but not as direct evidence of, in this case, intoxication

routine practice A business's regular response to a repeated specific situation.

at the time of the accident. If there is no other evidence serving as a basis for corroboration, evidence of habit is not admissible in Florida. *State v. Wadsworth,* 210 So. 2d 4 (Fla. 1968).

SUBSEQUENT REMEDIAL MEASURES

Logically, when attempting to prove the negligence of a defendant, it is relevant to show that the defendant made repairs or installed safety devices after an accident, actions that, had they been taken earlier, might have made the accident less likely to occur. On the other hand, it would not be fair to penalize a person or organization for taking measures to see that other persons are safe once an injury has occurred. Rule 407 is grounded on "a social policy of encouraging people to take, or at least not discouraging them from taking, steps in furtherance of added safety."[3]

Rule 407. Subsequent Remedial Measures

When, after an injury or harm allegedly caused by an event, measures are taken that, if taken previously, would have made the injury or harm less likely to occur, evidence of the subsequent measures is not admissible to prove negligence, culpable conduct, a defect in a product's design, or a need for warning or instruction. This rule does not require the exclusion of evidence of subsequent measures when offered for another purpose, such as proving ownership, control, or feasibility of precautionary measures, if controverted, or impeachment.

As with other rules of evidence, it is important to determine the purpose for which the evidence is offered. Rule 407 excludes evidence of subsequent remedial measures if the evidence is offered to prove negligence or culpable conduct in connection with an event. The evidence may survive an objection if it is argued to the judge that it is being offered to prove something other than negligence or culpable conduct. Evidence of subsequent remedial measures can be admitted to prove such things as ownership, control, or feasibility of precautionary measures, but only if the matter is in controversy. If the party admits ownership, subsequent remedial measures would not be admissible because ownership is not contested. Without another reason to admit the subsequent remedial measure, it falls under Rule 407, because its only purpose is to prove negligence. Nevertheless, it might still be useful on cross-examination to impeach a witness's testimony at trial. This usage is allowed by the rule, as shown in Illustration 6-5.

Illustration 6-5

In an action by a rape victim against the owners of the motel where the rape occurred, the motel owners offered testimony that peep holes and chain locks were not installed because they would give occupants a false sense of security. The court found that this testimony led to the inference that these devices would have created a lesser level of security if installed. Based on the testimony and this inference, the court held the feasibility of installation of peep holes and chain locks was in controversy. Thus, the plaintiff could offer evidence of installation of these devices after the rape (subsequent remedial measure) to prove feasibility and to impeach the credibility of the motel owners' contention the peep holes and chain locks would not be successful security measures. A limiting instruction to the jury to use the evidence to prove feasibility, and not negligence, could be provided under Rule 407. *Anderson v. Malloy,* 700 F.2d 1208, 1214 (8th Cir. 1983).

Finally, a Rule 403 objection that the evidence is more prejudicial than probative might still be successful if Rule 407 fails to stop admission of the evidence.

EVIDENCE OF COMPROMISE OF CLAIMS

There are two reasons why, as a general rule, evidence of offers to compromise a claim are not admissible to prove liability or invalidity of a claim or its amount. Relevance is debatable because the offer to compromise, or the act of compromise, may be motivated by reasons having nothing to do with admission of liability. The inference is not a fair one because the motive, even if explained to the jury, might still lead the jury to emphasize the evidence unfairly. More importantly, it is a matter of public policy to encourage settlement of disputed claims. If a party knew settlement discussions could be used against the party after a failure to reach agreement, there would be no incentive to compromise, and every reason not to discuss settlement.

The protection extends to statements of fact that are made during discussions. However, just because the facts are discussed does not necessarily lead to automatic exclusion. If evidence can be discovered in the normal discovery process under the Rules of Civil Procedure, the evidence can be offered at trial, subject to other objections that might apply.

Rule 408. Compromise and Offers to Compromise

Evidence of (1) furnishing or offering or promising to furnish, or (2) accepting or offering or promising to accept, a valuable consideration in compromising or attempting to compromise a claim which was disputed as to either validity or amount, is not admissible to prove liability for or invalidity of the claim or its amount. Evidence of conduct or statements made in compromise negotiations is likewise not admissible. This rule does not require the exclusion of any evidence otherwise discoverable merely because it is presented in the course of compromise negotiations. This rule also does not require exclusion when the evidence is offered for another purpose, such as proving bias or prejudice of a witness, negativing a contention of undue delay, or proving an effort to obstruct a criminal investigation or prosecution.

Evidence of offers to compromise or the compromise itself might be admissible for a purpose other than proof of liability or the amount of a claim. See Illustration 6-6 for an example of (1) appropriate notice to the jury that a settlement was made with a majority of defendants but (2) error in disclosing the amount of damages because of the prejudicial effect on the remaining defendant.

Illustration 6-6 _____

Ten-year-old Jerry Kennon was injured when his moped hit a hole in the road and a piece of the moped's windshield pierced his right eye. His parents brought suit on his behalf against the manufacturer of the windshield and the windshield wholesaler. The windshield retailer and manufacturer of the Lucite from which the windshield was made also became parties to the lawsuit. After the jury was selected, the Kennons settled with three of the four defendants. Because he believed the jury might speculate on the absence of the other defendants, the judge told the jury about the settlement, and further disclosed the nominal amount received from each defendant in the settlement. The remaining defendant objected, citing Rule 408.

The appellate court held there was no abuse of discretion by the trial court judge in revealing the fact of settlement. However, the appellate court found that disclosure of the amount of settlement invited the jury to consider the settlement in its deliberations to the detriment of the remaining defendant. The jury, knowing of the nominal settlements, could have taken that fact as a reflection of the case against the remaining defendant, and it also could have led the jury to believe compensation of the defendant could come only from the remaining defendant.

Rule 408, according to the court, can be invoked by a party who is not a party to the settlement because the fact or amount of settlement cannot be used as an offensive weapon that prejudices the substantial rights of the remaining defendant. The appellate court stated the defendant was entitled to a new trial. *Kennon v. Slipstreamer, Inc.,* 794 F.2d 1068, 1068–1071 (5th Cir. 1986).

PAYMENT OF MEDICAL AND SIMILAR EXPENSES _____

Again, social policy plays a role in the formulation of the Rules of Evidence. The law should not discourage humane efforts to alleviate the financial problems of someone who is injured. Rule 409 does not allow into evidence the fact that a defendant paid medical-related expenses of an injured person for the purpose of proving the defendant is liable for the injury.

Rule 409. Payment of Medical and Similar Expenses

Evidence of furnishing or offering or promising to pay medical, hospital, or similar expenses occasioned by an injury is not admissible to prove liability for the injury.

Rule 409 differs from Rule 408, which protects statements made in settlement discussions, in that it makes admissible any statements proving liability if those statements were not necessary to furnish payment. If a defendant tells the admissions clerk at the hospital the defendant will be responsible for medical expenses "because I ran the red light and crashed into the injured party," this statement is admissible because it was not necessary for responsibility for payment. It is an admission of fault.

PLEAS AND PLEA DISCUSSIONS

The public policy behind Rule 410 is to encourage defendants to negotiate pleas with the prosecuting authority. Rule 410 raises similar issues as offers to compromise. Furthermore, there are also constitutional considerations because criminal defendants are presumed innocent, and the burden is on the state to prove guilt beyond a reasonable doubt. Allowing statements from failed plea negotiations would jeopardize a fair trial.

Rule 410. Inadmissibility of Pleas, Plea Discussions, and Related Statements

Except as otherwise provided in this rule, evidence of the following is not, in any civil or criminal proceeding, admissible against the defendant who made the plea or was a participant in the plea discussion:

(1) a plea of guilty which was later withdrawn;

(2) a plea of nolo contendere;

(3) any statement made in the course of any proceedings under Rule 11 of the Federal Rules of Criminal Procedure or comparable state procedure regarding either of the foregoing pleas; or

(4) any statements made in the course of plea discussions with an attorney for the prosecuting authority which do not result in a plea of guilty or which result in a plea of guilty later withdrawn.

However, such a statement is admissible (i) in any proceeding wherein another statement made in the course of the same plea or plea discussions has been introduced and the statement ought in fairness be considered contemporaneously with it, or (ii) in a criminal proceeding for perjury or false statement if the statement was made by the defendant under oath, on the record and in the presence of counsel.

The vast majority of criminal defendants engage in plea negotiations that result in fewer trials and a reduction in cost and time. Rule 410 does not allow statements made during plea negotiations to be used at trial in the event the negotiations fail and the case is tried. However, voluntary statements are not protected when there is no **quid pro quo**. One party must give something in return for something from the other party, or there is no quid pro quo, and no plea negotiation. A quid pro quo exists where the defendant is willing to exchange a guilty plea if the government reduces the charges.

It also should be noted statements made during plea negotiations are not admissible in the criminal case that is tried when plea negotiations fail, nor are such statements admissible in civil cases that might arise out of the same circumstances that led to the criminal charge. It is common for civil litigation to

quid pro quo The exchange of one valuable thing for another.

result from an act that also resulted in criminal prosecution. For instance, a defendant facing a DUI manslaughter charge might negotiate a plea and later face a wrongful death action filed by the family of the victim in a civil case. Statements made during the plea negotiations are not admissible in the wrongful death action.

Also inadmissible are evidence of a guilty plea later withdrawn, a plea of **nolo contendere**, statements made pursuant to state and Federal Rules of Criminal Procedure, and statements made in the course of plea negotiations when made to an attorney with a prosecuting authority. As seen in Illustration 6-7, it is the defendant's perception of the government's negotiator that controls, not whether the government negotiator had actual authority or is in fact an attorney with a prosecuting authority.

Illustration 6-7 _____

The defendant offered to plead guilty to robbery charges if the government would drop murder charges. The discussion was with postal inspectors who "had all the trappings of officialdom." The ruling was, "When a defendant knows that the people to whom he or she is speaking cannot negotiate a plea, and when they have not intimated that they will communicate the defendant's statements to someone who does have negotiating authority," then the statements are not plea-related and are admissible at trial. *United States v. Herman,* 544 F.2d 791, 799 (5th Cir. 1977).

Finally, Rule 410 does not cover negotiations for lenience. The rule applies only where the defendant contemplates entering a plea to obtain a concession from the prosecutor, and the prosecutor contemplates making an offer to obtain the defendant's plea. See Illustration 6-8.

Illustration 6-8 _____

The defendant offered to cooperate in an investigation unrelated to the charges for which he was being held. He offered information in exchange for leniency and never contemplated pleading guilty to any charges that were or might have been brought against him. Because of this, statements he made regarding the investigation were admissible against him at a trial for making false material declarations before a grand jury. There was no quid pro quo, so Rule 410 did not apply. *United States v. Cross,* 638 F.2d 1375, 1380 (5th Cir. 1981).

LIABILITY INSURANCE _____

nolo contendere A plea of no contest by a defendant in a criminal case where the defendant does not admit guilt but agrees to some punishment.

The fact that a party had liability insurance, or did not have liability insurance, at the time an act occurred that resulted in injury is not relevant to the issue of negligence. Rule 411 recognizes that knowledge by a jury of coverage or lack of coverage by liability insurance might induce the jury to decide a case on improper grounds. The knowledge could also unfairly influence the amount of an award.

Rule 411. Liability Insurance

Evidence that a person was or was not insured against liability is not admissible upon the issue of whether the person acted negligently or otherwise wrongfully. This rule does not require the exclusion of evidence of insurance against liability when offered for another purpose, such as proof of agency, ownership, or control, or bias or prejudice of a witness.

Like the other rules related to relevancy, Rule 411, on liability insurance, makes evidence admissible if it is for a purpose other than proof of negligence. The rule lists some of the more common purposes, including proof of agency, ownership, or control.

A witness can be impeached with evidence of insurance by showing bias. This possibility sometimes occurs where an insurance investigator testifies on behalf of a defendant in an accident case. The bias of the investigator can be demonstrated on cross-examination with questions about employment and payment. The fact that a defendant has liability insurance is not offered to prove negligence, but only to attack the credibility of the witness's testimony. Of course, it is to the plaintiff's advantage for the jury to hear about the liability insurance. Legally, the jury cannot use the evidence on the issue of negligence, but in reality the jury may be influenced to some degree, so long as negligence is established with other evidence.

Generally, evidence of liability insurance is not admissible to prove the ability of a defendant to pay damages if awarded by a jury. Ability to pay normally is not an issue in a negligence case, so evidence of ability to pay is not relevant. But, again, it is possible a jury will keep in mind that a defendant has liability insurance when determining the damage award after learning of the insurance when evidence of liability insurance was offered for another purpose.

If it is particularly important to the plaintiff's case that evidence of liability insurance get to the jury, the paralegal, in preparation for trial, should research how the prohibition against evidence of liability insurance in Rule 411 can be overcome. At the same time, the defense should be prepared to argue for the prohibition in Rule 411, and also be ready to make a Rule 403 argument that any mention of liability insurance would be unfairly prejudicial. Consider the example in Illustration 6-9.

Illustration 6-9

The plaintiff alleged a lack of knowledge of the limitation of liability contained in a liability insurance policy and of the custom in the industry to limit liability. Evidence of insurance coverage thus became a critical issue in the case. Its probative value to the defendant was ruled to outweigh any prejudice that the plaintiff might suffer. *Posttape Associates v. Eastman Kodak Co.,* 537 F.2d 751, 758 (3d Cir. 1976).

VICTIM'S PAST SEXUAL BEHAVIOR

Rule 412 was first enacted in 1978 by Congress. Its principal sponsor and author was Representative Elizabeth Holtzman. The purpose of the rule was to limit the use of evidence of prior sexual experiences of a victim of sexual assault. Historically, victims of sexual assault were brutally cross-examined at the trial of the accused. The victim's morality was called into question rather than focusing on the guilt or innocence of the defendant. By the time Rule 412 passed in 1978, 30 states had already enacted statutes or rules affording some protection to victims of sexual assault who testified at criminal trials.[4] The federal rule followed the lead of these states.

In 1994 Rule 412 was amended to further protect victims of sexual misconduct. It was expanded to apply to all criminal cases (not just sexual assault cases) and, for the first time, to civil cases. Rule 412 generally excludes evidence of both the past sexual behavior and sexual predisposition of an alleged victim. Although the rule does allow this type of evidence in limited circumstances, neither reputation nor opinion evidence are ever admissible as methods to prove past sexual behavior and sexual predisposition. This is in contrast to Rule 405, which allows the use of reputation or opinion testimony when character evidence passes the Rule 404 test. Rule 412 supersedes Rules 404 and 405, so these two rules are not applicable to alleged victims of sexual misconduct.

Rule 412. Sex Offense Cases; Relevance of Alleged Victim's Past Sexual Behavior or Alleged Sexual Predisposition

---

(a) **Evidence generally inadmissible**—The following evidence is not admissible in any civil or criminal proceeding involving alleged sexual misconduct except as provided in subdivisions (b) and (c):

(1) Evidence offered to prove that any alleged victim engaged in other sexual behavior.

(2) Evidence offered to prove any alleged victim's sexual predisposition.

Criminal Cases

Rule 412 does allow evidence of specific instances of sexual behavior of the alleged victim, but only under the limited circumstances outlined in the rule. Before a party can use specific instances of sexual behavior, the party must file a motion detailing the proposed evidence. The hearing on the motion is **in camera** with all parties, and the victim is given the opportunity to be present. The record is sealed during the course of the trial and on appeal in order to ensure the privacy of the alleged victim in case the proffered evidence is held to be inadmissible.

Rule 412. Sex Offense Cases; Relevance of Alleged Victim's Past Sexual Behavior or Alleged Sexual Predisposition

---

(c) **Procedure to determine admissibility.**

(1) A party intending to offer evidence under subdivision (b) must—

in camera In the judge's chambers, with spectators excluded from the hearing.

> **(A)** file a written motion at least 14 days before trial specifically describing the evidence and stating the purpose for which it is offered unless the court, for good cause requires a different time for filing or permits filing during trial; and
>> **(B)** serve the motion on all parties and notify the alleged victim or, when appropriate, the alleged victim's guardian or representative.
>> **(2)** Before admitting evidence under this rule the court must conduct a hearing in camera and afford the victim and parties a right to attend and be heard. The motion, related papers, and the record of the hearing must be sealed and remain under seal unless the court orders otherwise.

Only limited purposes are outlined in Rule 412 to allow admission of evidence of the alleged victim's prior sexual behavior or predisposition. First, the evidence is admissible to prove someone other than the defendant was the source of semen, injury, or physical condition of the victim. Second, where the defendant raises consent as a defense, it may be admissible. Third, if constitutional rights of the defendant are affected, such as the right to confront adverse witnesses, the evidence may be admissible. Fourth, evidence of the sexual conduct of the victim can be offered by the prosecution.

Rule 412. Sex Offense Cases; Relevance of Alleged Victim's Past Sexual Behavior or Alleged Sexual Predisposition

(b) Exceptions.
> **(1)** In a criminal case, the following evidence is admissible, if otherwise admissible under these rules:
>> **(A)** evidence of specific instances of sexual behavior by the alleged victim offered to prove that a person other than the accused was the source of semen, injury or other physical evidence;
>> **(B)** evidence of specific instances of sexual behavior by the alleged victim with respect to the person accused of the sexual misconduct offered by the accused to prove consent or by the prosecution; and
>> **(C)** evidence the exclusion of which would violate the constitutional rights of the defendant.

Civil Cases

The standards for admissibility of an alleged victim's sexual behavior or sexual predisposition are different from those for criminal cases. Although opinion testimony is never admissible, reputation testimony may be admissible if the victim of sexual misconduct raises it first. However, specific instances are the most common form of evidence to prove sexual behavior or predisposition.

Rule 412. Sex Offense Cases; Relevance of Alleged Victim's Past Sexual Behavior or Alleged Sexual Predisposition

(b) Exceptions.
> **(2)** In a civil case, evidence offered to prove the sexual behavior or sexual predisposition of any alleged victim is admissible if it is otherwise admissible under these rules and its probative value substantially outweighs the

danger of harm to any victim and of unfair prejudice to any party. Evidence of an alleged victim's reputation is admissible only if it has been placed in controversy by the alleged victim.

Illustration 6-10 offers an example of the admissibility of prior sexual history where its probative value outweighed its prejudicial effect because of the nature of the plaintiff's claim. Rule 412 has been used to block admission of sexual history in civil cases involving sexual assault and sexual harassment, but this case involved transmission of genital herpes.

Illustration 6-10 _____

Lisa Beth Judd sued Dennis Rodman, alleging wrongful transmission of genital herpes. Over the objection of Judd's attorney at trial, the judge allowed evidence of Judd's sexual history and her long-time occupation as a nude dancer. The basis for the objection was Rule 412, and the probative value of the evidence was outweighed by its prejudicial effect.

The appellate court noted the central issue of the case was whether Judd contracted genital herpes from Rodman. Expert testimony established genital herpes can be dormant for long periods of time when a person would have no symptoms. Consequently, considerable evidence of her sexual history was properly admitted because it was highly relevant to Rodman's liability. And evidence of her nude dancing before and after she allegedly contracted the genital herpes from Rodman was probative as to damages she claimed. The Rule 412(b) balancing test favored Rodman, because the evidence was more probative than prejudicial. *Judd v. Rodman,* 105 F.3d 1339, 1343 (11th Cir. 1997).

Rule 412, as it applies to criminal and civil cases, is a product of social evolution. The law has changed to reflect modified assumptions about women and men where sexual misconduct is alleged. For the most part, the law now recognizes the character of victims of sexual misconduct as being rarely relevant to allegations of either criminal or civil sexual misconduct.

The need to protect alleged victims against invasion of privacy, potential embarrassment, and unwarranted sexual stereotyping, and the wish to encourage victims to come forward when they have been sexually molested do not disappear because the context has shifted from a criminal prosecution to a claim for damages or injunctive relief. There is a strong social policy in not only punishing those who engage in sexual misconduct, but in also providing relief to the victim. Thus, Rule 412 applies in any civil case in which a person claims to be the victim of sexual misconduct, such as actions for sexual battery or sexual harassment.[5]

It is important for the paralegal to understand the background of this rule and the social policy it reflects in order to frame arguments for admitting or not admitting evidence of sexual behavior or sexual predisposition. The distinction between criminal and civil cases with regard to admission of this type of evidence should also be remembered.

SIMILAR ACTS OR CRIMES INVOLVING SEXUAL ASSAULT OR CHILD MOLESTATION

Rules 413, 414, and 415 became effective July 9, 1995. These rules apply to civil or criminal cases involving sexual assault, child molestation, or sexual misconduct. The premise for these rules is that certain past acts of the defendant are relevant to current questions of culpability. This premise contradicts Rule 404, which states that character evidence is not admissible to prove conduct in conformity with a character trait.

Rule 413.   Evidence of Similar Crimes in Sexual Assault Cases

(a) In a criminal case in which the defendant is accused of an offense of sexual assault, evidence of the defendant's commission of another offense or offenses of sexual assault is admissible, and may be considered for its bearing on any matter to which it is relevant.

(b) In a case in which the Government intends to offer evidence under this rule, the attorney for the Government shall disclose the evidence to the defendant, including statements of witnesses or a summary of the substance of any testimony that is expected to be offered, at least fifteen days before the scheduled date of trial or at such later time as the court may allow for good cause.

(c) This rule shall not be construed to limit the admission or consideration of evidence under any other rule.

(d) For purposes of this rule and Rule 415, "offense of sexual assault" means a crime under Federal law or the law of a State (as defined in section 513 of title 18, United States Code) that involved—

(1) any conduct proscribed by chapter 109A of title 18, United States Code;

(2) contact, without consent, between any part of the defendant's body or an object and the genitals or anus of another person;

(3) contact, without consent, between the genitals or anus of the defendant and any part of another person's body;

(4) deriving sexual pleasure or gratification from the infliction of death, bodily injury, or physical pain on another person; or

(5) an attempt or conspiracy to engage in conduct described in paragraphs (1)–(4).

Rule 414.   Evidence of Similar Crimes in Child Molestation Cases

(a) In a criminal case in which the defendant is accused of an offense of child molestation, evidence of the defendant's commission of another offense or offenses of child molestation is admissible, and may be considered for its bearing on any matter to which it is relevant.

(b) In a case in which the Government intends to offer evidence under this rule, the attorney for the Government shall disclose the evidence to the defendant, including statements of witnesses or a summary of the substance of any testimony that is expected to be offered, at least fifteen days before the scheduled date of trial or at such later time as the court may allow for good cause.

(c) This rule shall not be construed to limit the admission or consideration of evidence under any other rule.

(d) For purposes of this rule and Rule 415, "child" means a person below the age of fourteen, and "offense of child molestation" means a crime under Federal law or the law of a State (as defined in section 513 of title 18, United States Code) that involved—

(1) any conduct proscribed by chapter 109A of title 18, United States Code, that was committed in relation to a child;

(2) any conduct proscribed by chapter 110 of title 18, United States Code;

(3) contact between any part of the defendant's body or an object and the genitals or anus of a child;

(4) contact between the genitals or anus of the defendant and any part of the body of a child;

(5) deriving sexual pleasure or gratification from the infliction of death, bodily injury, or physical pain on a child; or

(6) an attempt or conspiracy to engage in conduct described in paragraphs (1)–(5).

Rule 415. Evidence of Similar Acts in Civil Cases Concerning Sexual Assault or Child Molestation

(a) In a civil case in which a claim for damages or other relief is predicated on a party's alleged commission of conduct constituting an offense of sexual assault or child molestation, evidence of that party's commission of another offense or offenses of sexual assault or child molestation is admissible and may be considered as provided in Rule 413 and Rule 414 of these rules.

(b) A party who intends to offer evidence under this Rule shall disclose the evidence to the party against whom it will be offered, including statements of witnesses or a summary of the substance of any testimony that is expected to be offered, at least fifteen days before the scheduled date of trial or at such later time as the court may allow for good cause.

(c) This rule shall not be construed to limit the admission or consideration of evidence under any other rule.

Congresswoman Susan Molinari was the main proponent of these rules when they were considered by Congress in 1994. A report of the Judicial Conference of the United States on the rules opposed their adoption and urged the Congress to reconsider its decision to pass the rules or, in the alternative, to amend Rules 404 and 405 to include provisions similar to those in Rules 413 through 415. Congress declined, and the rules became effective in July 1995.

The rules allow the inference that the defendant committed the sexual assault or molested the child as alleged in the current case because the defendant acted similarly on an earlier occasion (action in conformity with character). A Rule 403 argument can still be made to try to exclude the evidence based on passage of too much time, lack of similarity of conduct, and because the incident was isolated. However, Illustration 6-11 demonstrates how a Rule 403 argument may not be successful.

Illustration 6-11 _____

Henry Lee Meachum was convicted in federal court of transporting a minor in interstate commerce with the intent to engage in sexual activity. On appeal, he challenged admission of the testimony of his adult stepdaughters that he molested them when they were under the age of 14, more than 30 years before the trial.

 The court noted there are no time limits beyond which evidence of prior sex offenses are inadmissible under Rule 414. The court went on to state that the Rule 403 balancing test is still applicable but that "under Rule 414 the courts are to 'liberally' admit evidence of prior uncharged sex offenses." The testimony of the stepdaughters was relevant to prove Meachum's intent to sexually molest the complaining witness in this case when she accompanied him on an interstate trip. The prejudicial effect of the testimony did not outweigh its probative value. *United States v. Meachum,* 115 F.3d 1488, 1491–1492 (10th Cir. 1997).

Under the rules, disclosure of the intent to use this type of evidence must be made 15 days before trial so there is an opportunity to prepare an objection. The objection is a good candidate for a **motion in limine**.

These rules affect few defendants, because they pertain only to federally prosecuted sex crimes committed on federal property or by Native Americans on Native American lands. The significance of these rules, though, lies in the possibility of individual states adopting similar provisions.[6] The paralegal must remain current with the evidentiary standards applicable in state court.

SUMMARY _____

Evidence may be relevant and yet not be admissible because of various limitations on the admissibility of relevant evidence.

Generally, evidence of character is not admissible to prove a person acted in conformity with a character trait. However, if character is an issue because it is an element of a claim in a civil case, a crime, or a defense, then evidence of a character trait is admissible as it relates to the element.

In a criminal case, a defendant can always offer evidence of good character, but the defendant risks an offer of rebuttal evidence by the prosecution. Furthermore, a prosecutor can offer character evidence against a defendant if it is to prove motive, opportunity, intent, preparation, plan, knowledge, identity, or absence of mistake.

Where evidence of character is admissible, it can be proven through testimony based on reputation or opinion. Specific instances of conduct can be used when the character of a person is an element of a charge, claim, or defense.

Generally, evidence of similar acts or occurrences is not admissible to prove the act or occurrence in issue. Yet the evidence might be admissible to prove a different issue in a case.

motion in limine A request for a court order, often before trial, to exclude reference at trial to anticipated evidence because the evidence allegedly violates a rule of law or a rule of evidence or procedure.

Habit and routine practice generally are admissible in both civil and criminal cases to prove action in conformity with the habit or routine practice. Unlike character evidence and evidence of similar acts or occurrences, evidence of habit or routine practice is deemed reliable in proving action in conformity.

Subsequent remedial measures generally are not admissible, because public policy dictates that people should not be discouraged from acts to make something safe.

Public policy is also behind the inadmissibility of evidence showing compromise of claims or offers to compromise, as well as the inadmissibility of the payment of medical and similar expenses. Pleas and plea negotiations are inadmissible as a general rule to further the policy of encouraging plea bargaining.

Evidence of liability insurance generally is not admissible because of the danger the jury would allow the evidence to overwhelm other substantive evidence (or lack of it) of a claim.

The most recent additions to the Federal Rules of Evidence are the rules related to admissibility of evidence of similar acts or crimes involving sexual assault or child molestation to prove action in conformity with similar prior behavior by the defendant. With regard to a victim's past sexual behavior, however, this evidence is not admissible in civil or criminal cases, particularly in sexual harassment and sexual assault cases.

Finally, the differences between the federal rules as they relate to relevance and state rules may be significant, so preparation for cases in state court require attention to state rules of evidence.

✔ CHECKPOINTS

❑ Character evidence

1. Character is a collection of traits that form an individual's disposition or nature.

2. Generally, evidence of character is not admissible to prove action in conformity with the character trait.

3. If character is an element of a claim, crime, or defense, the evidence of the character trait is admissible to prove action in conformity with the trait.

4. In a criminal case, a defendant can always introduce evidence of good character, but the prosecution can then offer rebuttal evidence.

5. In a criminal case, evidence of the victim's character is admissible to support a defense.

6. Prosecutors can use evidence of character to prove motive, opportunity, intent, preparation, plan, knowledge, identity, or absence of mistake.

❑ How to prove character

1. Testimony of witness as to the person's reputation.

2. Witness's opinion of the person's character.

3. On cross-examination, witnesses can be asked about specific instances reflecting the person's character.

❑ Similar acts or occurrences

1. Generally not admissible to prove an issue in current litigation.

2. May be admissible for another purpose.

❑ Habit and routine practice

1. Admissible to prove action in conformity with habit or routine practice.

2. People have habits; businesses have routine practices.

❑ Subsequent remedial measures
1. Generally not admissible to prove negligence.
2. May be admissible for another purpose.

❑ Compromise of claims
1. Generally, settlement negotiations are not admissible in subsequent trial.
2. May be admissible under limited circumstances.

❑ Payment of medical and similar expenses
1. Generally not admissible to prove liability.
2. Statements unrelated to the payment of expenses are admissible.

❑ Pleas and plea discussions
1. Evidence of plea bargaining not admissible at subsequent trial.
2. Must be quid pro quo with someone who is authorized to plea bargain with the defendant.

❑ Liability insurance
1. Generally not admissible because it might prejudice the jury to know the defendant did or did not have insurance.
2. Might be admissible for other purposes.

❑ Victim's past sexual behavior
1. Generally not admissible in criminal or civil cases.
2. Narrow exceptions exist that require an in camera hearing to determine admissibility.

❑ Similar acts or crimes involving sexual assault or child molestation
1. Evidence of prior acts admissible in civil and criminal cases as character evidence to prove the defendant acted in conformity with the character trait.

APPLICATIONS

Application 6-1

The following case provides an excellent review of Rules 104(a) and 104(b) and shows how they relate to the use of character evidence by the prosecution under Rule 404(b). It also incorporates two standards of proof, clear and convincing and preponderance of the evidence, and shows their relationship to the admissibility of evidence. In the discussion of these standards of proof in an earlier chapter, they were related to the standard a jury must use in deciding a case. Here they relate to the applicability of these standards to the determination of the admissibility of evidence for the jury's consideration at trial. The Supreme Court also discusses the appropriate role for Rule 403.

The defendant, Guy Rufus Huddleston, was charged with selling stolen goods in interstate commerce and possessing stolen property in interstate commerce. Since these charges were in violation of federal law, Mr. Huddleston was tried in the United States District Court in Michigan. He was convicted on the possession charge only. On appeal to the United States Court of Appeals for the Sixth Circuit, his conviction was reversed and then affirmed on a rehearing. The United States Supreme Court granted certiorari in order to resolve a conflict among the Circuit Courts of Appeals with regard to Rule 404(b) similar act evidence.

Huddleston v. United States
485 U.S. 681 (1988)

CHIEF JUSTICE REHNQUIST delivered the opinion of the Court.

Federal Rule of Evidence 404(b) provides:

"Other crimes, wrongs, or acts—Evidence of other crimes, wrongs, or acts is not admissible to prove the character of a person in order to show action in conformity therewith. It may, however, be admissible for other purposes, such as proof of motive, opportunity, intent, preparation, plan, knowledge, identity, or absence of mistake or accident."

This case presents the question whether the district court must itself make a preliminary finding that the Government has proved the "other act" by a preponderance of the evidence before it submits the evidence to the jury. We hold that it need not do so.

The evidence at trial showed that a trailer containing over 32,000 blank Memorex videocassette tapes with a manufacturing cost of $4.53 per tape was stolen from the Overnight Express yard in South Holland, Illinois, sometime between April 11 and 15, 1985. On April 17, 1985, petitioner contacted Karen Curry, the manager of the Magic Rent-to-Own in Ypsilanti, Michigan, seeking her assistance in selling a large number of blank Memorex videocassette tapes. After assuring Curry that the tapes were not stolen, he told her he wished to sell them in lots of at least 500 at $2.75 to $3 per tape. Curry subsequently arranged for the sale of a total of 5,000 tapes, which petitioner delivered to the various purchasers—who apparently believed the sales were legitimate.

There was no dispute that the tapes which petitioner sold were stolen; the only material issue at trial was whether petitioner knew they were stolen. The District Court allowed the Government to introduce evidence of "similar acts" under Rule 404(b), concluding that such evidence had "clear relevance as to [petitioner's knowledge]." App. 11. The first piece of similar act evidence offered by the Government was the testimony of Paul Toney, a record store owner. He testified that in February 1985, petitioner offered to sell new 12" black and white televisions for $28 apiece. According to Toney, petitioner indicated that he could obtain several thousand of these televisions. Petitioner and Toney eventually traveled to the Magic Rent-to-Own, where Toney purchased 20 of the televisions. Several days later, Toney purchased 18 more televisions.

The second piece of similar act evidence was the testimony of Robert Nelson, an undercover FBI agent posing as a buyer for an appliance store. Nelson testified that in May 1985, petitioner offered to sell him a large quantity of Amana appliances—28 refrigerators, 2 ranges, and 40 icemakers. Nelson agreed to pay $8,000 for the appliances. Petitioner was arrested shortly after he arrived at the parking lot where he and Nelson had agreed to transfer the appliances. A truck containing the appliances was stopped a short distance from the parking lot, and Leroy Wesby, who was driving the truck, was also arrested. It was determined that the appliances had a value of approximately $20,000 and were part of a shipment that had been stolen.

Petitioner testified that the Memorex tapes, the televisions, and the appliances had all been provided by Leroy Wesby, who had represented that all of the merchandise was obtained legitimately. Petitioner stated that he had sold 6,500 Memorex tapes for Wesby on a commission basis. Petitioner maintained that all of the sales for Wesby had been on a commission basis and that he had no knowledge that any of the goods were stolen.

In closing, the prosecution explained that petitioner was not on trial for his dealings with the appliances or the televisions. The District Court instructed the jury that the similar acts evidence was to be used only to establish petitioner's knowledge, and not to prove his character. The jury convicted petitioner on the possession count only.

We granted certiorari ... to resolve a conflict among the Courts of Appeals as to whether the trial court must make a preliminary finding before "similar act" and other Rule 404(b) evidence is submitted to the jury. We conclude that such evidence should be admitted if there is sufficient evidence to support a finding by the jury that the defendant committed the similar act.

Federal Rule of Evidence 404(b)—which applies in both civil and criminal cases—generally prohibits the introduction of evidence of extrinsic acts that might adversely reflect on the actor's character, unless that evidence bears upon a relevant issue in the case such as motive, opportunity, or knowledge. Extrinsic acts evidence may be critical to the establishment of the truth as to a disputed issue, especially when that issue involves the actor's state of mind and the only means of ascertaining that mental state is by drawing inferences from conduct. The actor in the instant case was a criminal defendant, and the act in question was "similar" to the one with which he was charged. Our use of these terms is not meant to suggest that our analysis is limited to such circumstances.

Before this Court, petitioner argues that the District Court erred in admitting Toney's testimony as to petitioner's sale of the televisions. [FOOTNOTE: Petitioner does not dispute that Nelson's testimony concerning the Amana appliances was properly admitted under Rule 404(b).] The threshold inquiry a court must make before admitting similar acts evidence under Rule 404(b) is whether that evidence is probative of a material issue other than character. The Government's theory of relevance was that the televisions were stolen, and proof that petitioner had engaged in a series of sales of stolen merchandise from the same suspicious source would be strong evidence that he was aware that each of these items, including the Memorex tapes, was stolen. As such, the sale of the televisions was a "similar act" only if the televisions were stolen. Petitioner acknowledges that this evidence was admitted for the proper purpose of showing his knowledge that the Memorex tapes were stolen. He asserts, however, that the evidence should not have been admitted because the Government failed to prove to the District Court that the televisions were in fact stolen.

Petitioner argues from the premise that evidence of similar acts has a grave potential for causing improper prejudice. For instance, the jury may choose to punish the defendant for the similar rather than the charged act, or the jury may infer that the defendant is an evil person inclined to violate the law. Because of this danger, petitioner maintains, the jury ought not to be exposed to similar act evidence until the trial court has heard the evidence and made a determination under Federal Rule of Evidence 104(a) that the defendant committed the similar act. Rule 104(a) provides the "[p]reliminary questions concerning the qualification for a person to be a witness, the existence of a privilege, or the admissibility of evidence shall be determined by the court, subject to the provisions of subdivision (b)." According to petitioner, the trial court must make this preliminary finding by at least a preponderance of the evidence.

We reject petitioner's position, for it is inconsistent with the structure of the Rules of Evidence and with the plain language of Rule 404(b). Article IV of the Rules of Evidence deals with the relevancy of evidence. Rules 401 and 402 establish the broad principle that relevant evidence—evidence that makes the existence of any fact at issue more or less probable—is admissible unless the Rules provide otherwise. Rule 403 allows the trial judge to exclude relevant evidence if, among other things, "its probative value is substantially outweighed by the danger of unfair prejudice." Rules 404 through 412 address specific types of evidence that have generated problems. Generally, these latter Rules do not flatly prohibit the introduction of such evidence but instead limit the purpose for which it may be introduced. Rule 404(b), for example, protects against the introduction of extrinsic act evidence when that evidence is offered solely to prove character. The text contains no intimation, however, that any preliminary showing is necessary before such evidence may be introduced for a proper purpose. If offered for such a proper purpose, the evidence is subject only to general strictures limiting admissibility such as Rules 402 and 403.

We emphasize that in assessing the sufficiency of the evidence under Rule 104(b), the trial court must consider all evidence presented to the jury. "[I]ndividual pieces of evidence, insufficient in themselves to prove a point, may in cumulation prove it. The sum of an evidentiary presentation may well be greater than its constituent parts." In assessing whether the evidence was sufficient to support a finding that the televisions were stolen, the court here was required to consider not only the direct evidence on that point—the low price of the televisions, the large quantity offered for sale, and petitioner's inability to produce a bill of sale—but also the evidence concerning petitioner's involvement in the sales of other stolen merchandise obtained from Wesby, such as the Memorex tapes and the Amana appliances. Given this evidence, the jury reasonably could have concluded that the televisions were stolen, and the trial court therefore properly allowed the evidence to go to the jury.

We share petitioner's concern that unduly prejudicial evidence might be introduced under Rule 404(b). We think, however, that the protection against such unfair prejudice emanates not from a requirement of a preliminary finding by the trial court, but rather from four other sources: first, from the requirement of Rule 404(b) that the evidence be offered for a proper purpose; second, from the relevancy requirement of Rule 402—as enforced through Rule 104(b); third, from the assessment the trial court must make under Rule 403 to determine whether the probative value of the similar acts evidence is substantially outweighed by its potential for unfair prejudice, and fourth, from Federal Rule of Evidence 105, which provides that the trial court shall, upon request, instruct the jury that the similar acts evidence is to be considered only for the proper purpose for which it was admitted.

Affirmed.

Class Discussion Questions

1. What was the only issue at trial that Mr. Huddleston claimed the prosecution failed to prove?

2. What was the evidence of "similar acts" that the prosecution presented over the objection of the defendant?

3. What was Mr. Huddleston's testimony with regard to his selling of the tapes, televisions, and appliances?

4. The Supreme Court outlined the appropriate analysis for a trial court judge to use in determining whether "similar act" evidence under Rule 404(b) should be admissible. In this case, the prosecution had to prove Mr. Huddleston had knowledge the tapes were stolen. To prove this, the prosecution wanted to use similar act evidence for the inference that the defendant had the requisite knowledge.
   a. What character trait could the jury conclude the defendant had after hearing the testimony of the two witnesses?
   b. Could the jury use the analysis that the defendant had a bad character and acted in conformity with that character with regard to the tapes in making its decision?
   c. What was the limiting instruction given to the jury by the trial court judge?
   d. How would you characterize the standard of proof—sufficient evidence—that a judge must use to determine whether similar act evidence is admissible? Where does the standard of sufficient evidence fall on the scale with clear and convincing, preponderance, and beyond a reasonable doubt?

5. What is the appropriate analysis to determine whether the similar act evidence that is offered is unduly prejudicial?

Application 6-2

The following excerpt from Carson v. Polley demonstrates how character evidence can be admissible for a purpose other than action in conformity with character; here a performance evaluation report was appropriate to prove intent, and another performance evaluation report was appropriate for impeachment purposes. Although character evidence is not admissible as a general rule, a party might open the door on the issue with questions prompting responses that essentially relate to a character trait of someone that has a bearing on the issues in the case. Here, Mr. Carson brought a civil rights action against county law enforcement officers, alleging the officers used excessive force when arresting and booking him. At the trial, Mr. Carson offered Sheriff's Department performance evaluation reports for officers Ellis and Polley. Polley's stated that Polley needed to "work on controlling temper and personal feelings," because "he tends to get into arguments with inmates, lets his temper flare up too quickly." Ellis's evaluation stated that Ellis was "a good officer, however he needs to learn to control his temper. This affects his public contact."

The trial court judge did not allow the jury to learn about either report based on Rule 404. The jury returned with a verdict against Mr. Carson, who on appeal to the Fifth Circuit alleged, among other things, that this ruling affected his substantial rights and thus he deserved another trial where the jury could learn about the reports. The Circuit Court agreed.

In reading this excerpt, note how the court carefully outlines how Rule 404 applies, or does not apply, to the reports.

Carson v. Polley
689 F.2d 562 (5th Cir. 1982)

Both performance evaluation reports were admissible, although for different purposes. The report as to Deputy Sheriff Polley tended to show Polley's *intent* to do harm to Carson when booking him at the jail, and, therefore, was admissible under the "intent" exception to the general against character. See Fed.R.Ev. 404(b); *United States v. Beechum,* 582 F.2d 898 (5th Cir. 1978) (en banc), cert. denied, 440 U.S. 920, 99 S.Ct. 1244, 59 L.Ed.2d 472 (1979). The performance report as to Ellis contradicted Ellis' testimony on a material issue, and, therefore, was admissible to impeach. Fed.R.Ev. 608(b); *United States v. Opager,* 589 F.2d 799, 802 (5th Cir. 1979). The district court abused its discretion in ruling otherwise.

We recently summed up the rules applicable to the admission of extrinsic character evidence for purposes other than to prove conduct in conformity with character:

> Rule 404(b) provides that "Evidence of other crimes, wrongs, or acts is not admissible to prove the character of a person in order to show that he acted in conformity therewith. It may, however, be admissible for other purposes, such as proof of motive, opportunity, intent, preparation, planning, knowledge, identity, or absence of mistake or accident." In *United States v. Beechum,* this Court construed the rule in light of the other rules of evidence and held that Rule 404(b) calls for a two-step test: First, it must be determined that the extrinsic evidence offense is relevant to an issue other than the defendant's character. Second, the evidence must possess probative value that is not substantially outweighed by its undue prejudice and must meet the other requirements of Rule 403."

Carson offered the performance evaluations as extrinsic evidence of the intent of two of the defendants to commit an assault and battery on Carson. Intent, of course, may be shown through extrinsic proof of prior acts. Fed.R.Ev. 404(b). The theory of Carson's case was that the force used by the deputy sheriffs was excessive and was prompted by irrational factors. The defendants countered by attempting to show that the deputy sheriffs responded coolly and reasonably to an obstreperous detainee. One key issue, therefore, was whether the sheriffs reacted to Carson with excessive and unfettered hostility, or with reason and control. This issue is, in part, a matter of intent. The question is whether the performance evaluations were relevant to this issue of intent.

In so applying *Beechum* to our case, we find that the performance evaluation report on Deputy Sheriff Polley was relevant to his intent. Loss of temper and consequent intentional hostility towards other detainees on earlier occasions made it more likely that a similar intent was present in Polley's conduct towards Carson. Moreover, in the Rule 403 balance, the report's probative value outweighs its possible prejudicial impact. The report was recent and specifically referred to Polley's relations with prisoners. It was of solid value in proving Carson's case, yet there were no horrifying details that would predictably inflame the jury's passion.

We reach a different conclusion, however, as to the relevance of the Ellis report to Ellis' intent. The Ellis report expressed only a general statement on Ellis' temper. It was recorded three years before the Carson arrest. It referred only in most general terms to "public contact," not solely with prisoners. The probative value of this report on Ellis' intent was slight. Because of the attenuated probative value, even the slight prejudice that the report might engender warranted excluding it.

Thus, the Polley performance evaluation report should have been admitted as substantive evidence of Polley's intent in his actions in connection with the arrest of Carson. The Ellis report was properly excluded from admission as substantive evidence under Fed.R.Ev. 403.

We now consider whether the reports should have been admitted to impeach the deputy sheriffs. We hold that one report was admissible to impeach Ellis' testimony on a material issue. Ellis testified at trial that he had no recollection of the events surrounding Carson's book-in at the Dallas County Jail. The following interchange then took place:

Q: And you're not testifying under oath today that it's impossible that you used excessive force and lost your temper while helping book in Mr. Carson, are you?

A: It's impossible that I lost my temper, sir.

Q: Well, you have had problems in the past with other prisoners; isn't that correct, learning to control your temper?

A: No, sir.

Ms. Legarde: Your honor, I object to this. I think that's improper, and I would object to it. I think he should restrict his questions to what happened in this case; those are the issues before the Jury.

The Court: Sustain the objection.

After this ruling, Carson sought to admit the performance evaluation report as extrinsic evidence that contradicted Ellis' testimony on a material issue. The district court refused to allow the evidence to be admitted.

Here, the likelihood that Ellis would lose his temper and overreact to a prisoner was a material issue in the case. Ellis' flat denial that it would be possible for him to lose his temper spoke to that issue. The district court should have allowed Carson to introduce contradictory extrinsic evidence on that point to impeach Ellis.

The impeachment value of Polley's performance evaluation report, however, stands on a different footing. Polley never testified one way or the other on the possibility that he would lose his temper with a prisoner. Carson points to several statements made by Polley that he claims contradicts the performance evaluation report. On review of the record, however, these statements were simply denials by Polley that he actually hit or kicked Carson, not denials of a hot temper. Thus, the performance evaluation report does not contradict Polley's testimony and was properly excluded as impeachment evidence, although as set out above, it should have been admitted as tending to prove intent.

Rule 404(a), Fed.R.Ev., bars the introduction of character evidence to show that a person acted in accord with his character on a particular occasion. The rule's exclusion of such evidence applies to both criminal and civil cases. Under the general policy of excluding character evidence, evidence of Polley's and Ellis' bad tempers would not be admissible to show that their actions toward Carson conformed to their bristly characters, even when self-defense is at issue.

Rule 404(a) contains three exceptions to the general ban on the use of character evidence to show action in conformity with character. The commentators have largely viewed the exceptions as applicable only to criminal cases, although the wisdom of this limitation has been questioned. We have held that when a central issue in a case is "close to one of a criminal nature," the exceptions to the Rule 404(a) ban on character evidence may be invoked.

The circumstances under which quasi-criminal conduct warrants the introduction of character evidence in a civil suit under Rule 404(a) may not always be easy to draw. Cf. *Croce v. Bromley Corp.,* 623 F.2d 1084 (5th Cir. 1980), cert. denied, 450 U.S. 981, 101 S.Ct. 1516, 67 L.Ed.2d 816 (1981) (allowing evidence of character traits in a civil negligence suit in order to present the case fairly to the jury). Here, however, we believe that the assault and battery with which the defendants in this suit are charged falls "close to one of a criminal nature." Therefore, we apply the character evidence exceptions of Rule 404(a). Even with the exceptions, however, the performance evaluation reports tendered by Carson are not admissible for showing conduct in conformity with character.

Of the three exceptions allowing the use of character evidence under Rule 404(a), only one has any bearing on Carson's exhibits. Rule 404(a)(1) allows an accused to introduce evidence on a pertinent trait of his character to defend against a criminal charge, and then permits the prosecution to rebut such evidence once the accused has presented it. Here, no substantial direct testimony was presented by the defendants as to their characters for temperaments of peacefulness. The only evidence even resembling an opinion on character came out on cross-examination when Carson elicited from Ellis a statement that it was impossible that Ellis could lose his temper. Ellis' simple statement, however, presents too tenuous a basis for holding that Ellis opened the door to an attack on his character for temperance. Even though this statement rendered Ellis subject to impeachment, as we have held above, it did not constitute a sufficient placing of his character at issue to justify the admission of extrinsic evidence to attack Ellis' character. As to Polley, there is no testimony even colorably resembling character evidence. The performance evaluation report, therefore, was not admissible to attack his character.

To sum up, the performance evaluation reports should have been admitted (a) against Polley to show his intent, and (b) against Ellis to impeach his denial that he could lose his temper. The reports were not admissible to show the character of either Polley or Ellis for the purpose of proving that each acted in conformity with his character. The evidentiary errors relating to these exhibits were of significance to plaintiff's case and require us to direct a new trial.

Class Discussion Questions

1. Why was the intent of the deputies an issue?

2. Why was Polley's report relevant with regard to intent, but Ellis's was not?

3. For what purpose was Ellis's report admissible?

4. Why could not Polley's report be used for impeachment purposes?

5. This is a civil, not criminal, case. Explain the reasoning of the court in applying Rule 404 exceptions.

EXERCISES

1. Assume you are assigned to the attorney in the law firm who handles personal injury and products liability cases. You are helping prepare for trial a products liability case where the client was injured by a portable circular saw. The defendant is the manufacturer of the saw. The cause of action is based on negligence and breach of warranty theories.

   The client was injured after using the saw to cut boards laid out on a workbench. After making a cut, the client contends he set the saw down on the floor. Since the saw was still rotating when it was laid on the floor, its momentum carried it toward the client's foot, which resulted in a cut in his right foot, partial amputation of a toe, and the laceration of another toe.

An important piece of evidence that needs to get before the jury is evidence of prior accidents to prove that the defendant had knowledge of the continuation of rotation of the blade after the saw was turned off (blade guard defect). This knowledge created a duty to warn the user of the saw, which warning was not made by the defendant. This evidence would also serve as proof of a blade guard defect, causation, and negligent design.

a. The defendant will attack admissibility of the evidence based on relevance unless careful preparation is made by the plaintiff. During discovery (when information can be obtained from the defendant on this and other issues), what information is needed from the defendant to survive an objection, based on relevance, to evidence of prior accidents?

b. Assume the only information asked of the defendant in discovery was the number of complaints involving personal injuries associated with the use of the saw before the date plaintiff was injured. It is this evidence that the plaintiff later proffers at trial. Explain the Rule 403 argument that the defendant can make to the judge (assuming relevance is conceded).

2. Assume you are employed by a law firm that represents a tire manufacturer. The case you are working on involves an allegation of a design defect in wheel components. The plaintiff tire mechanic was injured when, in the process of remounting a tire, the rim wheel assembly separated with explosive force, and he was struck in the head by the parts.

In your investigation of the case, you learn that the plaintiff had a reputation for drinking alcoholic beverages regularly. This evidence is relevant to the tire manufacturer's defense of assumption of risk and apportionment of liability, since the comparative negligence standard applies. This could be the key to exoneration, or at least to a reduction in any damage award.

In your research, you find a case in which four prior convictions over a three-and-one-half-year period for public intoxication were not admissible against a party because the convictions were used

to prove that the party acted in conformity with his character, and this evidence failed to constitute habit evidence. The court went on to state that although there is no precise formula to determine when behavior becomes so consistent that it rises to the level of habit, an important factor is "adequacy of sampling and uniformity of response." *Reyes v. Missouri Railroad Co.*, 589 F.2d 791 (5th Cir. 1979).

In your investigation, you learn the following.

(1) The plaintiff was at his present job for three years before the accident. Before that, he was employed for two years by an employer who tells you the plaintiff was fired because of drinking. The employer knew the plaintiff drank because of his slurred speech, wobbly walk, alcoholic breath, and complaints from customers. This employer heard talk that the plaintiff was a "happy" guy, but "he drank too much."

(2) The plaintiff stated in a deposition he carried a cooler of beer on his truck while at his current job and he would drink the beer between 9:00 a.m. and 5:00 p.m. However, he also stated he had nothing to drink on the day of the accident.

(3) The plaintiff's supervisor tells you the plaintiff routinely carried a cooler of beer on his truck and drank on the job, starting in the early morning hours. The supervisor also tells you he received complaints from customers regarding the plaintiff's drinking.

(4) You cannot find anyone to testify that the plaintiff was drinking the day of the accident. In fact, his current employer tells you the plaintiff did not have his cooler the day of the accident.

Based on this information, frame an argument that the testimony of the former employer and the current supervisor regarding plaintiff's drinking constitute evidence of habit, not character. Distinguish *Reyes*.

3. Review the evidence rules for your state. Can character be established by opinion, reputation, or specific instances?

4. How does your state deal with evidence of habit and routine practice?

5. What is the current status of your state's rules with regard to matters raised in Rules 413, 414, and 415 of the Federal Rules of Evidence?

RULES REFERENCED IN THIS CHAPTER

Rule 404. Character Evidence Not Admissible to Prove Conduct; Exceptions; Other Crimes

Rule 405. Methods of Proving Character

Rule 406. Habit; Routine Practice

Rule 407. Subsequent Remedial Measures

Rule 408. Compromise and Offers to Compromise

Rule 409. Payment of Medical and Similar Expenses

Rule 410. Inadmissibility of Pleas, Plea Discussion, and Related Statements

Rule 411. Liability Insurance

Rule 412. Sex Offense Cases; Relevance of Alleged Victim's Past Sexual Behavior or Alleged Sexual Predisposition

Rule 413. Evidence of Similar Crimes in Sexual Assault Cases

Rule 414. Evidence of Similar Crimes in Child Molestation Cases

Rule 415. Evidence of Similar Acts in Civil Cases Concerning Sexual Assault or Child Molestation

NOTES

[1] Fed. R. Evid. 406. See Advisory Committee Notes (1972 Proposed Rules), which quote McCormick, § 162, p. 340.

[2] Fed. R. Evid. 406. See Advisory Committee Notes (1972 Proposed Rules).

[3] Fed. R. Evid. 407. See Advisory Committee Notes (1972 Proposed Rules).

[4] Fed. R. Evid. 412. See Congressional Discussion of H.R. 4727.

[5] Fed. R. Evid. 412. See Advisory Committee Notes (1994 Amendments).

[6] Harvey Berkman. "Crime Bill Sex Rule Stirs Evidence Debate." *The National Law Journal,* September 5, 1994, p. A16.

CHAPTER

7

Authentication, Original Documents, and Exhibits

OUTLINE

INTRODUCTION

Evidence may be in the form of a witness's testimony, or evidence may be something that is **tangible**, such as an object, a document, handwriting, or data. Evidence also may be part of a separate medium, such as a tape-recorded voice or images in photographs or on video.

Before tangible evidence is admissible, the trial court judge must be satisfied the evidence is what the proponent claims it to be when the opponent objects to its admissibility. The party who objects to admission of tangible evidence may challenge the authenticity or the genuineness of the evidence. Or, if the evidence is an exhibit to illustrate the testimony of a witness, an objection can be raised based on the prejudicial effect the evidence might have on the jury.

This chapter deals with the authenticity and identification of tangible evidence, the use of original documents, and the use of exhibits by witnesses to illustrate the witness's testimony.

tangible evidence Non-testimonial evidence that can be touched or perceived by the senses; real evidence.

132

AUTHENTICATION AND IDENTIFICATION

Evidence may appear to be relevant, but it is relevant only if it can be **authenticated** or identified by a witness or through some other means. Not only must the evidence relate to and tend to prove a fact at issue in the case, but the proponent of the evidence must prove the evidence is what the proponent alleges it to be.

Sometimes issues related to authentication and identification are settled before the trial begins. As part of the discovery process before the case gets to the courtroom, *requests for admissions* may be used to establish the authenticity of a piece of evidence, such as a document. In many courts, **pretrial conferences** help define the disputed issues that will be contested at trial. This is not to say Rule 901 is unnecessary. The paralegal needs to understand Rule 901 in order to draft requests for admissions, and answers to requests for admission, as well as to help prepare for the pretrial conference.

Rule 901 outlines methods of authenticating or identifying evidence. Rule 901(b) includes nine nonexclusive illustrations of types of evidence and methods of establishing authenticity. Most of the illustrations have to do with documents, while some deal with verbal communications. Rule 901(b)(10) states there are other sources of methods of authentication in acts of Congress, Rules of Civil and Criminal Procedure, and bankruptcy rules. This subsection is a reminder that the Rules of Evidence cannot be read in a vacuum. The Rules of Evidence are only one set of guidelines; other procedural rules and statutes will also affect what a juror will see or hear at trial.

Furthermore, individual rules must be read in the context of all of the Rules of Evidence. A piece of evidence can pass the relevancy test and can have proper authentication, but another rule still might apply to bar admission of that evidence. For example, the evidence may fail the Rule 403 balancing test, or it may be hearsay and therefore subject to objection.

Rule 901. Requirement of Authentication or Identification

(a) **General provision.** The requirement of authentication or identification as a condition precedent to admissibility is satisfied by evidence sufficient to support a finding that the matter in question is what its proponent claims.

(b) **Illustrations.** By way of illustration only, and not by way of limitation, the following are examples of authentication or identification conforming with the requirements of this rule:

(1) **Testimony of witness with knowledge.** Testimony that a matter is what it is claimed to be.

(2) **Nonexpert opinion on handwriting.** Nonexpert opinion as to the genuineness of handwriting, based upon familiarity not acquired for purposes of the litigation.

(3) **Comparison by trier or expert witness.** Comparison by the trier of fact or by expert witnesses with specimens which have been authenticated.

(4) **Distinctive characteristics and the like.** Appearance, contents, substance, internal patterns, or other distinctive characteristics, taken in conjunction with circumstances.

(5) **Voice identification.** Identification of a voice, whether heard firsthand or through mechanical or electronic transmission or recording, by opinion

authentication The introduction of evidence that proves a document or object is what it appears to be.

pretrial conference A meeting with the trial judge and the parties to a lawsuit before the trial begins. Its purpose is to define the matters at issue and in need of resolution at trial.

based upon hearing the voice at any time under circumstances connecting it with the alleged speaker.

(6) Telephone conversations. Telephone conversations, by evidence that a call was made to the number assigned at the time by the telephone company to a particular person or business, if (A) in case of a person, circumstances, including self-identification, show the person answering to be the one called, or (B) in the case of a business, the call was made to a place of business and the conversation related to business reasonably transacted over the telephone.

(7) Public records or reports. Evidence that a writing authorized by law to be recorded or filed and in fact recorded or filed in a pubic office, or a purported public record, report, statement, or data compilation, in any form, is from the public office where items of this nature are kept.

(8) Ancient documents or data compilation. Evidence that a document or data compilation, in any form, (A) is in such condition as to create no suspicion concerning its authenticity, (B) was in a place where it, if authentic, would likely be, and (C) has been in existence 20 years or more at the time it is offered.

(9) Process or system. Evidence describing a process or system used to produce a result and showing that the process or system produces an accurate result.

(10) Methods provided by statute or rule. Any method of authentication or identification provided by Act of Congress or by other rules prescribed by the Supreme Court pursuant to statutory authority.

Some of the nine illustrations of authentication or identification in Rule 901 are more clear than others. The first illustration, testimony of a witness with knowledge, includes, for instance, the identification of an object as one found at a certain place. The identification involves proper **chain of custody.** For example, a weapon found next to a victim is taken by a law enforcement officer and put in an evidence bag that is sealed and marked with appropriate identifying information. The officer can then take the stand at trial and identify the weapon as the one found next to the victim.

The first illustration of Rule 901 also applies to material subject to laboratory analysis. Someone has to testify that what is presented as evidence in court by a party is what the party says it is. For example, a white substance put in an evidence bag, then sealed and checked into the evidence room, could be checked out and sent to a laboratory for analysis. The laboratory technician keeps track of the substance from the beginning while testing it. The laboratory technician can testify the white substance found at the scene tested as cocaine.

The chain of custody does not have to be established by the proponent as a perfectly connected set of links. Minor gaps in the links go to the weight of the evidence, not its admissibility. In other words, the judge should allow the evidence to be considered by the jury, who in turn will determine its reliability where the chain of custody has missing or imperfect links (see Illustration 7-1).

chain of custody The written record that establishes the location of physical evidence from the time it is collected until the time it is offered as evidence at trial.

Illustration 7-1 _____

Pursuant to a search warrant, detectives searched a house and found a bag filled with hypodermic needles, syringes, and various pills and tablets identified as controlled substances. A detective placed the items in a large plastic envelope, sealed the envelope, put it in a paper bag, and locked the bag in the vice squad vault.

The bag and its contents were later sent to the state crime laboratory for analysis and then returned to the vice squad vault, where it remained until trial.

On appeal, the defendant contended the chain of custody proven at trial when the contents of the bag were introduced into evidence was incomplete, calling into question the authenticity of the contents introduced at trial.

To be successful with such a contention, the defendant must allege reasons why it was possible that different items could have been substituted while the contents were held at the vice squad vault and the crime laboratory. Alternatively, the defendant must allege tampering occurred.

The court found that a perfect chain of custody was not established at trial but held that this fact goes to the weight of the evidence, not its admissibility. A presumption of regularity attaches to official duties, such as holding evidence. Without proof of specific allegations, the presumption is not overcome. *United States v. Jefferson*, 714 F.2d 689, 695–696 (7th Cir. 1983).

If an opponent of a piece of evidence can convince the court that it is likely the evidence is not what the proponent claims it to be, because of a serious break in the chain of custody owing to tampering, the judge may keep the jury from seeing the evidence. If evidence that is the basis for a criminal charge is not kept identifiable through the gathering and testing processes, the judge may sustain an objection to admissibility.

The testimony of a witness who saw a document signed, thus establishing that the document is what the proponent says it is, also falls within the purview of Rule 901(b)(1). In this way, a document offered at trial is authenticated or identified. This authentication might be of importance in a dispute centering on the validity of a contract.

The second illustration in Rule 901 deals with nonexpert opinion on handwriting. The rule allows a witness to testify that the handwriting on a document is that of a particular person. The questions the proponent asks the witness should establish that the witness has reason to recognize the handwriting, possibly from correspondence or business dealings.

The third illustration in Rule 901 also deals with experts on handwriting. They can compare an **authenticated specimen** against the document in question and testify regarding similarities and differences. The jury can also make the comparison and draw its own conclusions.

The fourth illustration in Rule 901 allows authentication of a document or verbal communication by inherent characteristics. A witness can testify to familiarity with a person's style of writing or voice in order to authenticate the document or voice as a product of or belonging to a particular person. On the other hand, this testimony can be used to prove the opposite, that the document was not the product of a particular person or the voice was not that of a particular person.

Voice identification is possible under the fifth illustration in Rule 901 when it is established by appropriate questions that a witness is familiar with a person's voice. Having heard a verbal communication either first-hand or recorded, the witness can testify that it is or is not the voice of a particular person.

authenticated specimen
A writing opposing parties agree is in fact written by a particular person; usually done by stipulation.

Telephone conversations are the subject of the sixth illustration in Rule 901. A voice can be identified, as we saw in the fourth illustration, by content of the communication. Or comparison by a person knowledgeable about the voice can be used under the fifth illustration. The sixth illustration deals with outgoing calls and identification of the answering voice. If a witness can testify that a specific number assigned to a person or business was called, then that is enough for identification purposes. But, remember, the credibility of the evidence is for the jury to decide.

Under the seventh illustration in Rule 901, public records or reports are admissible simply by proof of custody and regardless of the form in which the data may be stored. Anyone with knowledge of the procedures of the public office, such as an employee of the office, can testify that the record or report is from the public office. The record or report is then admissible into evidence as long as there is no successful objection on other grounds. Illustration 7-2 demonstrates the process.

Illustration 7-2 _____

Under federal law, individuals are required to register semiautomatic weapons with barrels less than 16 inches long with the National Firearms Registration Office. It is a federal crime to not register this type of weapon.

Before a defendant can visit the National Firearms Registration and Transfer Record room in Washington, DC, to challenge a witness/employee of the office who testifies that no registration was found in the name of the defendant, the defendant has to convince the judge the inspection is necessary because there is evidence the record keeping system is defective.

If there is no sufficiently serious challenge to the system's operation, it is within the discretion of the court to deny a motion to visit the facility. *United States v. Rose,* 695 F.2d 1356, 1358 (10th Cir. 1982).

Oftentimes parties stipulate to the authenticity of public records and reports before trial so there will be no need to call a witness at trial to authenticate the records or reports. In response to modern technology, the seventh illustration in Rule 901 also covers data stored in computers.

The eighth illustration in Rule 901 often is referred to as the *ancient document rule.* However, the "document" can be one that is electronically stored, in spite of the image of yellowed parchment paper that comes to mind with the title. The document is admissible as long as the document appears to be free from tampering, is found where one would expect to find the type of document, and has been in existence for 20 years or more at the time it is offered into evidence.

The last illustration in Rule 901, the ninth, allows the results of a process or system into evidence when there is testimony describing the process or system and affirming that accurate results are produced by that process or system. The ninth illustration encompasses, for instance, the production of x-rays and the manipulation of computer data. Items that would fit into this category commonly are stipulated to by the parties or are judicially noticed on motion by a party.

Self-Authenticating Documents

Rule 902 allows shortcuts to dispense with a showing of authenticity if documents are of a certain type. The document alone is admissible without the testimony of a sponsoring witness when the document meets requirements that make it self-authenticating.

Rule 902. Self-Authentication

Extrinsic evidence of authenticity as a condition precedent to admissibility is not required with respect to the following:

(1) Domestic public documents under seal. A document bearing a seal purporting to be that of the United States, or of any State, district, Commonwealth, territory, or insular possession thereof, or the Panama Canal Zone, or the Trust Territory of the Pacific Islands, or of a political subdivision, department, officer, or agency thereof, and a signature purporting to be an attestation or execution.

(2) Domestic public documents not under seal. A document purporting to bear the signature in the official capacity of an officer or employee of any entity included in paragraph (1) hereof, having no seal, if a public officer having a seal and having official duties in the district or political subdivision of the officer or employee certifies under seal that the signer has the official capacity and that the signature is genuine.

(3) Foreign public documents. A document purporting to be executed or attested in an official capacity by a person authorized by the laws of a foreign country to make the execution or attestation, and accompanied by a final certification as to the genuineness of the signature and official position (A) of the executing or attesting person, or (B) of any foreign official whose certificate of genuineness of signature and official position relates to the execution or attestation or is in a chain of certificates of genuineness of signature and official position relating to the execution or attestation. A final certification may be made by a secretary of an embassy or legation, consul general, consul, vice consul, or consular agent of the United States, or a diplomatic or consular official of the foreign country assigned or accredited to the United States. If reasonable opportunity has been given to all parties to investigate the authenticity and accuracy of official documents, the court may, for good cause shown, order that they be treated as presumptively authentic without final certification or permit them to be evidenced by an attested summary with or without final certification.

(4) Certified copies of public records. A copy of an official record or report or entry therein, or of a document authorized by law to be recorded or filed and actually recorded or filed in a public office, including data compilations in any form, certified as correct by the custodian or other person authorized to make the certification, by certificate complying with paragraph (1), (2), or (3) of this rule or complying with any Act of Congress or rule prescribed by the Supreme Court pursuant to statutory authority.

(5) Official publications. Books, pamphlets, or other publications purporting to be issued by public authority.

(6) Newspapers and periodicals. Printed materials purporting to be newspapers or periodicals.

(7) Trade inscriptions and the like. Inscriptions, signs, tags, or labels purporting to have been affixed in the course of business and indicating ownership, control, or origin.

(8) Acknowledged documents. Documents accompanied by a certificate of acknowledgment executed in the manner provided by law by a notary public or other officer authorized by law to take acknowledgments.

(9) Commercial paper and related documents. Commercial paper, signatures thereon, and documents relating thereto to the extent provided by general commercial law.

(10) Presumptions under Acts of Congress. Any signature, document, or other matter declared by Act of Congress to be presumptively or prima facie genuine or authentic.

Rule 902 describes the types of documents that are self-authenticated, including, in subsection 1, domestic and foreign public documents with the seal of a government entity affixed along with an appropriate signature. Subsection 2 provides for domestic public documents not under seal but signed by someone with authority. A public official with a seal can certify that the signatory has the official capacity to sign and the signature is genuine. See Illustration 7-3 for an example of the use of Rule 902(2) at trial.

Illustration 7-3 _____

In a lawsuit where E. Howard Hunt sued Liberty Lobby for damages for libel based on an article in a weekly newspaper published by Liberty Lobby, Liberty Lobby challenged the admissibility of affidavits of the custodian of particular records of the CIA.

The article stated Mr. Hunt was involved in a conspiracy to assassinate President John F. Kennedy and that the CIA had records to prove the contention.

Mr. Hunt offered into evidence affidavits of CIA employees stating that no such records could be found after a diligent search.

The court held that the affidavits met the requirements of Rule 902(2) because the affidavits were executed by a CIA employee and a certificate of the general counsel of the CIA was attached, certifying that the affiant occupied the position stated in the affidavit. The certificate of the general counsel also bore the agency's official seal, which was necessary for self-authentication under Rule 902(2). *Hunt v. Liberty Lobby,* 720 F.2d 631, 651 (11th Cir. 1983).

Rule 902(4) allows certified copies of public records where originals are not offered. Subsections 1, 2, and 3 encompass originals. However, not all certified copies of documents are self-authenticating the way documents under seal are. If a certified copy rather than a document under seal is going to be used in litigation, the paralegal needs to be certain that the document qualifies as self-authenticating under Rule 902(4).

Rule 902(7) recognizes official publications, newspapers, and periodicals as likely to be genuine, so they are self-authenticating. There is no need to call an editor or author to authenticate the material. Trade inscriptions are also self-authenticating as they are likely to be genuine, given that there are serious penalties for infringement. The law reflects common sense here; businesses go to a great deal of effort and expense to foster public recognition of trade inscriptions, so it should not be necessary to call a corporate executive to authenticate a product label. For an older view, demonstrating a contrary rule and its absurd consequences, see Illustration 7-4.

Illustration 7-4 _____

Carolyn Keegan ate green peas served by her mother. In eating the peas, a triangular piece of steel caught in her throat, causing her to choke. She sued Green Giant because of her injuries.

At trial, Green Giant objected to the admission of the actual can from which Ms. Keegan's peas were served. Ms. Keegan argued to the trial court judge that the can should be admitted because "it is self-evident that the Green Giant Company was the distributor." The can was needed to prove Green Giant was the distributor and for the inference that the can was packed by Green Giant. Keegan argued that this was a question for the jury to decide.

The trial court judge and the Maine supreme court agreed with Green Giant that the label was not enough to prove Green Giant was the distributor and canner of the peas, so the jury could not consider the labeled can as proof that Green Giant was the distributer and canner.

This gutted Ms. Keegan's case because there was then no link between Green Giant and the peas ingested by Ms. Keegan. The dissenting opinion pointed out the absurdity of the majority's reasoning, noting Green Giant went to great lengths to get consumers to accept its product through label recognition and advertising and that any risk of substitution or imitation was small under these circumstances. Rule 902(7) acknowledges the wisdom and common sense of the dissent. *Keegan v. Green Giant Co.,* 150 Me. 283, 110 A.2d 599 (1954).

Rule 902(8) includes documents signed in the presence of a notary public according to statutory requirements. **Acknowledged documents** are self-authenticating; generally there is no need to call the notary as a witness to testify to the circumstances of the signing.

Rule 902(9) applies to documents executed according to the Uniform Commercial Code or federal commercial law, whichever is appropriate. If the documents meet the requirements of the law, they are self-authenticating.

Subscribing Witnesses

Subscribing, or attesting, witnesses to a document do not have to testify to authenticate a document unless state or federal law requires it. For example, some contracts are signed by the parties and by attesting witnesses. If no statute requires the contract to have subscribing witnesses, then the contract can be introduced into evidence without calling any of the attesting witnesses. This is not the case when it comes to wills that have subscribing witnesses who attest to the execution of the will. The subscribing witnesses must be called to authenticate the will.

Many states now have statutes allowing self-authenticating wills using an **attestation clause.** In this case, attesting witnesses need not be called to testify to the authenticity of the will.

acknowledged documents Documents signed in the presence of a notary public, where the signing party declares the act of signing as the party's own, and the notary public attaches a formal statement acknowledging the party's act.

attestation clause A written statement acknowledging the witnessing of the signing of a document as well as the signing of the statement.

Rule 903. Subscribing Witness' Testimony Unnecessary

The testimony of a subscribing witness is not necessary to authenticate a writing unless required by the laws of the jurisdiction whose laws govern the validity of the writing.

The paralegal must be familiar with state law on this issue because it might control in a federal diversity case. Of course, the paralegal must be familiar with the state's rules of evidence and state statutory requirements for litigation in state court.

ORDER OF PROOF AND CONDITIONAL RELEVANCE _____

Recall from Chapter 3 that one of the duties of the judge is to control the order of proof in accordance with Rule 104(b).

Rule 104. Preliminary Questions

(b) Relevancy conditioned on fact. When the relevancy of evidence depends upon the fulfillment of a condition of fact, the court shall admit it upon, or subject to, the introduction of evidence sufficient to support a finding of the fulfillment of the condition.

Evidence, or proof of a claim, must be offered one piece at a time through the testimony of witnesses and presentation of tangible evidence. However, the testimony of a witness may be relevant only if someone else can testify to other matters related to the testimony of the initial witness. But since only one witness can testify at a time, the admission of the testimony of the initial witness is conditioned on other testimony establishing the connection to the matter being litigated. This situation involves **conditional relevancy.**

When the testimony of the initial witness is offered as evidence and is challenged because no evidence has yet been offered to connect the testimony to the issues being tried, the trial court judge generally will allow the evidence in, subject to the missing link being added by the proponent through later witnesses. If the proponent fails to provide the necessary evidence, the testimony of the initial witness can be stricken from the record, and the jury will be told not to use the testimony in its deliberations.

conditional relevance
Evidence not directly tied to a claim, charge, or defense is relevant only if subsequent testimony or tangible evidence ties the evidence to the claim, charge, or defense.

Conditional relevancy is necessary for the orderly presentation of evidence as proof of a claim, charge, or defense. The concept allows a party to choose the order of the presentation of evidence to the jury in the manner the party believes to be most advantageous. As long as the party connects initial evidence to the claim, charge, or defense with subsequent evidence, the initial evidence is not subject to being stricken by the trial court judge on a relevancy objection.

ORIGINAL DOCUMENT RULE

Rule 1002 was traditionally called the *best evidence rule*. However, a more accurate title is the *original document rule*. The rule applies only when the proponent of a writing, recording, or photograph wishes to prove the truth of the content. The rule does not apply if the writing, recording, or photograph is used by the witness merely to illustrate the witness's testimony.

Rule 1002.   Requirement of Original

To prove the content of a writing, recording, or photograph, the original writing, recording, or photograph is required, except as otherwise provided in these rules or by Act of Congress.

The original document rule means a proponent of the writing, recording, or photograph must use an **original** at trial, not a copy. The original document rule does not mean there is a hierarchy of evidence. A party is in no way required to prove an issue with types of evidence in a preordained order, as implied by the term "best evidence rule."

The purpose of the original document rule is to prevent inaccuracy and fraud when an attempt is being made to prove the contents of a recording, writing, or photograph. As long as a proponent of secondary evidence proves to the satisfaction of the judge that the original is lost or destroyed, any secondary evidence of content can be used by the proponent, including oral testimony, copies, or transcripts.

However, a proper foundation must be laid by the proponent. For instance, when an original document has been destroyed, a copy can prove the content of the original as long as a witness can testify that the copy is the same as the original because the witness saw the original and knows that the copy accurately reflects the content of the original. It is incumbent on the opponent of the copy to bring into question the credibility of the witness's testimony, and then it is up to the jury to decide whether the copy is credible.

Many times, the issue of the reliability of a copy is decided before trial, with the parties stipulating to the use of a copy rather than the original. But if a party objects to the use of a copy, Rule 1002 is the basis for the objection.

Definitions

The terms *writing, recording,* and *photograph* are defined in Rule 1001. Two other terms, *original* and *duplicate,* are also defined. These definitions are important, because duplicates are admissible to the same extent originals are admissible, unless authenticity is raised as an issue or if it would be unfair to a party to admit a duplicate.

Rule 1001.   Definitions

For purposes of this article the following definitions are applicable:

(1) Writings and recordings. "Writings" and "recordings" consist of letters, words, or numbers, or their equivalent, set down by handwriting, typewriting,

original Not copied or derived.

> printing, photostating, photographing, magnetic impulse, mechanical or electronic recording, or other form of data compilation.
>
> **(2) Photographs.** "Photographs" include still photographs, X-ray films, video tapes, and motion pictures.
>
> **(3) Original.** An "original" of a writing or recording is the writing or recording itself or any counterpart intended to have the same effect by a person executing or issuing it. An "original" of a photograph includes the negative or any print therefrom. If data are stored in a computer or similar device, any printout or other output readable by sight, shown to reflect the data accurately, is an "original."
>
> **(4) Duplicate.** A "duplicate" is a counterpart produced by the same impression as the original, or from the same matrix, or by means of photography, including enlargements and miniatures, or by mechanical or electronic recording, or by chemical reproduction, or by other equivalent techniques which accurately reproduces the original.

A **duplicate** is a reproduction of an original that is exactly the same as the original or reflects the original in another size. It is not the same as a copy, nor is it the same as an original, although a duplicate has the same effect as an original.

For instance, when a buyer and seller of real estate enter into a contract, multiple original documents are often signed. Each contract has exactly the same wording, and each is signed by the parties. Each of these contracts is an original, because the parties intend them to have the same effect as an original. Examples of duplicates would be the enlargement of a photograph or a tape recording re-recorded in every detail.

Copies, unlike duplicates, are not necessarily trustworthy. A **copy** is a reproduction of an original that may not be exact. For instance, a copy of a real estate contract could be reproduced by photocopying the original document, which would allow for careful alteration of the original document not apparent in the copy. The alteration could be masqueraded in the copying process.

A duplicate generally is admissible as if it were an original, unless an objection is raised by the opponent of the duplicate calling into question the authenticity of the original.

Rule 1003. Admissibility of Duplicates

> A duplicate is admissible to the same extent as an original unless (1) a genuine question is raised as to the authenticity of the original or (2) in the circumstances it would be unfair to admit the duplicate in lieu of the original.

duplicate Reproduction of an original that is exactly the same as the original.

copy Reproduction of an original that is an imitation and may not be exactly the same as the original.

Proof of Content without Original

Sometimes the original is not available to a party to prove the content of a writing, recording, or photograph for a variety of reasons.

If a party demonstrates to the trial court judge that the original was lost, destroyed, or cannot be obtained, then the content of the original can be proven using any kind of secondary evidence. The opponent of the secondary evidence can attack only the sufficiency of the secondary evidence, not its admissibility. The issue then becomes the weight the jury gives the evidence, not its admissibility, as in Illustration 7-5.

Illustration 7-5 _____

In a prosecution by the federal government of a defendant charged with knowingly making a false statement on a loan application, the government misplaced an original photocopy of a check. The trial court judge allowed into evidence a secondary photocopy of the check, made by the bank official who gave the first photocopy to the law enforcement. There was no issue with regard to the authenticity of the first photocopy.

The bank official and the law enforcement officer testified they had seen both the original photocopy and the secondary photocopy and that the second photocopy accurately reproduced the original photocopy.

The defendant did not dispute the government's contention that the original photocopy had been lost. However, the defendant argued there needed to be clear and convincing evidence of the trustworthiness of the secondary evidence, that is, the second photocopy.

The court held that no such proof of trustworthiness is necessary. Once the government showed to the satisfaction of the trial court judge that the original photocopy was lost, the government could use any secondary evidence it chose, as long as the government demonstrated to the trial court judge that the evidence was what it purported to be and reflected the content of the original photocopy. The government did demonstrate this through the testimony of the bank official and the law enforcement officer. The court then held that it was up to the jury to determine the weight to be given to the second photocopy. *United States v. Gerhart,* 538 F.2d 807, 809–810 (8th Cir. 1976).

Rule 1004. Admissibility of Other Evidence of Contents

The original is not required, and other evidence of the contents of a writing, recording, or photograph is admissible if—

(1) Originals lost or destroyed. All originals are lost or have been destroyed, unless the proponent lost or destroyed them in bad faith; or

(2) Original not obtainable. No original can be obtained by any available judicial process or procedure; or

(3) Original in possession of opponent. At a time when an original was under the control of the party against whom offered, that party was put on notice, by the pleadings or otherwise, that the contents would be a subject of proof at the hearing, and that party does not produce the original at the hearing; or

(4) Collateral matters. The writing, recording, or photograph is not closely related to a controlling issue.

If a writing, recording, or photograph is not essential to an issue in the case, then an original is not required, and other evidence of content is admissible. The original document rule does not apply in this event, and copies or other forms of evidence, like testimony, can be used to prove content.

Furthermore, the original document rule does not apply where the fact to be proven has an existence independent of any writing. Here the writing only memorializes a fact. For instance, birth, age, and death are facts existing independent of any certificate that might memorialize the event. On the other hand, a divorce can be proven only by a decree entered by a court. A person does not have to prove birth by a certificate but must prove a divorce by a written decree.

Public Records

Because it is unwise and impractical to remove official records from public offices, **certified copies**, or true copies in accordance with Rule 902(4), are admissible. Before other evidence of the contents can be used, a party must use "reasonable diligence" to obtain certified copies.

Rule 1005. Public Records

The contents of an official record, or of a document authorized to be recorded or filed and actually recorded or filed, including data compilations in any form, if otherwise admissible, may be proved by copy, certified as correct in accordance with Rule 902 or testified to be correct by a witness who has compared it with the original. If a copy which complies with the foregoing cannot be obtained by the exercise of reasonable diligence, then other evidence of the contents may be given.

Rule 1005 dictates the order of the type of evidence that can be used to prove an official record or document. Production of the actual record or document is impractical, so certified copies are mandated as the second choice; only after a party tries and fails to obtain a certified copy can other proof of the content of the official record be used.

Summaries

Rule 1006 is a practical rule that allows summaries of voluminous writings, recordings, or photographs to be presented to the jury in lieu of the actual material. The rule requires the material that is the basis for the summaries be available for examination, copying, and production in court in case the judge orders production.

Rule 1006. Summaries

The contents of voluminous writings, recordings, or photographs which cannot conveniently be examined in court may be presented in the form of a chart, summary, or calculation. The originals, or duplicates, shall be made available for examination or copying, or both, by other parties at reasonable time and place. The court may order that they be produced in court.

certified copy Officially approved document.

In *White Industries, Inc. v. Cessna Aircraft Co.,* 611 F.Supp. 1049, 1069 *et seq.* (W.D. Mo. 1985), a case from the Western District of Missouri, the court extensively discusses summaries and the criteria for admissibility. The summary must be based on material that is (1) voluminous, (2) itself admissible, (3) available to the opponent and the court, and (4) accurate.

Rule 1006 allows summaries of voluminous writings, recordings, or photographs. The summary can be in chart or graphic form. As long as a proper foundation is laid, and the voluminous material is available to the opponent and to the court, these summaries are admissible as substantive evidence.

Original Not Required

Article X of the Federal Rules of Evidence generally favors originals of writings, recordings, and photographs because originals are the most accurate proof of the content. However, under Rule 1007, the content can be proven by secondary evidence without telling the jury why the original was not used instead.

Rule 1007.   Testimony or Written Admission of Party

Contents of writings, recordings, or photographs may be proved by the testimony or deposition of the party against whom offered or by that party's written admission, without accounting for the nonproduction of the original.

The use of secondary evidence is possible when the party against whom it is offered testified in court or at a deposition—or made a written admission—that the content of the writing, recording, or photograph is the same as the original. Rule 1004 does not require special circumstances in order to apply, so there is no need to prove the original was lost or is not obtainable before secondary evidence is used.

Roles of the Judge and the Jury

Rule 1008 is similar to Rule 104 in that it says the judge should decide preliminary questions with regard to admissibility of evidence.

Rule 1008.   Functions of Court and Jury

When the admissibility of other evidence of contents of writings, recordings, or photographs under these rules depends upon the fulfillment of a condition of fact, the question whether the condition has been fulfilled is ordinarily for the court to determine in accordance with the provisions of Rule 104. However, when an issue is raised (a) whether the asserted writing ever existed, or (b) whether another writing, recording, or photograph produced at the trial is the original, or (c) whether other evidence of contents correctly reflects the contents, the issue is for the trier of fact to determine as in the case of other issues of fact.

The judge generally determines whether an original is lost, destroyed, or not obtainable. The judge also decides whether the writing, recording, or photograph is an issue in a case or a collateral matter. This type of decision is part of the judge's function as a filter for evidence.

However, when certain issues are raised that involve the writings, recordings, or photographs, the judge must allow the jury to determine the preliminary questions or risk taking the entire case from the jury. It is the judge's role to decide if there is *prima facie* evidence supporting the introduction of the writings, recordings, or photographs. Here the judge simply determines whether the jury could find that the writing, recording, or photograph did exist, leaving the ultimate decision to the jury on the existence of originals when that is in issue.

Rule 1008 lists three circumstances in which the matter should be left to the jury's determination. These include whether a writing, recording, or photograph ever existed, whether it is the original, or whether secondary evidence of the unavailable writing, recording, or photograph correctly reflects its content.

EXHIBITS

An **exhibit** is something tangible, such as a document or an object, that is used or placed into evidence by a party at trial, in deposition, or at a hearing. The exhibit is subject to a variety of objections related to the purpose for which it is used. Generally, when a party uses an exhibit, it is marked as, for example, Defendant's Exhibit No. 1. This marking is to identify it throughout the trial and on appeal.

If there is no successful objection to an exhibit offered into evidence, the judge will allow it into evidence after it is marked, which means the jury can consider it as substantive proof.

Before an exhibit is presented to the witness, a foundation is laid for use of the exhibit. The proponent asks the witness questions to establish the relevance and authenticity of the exhibit. The original document rule may come into play if the proponent uses a copy that the opponent challenges. As will be discussed in a later chapter, an objection might also be raised based on the hearsay rule. Thus, to summarize, the use of an exhibit is governed by the Federal Rules of Evidence dealing with relevancy, authenticity, original documents, and hearsay.

Objects used or offered as exhibits generally are identified by a witness who has knowledge of the source of the object and who can testify it is the same object or is in substantially the same condition as it was at the time of its source. This point was discussed earlier in regard to a weapon found at the scene of a crime. Rule 901(a) and Rule 901(b)(1) require the proponent to demonstrate to the judge that the object is what the proponent claims it to be, through the testimony of a witness who can identify the object.

Exhibits play an important role at trial because they enhance oral presentations. Jurors tend to remember testimony better if it is accompanied by a visual presentation. Exhibits can be illustrative or demonstrative. *Illustrative exhibits* help a witness testify using diagrams, charts, maps, models, and graphs to create a visual illustration of the witness's testimony. These exhibits help present a clear picture of the witness's testimony for the jury. They are an aid to testimony and are marked as exhibits, but they are not admissible into evidence, because they have no probative value independent of the witness's testimony.

exhibit Something tangible used or offered into evidence at trial, in a deposition, or at a hearing.

Demonstrative exhibits do more than illustrate testimony. These exhibits depict or represent something that is at issue in the trial. Demonstrative exhibits include photographs, scaled models, objects, and computer animation. They tend to prove something related to the contested issues at trial. Consequently, they are not only identified and marked as exhibits, but often are offered as substantive evidence to be considered by the jury independent of the witness's testimony.

If demonstrative evidence will be used at trial, the paralegal should carefully research issues of admissibility. Appellate court opinions reflect some confusion between illustrative and demonstrative evidence. "Many courts have followed the anomalous course of formally admitting illustrative evidence, while simultaneously instructing the jury that it is not evidence."[1] Careful research of prior cases in the circuit where the trial takes place is very important. Reference should also be made to the rationale of other circuit courts of appeals, particularly when the controlling circuit has not ruled on the issue.

The problem of distinguishing between illustrative and demonstrative evidence and determining whether the jury can use the evidence during deliberation is today compounded by new technology. Computer animation using laser disc technology is especially troublesome. Jurors might put unfair weight on the animation if allowed to "play with it" during deliberations. If computer animations or simulations are admitted into evidence over the opponent's objection, the opponent should ask the judge to allow the proponent to use it in open court but not supply it to the jury during deliberations.

A limiting instruction should be requested so that the jury will keep the animation or simulation in perspective. The paralegal for the proponent or opponent should have this issue thoroughly researched, with careful arguments outlined, before the matter is considered at trial or in a pretrial motion. For instance, the paralegal should have all the information on the data used to create a computer animation, because the computer animation is only as good as the data and the computer analysis used by the expert who created it.

Finally, exhibits may be created by companies that specialize in visual presentations at trial. The Demonstrative Evidence Specialists Association is an organization of professionals associated with companies providing such demonstrative evidence. This organization might be helpful as a resource for locating a company to meet litigation needs.[2]

Publications targeting attorneys often carry advertisements for specialists in visual presentations. The information in these advertisements can also be accessed on the Internet. Recommendations from other attorneys who have used particular companies are helpful to paralegals.

SUMMARY

Tangible evidence must be authenticated or identified before it is admissible. Evidence is authenticated if it is proven to be what the proponent claims it to be. Often authentication is done through the testimony of a witness who can testify about the tangible object, vouching for its authenticity.

If the authenticity of the tangible evidence is uncontested, the parties may stipulate to authenticity.

Rule 901 not only requires authentication, but also illustrates ways to authenticate evidence. Authentication or identification can be accomplished using the testimony of a witness or the opinion of an expert or nonexpert regarding handwriting. Rule 901 also discusses identification of voices. The process for authentication of public records is outlined, along with the authentication of ancient documents and data compilations. In addition, Rule 901 notes that evidence of a process or system is admissible when properly authenticated. And finally, the rule recognizes other ways of authenticating tangible evidence as found in the federal statutes or other rules promulgated by the Supreme Court.

It is possible to authenticate certain documents without the use of extrinsic evidence. If the evidence is a public domestic or foreign document, Rule 902 outlines the means of authentication. Documents such as official publications, newspapers, trade inscriptions, and commercial paper do not require additional evidence of authenticity. Documents accompanied by a certificate of acknowledgment conforming to statutory requirements need no additional evidence of authenticity.

Rule 903 relieves witnesses to the execution of documents from having to testify to the authenticity of the document as long as a statute does not require otherwise.

The parties can present their evidence in the order that best explains each party's contentions. If evidence is offered that is not relevant without the testimony of a later witness, the judge can conditionally admit the evidence. If the subsequent evidence is never offered, the trial court judge can strike the previous testimony and tell the jury not to use it as a basis for its decision.

The original document rule, sometimes referred to as the best evidence rule, requires that an original be used as evidence when the purpose is to prove the content of the document. However, if the proponent of the evidence satisfies the court that the original is not available, the proponent can use any type of evidence to prove the content of the missing original, including testimony or photocopies. The credibility of the secondary evidence is for the jury to weigh.

Rule 1001 provides definitions of key words related to the original document rule. Writings, recordings, and photographs are explained. An original is defined as the writing or recording itself. A duplicate is an original reproduced in such a way that it is exactly the same as the original. A copy is an imitation of an original, not necessarily an exact reproduction. Duplicates are admissible to the same extent and in the same manner as originals, but copies are not admissible into evidence unless the proponent satisfies the trial court judge the original is not available.

Copies of public records are admissible if they are certified by the appropriate government employee, or if the employee testifies to having compared the original to the copy and seeing that they were the same.

Summaries of voluminous records are admissible as long as the underlying data are available to opposing counsel.

The original of a document is not necessary if a party admits to the existence of the original in a deposition or in testimony.

If the judge cannot determine the issue of admissibility of a copy without usurping the role of the jury in deciding the dispute, the judge will make that determination only if there is a reasonable chance the jury could find that the original writing, recording, or photograph did exist when that existence is an issue in the case.

Exhibits can be illustrative or demonstrative. Illustrative exhibits are visual means of explaining the testimony of a witness and are used by the witness for that purpose. Illustrative exhibits are not admissible into evidence. Demonstrative exhibits often are admissible as evidence because they represent something at issue in the trial and tend to prove something contested at trial. Demonstrative exhibits are visual. For instance, a scaled model of a building that is the subject of the lawsuit might be demonstrative evidence used by the jury as substantive evidence of the building. The model does not just illustrate a witness's testimony; it is also substantive evidence in and of itself.

Tangible evidence is admissible, but it must be authenticated or identified, and originals usually are necessary to qualify as tangible evidence. Exhibits are important because of the impact on the jury of visual evidence. Although illustrative exhibits are not admissible, both demonstrative and illustrative exhibits are essential to a well-presented case.

✔ CHECKPOINTS

❑ Authentication and identification of evidence
1. Evidence is what the proponent claims it to be.
2. Some documents are self-authenticating when they are executed according to statutory requirements.
3. Subscribing witnesses need not testify unless statutorily required.

❑ Order of Proof
1. Evidence is presented in the order chosen by the party.
2. Evidence is only conditionally relevant if it needs subsequent evidence to make it relevant.
3. Trial court judge can conditionally admit evidence.
4. If a party never offers subsequent evidence, trial court judge can instruct jury to disregard conditionally admitted evidence.

❑ Original document rule
1. Originals are favored.
2. If original is not available, any secondary evidence can prove content of original.
3. Jury determines weight of secondary evidence.
4. Original is the document itself.

5. Duplicate is reproduction that is exactly like the original and is treated like the original.
6. Copy is imitation of the original and admissible only if the original is not available.
7. Public records are admissible if certified or if government employee testifies as to authenticity.
8. Summaries of voluminous records are admissible as originals as long as underlying data available.
9. If party admits to existence of original in deposition or testimony, original document does not have to be used.
10. Judge lets jury decide if original ever existed when its existence is contested.

❑ Exhibits
1. Illustrative: visual material such as charts, maps, and diagrams used to illustrate testimony.
2. Demonstrative: visual material such as scaled models, photographs, objects, and computer animations are admissible as substantive evidence.

APPLICATIONS

Application 7-1

United States v. Balzano
687 F.2d 6 (1st Cir. 1982)

PER CURIAM.

Anthony Balzano appeals from his conviction on two counts for the sale of "slugs" in violation of 18 U.S.C. §§ 491(b), 2. He argues that his conviction should be reversed because the district court permitted the government to play for the jury a copy of a tape, containing statements appellant made to an undercover agent, rather than the original tape.

The original tape was recorded on a Nigra tape recorder which was strapped to the undercover agent's body. The Nigra recorder had no capacity for audio replay. Therefore, the government transferred the contents of the Nigra tape to a Sony cassette, but because of the nature of the equipment, the original Nigra tape was erased in the process. The government knew at the time it made the copy that the original would be erased. At trial appellant objected to the introduction of the tape on the ground that it is not the original tape, and that the loss of the original was not inadvertent. The district court, after an extensive voir dire of the undercover agent and the United States Secret Service agent who placed the equipment on the undercover agent, found that the government had presented "prima facie evidence of regularity" and that "there is some guarantee of authenticity," and allowed a portion of the tape to be played for the jury. The court left it to appellant to show that the recording was not the original.

On appeal, appellant cites Rules 1002, 1003, and 1004 of the Federal Rules of Evidence and argues that the tape should not have been admitted because "[a] genuine question is raised as to the authenticity of the original" since "no one ever heard the original tape." Rule 1003 provides:

> A duplicate is admissible to the same extent as an original unless (1) a genuine question is raised as to the authenticity of the original or (2) in the circumstances it would be unfair to admit the duplicate in lieu of the original.

Appellant claims that the district court should not have admitted the tape because the court had no clear and convincing evidence of the accuracy of the tape. We disagree. The court had extensive testimony from the government's participants as to the mechanics of the original recording and the transcription, and the substance of the conversation during which appellant made the statements. Moreover, other than eliciting testimony that the tape was not the original, appellant presented no evidence which raised any question as to the authenticity of the original. "[T]he government made out a prima facie case, by clear and convincing evidence, that the tape [was] what it said ... [T]he tape [is] not inadmissible merely because 'one can conjure up hypothetical possibilities that tampering occurred.' " *United States v. Cortellesso,* 663 F.2d 361, 364 (1st Cir. 1981).

Appellant further argues that the tape should not be admitted under F.R.Evid. 1004 because the original was not inadvertently erased but was deliberately erased. However, Rule 1004 provides that originals are not required if they are lost or destroyed, unless "the proponent lost or destroyed them in bad faith." Appellant makes no allegation of bad faith here, nor can we see any basis for such an allegation. The district court did not abuse its discretion in admitting the tape.

Affirmed.

Class Discussion Questions

1. What was the "clear and convincing" evidence cited by the court that established the prosecutor's proof of the accuracy of the tape recording?

2. Is it enough for the opponent of evidence that is not the original recording to elicit testimony that the tape is not an original? In this case, what kind of evidence might have convinced the judge that the tape was not an original?

3. Is there a difference between deliberate erasure of a tape and erasure in bad faith? Explain your answer.

Application 7-2

In *Needham v. White Laboratories, Inc.,* Anne Needham brought an action against White Laboratories, the manufacturer of dienestrol, a synthetic estrogen. Ms. Needham was the daughter of a woman who took the drug while she was pregnant with Ms. Needham in 1952. In 1974 Ms. Needham learned that she had a rare form of vaginal cancer. In her lawsuit, Ms. Needham claimed that the dienestrol was the proximate cause of her cancer. A jury returned a verdict for Ms. Needham and awarded her $800,000. White Laboratories appealed.

One contention by White Laboratories on appeal was that the trial court erred in permitting an expert witness for Ms. Needham to read into evidence a list of medical titles. An excerpt from the case follows. Note the importance of getting evidence before the jury by establishing a proper foundation using the testimony of a witness.

Needham v. White Laboratories, Inc.
639 F.2d 394 (7th Cir. 1981)

... Dr. Shimkin testified on direct examination that the titles were of articles published before 1952 that discussed the possibility of a relationship between estrogen and cancer. Tr. at 183. On cross-examination he testified that he had not read all of the articles. The trial court accepted the list into evidence, over White's objection, for the limited purpose of showing that White should have known in 1952 that dienestrol could cause cancer. Tr. at 269.

A trial judge may admit a summary of voluminous writings into evidence. Fed.R.Evid. 1006. Admission of summaries is a matter that rests within the sound discretion of the judge. Before a summary is admitted, the proponent must lay a proper foundation as to the admissibility of the material that is summarized and show that the summary is accurate. Needham failed to satisfy either of these requirements.

First, Needham failed to lay a proper foundation as to the admissibility of the articles. The article titles were admitted for the limited purpose of showing that White should have known that dienestrol caused cancer because numerous articles published before 1952 tended to show a relationship between estrogen and cancer. Given this purpose, the articles were relevant only if they discussed a relationship between estrogen and cancer. Dr. Shimkin, the foundational witness, testified that he had not read all of the articles. Tr. at 243. He further testified that some titles on the list did not discuss the relationship between estrogen and cancer at all. Tr. at 254, 258, 265, 267. Dr. Shimkin's testimony failed to show that all the titles were relevant for the limited purpose of demonstrating notice of the relationship between estrogen and cancer.

In addition, Needham failed to show that the list of articles accurately summarized the material contained in the original articles. As a rule, one should not assume that titles are an accurate summation of article contents. Since Dr. Shimkin had not read some of the articles, he was unable to testify that the list of titles accurately reflected and summarized what was contained in the articles.

Because Needham failed to lay an adequate foundation or to demonstrate that the titles were an accurate summary of the articles, the list of article titles should not have been admitted. The trial court abused its discretion in permitting the jury to consider this summary for the limited purpose of showing that White should have known of the relationship between estrogen and cancer.

Class Discussion Questions

1. For what purpose did the trial court admit the list of titles of articles published before 1952?
2. Rule 1006 allows summaries of voluminous material. In this case, the titles of articles constituted a summary.
   a. Considering the purpose for which the article titles were offered, was the list relevant? Explain your answer.
   b. Was the list of titles accurate? Why or why not?

EXERCISES

1. Assume you are a paralegal for the United States Attorney's office in the Northern District of Florida. Your job is to help prepare for the trial of a defendant indicted for conspiracy to import, distribute, and possess marijuana and cocaine with intent to distribute. The trafficking operation engaged in by the defendant involved other parties. A law enforcement agency tape recorded conversations between the defendant and alleged co-conspirators. The tapes recorded incriminating conversations. Unfortunately, the tapes were destroyed by the law enforcement agency as part of standard operating procedure. However, transcripts are available. It is your assignment to develop an argument for admissibility of the transcripts.
   a. Generally, is the original tape required as proof of the contents of the tape? Cite the rule that supports your position.
   b. Cite the rule that provides an avenue for admissibility of the transcripts of the tape recordings, and explain the rationale for admissibility.
   c. Who makes the decision of whether the tape recordings were destroyed in good faith?
   d. What kinds of questions need to be prepared by the prosecutor to establish good faith?
   e. Suggest a witness who can be called to answer the questions in order to lay a proper foundation.
2. In preparing for trial, you are told by your supervising attorney that there is a need to introduce telephone records.
   a. What would constitute the original telephone records?
   b. Assume that the original telephone records are not obtainable. You contact the telephone company for its records of the calls at issue. Should the telephone company's records be characterized as copies or duplicates? Explain your answer, and cite the rule.
3. In preparing for a trial where the plaintiff claims a breach of warranty against a manufacturer of foam insulation that caused the plaintiff's business to be destroyed by fire, the plaintiff inadvertently failed to list a manufacturer's brochure similar to the one destroyed in the fire on the pretrial exhibit list. Because of this mistake, the judge has now sustained the manufacturer's objection to the admission of the brochure into evidence. The plaintiff needs to prove the content of the brochure because the content specifically discusses the manufacturer's warranty.

   Can the plaintiff take the stand and testify to the content of the brochure he read over the objection of the manufacturer? The manufacturer maintains that the testimony is not the best evidence of the contents of the brochure.

RULES REFERENCED IN THIS CHAPTER

NOTES

[1] David L. Schiavone and Reid L. Ashinoff. "Evidentiary Confusion Abounds." *The National Law Journal*. September 12, 1994, Sec. "C," pp. C1, C2.

[2] The telephone number is 1-800-552-DESA.

Witnesses

ROLE OF WITNESSES AT TRIAL

Witness testimony is the primary source of evidence in most trials. As we saw in Chapter 7, witnesses may use demonstrative or illustrative evidence along with their verbal communication. Witnesses tell parts of the story for each party and thus create the basis for the jury's decision.

Often it is the paralegal and investigator who will locate witnesses long before the beginning of the trial. The witnesses called to testify may have given a deposition, outlining the essence of their trial testimony, before the trial.

The parties to a civil suit often testify themselves, hoping to convince the jury of the merit of the claim or defense. In a criminal trial, defendants do not have to testify. Recall that the burden is on the government to offer enough evidence to convince a jury of a defendant's guilt beyond a reasonable doubt. Although the defendant need not testify, or even offer the testimony of others, the government will call witnesses to convince the jury of the defendant's guilt.

Before witnesses take the stand at the trial, the paralegal often has the job of preparing them for the court appearance. Depositions are reviewed and memories jogged. Exhibits are prepared and interpreters are readied when necessary. The witness is told what to expect in the courtroom, including information about exclusion from the courtroom during trial, the oath, and the direct and cross-examination.

The attorneys for the parties are not witnesses; anything that they say to the jury is argument, not evidence. Recall that when the trial begins, the attorneys have the opportunity to present opening statements. Opening statements are not evidence; they are more like a road map of the trial ahead given from the perspective of each party. At the end of the trial, each side makes its closing argument and, again, these are not evidence, either. Closing arguments merely summarize the evidence that was presented by and through the witnesses at trial, from the perspective of each side.

Once the opening statements are completed, the plaintiff in a civil case and the prosecutor in a criminal case begin the presentation of evidence by calling witnesses. The burden of presenting evidence so the case can move forward is on the plaintiff and prosecutor. There is no choice but to call witnesses to the stand or risk dismissal of the case on a motion made by the opponent to the trial court judge.

EXCLUSION OF WITNESSES

Before witnesses are called, one of the parties normally invokes Rule 615 and asks the judge to exclude witnesses who are scheduled to testify at trial. The judge has no discretion in granting the motion. **Exclusion**, sometimes called **sequestration of witnesses**, is required when requested by a party. The purpose is to keep witnesses from hearing other testimony and coloring their testimony accordingly. Rule 615 allows the judge to instruct the witnesses that they are not to discuss their testimony with other witnesses while they are sequestered. The witnesses gather in an area close to the courtroom to wait to be called to testify.

Rule 615. Exclusion of Witnesses

At the request of a party the court shall order witnesses excluded so that they cannot hear the testimony of other witnesses, and it may make the order of its own motion. This rule does not authorize exclusion of (1) a party who is a natural person, or (2) an officer or employee of a party which is not a natural person designated as its representative by its attorney, or (3) a person whose presence is shown by a party to be essential to the presentation of the party's cause.

Who Cannot Be Excluded

The judge can order exclusion even if the parties do not request sequestration of witnesses. Parties to the lawsuit cannot, however, be excluded, because their exclusion would violate constitutional requirements for a fair trial. If a party is

exclusion Keeping witnesses out of the courtroom during a trial.

sequestration of witnesses Keeping witnesses out of the courtroom during trial.

an entity and not a natural person, the entity must be allowed to have a representative present. Rule 615 also permits anyone who has acted as an agent in a transaction, or any expert who is needed to advise either of the party's attorneys on the management of the litigation, to remain present during the trial. Prosecutors are allowed to have the case investigator remain at the table.

The role of the paralegal is to assist the attorney in trial preparation, and this role often carries over to assistance at the trial itself. The attorney who wishes a paralegal to be present at counsel table should ask the judge for permission. Generally, permission is readily given, but it is not automatic. Some judges do not allow any persons not covered in Rule 615 to be present at counsel table. If it is known before trial that the presiding judge excludes paralegals, then other arrangements need to be made to be sure the paralegal is close to the attorney but beyond the bar, which is usually in the first row of spectator seats.

If there is a violation of Rule 615, the judge has several options. The judge can exclude the testimony of the offending witness, comment negatively to the jury on the witness's misconduct, hold the witness in contempt, or declare a mistrial if the conduct is detrimental to a party.

COMPETENCY OF WITNESSES

Generally, under the modern rules, any person called as a witness can testify, because every person is presumed to be a **competent witness**.

Rule 601. General Rule of Competency

Every person is competent to be a witness except as otherwise provided in these rules. However, in civil actions and proceedings, with respect to an element of a claim or defense as to which State law supplies the rule of decision, the competency of a witness shall be determined in accordance with State law.

This was not always the case. At common law, someone without religious beliefs or someone who was a convicted criminal could not testify at trial. Disqualification of atheists and felons was logical within the social context of the period, when the oath a witness took included a promise to tell the truth or risk the wrath of God. Someone without religious beliefs would have no fear of a punishing deity and so, it was thought, would have no compulsion to be truthful. Convicted criminals forfeited a number of rights including the ability to testify at trial.

Today, as long as a witness has the ability to observe, to recollect, to communicate, and to speak truthfully, the witness is deemed competent. Diminished **capacity** goes to the weight of the testimony, not admissibility. For example, a 32-year-old witness who has an intelligent quotient of 54, suffers from cerebral palsy and a severe hearing deficiency, and has the signing ability of a six- to eight-year-old can be found competent to testify.

At common law, parties also were not competent to testify. Again, this is not the rule in federal or state courts today.

competent witness A person legally qualified to testify at trial.

capacity In contract law, the mental ability to enter into a contract.

Oath or Affirmation

Before a witness takes the stand to testify, the witness must swear or affirm that all testimony given will be truthful. This oath or affirmation is to assure the court the potential witness understands the solemnity of the courtroom drama, as well as to demonstrate to the court the witness has an understanding of what it means to tell the truth. In *United States v. Looper*, 419 F.2d 1405, 1407 (4th Cir. 1969), the court cites an evidence treatise in a footnote to describe alternatives to the oath or affirmation statement. To qualify them to tell the truth, English courts permitted a Chinese witness to break a saucer, a Mohammedan to bow before the Koran and touch it to his head, and a Parsee to tie a rope around his waist.

Rule 603.   Oath or Affirmation

Before testifying, every witness shall be required to declare that the witness will testify truthfully, by oath or affirmation administered in a form calculated to awaken the witness' conscience and impress the witness' mind with the duty to do so.

The trial court judge cannot prescribe an oath or deny an alternative without risking violation of a witness's First Amendment rights under the free exercise clause. It is reversible error for a trial court judge to prevent a party from testifying on the basis of religiously based objections to the oath's form (see Illustration 8-1).

Illustration 8-1

The witness proposed an oath: "Do you affirm to speak with fully integrated Honesty, only with fully integrated Honesty and nothing but fully integrated Honesty?" The witness expressed his fervent belief that "fully integrated Honesty" was even more of a commitment to speak truthfully than "truth."

The trial court judge would not allow the witness to take his oath, noting the standard of "truth, whole truth, and nothing but the truth" had not changed for hundreds of years.

The appellate court stated the controlling factor is that the form of the oath needs to be meaningful to the witness. The defendant's conviction was reversed and the case remanded for a new trial. *United States v. Ward*, 989 F.2d 1015, 1017, 1019, 1020 (9th Cir. 1992).

Rule 603 does not prescribe the words for an oath, but generally the judge or clerk asks the witness, "Do you swear or affirm that the evidence you are about to give will be the truth, the whole truth, and nothing but the truth?" Some state rules prescribe the form of the oath or affirmation, although constitutional arguments can also be made in state court.

Failure to Administer Oath

It is possible for a witness to testify without an oath being administered. However, an objection to the failure to swear in a witness is waived unless it is made during or near the time of a witness's testimony. If a party chooses not to recall a witness to administer the oath and repeat the testimony, the lack of an oath is not a basis for an appeal.

The objection is notice to the judge of a mistake that can be corrected by swearing in the witness and allowing the testimony to be repeated under oath (see Illustration 8-2).

Illustration 8-2 _____

Mr. Hawkins was charged with criminal contempt for his failure to testify in a prior court proceeding. The presiding judge at the contempt trial was not the same judge as the original trial court judge.

The defendant appealed his conviction, claiming the state failed to prove his identity; that is, the defendant in the contempt proceeding was the witness who refused to testify in the first trial. The judge in the contempt proceeding asked the prosecutor (the same one for both proceedings) only whether Mr. Hawkins was the same person.

The prosecutor was not administered an oath before questioning by the judge. Since the defendant made a timely objection, the point was preserved for appeal. Because the identity testimony was not admissible owing to no oath being administered to the prosecutor before testifying, an element of the charge was not proven, and the defendant was entitled to a new trial. *United States v. Hawkins,* 76 F.3d 545, 550–552 (4th Cir. 1996).

Dead Man's Statutes

Although generally all witnesses are presumed competent to testify, there is one type of witness some states still recognize as not competent to testify, at least to some degree: persons who have a claim in a civil suit against a dead person's representative, where there are things to which the dead person might have testified. The prohibition is embodied in what traditionally was called the *Dead Man's Statutes*. The paralegal needs to research this issue when the lawsuit involves claims against an estate, not only for state court actions but also for federal actions, since state law applies in federal court with regard to this type of testimony.

Judge Determines Competency

Because witnesses are presumed competent to testify does not mean that their competency cannot be questioned. The trial court judge determines whether a witness is competent when a motion is made to disqualify a witness from testifying. The judge has a great deal of discretion in making the decision on competency, and the discretion usually is exercised in favor of allowing a witness to testify. The jury then determines the weight and credibility of the witness's testimony. The issue of competence is most often raised when the witness is a child or is physically or mentally impaired.

The role of the judge is simply to determine whether the witness has the ability to perceive the events that are the subject of the testimony, the ability to remember those events, and the ability to communicate to the judge and jury. Perception, memory, and communication do not have to be perfect.

Rule 602 addresses the need for the proponent of a witness's testimony to lay a foundation demonstrating the witness has the capacity to perceive accurately and remember what was perceived. In other words, the proponent must show that the witness has personal knowledge of the matter testified to because the witness saw, heard, or otherwise sensed something. If the witness's testimony is merely conjecture as to the matter testified to, then the witness does not have personal knowledge and should not be allowed to testify.

Rule 602.   Lack of Personal Knowledge

A witness may not testify to a matter unless evidence is introduced sufficient to support a finding that the witness has personal knowledge of the matter. Evidence to prove personal knowledge may, but need not, consist of the witness' own testimony. This rule is subject to the provisions of Rule 703, relating to opinion testimony by expert witnesses.

It is the judge who determines whether the proponent of the testimony establishes the witness's personal knowledge when an objection is made by the opponent of the testimony. If the judge determines the witness has the ability to perceive, remember, and communicate, then the jury gets to hear the testimony.

Interpreters Aid Communication

In order to facilitate communication by a witness, interpreters may be used.

Rule 604.   Interpreters

An interpreter is subject to the provisions of these rules relating to qualification as an expert and the administration of an oath or affirmation to make a true translation.

When interpreters are necessary, they must be qualified as **experts**, with a preliminary showing to the court that they have the requisite knowledge and skills. Questions related to education and experience lay the proper foundation for qualifications as an expert. The interpreter must also take an oath or affirm that the translation will be truthful.

Competency of Judge or Juror as a Witness

Although a judge is supposed to disqualify himself or herself from sitting in a case where the judge could be a material witness, Rule 605 makes it clear that in no event can a presiding judge testify in a trial as a witness where the judge is presiding. Neither party has to object; the objection is "automatic," and it is a basis for an appeal.

expert witness A witness who possesses special knowledge, training, or experience and whose testimony at trial includes an opinion.

Rule 605.   Competency of Judge as Witness

The judge presiding at the trial may not testify in that trial as a witness. No objection need be made in order to preserve the point.

A judge cannot provide evidence for either party in a lawsuit, including the gathering of evidence *sua sponte* (see Illustration 8-3).

Illustration 8-3

In a case where a malfunctioning pipe wrapping machine was at issue, the trial court judge sent his law clerk to visit the plant to observe the machine.

The appellate court remanded the case with directions to hold an evidentiary hearing to determine (1) the exact conduct of the judge and the law clerk and (2) whether the defendant knew about and approved of the visit.

The appellate court noted "a judge may not direct his law clerk to do that which is prohibited to the judge." *Price Brothers Co. v. Philadelphia Gear Corp.,* 629 F.2d 444, 447 (6th Cir. 1980).

A federal trial court judge has the power to explain, summarize, and comment on the facts and the evidence as long as the judge does not distort or add to the evidence. When judges exceed their rightful power, they are acting more in the role of a witness, and the verdict is subject to reversal if the error is found by the appellate court to be prejudicial.

Generally, it is inappropriate for a juror to testify in a case on which the juror sits. However, to keep such testimony from being given, opposing counsel must object, and counsel must be allowed to make the objection outside the hearing of the jury.

Rule 606.   Competency of Juror as Witness

(a) At the trial. A member of the jury may not testify as a witness before that jury in the trial of the case in which the juror is sitting. If the juror is called so to testify, the opposing party shall be afforded an opportunity to object out of the presence of the jury.

(b) Inquiry into validity of verdict or indictment. Upon an inquiry into the validity of a verdict or indictment, a juror may not testify as to any matter or statement occurring during the course of the jury's deliberations or to the effect of anything upon that or any other juror's mind or emotions as influencing the juror to assent to or dissent from the verdict or indictment or concerning the juror's mental processes in connection therewith, except that a juror may testify on the question whether extraneous prejudicial information was improperly brought to the jury's attention or whether any outside influence was improperly brought to bear upon any juror. Nor may a juror's affidavit or evidence of any statement by the juror concerning a matter about which the juror would be precluded from testifying be received for these purposes.

sua sponte The judge acts on his or her own, without the parties making a request.

If a party alleges a new trial is necessary because jurors used information not introduced into evidence, such as newspaper articles or books, jurors can testify at the hearing on the motion for a new trial. But the jurors cannot be asked questions related to internal deliberations of the jury. The purpose of Rule 606 is to protect jurors from harassment by the losing party and to bring litigation to an end.

THE JUDGE AND WITNESSES

Generally, the parties are the ones who call witnesses to the stand and who interrogate the witnesses. However, Rule 614 allows the judge to call and question a witness. The judge may also question a witness called by a party. A party may want to object to the action of the judge, especially if the questioning makes it appear the judge is biased. The objection can wait until the jury has left the courtroom, but the objection must be made in time to give the judge an opportunity to take corrective measures. If no objection is made, it is waived, as is the case with other objections, and cannot serve as a basis for an appeal.

Rule 614. Calling and Interrogation of Witnesses by Court

(a) **Calling by court.** The court may, on its own motion or at the suggestion of a party, call witnesses, and all parties are entitled to cross-examine witnesses thus called.

(b) **Interrogation by court.** The court may interrogate witnesses, whether called by itself or by a party.

(c) **Objections.** Objections to the calling of witnesses by the court or to interrogation by it may be made at the time or at the next available opportunity when the jury is not present.

In deciding whether a trial court judge's questioning is inappropriate, an appellate court considers the tone of the interruptions, not just the number. It also considers the extent to which each side is affected, any curative instructions given by the judge, and the nature of the evidence. The judge's conduct does not have to be perfect, but it must not taint the jury (see Illustration 8-4).

Illustration 8-4

The judge interrupted counsel 28 times through the course of a relatively short proceeding. From the transcript, the appellate court concluded the questions to the witnesses by the judge went beyond what a neutral arbiter would be expected to ask.

Although the appellate court refused to condone the conduct of the trial court judge, the questioning by the judge did not result in a reversal of Mr. Tilton's conviction, mainly because the court found the judge's interruptions affected both parties roughly to the same extent. *United States v. Tilton,* 714 F.2d 642, 644, 645 (6th Cir. 1983).

Examination of Witnesses

Each of the parties offers evidence to support its position in the litigation, and then it attempts to erode the opponent's case by cross-examining the opponent's witnesses.

Direct Examination

On **direct examination**, the party who calls the witness to the stand to testify asks questions to elicit responses that reflect the witness's knowledge of issues related to the litigated matter. The questions require responsive narrations from the witness. By the time the questioning is over on direct examination, the jury has learned more about the party's position and begins to form general notions about the merit of the calling party's case. See Illustration 8-5 for an example of how direct examination proceeds.

Illustration 8-5

Following is an observation on conducting direct examination from James W. McElhaney:

> Direct examination is probably the most difficult part of the trial to make come alive. That's because we are steeped in the traditions of formalism and wooden introductions and transitions.
>
> One of the easiest ways to get out of stultified direct examinations is to use the verbs of vision in your questions. For example:
>
> - Could you help the jury see what you saw when you came around the corner?
> - Would you help us picture how cousin Charles was acting when Uncle Waldo signed his will?
> - Doctor, would you let us look through your professional eyes for a moment to help us understand what this impact did to Nick Jensen's spine?
> - Ms. Williams, take us with you to that meeting. Could you show us how people reacted when the chairman announced that the company was going to start making assault rifles?
>
> Make it come alive, but don't milk it. Remember that visual emphasis is like highlighting in a book. Too much, and every page turns a bright yellow in which nothing stands out.[1]

direct examination Questioning of a witness by the party who called the witness to the stand to testify at trial.

cross-examination Questioning of an opposing party's witness during a trial.

Cross-Examination

Opposing counsel has the opportunity to discredit a witness's testimony given on direct examination by bringing out inconsistencies or by impugning the truthfulness of the witness. This process is **cross-examination** of the witness and impeachment (discussed in detail later in this chapter) of the witness's testimony. The credibility of every witness is at issue in a case.

Rule 611. Mode and Order of Interrogation and Presentation

(a) Control of court. The court shall exercise reasonable control over the mode and order of interrogating witnesses and presenting evidence so as to (1) make the interrogation and presentation effective for the ascertainment of the truth, (2) avoid needless consumption of time, and (3) protect witnesses from harassment or undue embarrassment.

(b) Scope of cross-examination. Cross-examination should be limited to the subject matter of the direct examination and matters affecting the credibility of the witness. The court may, in the exercise of discretion, permit inquiry into additional matters as if on direct examination.

(c) Leading questions. Leading questions should not be used on the direct examination of a witness except as may be necessary to develop the witness' testimony. Ordinarily leading questions should be permitted on cross-examination. When a party calls a hostile witness, an adverse party, or a witness identified with an adverse party, interrogation may be by leading questions.

If the attorney questioning the witness unduly harasses or attempts to embarrass the witness, the judge can step in and stop or limit the questioning without waiting for an objection. The judge is supposed to guide the courtroom proceedings so that the questioning of witnesses and the presentation of evidence can lead to the determination of truth in the case. The judge can also decide if the presentation of testimony is a waste of time and thus terminate it. Rule 403 can be the basis for an objection that evidence is a waste of time or a needless presentation of cumulative evidence.

Rule 611 also defines the scope of cross-examination. The party cross-examining the witness can ask questions relating to matters raised by the questions and answers from direct examination. Furthermore, the cross-examining party may inquire into matters that touch on the credibility of the witnesses in an attempt to get the jury to discount the witness's damaging testimony.

Rule 611 touches on the method of asking questions, as well. **Leading questions**, ones that suggest the desired answer and seem to put words in the mouth of the witness, are not appropriate on direct examination unless the questions are related to routine, uncontested matters like identification and background information. On cross-examination, leading questions are not only allowed, but are used extensively as a means to discredit the witness's testimony. Leading questions are also a means of allowing an orderly and predictable development of the evidence.

leading questions
Questions that suggest an answer; usually allowed only on cross-examination of a witness.

hostile witness A witness who shows so much hostility to the calling party that the witness can be treated as if called by the opposing party.

Hostile Witnesses

A party can use leading questions when it calls a **hostile witness**, which is one who does not favor the calling party and is therefore deemed a witness for the opposing party.

Preparation

Whether for direct or cross-examination, before trial, the paralegal can assist the attorney by outlining questions for each of the witnesses. For instance, on direct examination, there may be a need to lay a foundation before the major point of the testimony can be addressed. Because the parties have exchanged interrogatories, and witnesses may have been deposed, cross-examining counsel is aware of the weaknesses of the witness and of the witness's testimony. An attack on the witness's testimony can be planned carefully, and leading questions used effectively. The paralegal can help in this regard with pretrial planning and preparation, utilizing interrogatories, depositions, and investigator's background reports.

IMPEACHMENT

The truthfulness of the witness is of central importance in a trial. A criminal prosecution also has the added factor of the Sixth Amendment right to confront adverse witnesses. Rule 607 allows either party to **impeach**, or attack, the credibility of a witness, regardless of whether the party called the witness to the stand to testify.

Rule 607. Who May Impeach

The credibility of a witness may be attacked by a party, including the party calling the witness.

Rule 607 acknowledges that a party is not vouching for the truthfulness of a witness just by calling the witness.

There are a number of ways to impeach the credibility of a witness's testimony, including (1) offering evidence of the untruthful character of a witness (Rule 608); (2) offering evidence that the witness has been convicted of a crime (Rule 609); (3) offering evidence of prior inconsistent statements of the witness (Rule 613); and (4) generally bringing out the information that the witness is biased or prejudiced, has an interest in the litigation, or has an improper motive for testifying.

Although demonstrating bias is not explicitly addressed in the Rules of Evidence dealing with impeachment, it was allowed by case law predating the Rules of Evidence and is implied in them, as evidenced by the Advisory Committee Notes to Rules 608 and 610. See Illustration 8-6 for a discussion of bias.

Illustration 8-6

In affirming the use of testimony against a witness to impeach the witness's credibility, the United States Supreme Court defined bias:

Bias is a term used ... to describe the relationship between a party and a witness which might lead the witness to slant, unconsciously or otherwise, his testimony in favor of or against a party. Bias may be induced by a witness' like, dislike, or fear of a party, or by the witness' self-interest. Proof of bias is almost always relevant because the jury, as finder of fact and weigher of credibility, has historically been entitled to assess all evidence which might bear on the accuracy and truth of a witness' testimony.

impeach Demonstrate a witness is not telling the truth.

The Court allowed testimony regarding the witness's membership in a prison organization called Aryan Brotherhood. The Court also allowed a description of the tenets of the Aryan Brotherhood because they directly related to the veracity of the witness.

The witness called to impeach the prior witness's testimony alleged that the Aryan Brotherhood had a creed requiring members to deny its existence and to lie for each other. The impeaching testimony had a bearing on the truth of the prior witness's testimony because of the prior witness's membership in the Aryan Brotherhood. *United States v. Abel,* 469 U.S. 45, 48 (1984).

Religious Beliefs

Rule 610 makes it clear that evidence of religious beliefs or opinions cannot be used to impeach the credibility of a witness. On the other hand, religious beliefs cannot be used to enhance the credibility of a witness either.

Rule 610. Religious Beliefs or Opinions

Evidence of the beliefs or opinions of a witness on matters of religion is not admissible for the purpose of showing that by reason of their nature the witness' credibility is impaired or enhanced.

As has been noted throughout the text with regard to other types of evidence, evidence of religious beliefs or opinions might be admissible if offered for a purpose other than credibility of the witness. Religious beliefs could be relevant and probative on the issue of bias on the part of the witness. For instance, the church affiliation of a witness might be the church that is the party calling the witness.

Use of Character Evidence

Rule 608 allows character evidence to be used to impeach the credibility of a witness. Recall Rule 404 prohibits using character evidence to prove someone acted in conformity with a character trait. However, Rule 404 lists exceptions, citing Rules 607, 608, and 609. The definition of character used in Rules 404 and 405 also applies to Rule 608.

Rule 608. Evidence of Character and Conduct of Witness

(a) Opinion and reputation evidence of character. The credibility of a witness may be attacked or supported by evidence in the form of opinion or reputation, but subject to these limitations: (1) the evidence may refer only to character for truthfulness or untruthfulness, and (2) evidence of truthful character is admissible only after the character of the witness for truthfulness has been attacked by opinion or reputation evidence or otherwise.

(b) Specific instances of conduct. Specific instances of the conduct of a witness, for the purpose of attacking or supporting the witness' credibility, other than conviction of crime as provided in Rule 609, may not be proved by extrinsic evidence. They may, however, in the discretion of the court, if probative of truthfulness or untruthfulness, be inquired into on cross-examination of the witness (1) concerning the witness' character for truthfulness or untruthfulness, or (2) concerning the character for truthfulness or untruthfulness of another witness as to which character the witness being cross-examined has testified.

The giving of testimony, whether by an accused or by any other witness, does not operate as a waiver of the accused's or the witness' privilege against self-incrimination when examined with respect to matters which relate only to credibility.

Rule 608 outlines the parameters for using character evidence to impeach a witness. First, the opposing party can call an impeaching witness to testify as to the impeaching witness's opinion of the other witness's character for truthfulness. However, only if the other witness's character has been attacked can another witness testify to and vouch for the truthfulness of the witness's character. This approach is practical, because a trial could go on forever if parties were allowed to bolster the truthful character trait of witnesses without there being an initial attack.

Second, reputation testimony can be used to impeach the credibility of a witness. The impeaching witness is called to the stand and asked about the first witness's reputation in the community for truthfulness. The questioning is done after a proper foundation has been laid to show that the witness had reason to know of the witness's reputation in the community. There must be a demonstration through foundational testimony that the impeaching witness has a long acquaintance during a period of time proximate to the relevant time period related to the litigation.

Specific instances of conduct that point to the untruthful or truthful character of a witness cannot be cited by an impeaching witness. This dichotomy in the form of proof from opinion and reputation testimony versus testimony regarding specific instances was seen in the discussion of Rule 405. To rehabilitate an impeached witness, however, another character witness can be called after the one who did the impeaching, and the second character witness can testify to specific instances of conduct (see Figure 8-1).

Investigation of witnesses' backgrounds prior to trial provides the attorney with information to plan for the impeachment of testimony. The paralegal and the investigator can play an important role in finding appropriate information useful for impeachment.

Conviction of a Crime as Character Evidence

Rule 608 does have an exception to the general rule on proof of character by testimony regarding specific instances. The noted exception is Rule 609, which involves convictions of crimes, themselves specific instances of conduct.

IMPEACHMENT OF INITIAL WITNESS BY CHARACTER WITNESS

Character witness testifies to bad character of witness
with
Opinion and reputation testimony

CHARACTER WITNESS IMPEACHED
using
Specific instances of honest conduct

REHABILITATION OF INITIAL WITNESS
using
Testimony of character witness as to
honesty of initial witness

FIGURE 8-1

Impeached witnesses can be rehabilitated by other character witnesses.

Rule 609.   Impeachment by Evidence of Conviction of Crime

(a) **General rule.** For the purpose of attacking the credibility of a witness,
(1) evidence that a witness other than an accused has been convicted of a crime shall be admitted, subject to Rule 403, if the crime was punishable by death or imprisonment in excess of one year under the law under which the witness was convicted, and evidence that an accused has been convicted of such a crime shall be admitted if the court determines that the probative value of admitting this evidence outweighs its prejudicial effect to the accused; and
(2) evidence that any witness has been convicted of a crime shall be admitted if it involved dishonesty or false statement, regardless of the punishment.
(b) **Time limit.** Evidence of a conviction under this rule is not admissible if a period of more than ten years has elapsed since the date of the conviction or of the release of the witness from the confinement imposed for that conviction, whichever is the later date, unless the court determines, in the interests of justice, that the probative value of the conviction supported by specific facts and circumstances substantially outweighs its prejudicial effect. However, evidence of a conviction more than 10 years old as calculated herein, is not admissible unless the proponent gives to the adverse party sufficient advance written notice of intent to use such evidence to provide the adverse party with a fair opportunity to contest the use of such evidence.
(c) **Effect of pardon, annulment, or certificate of rehabilitation.** Evidence of a conviction is not admissible under this rule if (1) the conviction has been the subject of a pardon, annulment, certificate of rehabilitation, or other equivalent procedure based on a finding of the rehabilitation of the person convicted, and that person has not been convicted of a subsequent crime which was punishable by death or imprisonment in excess of one year, or (2) the conviction has been the subject of a pardon, annulment, or other equivalent procedure based on a finding of innocence.

(d) Juvenile adjudications. Evidence of juvenile adjudications is generally not admissible under this rule. The court may, however, in a criminal case allow evidence of a juvenile adjudication of a witness other than the accused if conviction of the offense would be admissible to attack on the credibility of an adult and the court is satisfied that admission in evidence is necessary for a fair determination of the issue of guilt or innocence.

(e) Pendency of appeal. The pendency of an appeal therefrom does not render evidence of a conviction inadmissible. Evidence of the pendency of an appeal is admissible.

Although Rule 609 allows the use of character evidence in the form of conviction of a crime for attacking the credibility of a witness, admissibility is subject to a number of limitations:

1. The witness against whom the evidence of conviction of a crime is used must be someone other than the accused.
2. The Rule 403 balancing test is applied predominantly in civil cases.
3. The crime that was the basis for the conviction must be punishable by imprisonment for more than one year or by death.
4. The conviction cannot be older than ten years from the date of the conviction or of the release of the witness from imprisonment to the date of the testimony, unless prior notice is given.
5. Evidence of juvenile adjudications cannot be used unless necessary for a fair determination of guilt of the defendant.

If a conviction is for dishonesty or false statement, the punishment the witness was subject to does not matter. The conviction can still be used to impeach the credibility of the witness. But a conviction cannot be used to impeach if the witness received a pardon based on rehabilitation or innocence. Only if the conviction is still in the appellate process at the time the testimony is solicited, can the conviction be used to impeach the witness, although here the proponent of the witness's testimony can bring out the fact of the appeal in an attempt to repair the damage to the witness's credibility. This effort would be made on **redirect examination**.

In a criminal case, the judge must apply a test that tends to favor exclusion of evidence of a conviction of a previous crime if the witness is the accused. There are constitutional considerations in a criminal case. The theory is the accused will not receive a fair trial when this type of impeachment is allowed because the jury will use it improperly. Therefore, if the jury could conclude from the prior conviction that the accused is guilty of the current charge, the evidence will be excluded. The prejudice of the prior conviction is too great.

When a criminal conviction can be used, it can be proven by cross-examining the witness or by introducing the public record of the conviction into evidence in the event the witness denies the criminal conviction. Often the use of a prior conviction is argued to the trial court judge before trial, since the balancing test may result in the exclusion of the prior conviction because of its unfair impact on the jury.

Whether done before or during trial, the paralegal should confirm relevant information and get copies of documents proving the conviction. It is not

redirect examination
Questioning of a witness by the party calling the witness after the witness has been cross-examined.

uncommon for individuals to have the same or very similar names. In a trial in state court in Florida, a party planned to offer evidence of a criminal conviction of a witness to impeach the witness's testimony. The proponent of the witness's testimony objected, claiming that the witness and the convicted felon were not the same person, even though the names were the same. The proponent of the witness's testimony offered to withdraw the objection to the impeachment evidence if the opposing party could prove the witness and the convicted felon were the same person. The judge ordered the witness fingerprinted but let cross-examination continue. The witness denied she ever had a criminal conviction, and she stated the social security number on the record was not hers. On redirect, the proponent of the witness got the fingerprints taken in court admitted into evidence. The fingerprints were not the same as those on the criminal record.

The judge had to instruct the jury to disregard any reference to a prior conviction because the criminal record did not belong to the witness. A motion for a mistrial was made because the proponent of the witness believed the jury could not disregard the issue of the mistaken identity.

This example illustrates poor preparation by the party impeaching the witness; that party should have verified that the record of the criminal conviction belonged to the witness.[2]

Assuming a felony conviction is used to impeach the character of a witness, basically the only question that can be asked by the impeaching party is whether the witness has been convicted of a felony. On redirect, the proponent of the witness can rehabilitate the witness by asking questions relating to the circumstances surrounding the conviction, which might take away some of the effectiveness of the conviction for impeachment purposes.

Prior Inconsistent Statements

Another way to impeach a witness's testimony is to show that the witness made a statement before the trial inconsistent with the witness's in-court testimony.

Rule 613. Prior Statement of Witnesses

(a) **Examining witness concerning prior statement.** In examining a witness concerning a prior statement made by the witness, whether written or not, the statement need not be shown nor its contents disclosed to the witness at that time, but on request the same shall be shown or disclosed to opposing counsel.

(b) **Extrinsic evidence of prior inconsistent statement of witness.** Extrinsic evidence of prior inconsistent statement by a witness is not admissible unless the witness is afforded an opportunity to explain or deny the same and the opposite party is afforded an opportunity to interrogate the witness thereon, or the interests of justice otherwise require. This provision does not apply to admissions of a party-opponent as defined in Rule 801(d)(2).

Under Rule 613, the statement can be oral or in writing. If the statement is in writing, it must be supplied to the attorney who called the witness to the stand. The prior oral or written statement is not admissible into evidence if it does not come under one of the exceptions to the hearsay rule or is not defined as non-hearsay. Rules 801, 803, and 804 are dealt with in the chapters on hearsay evidence. Even if the statement is hearsay, it can be effectively used to demonstrate the lack of credibility on the part of the witness. The statement can be used to impeach the testimony of the witness even though it cannot be used as substantive evidence by the jury.

REFRESHING THE MEMORY OF A WITNESS

Finally, a witness on the stand may suffer a lapse in memory on a particular issue and be unable to answer questions on direct examination. If this happens when the witness is on the stand, the questioning attorney can provide the witness with a document to jog the witness's memory. The document must be marked for identification (it is not admissible into evidence at this point) and shown to the witness. After the witness has read the document, and the witness's memory is refreshed, the witness should be able to proceed to answer the questions without reference to the document.

Rule 612.   Writing Used to Refresh Memory

Except as otherwise provided in criminal proceedings by section 3500 of title 18, United States Code, if a witness uses a writing to refresh memory for the purpose of testifying, either—
   (1) while testifying, or
   (2) before testifying, if the court in its discretion determines it is necessary in the interests of justice,
an adverse party is entitled to have the writing produced at the hearing, to inspect it, to cross-examine the witness thereon, and to introduce in evidence those portions which relate to the testimony of the witness. If it is claimed that the writing contains matters not related to the subject matter of the testimony the court shall examine the writing in camera, excise any portions not so related, and order delivery of the remainder to the party entitled thereto. Any portion withheld over objections shall be preserved and made available to the appellate court in the event of an appeal. If a writing is not produced or delivered pursuant to order under this rule, the court shall make any order justice requires, except that in criminal cases when the prosecution elects not to comply, the order shall be one striking the testimony or, if the court in its discretion determines that the interests of justice so require, declaring a mistrial.

Extra copies need to be made so a copy of the document can be given to opposing counsel. Opposing counsel can ask the trial court judge to admit part or all of the document into evidence, but the proponent of the evidence is not allowed to offer any part of the document.

Sometimes a witness will prepare for testimony by reading over documents before taking the stand. The paralegal who helps prepare witnesses before trial should caution the witnesses that any documents consulted to refresh memory for trial testimony can be obtained by the opposing party. It is within the discretion of the trial court judge to order production of the document for opposing counsel to review. Generally it is better to avoid the problem by cautioning witnesses during trial preparation about the use of documents to refresh their memories. If opposing counsel lays a proper foundation, showing that the witness relied on the documents or that the documents influenced the witness's testimony, the trial court judge likely will order the document be given to the opposing side.

SUMMARY

Article VI of the Federal Rules of Evidence can be divided into two categories. One category deals with eliciting testimony of witnesses in general. The other deals with impeachment and cross-examination (see Figure 8-2).

Generally, all persons are competent to testify at trial as long as they have personal knowledge of the events to which they are testifying, they can remember the event, they can communicate their testimony, and they appreciate what it means to be truthful. If a witness does not speak English, an interpreter can be used, but the interpreter must be qualified. The interpreter must also take an oath to interpret the witness's testimony truthfully.

WITNESS TESTIMONY IN GENERAL

Rule 601. General Rule of Competency
Rule 602. Lack of Personal Knowledge
Rule 603. Oath or Affirmation
Rule 604. Interpreters
Rule 605. Competency of Judge as Witness
Rule 606. Competency of Juror as Witness
Rule 611. Mode and Order of Interrogation and Presentation
Rule 612. Writing Used to Refresh Memory
Rule 614. Calling and Interrogation of Witnesses by Court
Rule 615. Exclusion of Witnesses

IMPEACHMENT AND CROSS-EXAMINATION

Rule 607. Who May Impeach
Rule 608. Evidence of Character and Conduct of Witness
Rule 609. Impeachment of Evidence of Conviction of Crime
Rule 620. Religious Beliefs or Opinions
Rule 613. Prior Statements of Witness

FIGURE 8-2

Article VI of the Federal Rules of Evidence includes rules for dealing with witness testimony in general and, specifically, with impeachment and cross-examination.

A presiding judge cannot be a witness at the trial. The trial court judge can call witnesses and question them as long as the judge does not demonstrate any bias.

Jurors can be called as witnesses only after the verdict has been rendered, when there is an allegation of improper use of material not introduced as evidence during the trial. Jurors cannot be questioned regarding internal deliberations.

Before testimony begins at trial, usually the witnesses are told to wait outside the courtroom until it is time to testify. However, parties or their representatives cannot be excluded from the proceedings.

The credibility of the testimony of any witness can be impeached with evidence of dishonesty, conviction of a crime, prior inconsistent statements, or actions demonstrating bias or prejudice. Unless indicative of bias in a particular case, religious beliefs or opinions cannot be the basis for impeachment of testimony.

The order in which witnesses are called to the stand is left to the parties to determine. If testimony by an early witness is never proven to be related to an issue in a case, the testimony can be stricken from the record and the jury instructed by the trial court judge to disregard the stricken testimony.

If a witness uses documents to refresh the witness's memory before trial, the documents can be obtained by opposing counsel, who then has the option to offer them into evidence.

✔ CHECKPOINTS

❑ Witnesses at trial
  1. Witnesses are often excluded from the courtroom.
  2. Witnesses are competent to testify under oath if they have the ability to perceive an event, recall it, and communicate it.
  3. Dead Man's Statutes, based on state law, govern who can testify in actions related to claims against a dead person.
  4. Judge determines competence to testify.
  5. Interpreters can be used.
  6. Presiding judge cannot be a witness.
  7. Jurors cannot testify regarding deliberations except in regard to allegations of use of material not admitted into evidence.

❑ Examination of witnesses
  1. Direct examination is by calling party.
  2. Cross-examination is by opposing party.

  3. Redirect examination is by calling party after cross-examination.
  4. Parties do not vouch for truthfulness of own witnesses, so all witnesses can be considered hostile and subject to cross-examination.

❑ Impeachment of witness's testimony
  1. Generally questions cannot be asked about religious beliefs.
  2. Character evidence can be used.
  3. Generally conviction of a crime can be used against witnesses other than accused.
  4. Prior inconsistent statements can be used.

❑ Refreshing memory before testimony at trial
  1. Documents used can be obtained by opponent.
  2. Opponent can offer documents into evidence.

✎ APPLICATIONS

Application 8-1

In the following case, Kenneth Varlack sued SWC Caribbean, Inc., doing business as Orange Julius Restaurant, and Bernett Cannings, an employee of Orange Julius. Mr. Varlack contended Mr. Cannings injured him when refusing to allow Mr. Varlack into the restaurant near closing time. Mr. Cannings hit Mr. Varlack with a two-by-four, leaving him so dazed and angry that he punched out a window and then accidently fell through another window. The injuries resulted in the amputation of Mr. Varlack's arm 8 inches below the shoulder. There was no jury; the judge decided matters of law as well as the facts.

When the complaint was first filed by Mr. Varlack, the employee who hit him was designated as "an Unknown Employee of Orange Julius Restaurant." Mr. Cannings was not substituted as a party until after the trial started. Mr. Varlack, on the first day of the trial, asked the court to sequester the witnesses. The court did so, excluding from the trial a representative of SWC Caribbean and Mr. Cannings. This was an issue on appeal raised by the defendants against whom the trial court judge entered a verdict.

Varlack v. SWC Caribbean, Inc.
550 F.2d 171 (3d Cir. 1977)

B.

Defendant's second argument is that the court violated F.R. Evidence 615 and the constitutional guarantee of due process to the extent it sequestered defendant, Cannings and Cyril Creque, the principal officer and owner of defendant SWC Caribbean, Inc.

1. Early on the first day of trial, Varlack's counsel requested that the witnesses be sequestered. When the court granted this request, counsel for SWC Caribbean, Inc. asked that an exception be made for Cyril Creque, whom he described as "a former owner of the corporation." The court refused, saying that "[i]f he is going to testify to the merits of the case, he must be sequestered." After Creque had testified, the court reversed its earlier decision and allowed him to sit at the counsel's table, saying that "I did not realize you were the owner of the place."

We conclude that SWC Caribbean's reliance on Rule 615 is misplaced. Since the company is not a natural person, it cannot make use of Rule 615(1). Moreover, sequestering Creque did not violate SWC Caribbean's rights under Rule 615(2), since the description of Creque by SWC's attorney as "a former owner of the corporation" did not designate him with sufficient clarity as a corporate representative. Finally, SWC Caribbean did not demonstrate on this record that Creque's presence was "essential to the presentation of [its] cause" within the meaning of Rule 615(3). Since SWC Caribbean did not describe Creque's present status with sufficient clarity, its due process claim is also groundless.

2. The district court's failure to allow defendant Cannings to be present at the trial until he had been formally named as a party raises different considerations.

The district court was apparently of the opinion that Cannings had no right to be present under Rule 615(1) until he had been formally named as a party. On the other hand, the court also felt that it was permissible to put off ruling on the motion to amend the Complaint to formally name Cannings until Varlack and an eyewitness of the events at Orange Julius had testified. Thus, Cannings was sequestered during some of the most important testimony in the case.

We conclude that the procedure employed by the district court impermissibly nullified Cannings' important right to be represented during trial; thus, the judgment of the district court as to him will be reversed, and the case remanded for a new trial as to him on all issues. Since Rule 615 requires reversal, we express no opinion on Cannings' due process argument.

The judgment of the district court as to Cannings will be reversed, and the case remanded for a new trial ...

Class Discussion Questions

1. What was the reasoning of the appellate court in concluding that Rule 615 was not violated when the trial court judge excluded Cyril Creque?

2. The appellate court found the trial court judge violated Rule 615 as it applied to Mr. Cannings because

Mr. Cannings was excluded (sequestered) for part of the trial. Explain the court's reasoning.

3. What were the consequences of the trial court judge's decision to exclude Mr. Cannings?

Application 8-2

United States v. Ell
718 F.2d 291 (9th Cir. 1983)

FERGUSON, Circuit Judge:

Henrietta Faye Ell appeals her conviction for uttering an altered government check. Ell contends that the district court committed reversible error during trial when it allowed the rebuttal testimony of government witnesses who were permitted to remain in the courtroom during the testimony of other witnesses. The defendant had requested that they be excluded pursuant to Rule 615 of the Federal Rules of Evidence. We agree that it was error for the district court not to exclude the witnesses from the courtroom upon defendant's request. We remand for a finding of whether allowing the testimony was harmless error.

FACTS

On April 16, 1982, defendant Ell cashed a United States Treasury check in the altered amount of $867.63. Government records indicated that the check had been made out for the sum of $67.63. Ell testified that when she received the check in the mail, the amount was already $867.63, and that she was not aware that the check had been altered at the time she cashed it. After a two-day jury trial, Ell was convicted of the felony of uttering an altered check. 18 U.S.C. § 495.

At trial, three of the prosecution's witnesses were Roberta DesRosier; Diana Wippert, Ell's sister-in-law; and Merlin Wippert, Ell's brother. During Ms. Wippert's testimony, Ell noticed that DesRosier, who had already testified in the prosecution's case-in-chief, was still present in the courtroom. The prosecution indicated that DesRosier might later be called as a rebuttal witness. Ell moved to have DesRosier excluded from the courtroom during the testimony of the other witnesses. The court denied the motion on the ground that DesRosier had already testified in the case-in-chief. Similarly, Ell's requests to have Diana Wippert and Merlin Wippert excluded from the courtroom after their testimony in the prosecution's case-in-chief were also denied. Ell renewed her objections when Ms. Wippert and DesRosier were allowed to give rebuttal testimony. Ell additionally moved for a mistrial and later for a new trial on the sequestration issue. These motions were also denied.

I. Application of Rule 615

Rule 615 of the Federal Rules of Evidence provides in pertinent part: "At the request of a party the court <u>shall</u> order witnesses excluded so that they cannot hear the testimony of other witnesses, and it may make the order on its own motion. ..." (Emphasis added). The rule makes the exclusion of witnesses a matter of right and the decision is no longer committed to the court's discretion as it once was. Fed. R. Evid. 615 advisory committee note. This circuit and others have applied the rule to rebuttal witnesses, although it is not clear from the cases whether the rebuttal witnesses also testified in the prosecution's case-in-chief.

The Government urges that Rule 615 is not applicable to rebuttal witnesses when those witnesses have already given testimony in the case-in-chief. It asserts that exclusion is not required because the jury will have the opportunity to weigh the credibility of the rebuttal testimony in light of the testimony previously given by the witness in the case-in-chief. We reject this contention. The purpose of the rule is to prevent witnesses from "tailoring" their testimony to that of earlier witnesses and to aid in detecting testimony that is less than candid. These concerns are just as valid for a rebuttal witness who has already testified in the case-in-chief as they are for a primary witness. A witness may wish to tailor rebuttal testimony to conform to that of other witnesses as well as to cover up inconsistencies in earlier testimony that have been revealed by the other witnesses. See 6 J. Wigmore, <u>Evidence</u> § 1840 (Chadbourn rev. 1976) ("[The time for sequestration] continues for each witness after he has left the stand, because it is frequently necessary to recall a witness in consequence of a later witness' testimony."). Thus, we hold that it was error for the district court to refuse to exclude the government witnesses from the courtroom upon Ell's request.

The Government next contends that even if it was error for the district court not to exclude the government witnesses, the error is not reversible since Ell has failed to demonstrate any significant prejudice.

This court has yet to adopt a standard of review for a trial court's noncompliance with Rule 615. This case is not controlled by those Ninth Circuit cases that consider the appropriate remedy when a witness violates an exclusionary order issued pursuant to Rule 615. Those cases commit to the discretion of the trial court the appropriate sanction for a witness' violation of an exclusionary order. In the above cases, the district court fully complied with Rule 615; the witnesses individually violated the court order issued pursuant to the rule. In the case at bar, however, the <u>court</u> failed to comply with Rule 615 when it refused to issue the exclusionary order.

A number of circuits have held that the district court's erroneous denial of an exclusion request does not mandate reversal absent a showing of prejudice. Other courts have suggested, without reaching the question, that noncompliance with the rule may mandate automatic reversal. Finally, several states have adopted an approach which presumes that a violation of the rule prejudiced the defendant and thus requires reversal unless the contrary is manifestly clear from the record or unless the prosecution proves that there was no prejudice.

We choose to adopt the last approach. Witness sequestration cases present the sort of situation in which it is grossly unfair to place the burden on the defendant to establish prejudice. It may be impossible to tell how a witness' testimony would have differed had the defendant's motion to exclude been granted. Therefore, we hold that when a court fails to comply with Rule 615, prejudice is presumed and reversal is required unless it is manifestly clear from the record that the error was harmless or unless the prosecution proves harmless error by a preponderance of the evidence.

On the basis of the record before us, we cannot conclude as a matter of law that allowing the rebuttal testimony of DesRosier and Ms. Wippert after they had been permitted to listen to the testimony of the other witnesses was harmless error. The credibility of both witnesses was at issue. Their rebuttal testimony may have served to rehabilitate them in the eyes of the jury. Therefore, we remand to the district court for a finding of whether the error was harmless. The prosecution will have the burden of proving harmless error by a preponderance of the evidence. Upon the district court's determination, the case will be returned to this panel.

REMANDED.

Class Discussion Questions

1. Generally, does Rule 615 apply to rebuttal witnesses? Does it matter if the rebuttal witness did not testify in a party's case-in-chief? Explain the reasoning of the appellate court.

2. For what period of time does the invocation of Rule 615 apply to witnesses? Explain why.

3. From this case, it appears that not all of the federal appeals courts agree on the consequences of erroneously denying an exclusion request. Explain the differences.

4. What are the consequences of a violation of Rule 615 by a federal trial court judge in your state?

Application 8-3

Government of the Virgin Islands v. Testamark
528 F.2d 742 (3d Cir. 1976)

OPINION OF THE COURT

ALDISERT, Circuit Judge.

This appeal, following sentence for a criminal conviction, raises questions relating to the impeachment of appellant's credibility ...

Appellant was charged with rape in the first degree, 14 V.I.C. § 1701(3), and unlawful entry, 14 V.I.C. § 445. A jury found him guilty of the lesser included offenses of aggravated assault and battery, 14 V.I.C. § 298(5), and trespass, 14 V.I.C. § 1741. The court imposed a concurrent sentence of one-year imprisonment. On appeal, appellant contends that the trial court improperly took judicial notice for impeachment purposes of a prior conviction for petit larceny; ... We reverse the judgment of conviction, for the evidentiary error only, and order a new trial.

The facts relevant to this appeal are not controverted. At trial appellant took the stand in his own defense. On cross-examination, the prosecutor deliberately asked appellant if he had previously been convicted in the Virgin Islands of petit larceny. Appellant said that he could not recall. The prosecutor sought to prove the conviction. The better practice would have been to present official copies of the conviction records. Instead, the district court took judicial notice of court records, stating: "[W]e will take judicial notice and accept as an established fact that on or about the 10th of December, 1966, Paul Leroy Testamark was convicted of petit larceny ..." We find no error in the procedure the court utilized to place the conviction before the jury for impeachment purposes. See Berkowitz v. Philadelphia Chewing Gum Corp., 303 F.2d 585 (3d Cir. 1962); F.R.Evid. 609(a) and 201(b).

Notwithstanding the foregoing, we do find reversible error in the district court's decision to place this evidence before the jury. Although this issue—the Government's use of petit larceny conviction for impeachment purposes—was not briefed, counsel did preserve the point at trial, and argued it to us.

We have held that a Virgin Islands conviction for petit larceny does not, ipso facto, qualify as a misdemeanor in the nature of crimen falsi so as to be admissible for impeachment purposes under the law of this circuit. Accordingly, such a conviction could not be used to impeach credibility in a trial conducted before the effective date of the new Federal Rules of Evidence; only conviction for felonies or for misdemeanors in the nature of crimen falsi could be used for such purposes. The trial in this case began on July 15, 1975—two weeks after the effective date of the new federal rules. But the new rules do not change this court's traditional rule relating to the types of misdemeanors which may be used for impeachment purposes. Rather, as we noted in Toto, supra, "the congressionally enacted Federal Rule tracks the substance of our long-standing practice." Accordingly, we hold that the district court erred in allowing evidence of the prior conviction for petit larceny to come in for the purpose of impeaching appellant's credibility. Because the jury's ultimate factual determinations in the case depended largely on its assessment of the credibilities of various witnesses, we cannot dismiss this error as harmless error.

The judgment of sentence and conviction will be reversed because of evidentiary error only. The proceedings will be remanded for a new trial.

Class Discussion Questions

1. What is the best way to prove a conviction that is used to discredit a witness's testimony?

2. Define *crimen falsi*.

3. What does it mean to say petit larceny is not in the nature of *crimen falsi*?

4. What is the significance of the court's holding that petit larceny (a misdemeanor) is not in the nature of *crimen falsi*?

5. Why was not proof of the conviction for petit larceny held to be harmless error?

EXERCISES

1. The firm's client is a defendant charged with the murder of a woman and the burglary of her apartment. The client contends that four other persons committed these acts and he merely remained in the car, thinking that the apartment was a "drug house" and the four were buying narcotics.

   As the paralegal assisting the defendant's attorney, you investigate the witnesses who will be called by the prosecutor to testify against the defendant. You learn that two of the main witnesses are addicted to drugs and used drugs near the time of the crime.

   You also learn that one of the witnesses has been diagnosed as schizophrenic. This witness also is unable to perform simple mathematical calculations and has a poor memory of recent events because of some amnesia. These problems are compounded by brain damage and a history of serious drug abuse.

   a. With regard to the witnesses who have admitted drug addictions, will the defendant's attorney be allowed to impeach the testimony of these witnesses by delving into their general use of heroin and the particular use of heroin on the night of the murder? Explain your answer, citing the appropriate rule.

   b. Frame an argument challenging the competency of the schizophrenic witness.

   c. Argue for the competency of this same witness.

2. The government's chief witness against your firm's client has a record of psychiatric disorders. She is the key witness in the government's case alleging fraud on the part of the client. The firm's client is an attorney who was an investor and founder of a company that provided physical therapy to injured persons pursuant to doctors' prescriptions.

   In your investigation, you have located medical records that hurt the credibility of the key witness. Excerpts of these records follow:

   (1) From a summary of a Minnesota Multiphasic Personality Inventory (MMPI) Report:

   > She is inclined to be overly sensitive to the responses and intentions of those around her. She chronically misinterprets the words and actions of others, which leads to difficulties in her interpersonal relationships.

   (2) From the medical file of the witness's treating psychiatrist:

   > A letter describing the patient as "very cynical about both doctors and lawyers and regales one with many very involved intrigues and treacheries of which she feels she has evidence in the medical and legal profession. She predicts that eventually she will kill herself. She is obviously very emotionally unstable with marked hysterical features."

(3) From the consultation report of another psychiatrist:

Conversion Reaction with dissociative traits. [The patient] has all the classical symptoms of a Hysterical Personality in all aspects of her past life history, her interpersonal relationships, her marital histories, and her personal psychological maladjustments.

The records were prepared during the period the witness instigated and participated in an investigation of the defendant.

a. Is this medical information evidence of character (moral inducements for truthfulness) or of mental capacity for truthfulness?
b. Which rule applies, Rule 607 and impeachment by cross-examination, or Rule 608 and impeachment by character evidence?
c. The government states these records are confidential and it is the better social policy that psychiatric medical records remain confidential. How should the defendant respond?

RULES REFERENCED IN THIS CHAPTER

Rule 615. Exclusion of Witnesses

Rule 601. General Rule of Competency

Rule 603. Oath or Affirmation

Rule 602. Lack of Personal Knowledge

Rule 604. Interpreters

Rule 605. Competency of Judge as Witness

Rule 606. Competency of Juror as Witness

Rule 614. Calling and Interrogation of Witnesses by Court

Rule 611. Mode and Order of Interrogation and Presentation

Rule 607. Who May Impeach

Rule 610. Religious Beliefs or Opinions

Rule 608. Evidence of Character and Conduct of Witness

Rule 609. Impeachment by Evidence of Conviction of Crime

Rule 613. Prior Statement of Witness

Rule 612. Writing Used to Refresh Memory

NOTES

[1] James W. McElhaney. "Making Evidence." *ABA Journal,* September 1995, pp. 84–85. Copyright (1995) by James W. McElhaney of Case Western Reserve University School of Law, Cleveland, Ohio. Reprinted with permission of the copyright holder.

[2] *State v. Divisconte,* Escambia County Court, First Judicial Circuit, Pensacola, Florida. February 10, 1995.

Lay and Expert Witnesses

WITNESSES AND OPINION TESTIMONY

Witnesses and their testimony in general were the subjects of Chapter 8. This chapter covers the rules that relate to witnesses who offer a specific type of testimony, testimony based on opinion.

Article VII of the Federal Rules of Evidence divides witnesses who offer testimony that incorporates an opinion into two categories: lay witnesses and expert witnesses. Rule 701 deals with nonprofessional people, or **lay witnesses** who give opinion testimony. Rules 702 through 705 apply to witnesses who qualify as **expert witnesses** because they have special knowledge or experience, and Rule 706 provides for the appointment of expert witnesses by the trial court judge.

lay witness A nonprofessional witness whose testimony at trial includes an opinion.

expert witness A witness who possesses special knowledge, training, or experience and whose testimony at trial includes an opinion.

OPINION TESTIMONY OF LAY WITNESSES

Lay opinion testimony often involves impressions and conclusions of nonprofessional witnesses. Generally, lay opinion testimony is admissible to prove such things as general appearance or condition of a person (elderly, strong, or drunk); sense recognition (heavy, purple, bitter in taste); identity or likeness of appearance, voice, or handwriting; speed of a vehicle; value of property; rationality of conduct; or nature of an agreement. A lay witness does not have to testify in the same manner as an expert witness.

> [A] witness who testifies that an individual whom he saw staggering or lurching along the way was drunk is spared the difficulty of describing, with the precision of an orthopedist or choreographer, the person's gait, angle of walk, etc. *Asplundh Manufacturing Division v. Benton Harbor Engineering,* 57 F.3d 1190, 1196 (3d Cir. 1995).

Of course, the matter that is the subject of the lay witness's testimony must be relevant to the lawsuit and what must be proven by a party.

Rule 701. Opinion Testimony by Lay Witnesses

If the witness is not testifying as an expert, the witness' testimony in the form of opinions or inferences is limited to those opinions or inferences which are (a) rationally based on the perception of the witness and (b) helpful to a clear understanding of the witness' testimony or the determination of a fact in issue.

Opinion Based on Personal Knowledge

Rule 701(a) requires, first, a witness have personal knowledge of the subject of the testimony and, second, the opinion be rationally based on personal knowledge. The requirement of personal knowledge by the witness is also seen in Rule 602, Lack of Personal Knowledge, discussed in Chapter 8. All witnesses must have the ability to perceive an event, remember the event, and communicate regarding the event. If a witness's testimony includes an opinion, the basis for the opinion must rationally relate to the knowledge of the event.

A rational basis for an opinion may be one grounded on experience or specialized knowledge, which is demonstrated when the questioning attorney lays a foundation with appropriate questions. The opinion testimony of this kind of lay witness is beyond impressions and conclusions, and it tends to approach expert opinion under Rule 702, particularly if the witness has specialized knowledge. The federal circuit courts have differed to some extent on how much of a lay witness's opinion testimony is allowable when the testimony is technical, especially where the lay witness "might have qualified" as an expert. The limit of lay opinion testimony appears to be reached when the questioning touches on hypothetical situations rather than matters within the personal knowledge of the lay witness.

Some states are more specific in their rules of evidence about lay opinions requiring no special knowledge, skill, experience, or training, in contrast to expert opinions. Thus, some state rules create a brighter line between lay and expert witness testimony than exists in federal court. This issue of lay versus expert opinion is one for the paralegal to research for state court where state rules apply. And if the case is in federal court, the relevant circuit court opinion must be researched, along with the decisions in other circuits in order to gain a full understanding of the admissibility of lay opinion testimony where the testimony is of a technical nature.

Opinion Helpful to Jury

Rule 701(b) outlines a second predicate to admissibility of opinion testimony by a lay witness. The trial court judge makes a preliminary determination that the opinion testimony will either help clarify for the jury the witness's testimony or will help the jury determine a fact disputed by the parties to the litigation.

Rule 701 is a practical rule, because witnesses tend to express themselves in terms of personal opinion or a conclusion based on personal knowledge. It is often difficult to distinguish between testimony relating facts and testimony relating opinions. The difficulty is short-circuited by Rule 701, which makes opinion testimony by nonexpert witnesses admissible as long as the witnesses have personal knowledge and the testimony is helpful in resolving issues in the case.

Opinion on Ultimate Issue

Rule 704 allows the lay witness to testify with an opinion even if it involves an issue that is an "ultimate issue" in a case and a matter for the jury to decide.

Rule 704. Opinion on Ultimate Issue

(a) Except as provided in subdivision (b), testimony in the form of an opinion or inference otherwise admissible is not objectionable because it embraces an ultimate issue to be decided by the trier of fact.

Rule 704(a) abolishes what was known as the *ultimate-issue rule:* if the witness's testimony was an opinion or conclusion that was a matter the jury had to decide to resolve a case, the witness could not testify with that opinion. Because the ultimate-issue rule was cumbersome and interfered with providing the jury with relevant testimony, it was abolished under Rule 704(a). The jury decides the credibility of a witness and a witness's testimony, and the jury is not bound by the opinion of a witness. So even when a lay witness testifies with an opinion on an ultimate issue in the case, the jury decides whether to accept the opinion. The jury is not bound by the opinion of the lay witness. The jury decides how much weight to give the testimony.

OPINION TESTIMONY OF EXPERT WITNESSES ⎯⎯⎯⎯⎯⎯

> An expert is someone who wasn't there when it happened, but who for a fee will gladly imagine what it must have been like.
>
> University of Texas law professor, Michael Tigar[1]

Unlike a lay witness, an expert witness need not have first-hand knowledge of an event as a basis for the expert's testimony. However, the witness must first qualify as an expert before the dispensation from personal knowledge becomes available.

Rule 702. Testimony by Experts

If scientific, technical, or other specialized knowledge will assist the trier of fact to understand the evidence or to determine a fact in issue, a witness qualified as an expert by knowledge, skill, experience, training, or education, may testify thereto in the form of an opinion or otherwise.

The witness, in order to be recognized by the trial court judge as an expert, must have scientific, technical, or some other specialized knowledge. The source of the knowledge can be from education, training, or acquired skill or experience. An expert witness might be a scientist, physician, architect, banker, appraiser, experienced English teacher, or mechanic (see Illustration 9-1).

Illustration 9-1 _____

Mr. Hammond was killed when he fell from a tractor and was crushed by the boom arm attached to the tractor.

In a lawsuit based on a theory of products liability brought against the manufacturer of the tractor by Mr. Hammond's widow, the court stated there was no abuse of discretion by the trial court judge when a witness was qualified as an expert, even though the witness had no degree in either engineering or physics.

The witness qualified as an expert based on knowledge and experience because he sold automotive and mechanical equipment, including agricultural equipment, and he had taught automotive repair and maintenance at a high school. *Hammond v. International Harvester Co.,* 691 F.2d 646, 652–653 (3d Cir. 1982).

Like the opinion testimony of a lay witness, the testimony of an expert witness must assist the jury in its understanding of evidence or its determination of a fact in issue. If the testimony does not meet this requirement, the testimony of a witness will not get through the judge as the filter of evidence, regardless of whether the witness qualifies as an expert. If no specialized knowledge is needed to form an opinion, and the jury can come to its own conclusions without the testimony of an expert, on motion, the expert witness will not be allowed by the trial court judge to testify as to the expert witness's opinion.

A Rule 403 argument may still be appropriate even where an expert is qualified to testify. If the expert's testimony is more prejudicial than probative, the testimony can be excluded by the trial court judge.

Rule 702 dispenses with the need for first-hand or personal knowledge of an underlying event. The witness who qualifies as an expert can use facts or data supplied to the witness before testifying at trial. The expert hired by the party might be supplied the necessary facts and data by the attorney with the assistance of the paralegal, and this information would be used as a basis for questions answered at trial by the expert. The equipment salesman in Illustration 9-1 could testify as to his opinion of the mechanics of the tractor that might have contributed to Mr. Hammond's death. The salesman did not witness the accident, but because he had special knowledge and experience, he could give his opinion regarding the accident.

Basis for an Expert's Opinion Testimony

The facts or data relied upon by an expert witness do not have to be admissible themselves into evidence as long as a foundation is laid to demonstrate that the facts or data forming the basis for the expert witness's opinion are of the type reasonably relied upon by experts in the particular field. As an example, an expert witness may testify regarding the results of a public opinion poll even though the opinions of those who answered the poll are inadmissible hearsay. Pollsters generally rely on answers to formulate their poll results. The document with the answers cannot be placed before the jury, but the witness can rely on the document in formulating an expert opinion regarding public opinion.

Rule 703. Bases of Opinion Testimony by Experts

The facts or data in the particular case upon which an expert bases an opinion or inference may be those perceived by or made known to the expert at or before the hearing. If of a type reasonably relied upon by experts in the particular field in forming opinions or inferences upon the subject, the facts or data need not be admissible in evidence.

If the opposing party objects to the admissibility of expert testimony, it is up to the trial court judge to determine whether the witness can testify. In this situation, the facts and data that support the expert's testimony will be needed for the trial court judge to determine whether the witness can testify. Once the trial court judge determines the testimony is admissible, the jury can hear the facts and data that are the basis of the expert's opinion, either disclosed on direct examination or through cross-examination.

The Rules of Civil Procedure contain provisions for discovery that allow opposing parties to obtain information so that a challenge to the qualifications of witnesses—and to the facts and data used to support the expert's opinion—can be formulated. Discovery also provides ample opportunity to prepare effective cross-examination in the event the judge allows the expert's testimony at trial. Cross-examination can focus on facts and data that contradict the opinion of the expert or cast doubt on whether there is a credible basis for the expert's opinion.

Rule 705. Disclosure of Facts or Data Underlying Expert Opinions

The expert may testify in terms of opinion or inference and give reasons therefor without first testifying to the underlying facts or data, unless the court requires otherwise. The expert may in any event be required to disclose the underlying facts or data on cross-examination.

The expert witness may base an opinion on first-hand knowledge instead of facts and data. For instance, the testimony of a treating physician is based on personal observation of a patient.

The actual questioning of a witness who has qualified as an expert need no longer be done using hypothetical questions, as was required before the adoption of the Federal Rules of Evidence. Hypothetical questions are permissible as a means of presenting the expert witness's testimony to the jury, but they are not required. But, remember, hypothetical questions cannot be posed to lay witnesses, because personal knowledge is required for lay witnesses to express an opinion. See Illustration 9-2 for an example of a witness who does not qualify as an expert, and note the basis for the lay opinion expressed.

Illustration 9-2 _____

A retailer sued a manufacturer supplier for breach of contract and won, but the retailer was unable to prove damages at trial because the judge refused to let the accountant for the retailer testify as to the amount of lost profits that resulted from the breach.

The trial court judge would not let the accountant testify because the retailer failed to comply with a pretrial order requiring identification of expert witnesses. The trial court judge would not let the accountant testify as a lay witness because the judge assumed the opinions of an accountant would necessarily constitute expert opinion testimony.

The appellate court noted that a lay witness had to have personal knowledge to give opinion testimony. Since the accountant had been employed by the retailer, and he was knowledgeable about the retailer's balance sheets for the time period in question, he could testify as to his opinion about how lost profits could be calculated, based on his perception of the retailer's accounting records. In other words, the accountant was not going to testify in reply to hypothetical questions. Since he had personal knowledge of the accounting records, he could testify as a lay witness with regard to lost profits. As a lay witness, he did not come under the pretrial order requiring disclosure of expert witnesses before they could be called at trial.

The retailer won a new trial, in which the accountant could offer opinion testimony to support the retailer's demand for money to compensate for lost profits. *Teen-Ed, Inc. v. Kimball International, Inc.,* 620 F.2d 399, 404 (3d Cir. 1980).

_____

Qualification of an Expert Witness

Generally, at trial, the witness is qualified as an expert by means of questions related to expertise and knowledge. Then questions are asked to solicit the expert witness's opinion. The examining attorney might also elicit the basis for the opinion. The paralegal can prepare the questions that lead to the qualification of the witness as an expert, using information on education and experience supplied by the witness. The paralegal can also prepare a list of facts and data supporting the opinion of the witness.

Opinion on Ultimate Issue

Like lay witnesses who offer opinions, expert witnesses can also testify to an opinion that embraces an "ultimate issue." The only exception to the expert witness's testimony in this regard is whether a defendant in a criminal case had the necessary mental state the prosecution must prove as an element of a crime. Only the jury can decide whether the defendant possessed **mens rea**. An opinion of an expert witness is not helpful to the jury in this case, because the jury hears the evidence itself and is capable of forming its own conclusions.

Rule 704. Opinion on Ultimate Issue

   (b) No expert witness testifying with respect to the mental state or condition of a defendant in a criminal case may state an opinion or inference as to whether the defendant did or did not have the mental state or condition constituting an element of the crime charged or of a defense thereto. Such ultimate issues are matters for the trier of fact alone.

For a comparison and summary of opinion testimony, see Figure 9-1.

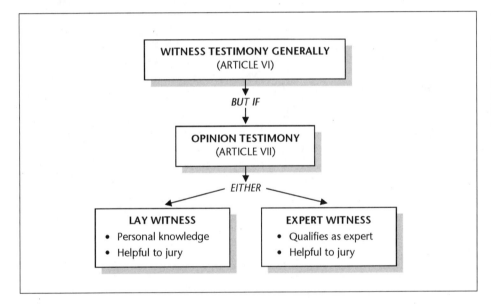

FIGURE 9-1

Article VI of the Federal Rules of Evidence covers witness testimony in general, and Article VII covers opinion testimony, both of lay witnesses and expert witnesses.

Scientific Evidence

The United States Supreme Court decision in *Daubert v. Merrell Dow Pharmaceuticals, Inc.* in 1993 settled a conflict among the circuits regarding the admissibility of scientific evidence through the testimony of an expert witness.[2] Rule 702 is the basis for determining whether expert testimony explaining scientific evidence is admissible. In *Daubert,* the Supreme Court held that the evidence or testimony of the witness must assist the jury in its understanding of the evidence or help the jury determine a fact in issue. Additionally, the court held that the testimony of the expert had to be valid scientific knowledge. In determining what is valid scientific knowledge, a trial court judge has a great deal of discretion, and the practical consequence is that more scientific evidence is admissible now in all federal trial courts.

mens rea The mental state necessary to the commission of a crime.

Prior to *Daubert,* some circuits followed the *Frye*[3] "general acceptance" test instead of relying on Rule 702 alone. The *Frye* test, used by ten of thirteen of the federal circuits before *Daubert,* was based on a Rule 403 analysis without utilizing Rule 702. *Frye,* decided long before the adoption of the Federal Rules of Evidence, set the standard for admission of scientific evidence in federal trials. Scientific evidence was admissible as competent and relevant if there were general acceptance in the particular field in which it belonged. In applying the *Frye* test, the trial court judge determined whether the theory or method propounded by the expert witness was generally accepted in the community to which the type of evidence related. The trial court judge made the preliminary determination, looking at relevant academic literature and case law.

After the adoption of the Federal Rules of Evidence, two circuit courts explicitly rejected the *Frye* test, reasoning that Rule 702 governed, allowing more testimony. However, in reading the *Daubert* opinion, one notices that the guidelines for implementing the *Daubert* test still ring of *Frye*—reliability of the scientific evidence includes a general acceptance standard and evidence of peer review. But the *Daubert* test does give the trial court judge more leeway in allowing the jury to hear innovative scientific evidence than does the *Frye* test.

Before *Daubert* was decided, fifteen states followed the *Frye* general acceptance test rather than a Rule 702 analysis. If a case is in federal court, the paralegal must be familiar with *Daubert* and its progeny in order to prepare for admission of scientific evidence, particularly if the scientific evidence is innovative or novel. In state court, the paralegal must determine whether the state follows the federal lead, or whether the more restrictive *Frye* general acceptance test is the standard. For instance, the Florida Supreme Court reaffirmed the use of the *Frye* test in Florida after *Daubert* was decided. See Illustration 9-3 for an example of the continued application of the *Frye* general acceptance test.

Illustration 9-3 _____

The defendant was convicted of sexually battering his mentally retarded nine-year-old daughter. The prosecution called a psychologist from the state child protection services office, who testified about the common characteristics of the home environment where child sexual abuse occurs and about the characteristics of abusers.

The defendant objected to the profile testimony of the psychologist.

The Florida Supreme Court found nothing in the relevant academic literature or case law to indicate that sexual offender profile evidence was generally accepted in the scientific community. The psychologist even conceded at trial that the profile could not be used to prove or disprove a person was a child abuser.

Novel or experimental scientific evidence is not admissible in Florida unless it meets the *Frye* general acceptance test.

Because the testimony was admitted as substantive evidence of guilt and it did not meet the *Frye* test, the trial should not have allowed the testimony. *Flanagan v. State,* 625 So. 2d 82, 828 (Fla. 1993).

_____

Regardless of whether the *Daubert* or the *Frye* test is used, certain scientific evidence is generally admissible but not conclusive, as only the jury can decide ultimate issues. Blood type comparison tests, for example, often used in paternity actions, are admissible. The expert can testify that fathers having certain blood types can produce children of only certain blood types and not others. Some states allow a rebuttable presumption of paternity if the tests show a statistical probability of paternity equal to or greater than 95 percent.

The courts also routinely allow experts to testify with regard to blood, breath, and urine tests for intoxication by alcohol or drugs. But with the rapid advance in technology, other techniques might be used, such as the detection of the use of illegal drugs after several weeks of abstinence through the testing of hair from the head. Admissibility of scientific evidence at trial might differ depending on the application of the *Daubert* test or the *Frye* test, since innovative science is not favored under the *Frye* general acceptance test.

Because of technological and scientific advancements, evidence from radar speed detection is greeted favorably by juries today, as is evidence from DNA printing. However, in preparing a case, the paralegal needs to investigate the basis for the particular technology and testing. The processes are not infallible; operators must be qualified and equipment calibrated on a scheduled basis. Experts can differ on statistical analyses and their meaning.

The results of a systolic blood pressure "deception test" (the precursor to the polygraph test) was the scientific evidence Mr. Frye attempted to introduce in his murder trial in 1923. He wanted to introduce the results of the testing because they showed he did not commit the murder. In establishing the general acceptance test, the circuit court held that "polygraph" evidence did not meet the standard.

> Just when a scientific principle or discovery crosses the line between the experimental and demonstrable stages is difficult to define. Somewhere in this twilight zone the evidential force of the principle must be recognized, and while courts will go a long way in admitting expert testimony deduced from a well-recognized scientific principle or discovery, the thing from which the deduction is made must be sufficiently established to have gained general acceptance in the particular field in which it belongs. *Frye,* 293 F. at 1014.

In 1995 an Arizona federal trial court judge allowed **exculpatory evidence** based on a polygraph test.[4] The analysis of the court was based on the flexible *Daubert* test, and on the application of Rule 403 with the imposition of specific restrictions. A trend in the federal circuits today reflects a challenge to the traditional stance that polygraph evidence is **per se** not admissible. See Illustration 9-4 for an example of differing results.

Illustration 9-4 _____

In 1989 the Eleventh Circuit noted there have been "tremendous advances" in polygraph instrumentation and technique. Because polygraph tests are used by many government agencies, the court also found that even under the *Frye* standard of general acceptance, polygraph evidence could be admissible.

This case was decided before *Daubert. United States v. Piccinonna,* 885 F.2d 1529, 1532 (11th Cir. 1989) (en banc). In 1995 the Sixth Circuit relied on Rule 403 to affirm the district court judge's decision to refuse to admit polygraph evidence on the basis that it was more prejudicial than probative.

exculpatory evidence
Evidence that tends to prove someone is free from blame.

per se In and of itself.

> The defendant took a privately commissioned polygraph test without the government's knowledge until after it was administered. The decision turned on the timing and notice to the government. *United States v. Sherlin,* 67 F.3d 1208 (6th Cir. 1995).

Advancing technology and novel scientific theories necessitate a vigilant search of legal authority and creative argument for inclusion or exclusion of proffered scientific evidence. Rule 702, along with *Daubert* and subsequent court decisions, offers an opportunity for novel and innovative scientific evidence to be heard by juries. This opportunity also exists in those states that follow the federal model in this regard. *Frye* lurks in the background in the modern analysis but is broadly expanded with the current application and interpretation of Rule 702 in *Daubert.*

COURT APPOINTED EXPERTS

Rule 706 allows a trial court judge to appoint an expert witness on motion from one of the parties or on the judge's own motion.

Rule 706. Court Appointed Experts

(a) Appointment. The court may on its own motion or on the motion of any party enter an order to show cause why expert witnesses should not be appointed, and may request the parties to submit nominations. The court may appoint any expert witnesses agreed upon by the parties, and may appoint expert witnesses of its own selection. An expert witness shall not be appointed by the court unless the witness consents to act. A witness so appointed shall be informed of the witness' duties by the court in writing, a copy of which shall be filed with the clerk, or at a conference in which the parties shall have opportunity to participate. A witness so appointed shall advise the parties of the witness' findings, if any; the witness' deposition may be taken by any party; and the witness may be called to testify by the court or any party. The witness shall be subject to cross-examination by each party, including a party calling the witness.

(b) Compensation. Expert witnesses so appointed are entitled to reasonable compensation in whatever sum the court may allow. The compensation thus fixed is payable from funds which may be provided by law in criminal cases and civil actions and proceedings involving just compensation under the fifth amendment. In other civil actions and proceedings the compensation shall be paid by the parties in such proportion and at such time as the court directs, and thereafter charged in like manner as other costs.

(c) Disclosure of appointment. In the exercise of its discretion, the court may authorize disclosure to the jury of the fact that the court appointed the expert witness.

(d) Parties' experts of own selection. Nothing in this rule limits the parties in calling expert witnesses of their own selection.

Rule 706 allows the trial court judge to appoint a neutral expert whom both parties are allowed to cross-examine. The rule details the procedure and the manner of compensation. The trial court judge may not necessarily allow disclosure to the jury that the expert is appointed by the court. This decision is discretionary; it depends on the impact the knowledge might have on the jury in its weighing of the evidence.

Rule 706 may have future use in litigation with complicated scientific or technological issues, especially in light of *Daubert,* which leaves the trial court judge with more discretion in admitting scientific evidence. The *Frye* test used peer review of the proffered scientific evidence as a basis for admissibility of scientific evidence, while *Daubert* opens the door to any scientific evidence that is helpful to the trier of fact, whether that trier of fact is a jury or a judge in a bench trial.

In the southern and eastern districts of New York, two federal trial court judges created a panel of neutral experts to advise them on scientific issues in silicone breast implant litigation which they were managing in their districts.[5] The authority for appointment of the panel is Rule 706, which offers judges the opportunity to gain general assistance in examining the admissibility of scientific evidence. In this case, evidence related to a causal connection between breast implants and serious health problems was examined. This pioneering effort may have implications in other breast implant litigation in the United States, and it may serve as a model for other litigation with underlying scientific disputes. It is incumbent on the paralegal to remain current on developments such as the one in New York, especially paralegals employed by litigation firms specializing in actions where state-of-the-art scientific evidence is subject to dispute.

SUMMARY

Whether the witness who offers an opinion is a lay witness or qualifies as an expert witness, the testimony must be helpful to the jurors in resolving the issues raised at trial. An expert witness is shown to be qualified by demonstrating to the trial court judge that the witness has the requisite education or experience. A lay witness must have personal knowledge. Unlike an expert witness, a lay witness cannot answer hypothetical questions.

The paralegal must learn the background of all witnesses in preparing for trial. Expert witnesses are hired to render opinions; lay witnesses generally are not. But both types of witnesses can have opinions that may have a strong impact on a jury in its determination of the facts. The trial court judge makes the preliminary determination of whether a witness can give an opinion, but it is the jurors who then determine the credibility of the witness and the weight to give that evidence in their deliberations.

Lay and expert witnesses can offer opinion testimony on the ultimate issue in a case, but the jury can ignore the testimony if it does not find the testimony credible.

All federal courts must apply the *Daubert* test, along with the Rule 403 balancing test. *Daubert* allows the admissibility of innovative or novel scientific evidence.

The *Frye* general-acceptance test is still applied in some states. It requires that scientific evidence be generally accepted in the scientific community, as seen in peer reviews and publications. The *Frye* test generally keeps novel and innovative scientific evidence from being heard by the jury.

Finally, the trial court judge can call expert witnesses to testify. Both parties are allowed to cross-examine the witness, and the jury is not told the witness was called by the judge.

✓ CHECKPOINTS

❑ Opinion testimony by lay witnesses
1. Witness must have personal knowledge.
2. Opinion must be helpful to jury.
3. Witness can offer opinion on ultimate issue, but jury decides weight of the evidence.

❑ Opinion testimony by expert witnesses
1. Witness must qualify as an expert based on scientific, technical, or other knowledge.
2. Opinion must be helpful to jury.
3. Witness can respond to hypothetical questions; personal knowledge of event is not necessary.
4. Opinion can be based on data or facts supplied to witness at trial.
5. Opinion can be based on personal knowledge.
6. Witness can offer opinion on ultimate issue, but jury decides weight of the evidence.

❑ Scientific evidence
1. Evidence is offered through an expert witness.

2. *Daubert* test based on Rule 702 is used; it favors novel and innovative science.
   ▪ Evidence must be helpful to jury.
   ▪ *Daubert* test is used in federal courts.
3. *Frye* general acceptance test looks to acceptance of science in its field.
   ▪ *Frye* test looks at peer evaluations and publications.
   ▪ *Frye* test is more restrictive of novel or innovative science than *Daubert* test.
   ▪ Evidence must be helpful to jury.
   ▪ *Frye* test is used in some state courts.
4. Polygraph tests are not *per se* inadmissible using *Daubert* test.

❑ Court-appointed experts
1. Trial court judge can call expert witnesses.
2. Both parties can cross-examine witnesses.
3. Jury is usually not informed of judge's role.
4. Experts are useful in class action liability cases involving complex scientific information.

🔨 APPLICATIONS

Application 9-1

In the following excerpt from *United States v. Powers,* Mr. Powers was convicted of aggravated sexual abuse of a minor in a federal trial court in North Carolina. Mr. Powers was charged under a federal statute because the alleged sexual abuse occurred on an Indian reservation. The substance of the charges was the repeated raping of his daughter over a ten-month period when she was nine and ten years old. He challenged his conviction based on a number of evidentiary rulings, including the exclusion of testimony of his expert witnesses. The appellate court incorporates the *Daubert* analysis in its examination of the propriety of excluding the expert witness testimony at trial.

United States v. Powers
59 F.3d 1460 (4th Cir. 1995)

IV.

Finally, Powers argues that the district court erred in excluding testimony of two experts who would have testified that Powers did not exhibit the characteristics of a fixated pedophile. Expert testimony explaining scientific evidence is admissible under Fed.R.Evid. 702 if it will assist the jury "to understand the evidence or determine a fact in issue." When determining admissibility under Rule 702, a trial judge must ensure that all scientific testimony or evidence admitted is both relevant and reliable, and that its evidentiary reliability is based upon scientific validity. *Daubert v. Merrell Dow Pharmaceuticals, Inc.,* _____ U.S. _____ at _____ & n. 9, 113 S.Ct. 2786 at 2795 & n. 9, 125 L.Ed. 2d 469 (1993). As we recently noted:

> [T]he *Daubert* Court set forth a two-part test which must be met in order for such expert testimony to be properly admitted under FRE: (1) the expert testimony must consist of "scientific knowledge"—that is, the testimony must be supported by appropriate validation; *and* (2) the evidence or testimony must "assist the trier of fact to understand the evidence or to determine a fact in issue."

United States v. Dorsey, 45 F.3d 809, 813 (4th Cir. 1995) (quoting *Daubert,* _____ U.S. at _____, 113 S.Ct. at 2795). We review the district court's refusal to admit scientific evidence for abuse of discretion. *Dorsey,* 45 F.3d at 814 ("[U]nder the *Daubert* analysis, a trial judge has a great deal of discretion in deciding whether to admit or exclude expert testimony."); *United States v. Bynum,* 3 F.3d 769, 773 (4th Cir. 1993), *cert. denied,* ___ U.S. _____, 114 S.Ct. 1105, 127 L.Ed.2d 416 (1994).

A.

The first question we must confront is whether the results of a penile plethysmography test meet the scientific validity prong of *Daubert.* Specifically, Powers argues that the district court erred in excluding the testimony of a clinical psychologist who would have testified that the results of a penile plethysmography test did not indicate that Powers exhibited pedophilic characteristics. The penile plethysmography, or arousal, test measured Powers' sexual arousal in response to pictures of nude females of various age groups. The district court excluded this evidence because, in its opinion, the test did not satisfy the "scientific validity" prong of *Daubert.*

In *Dorsey,* we enumerated the factors that the Supreme Court directed trial courts to consider when evaluating the scientific validity of proposed evidence:

1. Whether the theory or technique used by the expert can be, and has been, tested;

2. Whether the theory or technique has been subjected to peer review and publication;

3. The known or potential rate of error of the method used; and

4. The degree of the method's or conclusion's acceptance within the relevant scientific community.

Dorsey, 45 F.3d at 813 (discussing *Daubert,* _____ U.S. _____ – _____, 113 S.Ct. at 2796–97).

The evidence produced at trial clearly showed that these factors weighed against the admission of the penile plethysmograph test results. First, the Government proffered evidence that the scientific literature addressing penile plethysmography does not regard the test as a valid diagnostic tool because, although useful for treatment of sex offenders, it has no accepted standards in the scientific community. Second, the Government also introduced evidence before the judge that a vast majority in incest offenders who do not admit their guilt, such as Powers, show a normal reaction to the test. The Government argues that such false negatives render the test unreliable. Powers failed to introduce any indicia, let alone a sufficient level, of reliability to rebut the Government's evidence. Accordingly, in light of extensive, unanswered evidence weighing against the scientific validity of the penile plethysmograph test, we cannot say that the district court abused its discretion.

B.

Next, Powers argues that the district court abused its discretion in excluding the testimony of Dr. Anthony Sciara. Dr. Sciara would have testified that Powers did not demonstrate the psychological profile of a fixated pedophile. The district court ruled that Powers failed to establish either the relevance or the scientific validity of psychological profiling as applied to the facts at issue. The arguments on appeal, however, focus our attention on the second prong of *Daubert,* namely, whether the evidence is "relevant" to the issue under consideration.

Once again, *Dorsey* provides the analytical framework for our analysis:

> In determining whether the evidence meets the second prong of the two part test—that is, whether the evidence will be helpful to the trier of fact—the Supreme Court warned that throughout an admissibility determination, a judge must be mindful of other evidentiary rules, such as FRE 403, which permits the exclusion of relevant evidence "if its probative value is substantially outweighed by the danger of unfair prejudice, confusion or the issues, or misleading the jury." [*Daubert*], ＿＿ U.S. ＿＿, 113 S.Ct. at 2798.

* * *

[The *Daubert*] Court concluded:

> Conjectures that are probably wrong are of little use ... in the project of reaching a quick, final, and binding legal judgment—often of great consequence—about a particular set of events in the past. We recognize that in practice, a gatekeeping role for the judge, no matter how flexible, inevitably on occasion will prevent the jury from learning of authentic insights and innovations. That, nevertheless, is the balance that is struck by the Rules of Evidence designed not for the exhaustive search for cosmic understanding but for the particularized resolution of legal disputes.

Id. at ＿＿ – ＿＿, 113 S.Ct. 17 2798–99. *Dorsey,* 45 F.3d at 813–14.

Powers argues that Dr. Sciara's psychological profile on him meets the relevancy criteria due to the direct relationship between the subject matter of the test and the crime charged. Counsel for Powers proffered the following evidence concerning Dr. Sciara's psychological profile. Based on numerous interviews with child sex abusers and other research, Dr. Sciara has created a profile of the common characteristics of incest abusers. According to Sciara, the largest common denominator among incest abusers is that forty percent of the time they exhibit the characteristics of fixated pedophiles. Powers' tests, however, revealed that he did not share this characteristic. From this data, Powers argues that "[t]his testimony was clearly relevant for the purpose of demonstrating that [he] was psychologically unlikely to have committed the alleged crimes charged against him." *Brief of Appellant* at 19. We disagree.

The difficulty with Powers' argument is that he fails to provide a substantial link between the expert testimony and his theory of defense. At most, this evidence would have shown only that Powers did not belong to a group that comprised forty percent of incest abusers. Powers, however, was charged with statutory rape of his daughter—incest abuse—not with being a fixated pedophile. To be relevant, this testimony must show, in a very real way, that *because* Powers did not share characteristics common to a large minority of incest perpetrators, he was less likely to be an incest perpetrator himself. The District court clearly understood this fundamental flaw when the testimony was proffered:

> THE COURT: [L]et's say that we did allow [Dr. Sciara] now to testify [without basing his opinion on the results of the penile plethysmography test]. And all he's going to say is that this is not the kind of man who has a fixation on children.
>
> [DEFENSE COUNSEL]: Correct, Your Honor.
>
> THE COURT: What does that tell us?
>
> [DEFENSE COUNSEL]: Judge, I don't think it is end all and be all of our defense. I think it's an important piece of evidence for the jury to have.
>
> THE COURT: Why? ... [The Court questioned Defense Counsel about whether this evidence would really make it more likely than not that Powers did not commit the offense.]
>
> [DEFENSE COUNSEL]: ... I don't think there's any question that some people that aren't fixated pedophiles commit incest. But I think it would be a substantial percentage and I think it is information that is relevant.

(J.A. 174.) If Powers had offered supporting evidence showing that those who are not fixated pedophiles are less likely to commit incest abuse (the crime with which Powers was charged), Dr. Sciara's testimony might have been relevant. However, Powers offered no evidence to link a non-proclivity for pedophilia with a non-proclivity for incest abuse, even after the district court gave Powers ample opportunity to introduce evidence showing the relevance of Dr. Sciara's testimony. Accordingly, we find that the district court did not abuse its discretion in excluding this evidence because Powers failed to prove either its relevancy or "a valid scientific connection to the pertinent inquiry" of whether he committed incest. *Daubert*, _____ U.S. _____, 114 S.Ct. at 2796.

V.

For reasons stated above, we affirm the judgment of the district court.

AFFIRMED.

Class Discussion Questions

1. What was the basis for the appellate court's view that the penile plethysmograph test was not scientifically valid?

2. Dr. Sciara was ready to testify that Mr. Powers did not match the profile of a fixated pedophile. Dr. Sciara's research concluded that the largest common denominator among incest abusers is that 40 percent of the time they exhibit the characteristics of a fixated pedophile. Mr. Powers did not exhibit the characteristics of a fixated pedophile.

What was the basis for the court's holding that the testimony was irrelevant and without a valid scientific connection to the crime charged?

Application 9-2

Although the following case is from a state supreme court, the rule of evidence governing admissibility of expert witness testimony is modeled after federal Rule 702.

State v. Buller
517 N.W. 2d 711 (Iowa 1994)

HARRIS, Justice.

In this appeal from an arson conviction, the defendant challenges testimony concerning the reaction at the fire scene of a dog trained in fire accelerant detection. We find no error in the testimony and affirm.

I. We review questions of admissibility of evidence for an abuse of district court discretion, meaning that we accord wide latitude to the district court on the question of sufficiency of foundation. Established rules of evidence however cannot be ignored under the guise of trial court discretion.

II. Following a fire in his Muscatine apartment, defendant Roy Laverne Buller was charged with first-degree arson. Buller's appeal, following a jury's guilty verdict, assigns only one error: admitting descriptions of a dog's actions that indicated it detected the scent of a fire accelerant. This evidence was offered to show the fire was a result of arson.

Buller asserts the evidence lacks a proper foundation, noting the existence of two types of cases involving police dogs. The first involves the use of dogs to search for hidden drugs and explosives. See, e.g., *United States v. Place,* 462 U.S. 696, 102 S.Ct. 2637, 77 L.Ed. 2d 110 (1983). In these cases, the evidence was used to establish probable cause for a search and seizure, but does not directly speak to the guilt or innocence of the party. The second line of cases deals with testimony concerning the tracking abilities of dogs and the use of that testimony to identify a suspect. See, e.g., *Ramus v. State,* 496 So. 2d 121 (Fla. 1986). We believe the latter cases, those involving tracking, more closely resemble this case. Dog tracking evidence, like accelerant detection, is evidence of a defendant's ultimate guilt. Drug and explosive detection evidence is almost exclusively used to analyze probable cause in the context of search and seizure.

Although accelerant detection by dogs seems not to have been addressed by any state appellate court, a related question, the cases in the second mentioned group concerning dog-tracking evidence, has been. A thirty-two state majority has taken the view that evidence of trailing by dogs of one charged with a criminal offense is admissible to prove identity in a criminal prosecution, provided the proper foundation is laid. Five states, including Iowa, have ruled that evidence of the conduct of a dog who trailed the accused is inadmissible on a theory that it is too unreliable and dangerous.

Buller of course contends our holding in *Grba* is controlling and that it was error to admit evidence of the dog's accelerant detection. But *Grba* was decided more than seventy years ago, at a time when courts were considerably less friendly to expert testimony than they are today. Testimony of experts is now governed by Iowa rule of evidence 702. It provides:

> If scientific, technical, or other specialized knowledge will assist the trier of fact to understand the evidence or to determine a fact in issue, a witness qualified as an expert by knowledge, skill, experience, training, or education may testify thereto in the form of an opinion or otherwise.

We have a liberal tradition in the admission of opinion evidence under this rule. "The trend of our cases ... has been toward broadening the scope of admissibility of expert testimony." "The question is whether the proffered evidence will assist the jury in resolving the issue." "That determination necessarily requires a threshold finding of reliability 'because unreliable evidence cannot assist a trier of fact.' " There is no requirement that the expert be able to express an opinion with absolute certainty: "an expert's lack of absolute certainty goes to the weight of his testimony, not to its admissibility." *United States v. Cyphers,* 553 F.2d 1064, 1072–73 (7th Cir. 1977). The district court has discretion to determine the admissibility of expert opinion testimony and reversal is justified only when the court has abused its discretion.

The evidence in this case qualifies as expert testimony and is admissible under rule 702. Evidence of the reaction at a fire scene of a dog trained in accelerant detection is a type of specialized information that will assist a trier of fact. Accelerant detection by a trained dog is probative in arson cases in that it provides direct evidence that a crime has been committed.

In addition to rule of evidence 702, expert testimony must survive rule of evidence 403. Rule 403 requires that evidence, though relevant, should be excluded if its probative value is substantially outweighed by the danger of unfair prejudice. Iowa R.Evid. 403. We see little or no danger of unfair prejudice in the evidence here, certainly nothing that would outweigh its probative value on the question of the fire's origin.

Grba is out of step with rules of evidence 403 and 702 and with our present understanding of expert testimony. It is overruled.

Even so the challenged evidence is not automatically admissible. Under rule 702 (and also under the majority cases, previously cited, relating to dog-tracking evidence) a foundation is required for admissibility. Buller argues it was lacking.

Testimony of Michael Dean Hiles, the handler of Ty, the dog whose reactions were the subject of the challenged testimony, is a special agent with the state fire marshal's office, a division of the Iowa department of public safety. He served with the state patrol beginning in January 1974 and was transferred to the fire marshal's office in February 1980. He attended short courses in fire investigations, hazardous chemicals and other related subjects in Missouri and Maryland and has attended a number of other seminars and training sessions. He is a member of the International Association of Arson Investigators. He investigates between seventy and 100 fires per year and frequently testifies as an expert on his investigations.

According to the record there is no place he could have received training on the subject of training and using a dog to detect fire accelerant. The evidence indicates it is a specialty that Hiles developed himself with his own dog, Ty. The fact that Hiles obtained his expertise in training and handling dogs in fire accelerant detection is not bar to admissibility. Practical experience, in a proper case, will suffice to qualify an expert witness. Hiles is widely recognized as a pioneer in the field.

He bought Ty as a seven-week-old puppy in 1985 and trained him in general obedience. In the summer of 1986 Hiles began training Ty to detect and respond to the odor of gasoline, using training techniques adapted from those used by law enforcement officers to train dogs to detect illegal drugs and explosives.

Later that year Hiles began training Ty to detect samples of gasoline that he had placed in actual fire scenes. Hiles then used Ty to detect accelerant at the scene of suspected arson. Over the next few years Hiles trained Ty to respond to the odor of other flammable liquids, including diesel fuel, kerosene, charcoal lighter fluid, and alcohol. He continued to train Ty regularly, both in and away from fire scenes, and took Ty to many of the fires that he investigated.

Given his years of experience and training in working with Ty, Hiles was qualified to give the expert opinion testimony. The record also supports a finding that Ty was sufficiently trained to serve in the investigation. This was shown, first by Hiles' training of the dog, and was confirmed by evidence that the accuracy of Ty's reaction to accelerant scents was authenticated. This was done in several ways.

In a large percentage of cases, about three out of four, Ty's location by scent of accelerant was later confirmed by laboratory tests using a gas chromatograph. A seventy-five percent confirmation rate is perhaps not impressive until it is explained that the twenty-five percent of cases lacking laboratory confirmation can largely be attributed to human error in gathering the material sampled for analysis. It must be remembered too that the accelerant tends to dissipate from the sample while awaiting analysis.

In the present case later laboratory tests proved inconclusive, placing this analysis within the twenty-five percent group. But the State offered evidence strongly indicating that the laboratory analysis was considerably less reliable in detecting fire accelerant than trained dogs. There was no evidence that Ty would indicate the existence of an accelerant where no accelerant existed.

Ty's accelerant detection ability was frequently confirmed by visual observation of the dog's selection of its location. Fire investigators have long noted physical characteristics left from the ignition at a fire's source.

Investigators, as part of their expertise, "read patterns" often left by flames and flame residue. Ty of course had no human knowledge of these patterns. But the points he indicated by scent were consistently confirmed independently as the fire source on the basis of patterns. Finally, Ty has a distinguished record of accuracy from many fire investigations where other evidence later confirmed his selection of the fire's source.

Hiles and other investigators, by reading patterns in a mattress selected by Ty, independently confirmed Ty's reactions to be correct, lending specific authenticity to Ty's reaction here.

Foundation for expert testimony under rule of evidence 702 has been shown by evidence establishing: (1) the dog handler's expertise; (2) the dog's training; and (3) the general accuracy of the dog's investigations. This is sufficient foundation. In the present case it is further bolstered by evidence of accuracy in this particular investigation.

Buller's challenge to the foundation is without merit.

AFFIRMED.

Class Discussion Questions

1. Explain the defendant's argument against admissibility of the dog handler's expert testimony concerning reaction at the fire scene of Ty, who was trained in fire accelerant detection, assuming the *Frye* test applied.

2. How did the court appear to use a *Daubert* analysis in finding scientific validity?

Application 9-3

Otwell v. Motel 6, Inc.
755 F.2d 665 (8th Cir. 1985)

PER CURIAM.

Barbara Lou Otwell, executrix of her husband's estate, appeals from a jury verdict in favor of Motel 6 on a wrongful death claim. We affirm.

At approximately 1:00 a.m. on the night in question, Mr. Otwell left his room at the Motel 6 in Little Rock, Arkansas, to call a cab. He returned to the room and, a short while later, someone knocked on the door. The motel rooms were not equipped with standard security devices such as "peep-holes" or chain locks on the doors. Nor were the rooms equipped with telephones. Mr. Otwell looked out the picture window next to the door, and then opened the door. Two men forced their way into the room and robbed Mr. Otwell and his companion at gunpoint. Upon pursuing the criminals as they fled from the room, Mr. Otwell was fatally wounded.

Mrs. Otwell contends that the trial court committed several errors during trial. We consider each of them in turn.

Mrs. Otwell claims first that the trial court's exclusion of expert testimony constitutes reversible error. At trial Mrs. Otwell called as witnesses two experts in the field of hotel and motel security. The trial court allowed these witnesses to compare the security devices used and precautions taken by Motel 6 with those used and taken in other motels and hotels. However, the trial court did not allow the witnesses to testify to the incidence of crime at the Motel 6 as compared with the incidence of crime at other motels, the standard of care in the security industry, or the cause of the incident.

We find no abuse of discretion in the trial court's limitation on expert testimony. The jury had before it evidence which established that crimes had occurred previously at the Motel 6. It also was aware of how the security devices used and the precautions taken by Motel 6, or lack of them, compared with those used and taken by other motels. The answer to the question of what caused the incident was a matter within the knowledge and experience of laypersons. Thus, the jury had before it sufficient evidence to decide for itself whether Motel 6's practices fell below an acceptable standard of care and to determine the cause of this incident without expert assistance.

Because we find no reversible error in the trial record, the judgment of the district court is affirmed.

Class Discussion Questions

1. Why did the appellate court agree with the trial court judge that it was correct to limit the expert testimony with regard to the incidence of crime at the Motel 6 as compared with other motels, the standard of care in the security industry, and the cause of the death of Mr. Otwell?

2. What matters were the experts allowed to testify to at trial?

3. Why was this testimony allowed?

Application 9-4

In *Douglass v. Hustler Magazine, Inc.*, Robyn Douglass, an actress, sued Hustler Magazine for invasion of privacy because it published nude photographs of her. At trial, she called an expert witness to testify to the nature of Hustler Magazine as a basis for proving her damages claim.

Douglass v. Hustler Magazine, Inc.
769 F.2d 1128 (7th Cir. 1985)

The next trial error relates to the "slide show." An expert witness on the issue of *Hustler*'s offensiveness accompanied his testimony with a projection of 128 slides showing some of the vilest photographs and cartoons to have been published in *Hustler* over the years. The plaintiff argues that the slide show, which lasted almost an hour, was an intrinsic part of the expert's testimony; and *Hustler*'s first counter is that the expert was unqualified. But he was an experienced English teacher, writer, and editor; and if there are to be expert witnesses on tastelessness and vulgarity, he was well qualified to be one. It can be argued that such things do not lend themselves to expert testimony. Unlike an ordinary witness, an expert witness is allowed to express an opinion; he is not confined to observation; and it might seem that opinions on matters of taste have no objectivity and that to allow them to be pushed at juries is to invite censorship and undermine the First Amendment. But this view has been rejected with respect to obscenity, see *United States v. Bagnell*, 679 F.2d 826, 833–34 (11th Cir. 1982), and cases cited there, and we can think of no basis for distinguishing false-light cases. Expert testimony is not required on matters of taste, see *Pinkus v. United States*, 436 U.S. 293, 302 S.Ct. 1808, 1814, 56 L.Ed. 2d 293 (1978), but neither is it forbidden.

Putting constitutional concerns aside, therefore, as insubstantial, we note that Rule 702 of the Federal Rules of Evidence defines the scope of permissible expert testimony very broadly. The rule and accompanying Advisory Committee Note indicate that such testimony is admissible whenever it concerns a topic on which a lay jury would be assisted by such testimony, and that the term "expert" includes the skilled layman—and the witness here was more. Although we are skeptical that an expert should have been allowed to testify on so vague, subjective, and impressionistic an issue as offensiveness, we cannot say as a matter of law that expert testimony could not have helped the jury reach an intelligent decision. A particular jury cannot be assumed to be familiar with the world of "provocative" magazines and therefore able to make the nice discriminations on which Douglass's case rests.

But while the expert's testimony was admissible, the prejudicial effect of the parade of filth in the slide show so clearly outweighed its probative value as to require exclusion under Rule 403 of the Federal Rules of Evidence. The plaintiff could have given the jury representative issues of *Hustler* to study but instead she put in evidence just the issue in which "Robyn Douglass Nude" appeared, plus some issues of *Playboy*—and the slides. To pick out the 128 worst pictures from many years of the magazine (there is no pretense that the pictures are random or representative sample of the magazine's contents) was to assail the senses and distract the mind, especially since projecting the slides on a large screen magnified the visual impact of the pictures as they appear in the magazine itself. The pictures apparently were selected with a view to highlighting the most offensive features of the magazine. The viewer of the slide show would think the magazine wholly given over to racially offensive cartoons, grotesque photographs (e.g., of a hermaphrodite), foul language, and scatological as well as sexual obscenities. Of course these are aspects of the magazine and ones that legitimately distinguish *Playboy* from it. But bad as it is, *Hustler* is not so concentratedly outrageous as the slide show would make a viewer think.

Although the district judge enjoys a broad discretion in balancing prejudice and probative value under Rule 403, we think he exceeded the limits of that discretion in this instance, and note that he himself remarked after the slide show that he had made a mistake in allowing it. In another setting such a mistake might not warrant a new trial. But the Supreme Court has told us (most recently in the *Bose* case, see 104 S.Ct. at 1962) to be assiduous in protecting the press, even in its least worthy manifestations, from the fury of outraged juries.

Class Discussion Questions

1. Explain the First Amendment issue that was raised by Hustler Magazine with regard to the expert testimony of the English teacher.

2. What credentials qualified the English teacher as an expert witness on taste?

3. Did the appellate court find that the English teacher's testimony could be helpful to the jury? Explain.

4. The slide show used by the expert witness was demonstrative evidence. How was Rule 403 added to the Rule 702 analysis by the appellate court, and what was the result?

🔍 EXERCISES

1. Your firm represents the widow and child of a motorist killed when his pickup truck was struck by a train while at a railroad crossing. Your supervising attorney plans to file a lawsuit to recover for the death of the motorist. In your investigation of the case, you locate several members of the rural community where the crossing is located. These individuals have used the crossing regularly over many years, and they tell you that the crossing has been poorly marked and badly maintained for as long as they can remember. They are willing to testify to the condition of the crossing both before and right after the accident. Unfortunately, none of the witnesses has beyond a fourth-grade education.

If the defendant objects to these witnesses testifying as to their opinions with regard to the condition of the railroad crossing, should the judge sustain or overrule the objection? Explain your answer.

2. The firm's client is a widower whose wife was treated for cancer at a Bahamian clinic where treatment methods had never been approved by any United States government agency. None of the treatments had ever been proven as effective treatments for cancer.

   The couple's health insurance carrier has refused to pay for the treatments even though they appear to be covered by a group health insurance policy covering "reasonable medical expenses." The policy excluded reimbursement for care, treatment, services, or supplies that were not necessary for the treatment of a disease or were unreasonable.

   The insurance company refuses to pay the claim for payment for the treatments, so you are preparing the case for trial.

   You locate several persons who are willing to testify that they were treated by the same clinic after conventional treatments failed. They can testify that they had cancer before being treated at the clinic and that they now feel in good health. In the opinion of each of them, the treatment helped improve their conditions. Only one of these persons has any training in the sciences, and that was political science.

   a. Argue that the testimony of these potential witnesses is *not* admissible as expert witness testimony.

   b. Frame an argument that the testimony of these persons *is* admissible as opinion testimony of lay witnesses.

3. Review the rules in your state related to lay and expert opinion testimony. Is there a clear difference between a lay and expert witness in that the difference is based on special knowledge, skill, experience, or training?

4. Does your state follow the *Daubert* test or the *Frye* test in determining the admissibility of scientific evidence?

RULES REFERENCED IN THIS CHAPTER

Rule 701. Opinion Testimony by Lay Witnesses

Rule 702. Testimony by Experts

Rule 703. Bases of Opinion Testimony by Experts

Rule 704. Opinion on Ultimate Issue

Rule 705. Disclosure of Facts or Data Underlying Expert Opinions

Rule 706. Court Appointed Experts

NOTES

[1] Michael Tigar. Quoted in *ABA Journal*, August 1995, p. 39.

[2] *Daubert v. Merrell Dow Pharmaceuticals, Inc.*, 509 U.S. 579 (1993).

[3] *Frye v. United States*, 293 F. 1013 (D.C. Cir. 1923).

[4] *United States v. Crumby*, 895 F.Supp. 1354 (D.Ariz. 1995).

[5] Mark Hansen. "Panel to Examine Implant Evidence." *ABA Journal*. June 1996, p. 34.

The Hearsay Rule

OUTLINE

INTRODUCTION

Some of the more difficult rules of evidence to apply are the rules related to **hearsay** evidence. If a trial court judge determines that the testimony of a witness or the content of a document offered into evidence is hearsay, the judge will not let the jury hear or view the evidence unless an exception to the hearsay rule applies. The *hearsay rule* is an exclusionary rule, and it is similar to other rules of evidence used to exclude evidence at trial.

Role of the Paralegal

Application of the hearsay rule is often confusing to both judges and attorneys. Paralegals who assist in litigation can have an impact on what the jury ultimately will hear at trial by thoroughly preparing for the admission of evidence

hearsay A statement by a witness of what someone else said out of court, offered as evidence of the truth of the statement.

before the trial begins. With a working understanding of the hearsay rule, the paralegal can anticipate potential hearsay problems with critical pieces of evidence. Then the paralegal can prepare an outline so the attorney can argue in court for the admissibility of these pieces of evidence.

A basic understanding of the hearsay rule is necessary for the paralegal to recognize evidence that is arguably hearsay. Then the paralegal must examine the competence of the evidence, that is, whether the hearsay rule applies, which results in the exclusion or admission of the evidence.

Framework for Analysis

The following framework should be applied by the paralegal in determining whether something said by a witness or written in a document is hearsay evidence:

- *Hearsay evidence:* a statement by the witness about what someone else said, or a document, written by someone other than the witness testifying, offered to prove the truth of the matter referred to in the statement or document. [Rule 801(a)–(c)].
- *Not hearsay evidence:* a statement by the witness or a document that is not someone else's statement or, if it is someone else's statement, is not offered to prove the truth of the matter referred to in it.
- *Not hearsay evidence:* a statement or document that a rule of evidence defines as non-hearsay [Rule 801(d)].
- *Hearsay evidence but an exception applies:* a statement or document that is hearsay but is ruled admissible [Rules 803, 804, and 807].

With this framework established, the hearsay rule will now be explored in depth.

HEARSAY RULE

Hearsay evidence includes statements made by a **declarant** who is someone other than the **witness** on the stand. The statement of the declarant is repeated by the witness and offered by one of the parties to prove the truth of the facts contained in the statement (Figure 10-1). In this context, "witness" refers to the person on the stand willing to testify, and "declarant" refers to the person who

declarant A person who makes a statement.

witness A person who takes an oath and whose testimony is evidence.

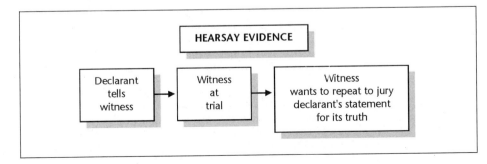

FIGURE 10-1

In hearsay evidence, a witness tells what someone else, out of court (a declarant), has said, offering it to prove the truth of what was said. A document can be offered as hearsay in the same way.

made an out-of-court statement and is not the same person as the witness. The witness is repeating what the declarant said. In some cases, witnesses may be repeating what they themselves said at an earlier time, which can also constitute hearsay evidence. This situation is dealt with separately later in the chapter.

Rule 801 states the formal definitions related to the hearsay rule.

Rule 801. Definitions

The following definitions apply under this article:
(a) **Statement.** A "statement" is (1) an oral or written assertion or (2) nonverbal conduct of a person, if it is intended by the person as an assertion.
(b) **Declarant.** A "declarant" is a person who makes a statement.
(c) **Hearsay.** "Hearsay" is a statement, other than one made by the declarant while testifying at the trial or hearing, offered in evidence to prove the truth of the matter asserted.

Sometimes legal definitions obscure meaning. Hearsay is simply unverified information gained from someone else, not part of the direct knowledge of the person reporting the information. In this light, some hearsay evidence might be characterized as gossip or rumor. The witness on the stand heard something from someone else, and the witness is trying to pass on what was heard to the jury as a fact (Figure 10-2).

Rule 602 requires a witness to have personal knowledge of a matter testified to in court.

Rule 602. Lack of Personal Knowledge

A witness may not testify to a matter unless evidence is introduced sufficient to support a finding that the witness has personal knowledge of the matter. Evidence to prove personal knowledge may, but need not, consist of the witness' own testimony ...

FIGURE 10-2

The hearsay rule determines whether out-of-court statements should be admitted as evidence or excluded.

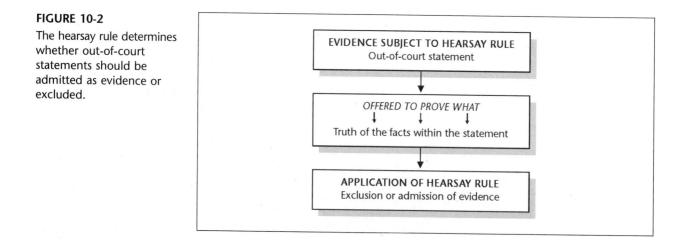

Since a witness can have personal knowledge of the making of a statement by someone else, Rule 602 does not exclude such a witness from testifying. Even though Rule 602 would prevent the witness from testifying about the subject matter of the statement told to the witness by someone else, it would allow the jury to hear the statement if not for Rules 801 and 805, which allow the trial court judge to exclude hearsay evidence.

The hearsay rule makes sense when put into the context of a trial. In Chapter 8, we learned that witnesses have to be competent, take an oath or affirmation to tell the truth, and have personal knowledge of the matter testified to at trial. The witness is then subject to cross-examination by the opposing party, who tests the perception, memory, and narration of the witness. If the person who actually made the statement (the declarant) is not the same person as the witness at trial, cross-examination to test how well the declarant observed the event, the declarant's memory of the events, and the ability of the declarant to relate the information under oath, becomes impossible (see Illustration 10-1).

Illustration 10-1 _____

WITNESS:	Declarant told me that the driver of the Mercedes truck ran the red light.
DEFENDANT:	Where was the declarant standing?
WITNESS:	I dunno.
DEFENDANT:	Was the declarant wearing eyeglasses?
WITNESS:	I dunno.
DEFENDANT:	How long after the accident was it that declarant told you this?
WITNESS:	About a month.
DEFENDANT:	Did declarant speak to anyone else about the accident before telling you this?
WITNESS:	I dunno.

The exchange in Illustration 10-1 demonstrates the impossibility of testing the declarant's statement when it is reported by a witness. It leaves the cross-examining party frustrated and at an unfair disadvantage, because the only reason the plaintiff is offering this testimony is to prove the driver of the Mercedes truck ran the red light, when, in fact, the declarant may have had a motive to lie.

In a personal injury action, this kind of testimony would be offered as proof of breach of duty. However, the nature of the proof is not helpful to the jury, and it gives the plaintiff an unfair advantage. The plaintiff should have to call the declarant to the stand, not someone else who will report second-hand to the jury, and whose testimony cannot be tested through cross-examination, during which the jury can observe the demeanor of the declarant.

A document can also be hearsay. For example, assume the witness in Illustration 10-1 received a letter from the declarant regarding the Mercedes truck running the red light. Not only is the witness's testimony as to the statement in the letter hearsay, but so is the letter itself, because it is a statement made out of court, offered to prove the fact it contains, that the Mercedes truck ran the red light. The letter cannot be cross-examined, just as its author cannot be cross-examined, because the author/declarant is not the witness. Examples of other hearsay documents are business records, certificates of marriage or baptism, public records, and medical records. Exceptions to the hearsay rule that deal with documents are discussed in Chapter 11.

If evidence is deemed hearsay, and an exception to the hearsay rule does not apply, the evidence may still have to be admitted. In a criminal case, the defendant's Sixth Amendment right to confront witnesses or the Fourteenth Amendment right to due process may dictate whether the testimony is admissible. A long line of Supreme Court cases deal with constitutional concerns in regard to hearsay evidence. The paralegal preparing a criminal case needs to thoroughly research the law in this regard (see Illustration 10-2).

Illustration 10-2 _____

The United States Supreme Court invalidated a Mississippi evidence rule that foreclosed the defendant from presenting hearsay testimony that could exonerate him. Three witnesses wanted to testify someone else claimed credit for the murder. The witnesses were all friends of the declarant.

The Supreme Court found the testimony of the three witnesses trustworthy because it was against the declarant's interest to tell his friends he murdered the victim, and he confessed to the friends spontaneously shortly after the murder. Other corroborating evidence included testimony of an eyewitness who saw the declarant shoot the victim, as well as testimony that the declarant owned the type of gun used to kill the victim and bought another gun after the murder like the one the declarant claimed he lost (the murder weapon was never found).

Furthermore, the declarant was available for cross-examination at trial. The Court held that the testimony of the witnesses was critical to Mr. Chambers' defense, and the evidentiary ruling of the trial court based on the Mississippi hearsay rule was an unconstitutional denial of the defendant's due process rights under the Fourteenth Amendment. *Chambers v. Mississippi,* 410 U.S. 284 (1973).

WITNESS AND DECLARANT NOT THE SAME PERSON _____

Rule 801(c) defines hearsay, while Rule 801(a) and Rule 801(b) explain two terms used in the definition of hearsay. The declarant is the person who intends to state something. The statement can be oral, written, or nonverbal conduct as long as the declarant has the requisite intent to state something.

A statement by a declarant is hearsay when a witness at trial repeats it for the purpose of proving the truth of the facts that make up the substance of the statement. The facts that make up the substance of the statement by the declarant constitute the "truth of the matter asserted." The witness on the stand is reporting the statement made by someone else, the declarant. This results in the classic example, "Mr. Garfield told me the Mercedes truck ran the red light."

Nonverbal Conduct

The form of the statement may also be nonverbal as long as the declarant's conduct is meant to convey substantive meaning. The declarant might have nodded up and down or raised a middle finger. As long as the declarant had the intent to convey meaning, the nonverbal conduct is a statement. If the nonverbal conduct is reported by a witness on the stand, it is hearsay and subject to objection.

Generally, verbal communication is always intended as an assertion. People do not speak unless they intend to convey something with the words. It may be debatable whether nonverbal conduct is meant as an assertion. Certainly an involuntary action, such as a sneeze, is not an assertion. But if the nonverbal conduct is challenged by the opposing party on the basis that the declarant intended to "say something" with the conduct, the judge makes the preliminary determination of whether the nonverbal conduct was an assertion. The judge decides if the jury will hear the witness report the conduct of the declarant. If the judge decides the testimony is hearsay, the witness will not be able to report the nonverbal conduct of the declarant to the jury unless an exception to the hearsay rule applies. This is the same result as when a verbal communication by a declarant is successfully challenged as hearsay. The rule also applies if the statement is written hearsay.

Written Document

The statement can be in the form of a written document. If the document was prepared by someone other than the witness on the stand, and it is offered to prove the truth of the facts contained in the document, it is subject to a hearsay objection. For instance, if a witness is questioned about the contents of a report prepared by someone else, the testimony is objectionable as hearsay, because the person who prepared the report is not the witness, but the out-of-court declarant.

STATEMENTS NOT OFFERED FOR THEIR TRUTH

Since a statement is hearsay only if offered to prove the truth of the facts that are the substance of the statement, a statement is not hearsay if it is offered for another purpose. For instance, at a competency proceeding, a witness may be called to testify the alleged incompetent person (the declarant) said to the witness a week before the proceeding, "I'm a federal agent in charge of domestic terrorism and I'm investigating the family next door." If the statement were offered to prove the alleged incompetent was a federal agent, the statement would be hearsay. However, if the purpose of offering the witness's testimony is to prove that the alleged incompetent is delusional, then the statement is not being offered to prove the truth of the content of the statement, so the testimony is not hearsay. Whether the content of the statement is true does not matter. It only matters that the declarant made the statement, which can then be used to infer that the alleged incompetent suffers from delusions.

Legally Operative Words

This rationale of offering evidence for reasons other than proving the truth of what is stated or written also operates for statements by a declarant that are **legally operative words** or **verbal acts**. Legal requirements exist for such

legally operative words
Words that have significance as part of a transaction.

verbal acts Words that have legal significance as part of a transaction.

things as the formation of contracts, the making of gifts, and the making of defamatory statements. For an oral contract, certain words must be uttered, or certain acts taken by the parties, that take their discussion from negotiation to binding contract. For example, "That's a deal," are legally operative words that demonstrate the parties have come to a meeting of the minds and have agreed to be bound to their promises. If no words are heard by a witness, but the witness sees the parties shake hands, this act indicates the same intent by the parties to be bound by their promises.

The same is true for **gifts**. For example, "I want you to have this diamond ring," and handing the ring to the recipient are legally operative words and a verbal act signifying a gift.

Likewise, in an action based on **defamation**, words are a necessary component of the plaintiff's case. If the plaintiff is suing the defendant for **libel** because the defendant wrote that the plaintiff cheats investors, the plaintiff offers the writing into evidence for the fact the defamatory statement was made, not for its truth.

How does the paralegal know if words or acts have independent legal significance that take them outside the hearsay rule? The paralegal applies the knowledge of the elements that constitute the substantive law of contracts, gifts, or other legal relationships to the evidence learned through informal and formal discovery. As part of this application, the paralegal researches relevant statutes and cases in order to frame an argument for the admissibility of legally operative words or verbal acts. The argument must be tied to material issues in a case. A declarant's statement offered only "to prove it was made" is not enough if the statement does not relate to an issue in the case that is in dispute.

Words Affecting the Listener

Sometimes a statement is offered to prove the state of mind of the person who heard the statement. If the effect on the mind of the person who heard the statement is an issue in the case, then the evidence is admissible (see Illustration 10-3).

gift Property or money transferred without payment or expectation of benefit.

defamation False statements, made in writing or verbally, that injure a person's reputation, property, or business.

libel Statements that are false and publically communicated, injuring a person's reputation, property, or business.

Illustration 10-3 _____

Mr. Cline was charged with second-degree murder. He was found guilty of the lesser, included offense of voluntary manslaughter. He appealed his conviction, claiming that the testimony of Delbert Pumpkinseed, who reported statements made by the victim, was hearsay.

PROSECUTOR:	What did Roger [Cline] say and what did Hobert [victim] say and then what did Roger say?
PUMPKINSEED:	Hobert came to get some gas—
PROSECUTOR:	Okay.
PUMPKINSEED:	—and Roger said he was tired of giving him gas on credit. Then Hobert says he is going to come up here and turn him in.
PROSECUTOR:	Come up here to Rapid City and turn him in?
PUMPKINSEED:	Yes.
PROSECUTOR:	Did he say to whom he was going to turn him in?

PUMPKINSEED: To the United States Marshals.

PROSECUTOR: As I understand it, Roger was complaining about giving gas and Hobert said, "If you don't give me gas, I am going to Rapid City and turning you in to the United States Marshal"?

PUMPKINSEED: Yes.

PROSECUTOR: Did he give him gas then?

PUMPKINSEED: Yes.

PROSECUTOR: And give him some money?

PUMPKINSEED: Yes.

The appellate court stated that the testimony of Pumpkinseed was relevant to show ill feelings existed between the victim and Mr. Cline. It did not make any difference whether the matter stated was true or not, that is, whether the victim turned Mr. Cline over to the marshals. From Mr. Pumpkinseed's testimony, the jury could infer that Mr. Cline had a motive for killing the victim.

The court went on to say there was no need to test the victim's statements because their truth did not matter. Mr. Pumpkinseed could be cross-examined as to whether the words were spoken or not, and this was enough. So Mr. Pumpkinseed's testimony was non-hearsay under Rule 801(c) with regard to out-of-court statements made by the victim. *United States v. Cline,* 570 F.2d 731, 734–35 (8th Cir. 1978).

Nonassertive Conduct

The drafters of the Federal Rules of Evidence intended that the definition of hearsay be read narrowly in order to allow more evidence to be heard by the jury. If an out-of-court statement by a declarant does not come within the definition of hearsay, then the in-court witness's testimony passes through the trial court judge's filter to the jury for its use in determining which party should prevail. If the hearsay rule is read narrowly, statements that are implied assertions are outside the hearsay rule because they are not properly characterized as hearsay. Thus, testimony by a witness that the defendant ran from the scene of the crime is not hearsay, because the defendant did not intend to make a statement. Flight implies guilt, so the correctness of the inference can be proven by the nonassertive conduct of fleeing from the scene of a crime.

Implied Assertions

The paralegal needs to recognize that a statement is not hearsay when it is not offered for the truth of the facts contained in the statement. If the in-court witness's testimony is offered as a basis for inferring something beyond what the words actually state, then the statement is not hearsay.

If a broader definition of hearsay is applied to statements characterized as **implied assertions**, the trial court judge would have to filter more evidence than currently is done in the federal courts. The paralegal must research the law of the state where state rules apply in order to find out if the state has adopted a narrow or a broad interpretation of the hearsay rule with regard to implied assertions.

implied assertion Inference from a statement.

NON-HEARSAY

Although Rule 802 serves as a basis for the exclusion of hearsay evidence as defined in Rule 801(a), (b), and (c), the rule also opens the door to the admissibility of evidence that in fact meets the terms of the definition of hearsay.

Rule 802. Hearsay Rule

Hearsay is not admissible except as provided by these rules or by other rules prescribed by the Supreme Court pursuant to statutory authority or by Act of Congress.

If other rules in the Federal Rules of Evidence or other rules prescribed by the United States Supreme Court allow hearsay to be admitted at trial, then the trial court judge must overrule a hearsay objection. This is another example of how the Federal Rules of Evidence do not act in a vacuum. The paralegal must be familiar with the whole trial process and all of the relevant rules: rules of civil and criminal procedure, as well as statutes that dictate the admissibility of evidence, regardless of its hearsay quality. The evidence reported by a witness may be admissible, even though it is hearsay, because other rules or statutes dictate the result. Depositions and affidavits for various purposes, which otherwise would be objectionable as written hearsay, could be admissible because other rules of civil and criminal procedure allow them into evidence.

Rule 802 opens the door to more than two dozen possible exceptions to the hearsay rule, listed in Rule 803 and covered in Chapter 11. Rule 804 is similar to Rule 803, but it has fewer exceptions, and they are applicable only if the declarant is not available to testify at trial. Rule 801 itself allows admission of evidence that meets the definition of hearsay simply by defining two types of statements as non-hearsay. Logically, prior statements by a witness and admissions by party-opponents meet the parameters of the definition of hearsay, but by the definitional provisions in Rule 801, these statements are excluded from the hearsay rule.

Rule 801. Definitions

(d) Statements which are not hearsay. A statement is not hearsay if—

(1) Prior statement by witness. The declarant testifies at the trial or hearing and is subject to cross-examination concerning the statement, and the statement is (A) inconsistent with the declarant's testimony, and was given under oath subject to the penalty of perjury at a trial, hearing, or other proceeding, or in a deposition, or (B) consistent with the declarant's testimony and is offered to rebut an express or implied charge against the declarant of recent fabrication or improper influence or motive, or (C) one of identification of a person made after perceiving the person; or

(2) Admission by party-opponent. The statement is offered against a party and is (A) the party's own statement in either an individual or a representative capacity or (B) a statement of which the party has manifested an adoption or belief in its truth, or (C) a statement by a person authorized by the party to make a statement concerning the subject, or (D) a statement by the party's agent or servant concerning a matter within the scope of the agency or employment, made during the existence of the relationship, or (E) a statement by a coconspirator of a party during the course and in furtherance of the conspiracy. The contents of the statement shall be considered but are not alone sufficient to establish the declarant's authority under subdivision (C), the agency or employment relationship and scope thereof under subdivision (D), or the existence of the conspiracy and the participation therein of the declarant and the party against whom the statement is offered under subdivision (E).

Rule 801(d) says that prior statements by a witness and admissions by a party-opponent are not hearsay as long as certain conditions are met.

Declarant as Witness

Generally, if the declarant is also the witness who wants to testify to an out-of-court statement made by the declarant/witness, the testimony constitutes hearsay. The out-of-court statement is offered to prove the truth of its content. All witnesses must testify as to what the witness personally knows. The knowledge may come from personal observation in the past, but the witness is testifying from current recollection and, in so doing, avoids a hearsay objection. Opposing counsel can effectively cross-examine the witness on what the witness saw, whereas no cross-examination could be made of what a declarant/witness told someone else.

ATTORNEY A:	Tell the jury about the Mercedes truck.
WITNESS:	I told Mr. Garfield that the Mercedes truck ran the red light.
ATTORNEY B:	Objection, Your Honor. Move to strike. Hearsay.
JUDGE:	Sustained. Rephrase the question, counselor.
ATTORNEY A:	What did you see at the intersection of Fairfield Drive and Ninth Avenue on June 15, 1997 at around noon?
WITNESS:	I saw the Mercedes truck run the red light.

Sometimes the witness does not remember the underlying events that form a basis for the witness's testimony but might remember saying something to someone else at the time of those events. That statement as reported by the witness/declarant is hearsay when it is offered for the truth of its content. The witness/declarant cannot be effectively cross-examined on it, because the witness/declarant cannot answer questions regarding perception at the time of the events and the memory of those perceptions. If the witness's only response is, "I just remember telling Mr. Garfield the Mercedes truck ran the red light," a hearsay objection would be sustained.

Rule 801(d)(1) exempts from hearsay three situations where the declarant is the witness. This provision allows prior statements by the declarant/witness to be used as **substantive evidence** in the jury's determination of the litigated matter.

Prior Inconsistent Statement

The first situation in which prior statements can be used as substantive evidence involves prior *inconsistent* statements. Here an out-of-court statement made by the declarant/witness is inconsistent with the in-court testimony

substantive evidence
Evidence used as proof of facts.

of the declarant/witness, plus the inconsistent statement was given when the declarant/witness was under oath and subject to the penalty of perjury at a trial, hearing, other proceeding, or in a deposition. Both these conditions must be met, and if they are, the jury will hear about the prior inconsistent statement and can choose to believe it rather than the testimony offered in court (see Illustration 10-4).

Illustration 10-4 _____

Mr. Moore gave a statement to two Internal Revenue Service (IRS) agents after he was assured he was not the target of any pending criminal investigation and after he was given a *Miranda* warning. In the statement, Mr. Moore cast himself as an uneducated country boy duped by the other two defendants in the business affairs under criminal investigation. Mr. Moore called one of the defendants a "damned crook" and accused the other of being the primary perpetrator of a check conversion scheme.

At trial, the judge overruled hearsay objections by the two defendants and allowed the government to introduce the statements as substantive evidence under Rule 801(d)(1)(A) when Mr. Moore's in-court testimony contradicted his statement to the IRS agents.

The appellate court noted the government offered no proof of either IRS agent having the authority to administer an oath that would invoke the penalty of perjury. Furthermore, the appellate court found the statement was given under circumstances more aptly described as a station house interrogation and was not an "other proceeding."

The trial court judge's error in allowing the jury to hear the statement and to use it as substantive evidence to convict was reversible error because the statement did not meet the requirements of Rule 801(d)(1)(A). *United States v. Day,* 789 F.2d 1217, 1220–21, 1223 (6th Cir. 1986).

_____

The jury can use the prior inconsistent statement as substantive evidence, that is, accept as true the facts in the prior inconsistent statement and use those facts as a basis for its verdict. Under Rule 801(d)(1), prior inconsistent statements made under oath are exempt from the hearsay definition. The trial court judge has considerable discretion in determining whether testimony is "inconsistent" with prior statements. Inconsistency is not limited to diametrically opposed answers; it may also be found in evasive answers, inability to recall, silence, or changes of position.

In order to introduce a prior inconsistent statement, a proper foundation must be laid. The witness has to be given the opportunity to explain or deny the statement. If the witness claims lack of memory with regard to the prior inconsistent statement, the statement can be read to the jury. It is within the discretion of the trial court judge to admit the statements as substantive evidence or to limit their use to impeachment. In making this decision, the judge incorporates a Rule 403 analysis, weighing undue prejudice against probativeness.

Prior Consistent Statement

The second situation in which prior statements can be used as substantive evidence involves prior *consistent* statements. Here the prior out-of-court statement by the declarant/witness is consistent with in-court testimony. However, a prior consistent statement is admissible only if it is offered in response to an express or implied charge of (1) recent fabrication, or (2) improper influence or motive. Otherwise, prior consistent statements are inadmissible hearsay whose only purpose is to bolster the testimony of the witness. As a practical matter, such statements would result in a waste of time and much longer trials.

Identification

The third situation in which prior statements can be used as substantive evidence involves *identification*. Here the declarant/witness made an out-of-court identification of a person after seeing the person. Now, on the stand, the declarant/witness wants to report the earlier identification. If identification were not involved, this statement would be considered a prior consistent statement and therefore inadmissible hearsay unless the opposing party alleged recent fabrication or improper motive or influence. The reporting of the earlier identification is exempt from the hearsay definition and admissible as substantive evidence under Rule 801(d)(1)(C). When a witness in a criminal case wants to testify to a prior identification of the defendant, constitutional considerations become relevant (see Illustration 10-5).

Illustration 10-5 _____

Mr. Owens was a prisoner who was convicted of assault with intent to commit murder. In part, his conviction was based on the testimony of the victim, Mr. Foster, who was a correctional counselor at a federal prison where the attack took place.

Mr. Owens challenged the prior out-of-court identification testimony of Mr. Foster because Mr. Foster could not explain the basis for the identification, having suffered memory loss attributed to the head injuries he suffered in the attack. He remembered only that he had identified Mr. Owens from an array of photographs presented by an FBI investigator. At the time of the identification, he could remember the attack. By the time of the trial, though, his memory of the attack and the assailant had faded. The government argued the testimony was nevertheless admissible under Rule 801(d)(1)(C) and because Mr. Foster was available at trial for cross-examination.

The Supreme Court stated that the purpose of Rule 801(d)(1)(C) was to prefer out-of-court identifications because they can be more reliable than in-court identifications. Mr. Owens had the opportunity to effectively cross-examine Mr. Foster and impugn the credibility of his identification testimony and memory loss. The confrontation clause requires no more than this. *United States v. Owens*, 484 U.S. 554, 560–64 (1988).

The United States Supreme Court has held that once a defendant has been charged, any proceedings prejudicial to the defendant are not admissible, including lineups where the defendant is not represented by an attorney.[1] This is an example of constitutional concerns superseding the hearsay rule in criminal cases.

A witness who is other than the declarant who made the out-of-court identification cannot testify to the declarant's out-of-court identification of a person. In other words, a police investigator cannot testify that the victim identified the defendant during the investigation. The victim must testify, so the defendant will have the opportunity to cross-examine the victim who made the identification.

Cross-Examination and Impeachment

The rationale for allowing certain prior statements into evidence under Rule 801(d)(1) rests to some degree on the availability of the declarant/witness for **cross-examination**. If the declarant and the witness are one and the same, effective cross-examination regarding memory, perception, and narration are possible. This cross-examination assists the jury in determining the weight and credibility of the prior statements and the in-court testimony. Furthermore, the prior statements are admissible only within defined parameters with this safeguard, and because the testimony can be reliable evidence and helpful to the jury in making its determination, prior statements as defined in Rule 801(d)(1) are exempt from the hearsay definition.

Prior inconsistent statements not meeting the requirements of Rule 801(d)(1) can sometimes still be used at trial. The jury may hear about the prior inconsistent statements if those statements are used to impeach the credibility of the witness's testimony. The prior inconsistent statement cannot be relied upon by the jury as a basis for its verdict when it is used for **impeachment** purposes only. With impeachment, the jury uses the prior inconsistent statement to determine credibility and weight, while substantive use of the prior inconsistent statement goes much further, allowing the jury to not only reject the in-court testimony but also to rely on the out-of-court statement as substantive proof of a party's claim or defense.

Statement of Party-Opponent

While Rule 801(d)(1) deals with prior statements of witnesses who were also the declarants, Rule 801(d)(2) deals with statements made by a party to a civil or criminal action. The rule uses the phrase "admission by party-opponent," but, in fact, the rule covers any statement of a party-opponent, regardless of whether the party-opponent admits anything, or meant to admit anything. The only requirement is that the party-opponent made a statement, as defined in Rule 801(a). Any witness can report what the declarant said out of court, as long as the declarant is a party. The jury can use the out-of-court statement as substantive evidence.

In a civil action, a party is any of the named plaintiffs or defendants. In a criminal action, a party is the defendant, because it is the government entity, whether state or federal, that prosecutes the defendant. Again, the admission need only be a statement as defined in Rule 801(a). The party did not have to admit any kind of culpability when making the out-of-court statement. It also does not matter if the statement was in the party's interest or against the party's interest when it was made. Whatever the statement was, as long as it is relevant, it can be reported through the testimony of any witness who heard it, when such witness is called by the opposing party for the purpose of using the statement against the party who made the statement.

Rule 801(d)(2) details what is meant by a "party," to include other persons who speak on behalf of, or in the stead of, a party. Others who can stand in the

cross-examination Questioning of an opposing party's witness during a trial.

impeach Demonstrate a witness is not telling the truth.

shoes of a party, and whose statements can be used against that party as if made by that party, include (1) anyone in a **representative capacity**; (2) anyone authorized by a party to make a statement; (3) an **agent** or employee of the party who makes a statement in the scope of and during the agency or employment (vicarious admission or statement); and (4) a co-conspirator speaking while participating in the **conspiracy** and in furtherance of a conspiracy to commit a crime or civil wrong. Figure 10-3 summarizes all the types of statements covered by Rule 801(d)(2).

RULE 801(d)(2)   NON-HEARSAY EVIDENCE

Statement by party-opponent means

- Party's own statement in individual or representative capacity
- Adopted statement
- Authorized statement
- Agent or employee's statement within scope and during relationship
- Co-conspirator's statement during and in furtherance of conspiracy

---

FIGURE 10-3
Rule 801(d)(2) details the types of statements made by a party-opponent that qualify as non-hearsay evidence.

Finally, if a party adopts someone else's statement (whether oral or written) as the party's own, the statement can be reported by a witness on the stand at trial. Illustration 10-6 gives an example.

Illustration 10-6 _____

Ms. Grundberg filed suit against The Upjohn Company alleging injuries from the drug Halcion. As part of the discovery process, she requested a copy of a clinical study conducted by Dr. Oster because she believed it would help to prove her case. Upjohn objected, claiming Dr. Oster was not its agent and the study was not conducted under its control, so the study was irrelevant and should be inadmissible at trial as hearsay evidence.

Dr. Oster's clinical study of Halcion was submitted by Upjohn to the Food and Drug Administration (FDA) as support for its application for approval of a new drug. Although Dr. Oster's status as it related to Upjohn was unclear, Upjohn manifested its acceptance of the Oster study when it submitted the study to the FDA with the application.

Furthermore, the clinical study was conducted at a facility provided by Upjohn. Based on these factors, the court held that Upjohn had adopted the study as its own and the clinical study was therefore admissible as non-hearsay evidence under Rule 801(d)(2)(B). *Grundberg v. Upjohn Co.*, 140 F.R.D. 459 (D. Utah 1991).

_____

The burden of proving that the declarant stands in the shoes of a party is on the proponent of the testimony. The proponent must establish, for instance, that the declarant adopted or authorized the statement. If the proof fails, the trial court judge will sustain the hearsay objection because Rule 801(d)(2) does not apply.

representative capacity
Standing in the place of someone else.

agent Someone authorized to act on behalf of another.

conspiracy A plan with an illegal purpose.

Think of 801(d)(2) as the rule that leads to words coming back to haunt a person when the person becomes a plaintiff or defendant in a court action. By definition, the Federal Rules of Evidence treat this statement by a person who is a party to a lawsuit as non-hearsay and therefore not subject to a hearsay objection. Note, however, that some states classify statements or admissions by party-opponents as exceptions to the hearsay rule. For instance, in Florida, statements of a party offered against the party are admissible into evidence even though such statements are classified as hearsay, because these statements fall within the exceptions to the hearsay rule.[2] Whether statements by party-opponents are defined as non-hearsay, as in the federal rules, or listed as an exception to the hearsay rule, as in Florida, the result is the same. The testimony is admissible into evidence (see Illustration 10-7).

Illustration 10-7 _____

In a murder case, the defendant's former girlfriend was called as a witness by the prosecutor. She testified the defendant told her, two days after the victim's death, that he recently "took a man by the throat and squeezed the life out of him."

Even though the witness went on to say the defendant did not say exactly when the murder occurred or who was killed, the evidence was admissible as an admission by a party-opponent. *State v. Hendrix,* Florida First Judicial Circuit, Circuit Court, Escambia County, August 1988.

SPECIAL CONSIDERATIONS _____

Two other rules within Article VIII of the Rules of Evidence cover special circumstances related to the hearsay rule. Rules 805 and 806 explain how to handle issues related to the hearsay rule.

Hearsay within Hearsay

Rule 805 offers guidance in situations where verbal or documentary evidence falls outside the hearsay rule either by definition or because an exception applies, yet the statement or document itself may contain statements that are themselves hearsay. See Illustration 10-8 for an example of the application of Rule 805.

Illustration 10-8 _____

Ms. Cedeck wanted to testify that the branch manager of the bank where she was employed told her, "Ginnie, I'm sorry, I was told that, 'Yes, we know she's qualified, but unless she's flat-chested and wears pants, there's no way.' " Ms. Cedeck was suing her employer, alleging sex discrimination in her failure to be promoted and in her discharge.

Generally, a statement by an employee concerning a matter within the scope of employment is not hearsay [Rule 801(d)(2)(D)]. However, because the branch manager's statement contained a reiteration of what someone else told him, Ms. Cedeck could not testify as to what the branch manager said, because the identity of the declarant the branch manager quoted was unknown.

This is hearsay within hearsay, treated in Rule 805. *Cedeck v. Hamiltonian Federal Savings & Loan Assn.,* 551 F.2d 1136 (8th Cir. 1977).

Rule 805. Hearsay within Hearsay

Hearsay included within hearsay is not excluded under the hearsay rule if each part of the combined statements conforms with an exception to the hearsay rule provided in these rules.

An example of *hearsay within hearsay* is when a witness testifies using a report, and the trial court judge determines that either the report itself is not hearsay or that a hearsay exception applies. The contents of the report must also be non-hearsay or covered by an exception. Otherwise, the witness cannot testify to the matters in the report that are hearsay, only to those matters in the report not characterized as hearsay. Sometimes this situation may occur with verbal communications, but typically Rule 805 is applicable only when documents are offered into evidence.

When documents are going to be offered into evidence, the paralegal should carefully review them to determine (1) is the document itself hearsay, and if so, does a hearsay exception apply; and (2) if an exception applies, can it be argued that statements within the document are hearsay, and if so, does an exception apply to those statements? Just because some statements may be excluded because they are hearsay does not mean the whole document is inadmissible. The offending portion can be removed and the jury allowed to see the unobjectionable parts of the document.

Credibility of a Declarant

Rule 806 allows a party to attack the **credibility** of a declarant after a witness testifies to what the declarant said. Like the witness who takes the stand in court, the declarant is a witness once the declarant's statement is reported.

Rule 806. Attacking and Supporting Credibility of Declarant

When a hearsay statement, or a statement defined in Rule 801(d)(2), (C), (D), or (E), has been admitted in evidence, the credibility of the declarant may be attacked, and if attacked may be supported, by any evidence which would be admissible for those purposes if declarant had testified as a witness. Evidence of a statement or conduct by the declarant at any time, inconsistent with the declarant's hearsay statement, is not subject to any requirement that the declarant may have been afforded an opportunity to deny or explain. If the party against whom a hearsay statement has been admitted calls the declarant as a witness, the party is entitled to examine the declarant on the statement as if under cross-examination.

To impeach a declarant's statement, Rule 806 allows a party to use all of the ways normally available to impeach any other witness. Prior inconsistent statements of the declarant can be used whether or not the requirements of Rule 613(b) can be met.

credibility Trustworthiness.

Rule 613. Prior Statements of Witnesses

> **(b) Extrinsic evidence of prior inconsistent statement of witness.** Extrinsic evidence of a prior inconsistent statement by a witness is not admissible unless the witness is afforded an opportunity to explain or deny the same and the opposite party is afforded an opportunity to interrogate the witness thereon, or the interests of justice otherwise require. This provision does not apply to admissions of a party-opponent as defined in Rule 801(d)(2).

The declarant does not have to get the opportunity to deny bias, prejudice, interest, or improper motive before the opposing party launches into an attack on the credibility of a declarant's statement. Extrinsic evidence is the usual mode for attacking the declarant, which means other witnesses can testify, or contrary documents can be presented. See Illustration 10-9 for an example of how this works.

Illustration 10-9

Rickett and Finch were defendants in a criminal trial where neither testified, but one sought to impeach the other during cross-examination of a third party, Nichols. Nichols testified as to out-of-court statements made by Finch about Rickett's drug activity (statement by a party-opponent). Rickett then impeached Finch's credibility as a hearsay declarant by introducing certified records of Finch's prior convictions.

Finch objected to the introduction of the convictions, claiming the convictions constituted inadmissible character evidence and were highly prejudicial.

Citing Rule 806, the appellate court noted Finch's credibility as an out-of-court declarant could be impeached as if he were a witness in court who made the statements about Rickett. The court added Rule 609 to the analysis, which allows prior convictions for impeachment purposes.

The trial court judge appropriately instructed the jury the prior crimes could not be considered as evidence of Finch's guilt but rather only to discredit the accuracy of his out-of-court statements. Admitting the evidence was not an abuse of the trial court judge's discretion. *United States v. Bovain,* 708 F.2d 606 (11th Cir. 1983).

The declarant can also be called to the stand by the attacking party, and the attacking party can question the declarant as if on cross-examination, that is, with leading questions as a means of impeachment. On the other hand, once the declarant has been attacked, the proponent of the evidence can offer evidence to rehabilitate the declarant.

SUMMARY

If the testimony of a witness reports the substance of someone else's statement for its truth, the testimony is subject to a hearsay objection. Rule 801 defines hearsay and the components of the definition. Sometimes a witness can be the declarant and that in-court testimony objectionable as hearsay.

Rule 801 also defines certain prior statements of witnesses and statements by party-opponents as non-hearsay and thus admissible into evidence as long as the testimony is not subject to another objection.

Just as Rule 801(d)(1) and (2) reflects the desirability of admitting certain testimony because its importance outweighs hearsay considerations, Rule 803 lists twenty-three exceptions to the hearsay rule. Rule 807 is a catch-all provision leaving the door open to other hearsay evidence. As we will see in the next chapter, the exceptions to the hearsay rule almost consume the rule itself.

It is incumbent on the paralegal to understand what type of evidence is subject to a hearsay objection and to then determine whether an exception to the rule will give the trial court judge the opportunity to overrule the objection and admit the evidence. Rule 801 defines hearsay, and Rule 802 excludes hearsay evidence generally, subject to other rules and statutes. Rules 803 and 804 allow the jury to consider hearsay evidence if the evidence falls within the requirements of either of these two rules. These two rules create huge holes in not only the hearsay rule, but in the trial court judge's ability to keep the jury from hearing evidence. Remember, though, just because a hearsay objection is overruled because there is an applicable exception does not mean there is no other way to keep the evidence from the jury. Rule 403 remains an excellent fall-back argument.

The paralegal who carefully assists in trial preparation and recognizes potential hearsay problems with evidence should not be surprised at trial when the opposing party fails to object to evidence that is arguably hearsay. Opposing counsel may decide, for tactical reasons, to forgo any objection to certain testimony or other evidence. On the other hand, opposing counsel may not have the able assistance of a well-trained paralegal to help the overworked attorney prepare thoroughly for trial. And if an objection is made by opposing counsel, again, do not be surprised when opposing counsel cannot competently articulate the hearsay argument. Although you and your supervising attorney may believe the chances are good the trial court judge will sustain a hearsay objection to your proffered evidence, if opposing counsel's argument stumbles while your attorney makes a cogent argument, the trial court judge may overrule the objection just because one attorney sounds so much better. Judges can be weak on the hearsay rule and hence rely on the arguments of the trial attorneys. Even though the ruling by the trial court judge may be wrong, if it is later appealed, the appellate court likely will note the error but find it harmless (as explained in Chapter 2).

✔ CHECKPOINTS

❏ Hearsay analysis
1. Hearsay evidence: testimony by a witness or something written in a document that is based on an out-of-court declarant's statement and is offered to prove the truth of what was stated.
2. Not hearsay evidence: testimony by a witness or something written in a document that is not the statement of someone else, or if it is, is not offered to prove the truth of the statement's content.
3. Not hearsay: by definition in the Federal Rules of Evidence.
4. Hearsay but admissible: an exception to the hearsay rule applies.

❏ Witness and declarant not the same person

1. Nonverbal conduct is a statement when it is intended to convey meaning.

2. Written document: hearsay evidence if prepared by someone other than the witness and offered for its truth.

❏ Statements not offered for their truth

1. Legally operative words.

2. Words affecting the listener.

3. Nonassertive conduct.

4. Implied assertions.

❏ Non-hearsay

1. Declarant as witness if witness has personal knowledge and current recollection.

2. Prior inconsistent statements.

3. Prior consistent statements, but only if in response to charge of recent fabrication or improper influence or motive.

4. Out-of-court identification if witness is the one who made the identification.

5. Statements used for cross-examination and impeachment, but they cannot be substantive evidence.

6. Statements of party-opponent.

❏ Special considerations

1. Hearsay within hearsay rule applies when evidence is a document.

2. Credibility of declarant can be attacked as if the declarant were a witness, using extrinsic evidence.

APPLICATIONS

Application 10-1

United States v. Russell
712 F.2d 1256 (8th Cir. 1983)

PER CURIAM.

Robert Russell appeals his conviction for three counts of aiding and abetting the passing and uttering of forged and altered United States postal money orders in violation of 18 U.S.C. §§ 2(a) and 500. Russell asserts the trial court improperly admitted prior inconsistent statements made by the government's chief witness to the grand jury and to investigating agents from the United States Postal Service. Russell also challenges the sufficiency of the evidence against him. We affirm.

In February of 1982, a burglar stole seventy-two United States postal money orders and other items from the Oxley, Missouri post office. The following month, the postal authorities apprehended Kenneth Polin after he cashed five of the stolen money orders in and around Poplar Bluff, Missouri. In a handwritten statement to the postal authorities, and later before a federal grand jury, Polin stated that Russell had asked him to cash the money orders in return for half of the money. Polin also stated that Russell had prepared the money orders, driven him to the stores where they were cashed, and provided him with fake identification. Polin pleaded guilty to two counts of passing and uttering forged money orders. The government dropped the other counts and recommended a three year sentence in exchange for Polin's cooperation.

When the government called Polin as a witness at Russell's trial, Polin said he could not remember having any contact with Russell around February 15, 1982, the approximate date the money orders were cashed. The trial court declared Polin a hostile witness and allowed the government to introduce into evidence his prior statements to the federal grand jury and the postal authorities.

Polin's grand jury testimony is clearly admissible under the federal rules as substantive evidence. Rule 801(d)(1)(A) provides that a statement is not hearsay if the declarant testifies at trial, is subject to cross-examination concerning the statement, and the statement is "inconsistent with his testimony, and was given under oath subject to the penalty of perjury at a trial, hearing, or other proceeding." Grand jury testimony comes within the scope of this rule. *United States v. Dennis*, 625 F.2d 782, 795 (8th Cir. 1980); *United States v. Mosley*, 555 F.2d 191, 193 (8th Cir.), *cert. denied*, 434 U.S. 851, 98 S.Ct. 163, 54 L.Ed. 2d 120 (1977).

Russell maintains Polin's grand jury testimony should have been excluded because it was not inconsistent with his testimony at trial. We do not agree. "The trial judge has considerable discretion in determining whether testimony is 'inconsistent' with prior statements; inconsistency is not limited to diametrically opposed answers but may be found in evasive answers, inability to recall, silence, or changes of position." *United States v. Dennis, supra*, 625 F.2d at 795. Polin's statement on the stand that he could not recall having any contact with Russell around the time he cashed the forged postal money orders is sufficiently inconsistent with his grand jury testimony for the court to admit the previous testimony.

Nor did the admission of Polin's prior testimony violate Russell's right to confrontation. The use of out-of-court statements does not violate the confrontation clause as long as the declarant is testifying as a witness and subject to full and effective cross-examination. *California v. Green*, 399 U.S. 149, 158, 90 S.Ct. 1930, 1935, 26 L.Ed. 2d 489 (1970).

Polin's prior statements to the postal authorities are not within the scope of Rule 801(d)(1)(A) and were admissible only for impeachment purposes. Ordinarily, the trial court should instruct the jury on the limited purpose of such testimony to reduce potential prejudice. Russell failed to request a limiting instruction, however, so the issue is whether the lack of such an instruction amounted to plain error. The statements to the postal authorities had little if any prejudicial effect since they were repeated in the grand jury testimony which was properly admitted. The trial court was thus not obliged to give a limiting instruction on its own motion.

Finally, we find the evidence introduced at trial sufficient to sustain the conviction. Other evidence corroborated Polin's grand jury testimony. Witnesses at the stores where Polin cashed the money orders testified that another man waited in a pickup truck while Polin went into the stores. The truck was traced to Russell. In addition, Russell's fingerprints were found on one of the money orders.

The judgment of conviction is affirmed.

Class Discussion Questions

1. What was the court's rationale for holding that the grand jury testimony of Polin fell within Rule 801(d)(1)(A)?

2. Could the jury use the grand jury statements as substantive evidence, that is, as a basis for convicting Mr. Russell? Explain your answer.

3. What part of Mr. Polin's testimony at trial was inconsistent with his statements to the grand jury?

4. Why did the handwritten statement to the postal authorities not fall within the scope of Rule 801(d)(1)(A)?

5. For what purpose was the statement to the postal authorities admissible?

Application 10-2

Estate of Shafer v. Commissioner, Internal Revenue Service
749 F.2d 1216 (6th Cir. 1984)

This appeal concerns the includability of the value of a parcel of property in the gross estate of Arthur C. Shafer (Arthur). The Commissioner of the Internal Revenue Service, contending that pursuant to I.R.C. § 1036(a) (1982) the value of the property should have been included in Arthur's gross estate, filed a notice of deficiency against the estate. The decedent's two sons, Arthur Chase Shafer (Chase) and Robert Resor Shafer (Resor), in their capacity as co-executors of their father's estate, petitioned the United States Tax Court for a redetermination of the deficiency. The co-executors argued that the property was not includable because Arthur had not paid for the lot and because no "transfer" within the meaning of Section 2036(a) had occurred. The Tax Court, relying upon affidavits executed by Chase and Resor and a letter from Chase to an Internal Revenue agent, concluded that Arthur had paid for the property and that there had been a "transfer" for federal estate tax purposes; consequently, the Tax Court upheld the Commissioner's notice of deficiency. Chase and Resor, asserting that the court admitted improperly into evidence the two affidavits and letter and erred in defining "transfer" for purposes of Section 2036(a), appeal from the Tax Court's determination. We conclude that the challenged documents were admitted properly into evidence and that the Tax Court, 80 T.C. 1145, interpreted correctly Section 2036(a). Accordingly, we affirm.

On June 8, 1939, Charles Whidden and Leslie Flanders conveyed by deed Lot No. 436 to Arthur C. Shafer and his wife, Eunice Shafer, for life with a remainder in Chase and Resor as tenants in common. The deed stated that the consideration had been paid by "Eunice C.R. Shafer, Arthur C. Shafer, and Arthur Chase Shafer and Robert Resor Shafer." On July 30, 1973, Eunice Shafer predeceased Arthur, Chase and Resor were appointed as co-executors of their mother's estate. The question arose at this time as to whether Lot No. 436 was includable in Eunice's gross estate. Because an Internal Revenue agent was unable to determine who paid for the lot, he requested Chase and Resor to execute affidavits concerning this matter. In compliance, Chase, who was an attorney, drew up affidavits which both he and Resor executed. Resor, in the pertinent portion of his affidavit, stated, "To the best of my memory, in all conversations with my father, he stated that he was the sole purchaser of [Lot No. 436] and the houses thereon." Similarly, in his affidavit, Chase stated, "Throughout my life both my mother and father referred to [Lot No. 436] as 'belonging' to my father. ... My father always said that he had bought and paid for [Lot No. 436], and I never heard my mother contradict him when he said so." Based upon these affidavits, the Internal Revenue agent determined that the property was not includable in Eunice's gross estate.

Within one year of Eunice's death, Arthur died. Chase and Resor, again named as co-executors, failed to include the value of Lot No. 436 in their father's gross estate. In response to an inquiry by an Internal Revenue agent as to why the lot had not been included in Arthur's gross estate, Chase, in a letter dated September 15, 1976, indicated that he did not believe that Arthur had made a "transfer" within the meaning of Section 2036(a). Within this letter, however, Chase noted parenthetically, "It will amuse you to know that [Arthur] bought Lot 437 for $600, put up a small camp on it, only to find that he had put the camp on Lot 436, which he then bought for $1,200." Based upon this statement and the affidavits executed in regard to Eunice's estate, the Commissioner filed a notice of deficiency against Arthur's estate contending that under Section 2036(a) the value of the property was includable in Arthur's gross estate. The Tax Court upheld the notice of deficiency.

Since the Tax Court allowed the statements in the two affidavits and letter to be introduced both for impeachment purposes and as substantive evidence, we must, as an initial matter, determine if they were admitted properly. [FN2. The Federal Rules of Evidence apply to proceedings before the Tax Court. I.R.C. § 7453 (1982)]. Generally, statements such as those in the affidavits and letter would be inadmissible as hearsay. *See* Fed.R.Evid. 801(c). Certain statements made by parties, however, fall outside of the hearsay definition if the statements are offered against a party and the statements are made in the party's individual or representative capacity. [FN3. In order to be an admission within rule 801(d)(2)(A), the statements do not have to be adverse to the party's interests when made. Fed.R.Evid. 801(a) & 801(d)(2)(A). We first consider whether the Chase letter of September 15, 1976 meets these two requirements.

Initially, in order for the letter to be admissible, Chase must be a "party" to this action. An executor of an estate was considered a "party" to the action under the restrictive common law rule of representative admissions. Since the purpose of Rule 801(d)(2)(A) is to increase the admissibility of representative admissions, *see* Fed.R.Evid. 801(d)(2) advisory committee note ("calls for generous treatment of this avenue to admissibility"), *a fortiori* an executor must be a "party" within the Rule. Accordingly, since Chase is a co-executor of Arthur's estate, he is a party for purposes of Rule 801(d)(2)(A). [FN5. Since Resor is also a co-executor, this reasoning applies equally to him].

Having determined that Chase is a "party" to this action, the next inquiry concerns the extent to which Rule 801(d)(2)(A) has expanded upon the admissibility of representative admissions. The history of the rule is relevant to this question. Rule 801(d)(2)(A) was meant to overturn the prior law which permitted admissions by a representative to be introduced only if the statements were made in the representative capacity. In contrast, the plain language of Rule 801(d)(2)(A) encompasses statements made in "either [the executor's] individual *or* a representative capacity." Fed.R.Evid. 801(d)(2)(A) (emphasis added). Thus, whether Chase was acting in his capacity as executor of his father's estate or in his individual capacity when he executed the letter is irrelevant; in either case, the letter is admissible under Rule 801(d)(2)(A) as a party-admission. The Tax Court, therefore, held properly that the letter was an admission within Rule 801(d)(2)(A).

Since the affidavits contain not only direct statements by Chase and Resor, but also statements attributed by Chase and Resor to Arthur, they present an additional hearsay problem. In order to be admissible, both levels of statements within the affidavits must be excluded from the hearsay definition. Fed.R.Evid. 805. As previously discussed, the direct statements made by Chase and Resor are party-admissions. In our view, the statements are a "classic example of an admission." Fed.R.Evid. 801(d)(2)(A) advisory committee note. Thus, the Tax Court held correctly that the affidavits were admissible under the Federal Rules of Evidence.

The includability of Lot No. 436 in Arthur C. Shafer's gross estate has presented this court with several evidentiary issues as well as a statutory interpretation question. As to the evidentiary issues, we conclude that the Tax Court did not abuse its discretion in interpreting its own Rule of Practice and Procedure 143(b) and Fed.R.Evid. 801(d)(2)(A) in a manner which permitted the two affidavits and letter to be admitted into evidence. Also, we conclude that the Tax Court interpreted properly the term "transfer" in Section 2036(a).

The decision of the Tax Court is, accordingly, affirmed.

Class Discussion Questions

1. Why did Resor and Chase execute the affidavits with regard to Lot 436?

2. What statement did Chase make in his September 15, 1976, letter to the IRS that came back to haunt him?

3. On what rule did the IRS base its argument that the affidavits and the letter were admissible into evidence?

4. There were three petitioners in this action before the United States Tax Court: the Estate of Arthur Shafer, Chase Shafer, and Resor Shafer, who were listed as co-executors of the estate. Did it matter whether Chase wrote the letter as the co-executor or as an individual? Explain your answer.

5. What was the hearsay within hearsay problem presented by the affidavits?

6. What was the reasoning of the court when it held that the statements attributed to Arthur were not hearsay?

Application 10-3

In the following case, Mr. Hill was terminated from his employment with Spiegel, Inc., in what the company characterized as a cost-effective reorganization. Mr. Hill claimed the firing was based on his age, in violation of the Age Discrimination in Employment Act. At trial, Mr. Hill called Mr. Baker to testify in support of his claim. Mr. Baker also was an employee of Spiegel. An excerpt from the appellate court opinion follows.

Hill v. Spiegel, Inc.
708 F.2d 233 (6th Cir. 1983)

III.

We now address the district court's admission of testimony pursuant to Rule 801(d)(2)(D) of the Federal Rules of Evidence. This Rule provides that a statement is not hearsay if it is offered against a party and is "a statement by his agent or servant concerning a matter within the scope of his agency or employment, made during the existence of the relationship ... ."

Spiegel argues on appeal, as it did at trial, that testimony of Matthew Baker constituted hearsay in that it fell outside the coverage of Rule 801(d)(2)(D). We agree. Baker, a former Spiegel district manager employed under Hill's supervision, testified in behalf of Hill to conversations he had with several other Spiegel employees concerning Hill's discharge. The essence of Baker's testimony was that he was told by Spiegel employees Ed Williams, Danny Seligman, and George Phillips, that Hill had been discharged because of his age and income. Baker further testified as to how these men relayed to him the terrible and traumatic experience of Hill's discharge, and its effect on incumbent management.

Spiegel submits that there was no evidence that these declarants, as to whose comments Baker testified, were involved in the decision to discharge Emery Hill. Spiegel argues, and we agree, that since there was no evidence that either Williams, Seligman, or Phillips had any involvement in the decision to discharge Hill, there was no basis for finding that the statement of these declarants concerned "a matter within the scope of [their] agency." Rule 801(d)(2)(D). We recognize that under this Rule, as is pointed out in the Notes of the Advisory Committee, it is not necessary to show that the declarant had authority to make the statement. But it is necessary, we repeat, to show, to support admissibility, that the content of the declarant's statement concerned a matter within the scope of his agency. The evidence of record tends to establish that Williams was an "operations manager" at Spiegel, about whose duties and responsibilities Baker testified he was uncertain. Baker further testified that Seligman was employed as a "catalog distribution manager," involved in the requisition and circulation of catalogs. Finally, Baker testified that George Phillips became a regional manager of the COS division upon Hill's discharge. The mere fact that each of these men was a "manager" within the expansive Spiegel organization is clearly insufficient to establish that matters bearing upon Hill's discharge were within the scope of their employment. Their statements to Baker concerning Hill's discharge cannot, on this record, be considered as vicarious admissions by Spiegel. We conclude that the admission of this evidence on this record was reversible error.

Accordingly, for the reasons stated herein, we vacate the judgment of the district court and remand for a new trial and such other proceedings as may be required.

Class Discussion Questions

1. What position did Mr. Baker have with Spiegel?

2. What was the content of his testimony?

3. Explain Spiegel's hearsay objection.

Application 10-4

The case that follows provides an excellent discussion of Rule 801(d)(2) on the issues of burden of proof and what is meant by the terms "authorized" [801(d)(2)(C)] and "scope of employment" [801(d)(2)(D)]. Ms. Wilkinson sued Carnival Cruise Lines for injuries she received when an automatic sliding door on board a cruise ship ran over the toes on her right foot. Because federal maritime law governed the case, she had to provide evidence that Carnival had actual or constructive notice of the door's alleged propensity to malfunction in order to prove negligence.

The only evidence of notice that Ms. Wilkinson had was contained in a deposition of her on-board roommate, who stated that she was told by a cabin steward shortly after the accident that "they had been having problems with the door and that he was, you know, hoping they would get it fixed before it happened to a child." Carnival objected to the statement of the cabin steward (who was never identified) as hearsay. Ms. Wilkinson claimed that it was a "vicarious admission" under 801(d)(2)(D) and therefore non-hearsay.

Carnival countered with an affidavit that room stewards were the most junior employees on board ship, that their only function was to clear rooms, that they were not authorized by Carnival to speak on behalf of the company or to work on or about electrically operated sliding glass doors. Furthermore, room stewards were restricted to crew areas of the ship and were not permitted in the passenger areas where the incident occurred.

The trial court judge allowed the deposition into evidence. The jury found in favor of Ms. Wilkinson, and Carnival appealed, arguing that the trial court judge erred in overruling its objection to the deposition statement.

The appellate court reversed the judgment of the trial court and remanded the case for a new trial. If Ms. Wilkinson had not raised the possibility of using Rule 803(24), the "catch-all" exception, the appellate court would have reversed the decision and entered judgment for Carnival. But since Ms. Wilkinson did raise this exception—which was not fully argued, because the trial court judge held that Rule 801(d)(2)(D) applied—the appellate court remanded the case so the trial court judge could determine whether the deposition statements were admissible under Rule 803(24).

Wilkinson v. Carnival Cruise Lines, Inc.
920 F.2d 1560 (11th Cir. 1991)

DISCUSSION

I. *Admissibility of the Cabin Steward's Hearsay Statement*

We first consider the admissibility of certain alleged comments by a room steward, identified only as "Fletcher," to the effect that the Tropicale "had been having problems with the door and that [the steward] was ... hoping they would get it fixed before it happened to a child." This testimony, adduced at trial through the video deposition of Tracie Sanders, was vital to the plaintiff's case, as it was the only evidence offered to prove that Carnival had actual or constructive notice of the risk-creating condition, i.e. previous problems with the sliding door in question.

The district court admitted the Fletcher statements as relevant, non-hearsay testimony pursuant to Rule 801(d)(2)(D) of the Federal Rules of Evidence. This Rule provides that a statement is not hearsay if it is offered against a party and is "a statement by the party's agent or servant concerning a matter within the scope of the agency or employment, made during the existence of the relationship." Fed.R.Evid. 801(d)(2)(D). Carnival contends that such a ruling was reversible error, and that the district court should have adopted the evidentiary recommendation of the magistrate, who found that the cabin steward Fletcher's statement to Tracie Sanders did not concern a matter within the scope of his agency or employment, and was therefore inadmissible hearsay. We agree.

Nothing in Rule 801(d)(2)(D) prevents the out-of-court statements of low-level employees from coming into evidence as non-hearsay admissions of a party-opponent in appropriate factual scenarios. *See, e.g., Zenith Radio Corp. v. Matsushita Elec. Ind. Co.,* 505 F.Supp. 1190, 1247 (E.D. Pa. 1980) (requirement "of managerial responsibilities, if it remains valid after the enactment of the [Federal Rules of Evidence], is pertinent only to authorized admissions" under 801(d)(2)(C), and "not to vicarious admissions" under 801(d)(2)(D)). We wholeheartedly agree with the district court that "the position of the individual in the so-called corporate hierarchy is not in and of itself determinative of an 801(d)(2)(D) type of issue." From this observation, however, the district court concluded that simply because Fletcher was a member of the Tropicale's crew, his statement to Ms. Sanders was covered by the language of Rule 801(d)(2)(D). Respectfully, we believe that such a conclusion begs the question.

The appropriate focus is instead upon whether the cabin steward's statement concerned a "matter within the scope of [his] agency or employment" with Carnival. We recognize, as suggested in the Notes of the Advisory Committee, that Rule 801(d)(2)(D) broadened the traditional view so that it is no longer necessary to show that an employee or agent declarant possesses "speaking authority," tested by the usual standards of agency law, before a statement can be admitted against the principal. But it is necessary, in order to support admissibility, that the content of the declarant's statement concerned a matter within the scope of his agency. *Hill v. Spiegel, Inc.,* 708 F.2d 233, 237 (6th Cir. 1983); see, e.g. *Tallarico v. Trans World Airlines, Inc.,* 881 F.2d 566, 572 (8th Cir. 1989) (in tort suit brought by handicapped minor against airline, trial court did not abuse discretion in refusing to admit derogatory remarks of airline employees as vicarious admissions, where employees were non-management personnel who were not involved in decision to keep minor from boarding aircraft); *Staheli v. Univ. of Mississippi,* 854 F.2d 121, 127 (5th Cir. 1988) (in decision affirming denial of university professor's tenure, proffered testimony of fellow accounting professor was not an admission where accounting professor had nothing to do with tenure decision and testimony did not concern matter within scope of his agency); *Miles v. M.N.C. Corp.,* 750 F.2d 867, 874–75 (11th Cir. 1985) (in plaintiff's Title VII suit against employer, nature of supervisory positions held by declarant determined admissibility of evidence of alleged racial slur as vicarious admission of employer); *Cebula v. General Elec. Co.,* 614 F.Supp. 260, 266 (D.C.Ill. 1985) (in age discrimination suit against employer, statements of low-level co-workers could not be attributable to employer as admission, and thus constituted inadmissible hearsay, where plaintiff offered no evidence to suggest that any of the co-workers was involved in the termination decision, or was speaking as to a matter within the scope of their agency or employment).

Thus, the inquiry is whether Fletcher was authorized to act for his principal, Carnival, concerning the matter about which he allegedly spoke. In this case, in support of its Reply to Plaintiff's Response to Motion for Summary Judgment, Carnival attached the affidavit of Jack Stein, one of its Operations Department employees. Stein stated, in pertinent parts:

5.   The function of a room steward is to clean rooms. Room stewards do not work in the engineering department. They are not mechanics, electricians, ships's officers or sliding glass door repairmen.

6.   Room stewards are restricted to crew areas of the ship except for those areas in which they work. A cabin steward such as the "Fletcher" described in the deposition of Tracie Sanders could only work in the passenger area where rooms he serviced were located and in the adjacent service areas (to get ice, food, etc.). Room stewards are not authorized to be in the area of the sliding glass door (near the swimming pool) where Ms. Wilkinson says she was when injured. That is a passenger area.

(R4-65). The magistrate found, and we agree, that Stein's affidavit established "that the statement made by a room steward to Ms. Sanders did not concern a matter within the scope of his agency or employment," and therefore was hearsay. [FN11. Absent conformity with one of the categories of non-hearsay statements listed in Rule 801(d), the Fletcher statement is clearly hearsay, since it is a statement, other than one made by the declarant Fletcher testifying at trial or hearing offered in evidence by plaintiff to prove the truth of the matter asserted, i.e. that Carnival had prior notice of problems with the sliding glass door. See Fed.R.Evid. 801(c).]

Plaintiff argues that Carnival has not properly preserved the issue on appeal, because "at no point from the beginning of the trial until the time of the jury's verdict did Carnival ever object to the 'Fletcher' statement on the specific ground that cabin stewards were not permitted to be on the deck where Mrs. Wilkinson was injured." *Brief of Appellee* at 10. On this point, plaintiff has apparently misunderstood its burden. It is well established that "Rule 801(d)(2)(D) requires the *proffering party* to lay a foundation to show that an otherwise excludible statement relates to a matter within the scope of the agent's employment." As one district court has aptly observed with regard to Rule 801(d)(2):

[A]lthough the necessary proof may certainly be circumstantial, there must be an adequate foundational showing, as to subsection (C), that the agent or servant was in fact authorized to make the statement in question, or as to subsection (D), that the subject of the statement 'concerned a matter' which was within [the] scope of the speaker's agency or employment. Merely showing that a statement was made by one who is identified generally as an agent or employee of the party, without some further proof as to the extent of his authority to make the statement (for purposes of subsection (C)) or as to the scope of his employment (for purposes of subsection (D)), establishes neither.

Carnival has consistently objected to the admissibility of the Fletcher statements as hearsay, and plaintiff has offered not one whit of evidence at any phase of this proceeding to lay a predicate for the admissibility of the statement, or to contradict Stein's assessment of the scope of Fletcher's employment as a cabin steward aboard the Tropicale. [FN12. To be sure, plaintiff speculates that even if cabin stewards were not generally authorized to be in passenger areas, there are a number of ways in which Fletcher might have legitimately acquired knowledge of the defective door in the course and scope of his employment, e.g. he might have been ordered to the area in question, or told of the problems with the doors in connection with his duties. Unfortunately, such speculation does not relieve plaintiff of its evidentiary burden to establish a predicate for the admissibility of Fletcher's statement.] Consequently, the admission of Tracie Sanders' testimony regarding Fletcher under Rule 801(d)(2)(D) was reversible error.

CONCLUSION

For the foregoing reasons, the judgment of the district court is REVERSED and REMANDED for a new trial.

Class Discussion Questions

1. Generally, can out-of-court statements by low-level employees be admitted under Rule 801(d)(2)(D) as admissions of a party-opponent?

2. What is the critical factor in determining whether an agent's or employee's statement comes within Rule 801(d)(2)(D)?

3. Give four examples of situations where the courts have dealt with the issue of scope of agency or employment.

4. Why did the trial court judge err in allowing Ms. Wilkinson to get the deposition statement into evidence?

5. Under Rule 801(d)(2)(C), what must be proven by the proponent of an apparent hearsay statement in order to get the out-of-court statement before the jury?

EXERCISES

1. You work in a firm that is defending a corporate client in a claim of discrimination based on national origin and age. The plaintiff alleges he was subjected to a variety of forms of disparate treatment by his corporate employer, amounting to discrimination based on national origin and age in violation of federal law. He claims that this treatment caused him to resign from the company after ten years of employment because, as a result of the discrimination, he received no raises or promotions in that time.

   A manager and supervisor of the defendant while he was employed at the corporation can testify she received multiple complaints from persons who worked with the plaintiff. You recognize that this testimony could be subject to a hearsay objection at trial. On the other hand, it is important to the corporation's defense against the plaintiff's claim of discrimination, so the defense will try to get it admitted.
   a. How can this testimony be construed as hearsay?
   b. Using the definition of hearsay, make an argument the testimony is not hearsay.
   c. What is the relevance of the complaints about the plaintiff?

2. You are preparing for a trial in which the firm's client is suing an apparel company that had contracted to sell its product. Among other claims, the client is alleging fraud in that the protective apparel did not function as promised and he was seriously injured while demonstrating the use of the apparel.

   The client gave you reprints of newspaper articles that the apparel company gave to him during negotiations. The reprints contain statements about the company's financial situation that are inflated representations. The reprints are relevant as evidence of the fraud.
   a. Characterize the reprints as hearsay evidence.
   b. Outline an argument for admissibility, based on Rule 801(d)(2).

3. The firm's client is a former employee of a corporation, and claims severance compensation under the corporation's personnel policy. Unfortunately, the client resigned from the corporation, and therefore lost the severance compensation. The client seeks to rescind that resignation, alleging that he was tricked into it.

   In the investigation of the case, you found a witness who overheard a telephone conversation between the client's supervisor and an unknown person, in which the supervisor stated, "You don't have to worry about paying him severance pay, because I'll make him quit." If the witness testifies, a hearsay objection is guaranteed. The supervisor is not a party to the lawsuit.

Outline an argument for admissibility of the evidence, citing the appropriate rule and subsection.

4. How does your state characterize implied assertions? Are statements that are implied assertions hearsay?

RULES REFERENCED IN THIS CHAPTER

Rule 801. Definitions
Rule 802. Hearsay Rule
Rule 805. Hearsay within Hearsay

Rule 806. Attacking and Supporting Credibility of Declarant
Rule 602. Lack of Personal Knowledge
Rule 613. Prior Statements of Witnesses

NOTES

[1] *United States v. Wade,* 388 U.S. 218 (1967); *Gilbert v. California,* 388 U.S. 263 (1967).

[2] Fla. Stat. § 90.803(18) Admissions.

Exceptions to the Hearsay Rule

OUTLINE

INTRODUCTION

In the last chapter, the hearsay rule was defined as in Rule 801(a)(b)(c), then immediately "excepted." Rule 801(d) lists the type of evidence that appears to be hearsay, yet is defined as non-hearsay and therefore beyond the strictures of the hearsay rule (Rule 802). From Rule 802, we also learned how other rules of court and statutes "except" evidence that would otherwise be hearsay, paving the way to admissibility.

Rule 803 lists twenty-three hearsay examples that are excluded from the hearsay rule even though the examples meet the definition of hearsay. And Rule 804 includes five more exceptions to the hearsay rule where the declarant is not available as a witness. Furthermore, Rule 807 is a "catch-all" provision allowing a proponent of hearsay evidence to argue to the trial court judge that other hearsay evidence should be excepted from the hearsay rule.

If evidence meets the parameters of one of the exceptions listed in Rule 803, then the evidence will pass through the filtering trial court judge to the jury for its consideration, along with all the other evidence presented at trial. The jury can hear a witness testify to what a declarant stated out of court, and that testimony can be used as substantive evidence. Even if the declarant is sitting in the courtroom, ready and able to testify, the witness can repeat the statement of the declarant as long as the statement falls within an exception. The reason the witness is allowed to do this is that, as a matter of common sense, a statement made under the circumstances defined in each exception is reliable, sometimes more reliable than the testimony of the declarant would be if the declarant took the stand. The exceptions in Rules 803 and 804 are a refinement of what existed in case law prior to the creation of the Federal Rules of Evidence.

As we have seen with the other rules of evidence, there may be a valid way to circumvent this rule. A Rule 403 objection, for instance, may be sustained even if the evidence appears admissible as an exception to the hearsay rule (Figure 11-1).

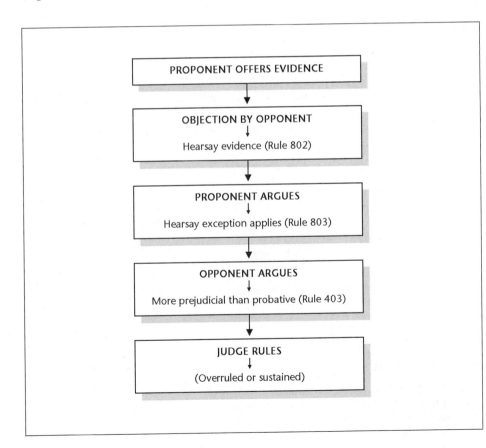

FIGURE 11-1

Hearsay evidence admitted on the basis of a Rule 803 exception can be objected to on the basis of being more prejudicial than probative (Rule 403).

EXCEPTIONS: AVAILABILITY OF DECLARANT IMMATERIAL ———

Rule 803 allows evidence that would otherwise meet the definition of hearsay to be offered as an exception to the application of the hearsay rule, whether or not the declarant is available to be called as a witness (Figure 11-2).

FIGURE 11-2

Rule 803 provides exceptions to the hearsay rule for many types of evidence.

**RULE 803. HEARSAY EXCEPTIONS:
AVAILABILITY OF DECLARANT IMMATERIAL**

Not excluded by the hearsay rule
even though declarant available to testify

(1)　Present sense impression

(2)　Excited utterance

(3)　Then existing mental, emotional, or physical condition

(4)　Statements for purposes of medical diagnosis or treatment

(5)　Recorded recollection

(6)　Records of regularly conducted activity

(7)　Absence of entry in records kept in accordance with the provisions of paragraph (6)

(8)　Public records and reports

(9)　Records of vital statistics

(10)　Absence of public record or entry

(11)　Records of religious organizations

(12)　Marriage, baptismal, and similar certificates

(13)　Family records

(14)　Records of documents affecting an interest in property

(15)　Statements in documents affecting an interest in property

(16)　Statements in ancient documents

(17)　Market reports

(18)　Learned treatises

(19)　Reputation concerning personal or family history

(20)　Reputation concerning boundaries or general history

(21)　Reputation as to character

(22)　Judgment of previous conviction

(23)　Judgment as to personal, family, or general history, or boundaries

---

Present Sense Impression and Excited Utterance

Where the witness is asked to testify as to what an out-of-court declarant said, the exception for *present sense impression* is useful as long as the reported statement was made very close to the time of the event that gave rise to the statement. The premise for this exception is the statement probably is trustworthy because there is not enough of a time lapse between the event and the statement to allow the declarant to consciously misrepresent the event in the statement. Cross-examination is possible because the witness can be questioned about the circumstances surrounding the making of the statement by the declarant. The jury then has the opportunity to evaluate the credibility of the testimony.

Rule 803. Hearsay Exceptions: Availability of Declarant Immaterial

(1) Present sense impression. A statement describing or explaining an event or condition made while the declarant was perceiving the event or condition, or immediately thereafter.

If the witness is also the declarant, reporting the statement that the witness made as a declarant after an event also would be hearsay but for this exception. The witness/declarant can be cross-examined as could any witness reporting a declarant's statement.

The declarant who makes a statement because of an event does not have to have been a participant in the event. The declarant needs only to describe or explain the event that was the basis for the statement.

In some states, present sense impression is called *spontaneous statement,* but the meaning is the same as in the federal rules.

The *excited utterance exception* is similar to present sense impression, but it requires that a level of excitement exist as a result of a startling event and that the declarant reacted under the stress of the event. In one sense, the excited utterance exception is broader than present sense impression, because the time lapse can be longer. But in another sense, the exception is narrower, because the event must be startling. The reasoning behind this rule is that a statement made after a startling event is one that leaves little room for fabrication, so the statement likely is trustworthy. Cross-examination considerations are the same for excited utterances as they are for present sense impression.

Rule 803. Hearsay Exceptions: Availability of Declarant Immaterial

(2) Excited utterance. A statement relating to a startling event or condition made while the declarant was under the stress of excitement caused by the event or condition.

As with present sense impression, the declarant of an excited utterance does not have to be a participant in the exciting event. More statements may be admissible under the excited utterance exception than the present sense impression exception, because the excited utterance need only relate to the exciting event, not necessarily describe or explain the event. A foundation needs to be laid by the proponent of the evidence to establish that the event was startling and the statement was connected to the event.

Between these two exceptions, a witness can testify to a declarant's statement over the objection of the opponent of the evidence because the proponent can argue either exception (Figure 11-3).

FIGURE 11-3

The hearsay exception of present sense impression assumes that a statement made very close to an event is likely to be true. The exception of excited utterance assumes that a statement made under the stress of an exciting event is likely to be true.

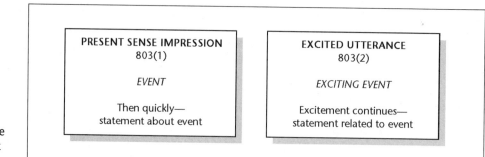

Mental, Emotional, or Physical Condition

The third exception under Rule 803 allows into evidence a declarant's statement relating to the declarant's then existing state of mind, emotional condition, or physical condition. The key factor is the statement must relate to the declarant's mental, emotional, or physical condition as it existed at the time the statement was made. If the statement by the declarant relates to the declarant's mental, emotional, or physical condition at a time before the statement was made—that is, a past mental or emotional condition—then the exception does not apply. A statement about a past condition does not have the same reliability as a statement describing a present condition as it occurs. The statement must be contemporaneous with the underlying condition giving rise to the statement.

Rule 803. Hearsay Exceptions: Availability of Declarant Immaterial

(3) Then existing mental, emotional, or physical condition. A statement of the declarant's then existing state of mind, emotion, sensation, or physical condition (such as intent, plan, motive, design, mental feeling, pain, and bodily health), but not including a statement of memory or belief to prove the fact remembered or believed unless it relates to the execution, revocation, identification, or terms of declarant's will.

This exception allows in as evidence statements about the declarant's mental and emotional health and physical condition. The statements can be repeated by anyone who heard them. The witness does not have to be a medical professional or family member, as is the case with the fourth exception, Rule 803(4), which involves medical treatment or diagnosis.

A statement by a declarant describing the declarant's intent to do something in the future is admissible as circumstantial evidence that, in fact, the declarant did what the declarant said was intended. This exception allows a statement of future intent but not of past condition or intent, except where the statement relates to the execution, revocation, identification, or terms of a declarant's will. So the witness can testify the declarant (now dead) stated, "I revoked my will last week." As the issues relating to a will arise only after a declarant's death, the need for the statements outweighs hearsay considerations.

Statements of future intent of the declarant can be reported by the witness at trial. For instance, the witness can testify the declarant said, "I am going to Denver next week." This statement is admissible to prove the declarant did go to Denver the following week. Long before the Federal Rules of Evidence were adopted, the United States Supreme Court, in *Mutual Life Ins. Co. v. Hillmon*, articulated this view.[1]

The *Hillmon* doctrine allows the jury to infer from the state of mind of the declarant that (1) the declarant acted in accordance with what was said by the declarant and (2) any person referred to in the statement also acted in accordance with what was in the statement. See Illustration 11-1 for a modern example of the application of the *Hillmon* doctrine.

Illustration 11-1 _____

The defendant, Angelo Incisco, was tried on federal charges related to the kidnapping of a 16-year-old boy. The boy's friends testified the teenager told them as they sat around in a restaurant, "I am going to meet Angelo in the parking lot to get a pound of grass."

The portion of the statement expressing the teenager's intent was admissible to prove he went to the parking lot. The court, applying the *Hillmon* doctrine, also allowed the statement to prove that Angelo was in the parking lot to meet the teenager.

The teenager's statement was evidence of his state of mind, that is, his intent to go to the parking lot to meet Angelo and get a pound of marijuana. It was also evidence Angelo intended to meet him in the parking lot and, by inference, did meet him. *United States v. Pheaster*, 544 F.2d 353, 377 (9th Cir. 1976).

_____

Hillmon is part of the federal common law predating the Federal Rules of Evidence. It is still applied by the federal courts because the doctrine remains viable. However, many states that have adopted a similar exception limit the applicability of the rule and of the *Hillmon* doctrine to using the declarant's statement as circumstantial evidence of the declarant's future act or condition. That is, the doctrine cannot be used in these states to prove someone else did something. "Elvin and I are going to Denver next week" is admissible to prove the declarant went to Denver that week but not that Elvin went.

In analyzing whether a statement meets this exception to the hearsay rule, a necessary element to consider is whether the state of mind of the declarant is relevant. Where a police officer is a witness and is asked about a conversation with someone other than the defendant, a hearsay objection is in order, because the police officer is testifying to what someone else said. If the proponent of the testimony argues that the statement relates to the state of mind of the police officer, that argument should fail to sway the trial court judge. In a criminal case, the state of mind of a law enforcement officer is not a material issue. The state of mind of the defendant might indeed be at issue. For instance, whether the defendant had the requisite intent to commit the illegal act might be at issue. But the state of mind of the officer is not a material issue that the prosecution must prove. The trial court judge should therefore sustain a hearsay objection.

Similarity of Rule 803(1), (2), and (3) Exceptions

The exceptions in Rule 803(1), (2), and (3) are similar because they all relate to a statement by a declarant regarding either a perception of an event or the condition or intent of the declarant. The three exceptions are avenues for admissibility of statements by a declarant that otherwise would be hearsay and lost to the jury. As there is a measure of reliability and trustworthiness in these statements, an exception is appropriate so that the hearsay rule will not block important and useful evidence from being presented to the jury.

Medical Diagnosis or Treatment

When a declarant tells a doctor about matters relating to present and past medical history, and when the statements are for the purpose of medical diagnosis or treatment, the statements are not hearsay when repeated by the doctor on the stand. Furthermore, when the declarant is speaking about matters related to medical diagnosis or treatment, other medical personnel and family members may also testify as to those statements. The premise is the statements are reliable because a person is not likely to lie about matters related to the need for medical diagnosis and treatment.

Rule 803. Hearsay Exceptions: Availability of Declarant Immaterial

  (4) Statement for purposes of medical diagnosis or treatment. Statements made for purposes of medical diagnosis or treatment and describing medical history, or past or present symptoms, pain, or sensations, or the inception or general character of the cause or external source thereof insofar as reasonably pertinent to diagnosis or treatment.

Statements made for purposes of medical diagnosis or treatment are trustworthy because it is assumed a patient has a strong motive to tell the truth. As long as it is reasonable for the doctor to rely on the information in diagnosis or treatment, the statements by the patient to the doctor can be reported by the doctor/witness, whether by testifying or as part of the hospital record. If statements related to fault that are not necessary for treatment or diagnosis are included in the testimony or record, those statements are deemed hearsay, and the trial court judge will not allow the jury to hear them.

Rule 803(4) also allows a doctor who is hired as an expert regarding a person's condition to testify about what the person stated regarding medical condition and history. This exception dovetails with Rule 703, which allows expert witnesses to testify to matters ordinarily relied upon by experts in order to render an opinion. Again, if the declarant's statement includes matters not necessary to medical diagnosis or treatment, such as fault or identity, that portion of the statement is inadmissible hearsay.

Recorded Recollection

When a person records an event near the time the event occurred, and later the recorded statement is offered into evidence at trial, the recorded statement falls within the exception for recorded recollections, Rule 803(5), if the declarant can no longer sufficiently recall the event. After the proponent of the evidence lays a foundation, the trial court judge determines whether the witness's memory of the event is so faded that an accurate report of the event is impossible. If the judge is satisfied the event is no longer remembered, the recorded statement can be read by the witness to the jury. However, if the recorded statement is enough to jog the memory of the witness, then the witness must testify to the events independently of the statement, and the recorded statement is not admissible.

Rule 803. Hearsay Exceptions: Availability of Declarant Immaterial

(5) **Recorded recollection.** A memorandum or record concerning a matter about which a witness once had knowledge but now has insufficient recollection to enable the witness to testify fully and accurately, shown to have been made or adopted by the witness when the matter was fresh in the witness' memory and to reflect that knowledge correctly. If admitted, the memorandum or record may be read into evidence but may not itself be received as an exhibit unless offered by an adverse party.

It is not necessary that the statement itself be prepared by the witness. If there is evidence the witness adopted the statement based on personal knowledge of the underlying events after it was prepared, and the witness no longer has sufficient memory of the contents of the statement, the statement falls within this exception. This is a common occurrence because trials often are scheduled years after the event which led to litigation.

In order to take advantage of the recorded recollection exception, the paralegal needs to prepare an outline so a proper foundation can be established by the attorney at trial. The attorney needs to establish with the witness that (1) the witness has no present recollection, (2) the witness can authenticate the statement as one made at or soon after the relevant event, (3) the witness had personal knowledge of the facts in the statement at one time, (4) the witness's memory was fresh at the time the statement was prepared or adopted, and (5) the witness's knowledge at the time is accurately reflected in the statement.[2]

Once the foundation requirement is met, the witness can read the statement to the jury. The jury will not get to see the document, because its value is the same as any testimonial evidence and no better. However, the opponent of the evidence has the option of introducing the actual document for tactical reasons. Furthermore, the proponent of the evidence can still attempt to get the written statement admitted under another hearsay exception, such as Rule 803(6), which allows as evidence business records. Figure 11-4 summarizes the provisions of Rule 803(5).

Records of Regularly Conducted Activity

The exception for records of regularly conducted activity is based on the idea that businesses prepare documents and reports on a regular basis and that accuracy is important to the perpetuation of the business. Consequently, business

FIGURE 11-4

One of the hearsay exceptions allows recorded recollections to be admitted provided they meet certain requirements.

RULE 803(5)   RECORDED RECOLLECTION

- Witness has no present recollection of event
- "Declarant" is the witness's written statement
- Witness verifies written statement true when made
- Witness can read written statement, BUT written statement not admissible

---

records are deemed reliable and trustworthy enough to pass through the trial court judge's filter to the jury for its consideration.

Rule 803.   Hearsay Exceptions: Availability of Declarant Immaterial

(6) Records of regularly conducted activity. A memorandum, report, record, or data compilation, in any form, of acts, events, conditions, opinions, or diagnoses, made at or near the time by, or from information transmitted by, a person with knowledge, if kept in the course of a regularly conducted business activity, and if it was the regular practice of that business activity to make the memorandum, report, record, or data compilation, all as shown by the testimony of the custodian or other qualified witness, unless the source of information or the method or circumstances of preparation indicate lack of trustworthiness. The term "business" as used in this paragraph includes business, institution, association, profession, occupation, and calling of every kind, whether or not conducted for profit.

To qualify for this exception, the document must be a writing or data compilation that records the activities of a business. The record must be made in the ordinary course of a regularly conducted activity and be prepared by a person who has personal knowledge of the contents of the record. The record must be prepared at or near the time of the event that is the subject of the record.

The term "business" has broad application. It includes for-profit and not-for-profit organizations, sole proprietorships, schools, hospitals, associations, professions, and occupations. Opinions and diagnoses can be part of the record, as long as the person providing them is qualified to give opinions and diagnoses.

The key to admissibility under this exception is preliminary proof to the judge that the record is reliable and trustworthy. The proponent must lay a foundation (1) demonstrating that preparation of the record is something done regularly by the business and concerns business activities, (2) disclosing the source of the information, and (3) pinpointing when the record was made in relation to the event.

Generally, admission of business records is favored. Regularity of preparation of the business record is construed generously to favor admission. In determining whether business records should be admitted, the judge does not "independently analyze the procedures used by a business or its employees in making regularly kept records of regularly conducted business activity. The principal basis of reliability is that reliance on routine record keeping is essential to ongoing business activity."[3]

If there are ambiguities in a business record, the record should be admitted, and then the parties can argue the ambiguities to the jury (see Illustration 11-2).

Illustration 11-2 _____

In an action against Japanese manufacturers where it was alleged antitrust, tariff, and antidumping violations occurred, notebooks kept by a Japanese high-management official were admissible under the business records exception to the hearsay rule.

Attendance at the meeting was within the scope of his authority, and he reported to his superiors what happened at the meetings. The notebooks were diaries containing notes of the meetings consistent with the types of notations that someone reporting to superiors for final decision making would make.

Although sometimes unintelligible, the notebooks were admissible on the antitrust and other alleged violations. All entries were made based on the personal knowledge of the employee. *In re Japanese Electronic Products Antitrust Litigation,* 723 F.2d 238, 290–291 (3d Cir. 1983).

Just because a record is created by a business does not mean it comes within the exception in its entirety. First the paralegal must identify the type of business that is conducted, then compare the information contained in the record to what is necessary to conducting the business. If the record contains information not germane to the business, the hearsay objection may be partially successful, and the record will have to be edited.

Furthermore, persons supplying information used in the record must have a business duty to report the information. Generally witnesses who provide information to law enforcement officers do not have a business duty to provide information to the officer for the officer's report. A hearsay objection as to those statements should be sustained.

As a general rule, if a record is prepared by a business for the purpose of litigation, it does not qualify for this exception. Self-serving motivation puts into serious question the trustworthiness of such a record. Most businesses do not function for the purpose of litigation. Their purpose is to do things such as treat patients, provide goods or services, or educate students.

Rule 803. Hearsay Exceptions: Availability of Declarant Immaterial

   (7) Absence of entry in records kept in accordance with the provisions of paragraph (6). Evidence that a matter is not included in the memoranda reports, records, or data compilations, in any form, kept in accordance with the provisions of paragraph (6), to prove the nonoccurrence or nonexistence of the matter, if the matter was of a kind of which a memorandum, report, record, or data compilation was regularly made and preserved, unless the sources of information or other circumstances indicate lack of trustworthiness.

The exception in Rule 803(7) is the flip side of the one in Rule 803(6). Evidence that there is no business record as defined in Rule 803(6) is proof of its nonexistence. For this exception to be utilized, the proponent of the lack of record must lay a foundation demonstrating that a record of the type in issue is normally prepared in the regular course of business. A knowledgeable witness must testify to the nonexistence of the record after explaining how the records normally are kept.

Public Records

The exception for public records and reports deals with those documents that describe the activities of an agency or an office. Public records and reports can also describe facts or events observed by a public official, but only if the official had a legal duty to report. However, if the opponent of the evidence can convince the trial court judge that the source of the information for the report, or the circumstances surrounding the creation of the report, are untrustworthy, then the judge may sustain the opponent's objection.

Rule 803.   Hearsay Exceptions: Availability of Declarant Immaterial

(8) Public records and reports.   Records, reports statements or data compilations, in any form, of public offices or agencies, setting forth (A) the activities of the office or agency, or (B) matters observed pursuant to duty imposed by law as to which matters there was a duty to report, excluding, however, in criminal cases matters observed by police officers and other law enforcement personnel, or (C) in civil actions and proceedings and against the Government in criminal cases, factual findings resulting from an investigation made pursuant to authority granted by law, unless the sources of information or other circumstances indicate lack of trustworthiness.

Generally, public reports are perceived as reliable because they are the result of a duty imposed on a public employee to prepare the reports. The assumption is the public employee is neutral, having no reason to favor anyone in preparing the report.

More specifically, the exception covers reports, statements, or data compilations in whatever form they might be available, as long as they are related to the functions of a public office or agency. Three possible applications of this exception are: (1) the material relates to the activities of the public office or agency; (2) the public official has a duty imposed by law to report the matters, excluding those matters observed by law enforcement officers in criminal cases; or (3) the factual findings are a result of an investigation based on authority granted by law (see Illustration 11-3).

Illustration 11-3 _____

Some states do not include evaluative reports as an exception to the hearsay rule. For instance, in Florida, a witness with personal knowledge of the facts must be called to the stand to testify. A record containing evaluations or statements or opinion cannot be substituted as is allowed in federal court.

In the third application, the material can be used in any civil action, but not in criminal cases unless used against, not by, the government. Under Rule 803(8)(C), official reports of investigations are presumed to be reliable, and the burden is on the opponent of the evidence to prove otherwise. In determining whether a government investigative report is prepared according to a duty imposed by law, the paralegal must consult the statute or regulation containing the standards for conducting the investigation and see if those standards were followed in preparing a particular report. If the government official complied with statutory requirements, trustworthiness of the report is not compromised, even if the government official relied on facts not directly observed by the government official.

The opponent of the investigative report has the burden of proving that the procedures outlined in the statute are a professionally unreliable means of ascertaining facts. As long as the government official had the legal duty to conduct the investigation for an important government purpose, and in compliance with the authorizing statute, the investigative report meets the trustworthiness requirement. However, if the opponent of the factual findings can convince the trial court judge of circumstances making the material untrustworthy, then the opponent's objection to the evidence can be sustained.

When the paralegal recognizes that the public records exception will be utilized at trial to admit or exclude evidence, the paralegal can prepare an outline of the foundation to be established before the exception applies. The outline should reflect facts that support the following:

1. The public official has personal knowledge of the matters in the reports, statements, or data compilations.
2. If the public official was supplied the material included in the report, statements, or data compilation, the person supplying the material must have had a business duty to give the material to the public official.
3. The reports, statements, or data compilations are trustworthy, as evidenced by the following facts:
   a. Investigation was timely.
   b. A knowledgeable or experienced public official performed the investigation.
   c. A hearing within the agency was held.
   d. The materials were not prepared for possible litigation.

Illustration 11-4 demonstrates the process.

Illustration 11-4 _____

The United States Supreme Court settled a controversy over reports that contained conclusions and opinions, holding that "factually based conclusions or opinions are not on that account excluded from the scope of rule 803(8)(C)." *Beech Aircraft Corp. v. Rainey,* 488 U.S. 153 (1988).

The Court concentrated on the trustworthiness of the report rather than on what constitutes facts or opinions, relying on Rule 403. Furthermore, the Court noted the opponent of the evidence has the right to present evidence undermining the evaluative report.

The business record exception contained in Rule 803(6) can apply to the same material that qualifies under Rule 803(8). However, reports by law enforcement officers, which do not meet the requirements for admissibility under Rule 803(8), may not be admissible under Rule 803(6). Therefore, unlike other evidence that might be admissible under either 803(6) or 803(8), or both, law enforcement reports disqualified under 803(8) may not be admissible under 803(6) either. This is an issue the paralegal must research carefully, because the appellate courts are in disagreement (see Illustration 11-5).

Illustration 11-5

In *United States v. Oates,* 560 F.2d 45 (2d Cir. 1977), the court discussed in detail the legislative history of Rules 803(8)(B) and (C) and 803(6). In order to avoid a collision between the Federal Rules of Evidence and the Constitution—specifically the confrontation clause of the Sixth Amendment—the Second Circuit concluded that the intent of Congress was to render law enforcement reports and evaluative reports absolutely inadmissible against defendants in criminal cases under Rule 803(8)(B) and (C). To allow these law enforcement reports to come into evidence under another exception, such as Rule 803(6), would subvert the demonstrated intent and set up a conflict with the Sixth Amendment right to confront witnesses who testify against a defendant.

However, in *United States v. Sokolow,* 91 F.3d 396, 405 (3d Cir. 1996), the Third Circuit agreed with the Seventh and Tenth Circuits and held that Rule 803(8)(C) does not compel the exclusion of documents admitted under 803(6), so long as the author testifies.

Unlike the court in *Oates,* other circuit courts of appeal have not ruled that the application of Rule 803(8) absolutely excludes the use of other exceptions to the hearsay rule.

Records of vital statistics, by their very nature, are trustworthy and so qualify as an exception to the hearsay rule. It is unlikely that the public office charged by law with the duty to keep statistics on the population in the community would be biased in any way bearing on the litigation. The records of births, fetal deaths, deaths, and marriages are admissible in whatever form that they are kept by the public office, including paper copies or computer disks. A public official can testify, or a certified copy of the record can be used, in accordance with Rule 902(4), which deals with certified copies of public records.

Rule 803. Hearsay Exceptions: Availability of Declarant Immaterial

(9) Records of vital statistics. Records or data compilations, in any form, of births, fetal deaths, deaths, or marriages, if the report thereof was made to a public office pursuant to requirements of law.

Because certain reports, statements, data compilations and records compiled in public offices or agencies are kept by law, if it can be demonstrated there is no such public entry or record, this can be proof of the absence of the information.

Rule 803. Hearsay Exceptions: Availability of Declarant Immaterial

(10) Absence of public record or entry. To prove the absence of a record, report, statement, or data compilation, in any form, or the nonoccurrence or nonexistence of a matter of which a record, report, statement, or data compilation, in any form, was regularly made and preserved by a public office or agency, evidence in the form of a certification in accordance with Rule 902, or testimony, that diligent search failed to disclose the record, report, statement, or data compilation, or entry.

The exception in Rule 803(10) can be applied two ways. First, a public official can testify that a diligent search was conducted and it failed to produce the required information. Or, second, a self-authenticating document as described in Rule 902 can be introduced as evidence of the absence of the public record. Illustration 11-6 is an example of how this works.

Illustration 11-6

In a libel action where E. Howard Hunt sued Liberty Lobby for publishing an article linking Mr. Hunt to the assassination of President John F. Kennedy as a CIA operative, Mr. Hunt had to prove the falsity of the published statements.

In order to prove he was not a CIA operative, Mr. Hunt introduced into evidence affidavits to show the CIA memorandum referred to in the Liberty Lobby article did not exist. Mr. Hunt did this by offering affidavits in which the affiant stated he was the custodian of particular records at the CIA and, after a diligent search, was unable to locate any evidence of CIA memoranda indicating that Mr. Hunt was in Dallas on November 22, 1963, or any memoranda discussing the need to explain Mr. Hunt's whereabouts on that date.

The certificate of the General Counsel of the CIA was attached to each affidavit certifying the position held by the affiant, and the certificates bore the CIA's official seal. The court held that the affidavits were properly admitted under Rule 803(10) [absence of record or entry] and that they were self-authenticating as provided for under Rule 902. *Hunt v. Liberty Lobby,* 720 F.2d 631, 651 (11th Cir. 1983).

Rule 803(10) can apply to information that falls under Rule 803(8), concerning public records and reports, and Rule 803(9), concerning records of vital statistics. Essentially, Rule 803(10) accomplishes the same thing as Rule 803(7) does for the business records exception under Rule 803(6).

Religious Organizations

Rule 803(11), the exception for records of religious organizations, allows into admission records of personal or family history that are regularly kept by a religious organization. This exception goes beyond Rule 803(6), which allows business records, because this exception does not require that the entry in the organization's records be made at the same time of the event (such as birth, marriage, divorce, or death). The person making the entry does not have to have personal knowledge of the event recorded, either.

Rule 803.   Hearsay Exceptions: Availability of Declarant Immaterial

(11) Records of religious organizations.   Statements of births, marriages, divorces, deaths, legitimacy, ancestry, relationship by blood or marriage, or other similar facts or personal or family history, contained in a regularly kept record of a religious organization.

The underlying assumption of Rule 803(11) is familiar. It is unlikely the event would be recorded by a religious organization unless the event occurred. The proponent can therefore prove personal or family history with a religious organization's records.

Certificates and Family Records

When a person is authorized by law or by a religion to conduct a baptism or marriage in a religious ceremony, a certificate memorializing the event can be admitted to prove any fact contained in the certificate. The proponent of the evidence must be able to establish that the certificate was completed very close to the time of the ceremony.

Rule 803.   Hearsay Exceptions: Availability of Declarant Immaterial

(12) Marriage, baptismal, and similar certificates.   Statements of fact contained in a certificate that the maker performed a marriage or other ceremony or administered a sacrament, made by a clergyman, public official, or other person authorized by the rules or practices of a religious organization or by law to perform the act certified, and purporting to have been issued at the time of the act or within a reasonable time thereafter.

Like records of religious organizations, family records do not have to be completed contemporaneously with the personal or family history recorded. But a witness must be able to authenticate the record, for instance, by providing testimony that the book is the family Bible and family members have never disputed any of the entries.

Rule 803.   Hearsay Exceptions: Availability of Declarant Immaterial

(13) Family records.   Statements of fact concerning personal or family history contained in family Bibles, genealogies, charts, engravings on rings, inscriptions on family portraits, engravings on urns, crypts, or tombstones, or the like.

Property Records

The law of the state where the public office sits applies to the recording of documents related to property. If the document is recorded in accordance with state law, then the document can be admitted under the exception for records of documents affecting an interest in property. Rule 902 is helpful, because it allows a certified copy of the document to be used. In this way, issues related to property interests can be proven by the records.

Rule 803. Hearsay Exceptions: Availability of Declarant Immaterial

(14) Records of documents affecting an interest in property. The record of a document purporting to establish or affect an interest in property, as proof of the content of the original recorded document and its execution and delivery by each person by whom it purports to have been executed, if the record is a record of a public office and an applicable statute authorizes the recording of documents of that kind in that office.

The exception in Rule 803(15) for statements in documents affecting an interest in property is broader than Rule 803(14). The document that relates to an interest in property does not have to be recorded in order for the recitals of fact contained in the document to be excepted from the hearsay rule. Rule 803(15) does require, however, a foundation establishing that the statements contained in the document relate to the purpose for which the document was created. Furthermore, any dealings with the property after the document was created have to be consistent with the purpose for which the document was created. These two foundational requirements establish that the document and the statements it contains are trustworthy.

Rule 803. Hearsay Exceptions: Availability of Declarant Immaterial

(15) Statements in documents affecting an interest in property. A statement contained in a document purporting to establish or affect an interest in property if the matter stated was relevant to the purpose of the document, unless dealings with the property since the document was made have been inconsistent with the truth of the statement or the purport of the document.

Rule 803(15) generally is useful when none of the signing witnesses are alive to prove the recitations of facts in a very old deed or will. With self-authenticating wills being relatively new in many states, this exception is helpful for the admission of a will properly witnessed but not self-authenticating.

Ancient Documents, Published Compilations, and Treatises

The *ancient document exception* applies to a multitude of documents as long as the document was created twenty years or more in the past. Documents that might fall under the exception include maps, contracts, records, certificates, letters, newspaper articles, and title documents. The age requirement for the document is thought to guarantee that the document was not prepared with current litigation in mind and so is trustworthy.

Rule 803. Hearsay Exceptions: Availability of Declarant Immaterial

(16) Statements in ancient documents. Statements in a document in existence twenty years or more the authenticity of which is established.

The proponent of the document must authenticate it according to the requirements of Rule 901(b)(8).

Rule 901. Requirement of Authentication or Identification

(b) Illustrations ...

(8) Ancient documents or data compilation. Evidence that a document or data compilation, in any form, (A) is in such condition as to create no suspicion concerning its authenticity, (B) was in a place where it, if authentic, would likely be, and (C) has been in existence 20 years or more at the time it is offered.

The authentication requirements of Rule 901(b)(8) substitute for the personal knowledge of someone who was associated with the document at its creation.

When compilations are prepared for use by the public, or for certain segments of the public, they are presumed to be accurate because those creating them have a business interest in their accuracy. Publications such as market reports, telephone books, city directories, newspapers, and actuarial material are included under this exception.

Rule 803. Hearsay Exceptions: Availability of Declarant Immaterial

(17) Market reports, commercial publications. Market quotations, tabulations, lists directories, or other published compilations, generally used and relied upon by the public or by persons in particular occupations.

Finally, the compilations do not have to be just factual. Interpretive or evaluative reports relied upon by an agency may also be admissible under the exception in Rule 803(17).

Before a learned treatise can be used at trial, a foundation is required to establish that the treatise was written impartially for professionals subject to a review for accuracy and hence the treatise is authoritative. The treatise cannot be offered without being sponsored by an expert witness called on direct examination who can explain the application of the treatise to the jury (see Illustration 11-7).

Illustration 11-7

A former installer of asbestos insulation products brought a products liability action against various manufacturers for damages suffered as a result of exposure to the asbestos products. The plaintiff introduced several articles from various publications over the objection of defendants.

The appellate court explained the trial court judge's error in allowing the evidence to be heard by the jury:

> Plaintiff's medical expert did not testify about the disputed articles. Moreover, these articles were admitted as exhibits and apparently given to the jury. Such action was improper. The reason for the Rule's restrictions on the use of learned treatises is to avoid the possibility that the jury will

misunderstand and misapply the technical language within such an article if they are allowed to consider the publication itself instead of receiving the information through the testimony of an expert in the field. Fed.R.Evid. 803(18) advisory committee note. *Dartez v. Fiberboard Corp.,* 765 F.2d 456, 465 (5th Cir. 1985).

Excerpts can only be read from the treatise. The jury is not provided written copies, although the material discussed by the expert witness can be used as substantive evidence by the jury in its determination of who should prevail.

Rule 803.   Hearsay Exceptions: Availability of Declarant Immaterial

(18) Learned treatises.   To the extent called to the attention of an expert witness upon cross-examination or relied upon by the expert witness in direct examination, statements contained in published treatises, periodicals, or pamphlets on a subject of history, medicine, or other science or art, established as a reliable authority by the testimony or admission of the witness or by other expert testimony or by judicial notice. If admitted, the statements may be read into evidence but may not be received as exhibits.

The treatise can also be used on cross-examination to call into question the testimony of the expert witness. If the jury chooses to believe the treatise instead of the testimony of the expert witness, the jury can use the treatise as substantive evidence. The witness is not required to concede the treatise is authoritative before cross-examination begins. A witness could deny authoritativeness to block questioning based on the treatise if this were required.

However, the questioning party must satisfy the trial court judge of the authoritativeness of the treatise before cross-examination through another expert witness. In the alternative, the cross-examining party can ask the trial court judge to take judicial notice that the treatise is authoritative, supplying the judge with the necessary information to allow judicial notice under Rule 201.

If the paralegal is told during trial preparation that a treatise may be used, the paralegal needs to understand the treatise enough to recognize whether it contains conflicting statements on the matter for which it is being used. Of course, the paralegal can discover this in a discussion with the expert witness retained by the paralegal's firm for the trial. Furthermore, the paralegal needs to be sure the author of the treatise did not write subsequent to the treatise a reconsideration of the relevant point. Some library research could save embarrassment at trial.

Not all states include learned treatises as an exception to the hearsay rule. For example, in Florida, a treatise can be used only for impeachment purposes, that is, to attack the credibility of an expert witness. Otherwise, the treatise is hearsay and subject to an objection, for which no exception applies.

Reputation

Reputation in a community is within spheres of activity such as employment, religious affiliation, social activity, and any other sphere of activity where people can have an opinion on someone's reputation. The sphere can be as small as a family, as broad as the number of associates a person has, or as inclusive as a town or other geographic unit. The reputation testimony involves what the witness has heard in the defined sphere about the person's family or personal history.

Rule 803. Hearsay Exceptions: Availability of Declarant Immaterial

(19) Reputation concerning personal or family history. Reputation among members of a person's family by blood, adoption, or marriage, or among a person's associates, or in the community, concerning a person's birth, adoption, marriage, divorce, death, legitimacy, relationship by blood adoption, or marriage, ancestry, or other similar fact of personal or family history.

Reputation testimony is classic hearsay, but the exception for reputation concerning personal or family history allows such testimony when the witness is a member of the family, an associate, or part of the same community. It must be established that the witness is familiar with the person's reputation and has heard that reputation discussed or has discussed the matter with others in the relevant sphere.

Reputation as to property in a community, or events of general history in a community, state, or the nation, is also hearsay but is admissible under the exception in Rule 803(20). The testimony can include matters related to boundaries of property before the underlying controversy erupted.

Rule 803. Hearsay Exceptions: Availability of Declarant Immaterial

(20) Reputation concerning boundaries or general history. Reputation in a community, arising before the controversy, as to boundaries of or customs affecting lands in the community, and reputation as to events of general history important to the community or State or nation in which located.

If an event is widely discussed in a community, it is assumed the event was important to the community. On this basis, a witness can testify to events as long as it is clear from the testimony the historical event was widely discussed and the witness was a participant in those discussions or heard those discussions.

Although Rule 803(21) allows reputation testimony regarding a person's character, other limitations on the admissibility of character evidence are found in Rules 404 and 608. The exception reiterates Rule 405(a), emphasizing that reputation testimony with regard to character is not going to be stopped by a hearsay objection if it is otherwise admissible.

Rule 803. Hearsay Exceptions: Availability of Declarant Immaterial

(21) Reputation as to character. Reputation of a person's character among associates or in the community.

Judgments

A conviction in a criminal case can be used in a subsequent civil or criminal case as proof of essential facts, that is, those facts necessary for the jury to convict the defendant. The exception also applies to guilty pleas (but not pleas of nolo contendere) and to those facts necessary to support the plea. The crime must have been punishable by either imprisonment for more than a year or death. Note this exception allows the essential facts proven in the previous criminal case to be used as substantive proof in the subsequent litigation.

Rule 803. Hearsay Exceptions: Availability of Declarant Immaterial

   (22) Judgment of previous conviction. Evidence of a final judgment, entered after a trial or upon a plea of guilty (but not upon a plea of nolo contendere), adjudging a person guilty of a crime punishable by death or imprisonment in excess of one year, to prove any fact essential to sustain the judgment, but not including, when offered by the Government in a criminal prosecution for purposes other than impeachment, judgments against persons other than the accused. The pendency of an appeal may be shown but does not affect admissibility.

   The use of judgment of a previous conviction as a hearsay exception is not the same as the use of evidence of a previous conviction for impeachment purposes under Rule 609.

   The exception in Rule 803(23) for judgments as to personal, family, or general history, or property boundaries, has to be read in conjunction with the exceptions in Rule 803(19) and (20), because it allows as a hearsay exception only those facts proven by reputation evidence in an earlier judgment. The judgment must have been one relating to personal, family, or general history, or to property in a community.

Rule 803. Hearsay Exceptions: Availability of Declarant Immaterial

   (23) Judgment as to personal, family, or general history, or boundaries. Judgments as proof of matters of personal, family or general history, or boundaries, essential to the judgment, if the same would be provable by evidence of reputation.

EXCEPTIONS: DECLARANT UNAVAILABLE

Rule 804 encompasses a second list of exceptions to the hearsay rule (Figure 11-5). However, in order to utilize one of the listed exceptions, there must be a threshold showing the declarant's testimony is not obtainable for presentation at trial. Recall that under Rule 803, the declarant could be sitting in the courtroom while a witness reported to the jury what the declarant said if a Rule 803 exception applied. Under Rule 804, such is not the case unless the declarant has an impairment that inhibits the declarant's ability to testify.

FIGURE 11-5

In order for the hearsay exceptions of Rule 804 to apply, the declarant's testimony must be unavailable.

RULE 804
FOUNDATION: UNAVAILABILITY OF THE DECLARANT'S TESTIMONY

THEN APPLICATION OF

Hearsay exceptions: (1) Former testimony
(2) Dying declaration
(3) Statement against interest
(4) Personal or family history
(5) [Transferred to Rule 807]
(6) Forfeiture by wrongdoing

"Declarant unavailable" means the testimony is unobtainable at trial. The reason the testimony is unobtainable may be because a privilege applies, a person refuses to testify even when ordered by the court, a person can no longer remember the earlier statement, or the person is dead or physically or mentally ill.

Also, if a person cannot be required to attend because the person is outside the jurisdiction of the court, then that witness is unavailable for the purposes of Rule 804, and one of the exceptions in Rule 804(b) can be utilized.

If a party wrongfully keeps a person from testifying, the person does not qualify as being unavailable, but Rule 804(b)(6) allows the statement to be offered as an exception to the hearsay rule.

Evidence offered under Rule 804 is not considered as trustworthy as evidence offered under Rule 803, hence the added condition that the declarant be unavailable. Although the hearsay evidence meeting the requirements of the exceptions listed under Rule 804 is not as reliable, it is too helpful to exclude entirely.

Rule 804. Hearsay Exceptions: Declarant Unavailable

(a) Definition of unavailability. "Unavailability as a witness" includes situations in which the declarant—

(1) is exempted by ruling of the court on the ground of privilege from testifying concerning the subject matter of the declarant's statement; or

(2) persists in refusing to testify concerning the subject matter of the declarant's statement despite an order of the court to do so; or

(3) testifies to a lack of memory of the subject matter of the declarant's statement; or

(4) is unable to be present or to testify at the hearing because of death or then existing physical or mental illness or infirmity; or

(5) is absent from the hearing and the proponent of a statement has been unable to procure the declarant's attendance (or in the case of a hearsay exception under subdivision (b)(2), (3), or (4), the declarant's attendance or testimony) by process or other reasonable means.

A declarant is not unavailable as a witness if exemption, refusal, claim of lack of memory, inability, or absence is due to the procurement or wrongdoing of the proponent of a statement for the purpose of preventing the witness from attending or testifying.

(b) **Hearsay exceptions.** The following are not excluded by the hearsay rule if the declarant is unavailable as a witness:

(1) **Former testimony.** Testimony given as a witness at another hearing of the same or a different proceeding, or in a deposition taken in compliance with law in the course of the same or another proceeding, if the party against whom the testimony is now offered, or, in a civil action or proceeding, a predecessor in interest, had an opportunity and similar motive to develop the testimony by direct, cross, or redirect examination.

(2) **Statement under belief of impending death.** In a prosecution for homicide or in a civil action or proceeding, a statement made by a declarant while believing that the declarant's death was imminent, concerning the cause or circumstances of what the declarant believed to be impending death.

(3) **Statement against interest.** A statement which was at the time of its making so far contrary to the declarant's pecuniary or proprietary interest, or so far tended to subject the declarant to civil or criminal liability, or to render invalid a claim by the declarant against another, that a reasonable person in the declarant's position would not have made the statement unless believing it to be true. A statement tending to expose the declarant to criminal liability and offered to exculpate the accused is not admissible unless corroborating circumstances clearly indicate the trustworthiness of the statement.

(4) **Statement of personal or family history.** (A) A statement concerning the declarant's own birth, adoption, marriage, divorce, legitimacy, relationship by blood, adoption, or marriage, ancestry, or other similar facts of personal or family history, even though declarant had no means of acquiring personal knowledge of the matter stated; or (B) a statement concerning the foregoing matters, and death also, of another person, if the declarant was related to the other by blood, adoption, or marriage or was so intimately associated with the other's family as to be likely to have accurate information concerning the matter declared.

(5) [Transferred to Rule 807]

(6) **Forfeiture by wrongdoing.** A statement offered against a party that has engaged or acquiesced in wrongdoing that was intended to, and did, procure the unavailability of the declarant as a witness.

Rule 804(a) lists five circumstances meeting the definition of unavailability. But the list is only illustrative. If the proponent of hearsay evidence can prove unavailability under these five circumstances, or base unavailability on other circumstances acceptable to the trial court judge, a foundation exists for the introduction of hearsay evidence that falls under the exceptions listed in Rule 804(b). The list is not exclusive; other circumstances of unavailability can be argued by the proponent of the hearsay evidence. The list is useful because each of the circumstances, if proven to the court, is *per se* unavailability for purposes of the exceptions listed in Rule 804(b).

Not surprisingly, a proponent of hearsay evidence cannot instigate the unavailability of a witness. Under Rule 804(b)(6), if the opponent can demonstrate to the trial court judge that this was the case, then the proponent cannot offer into evidence matters related to former testimony, a statement under

per se In and of itself.

belief of impending death, a statement against interest, or a statement of personal or family history, because a hearsay objection will be sustained.

Assuming the proponent of hearsay evidence establishes to the satisfaction of the court that a declarant's testimony is not obtainable, the proponent then has available four avenues for arguing that a witness should be able to testify as to what a declarant said out of court.

Former Testimony

Rule 804(b)(1) provides that former testimony given under oath at a prior proceeding that dealt with the same issue as the one at hand is admissible. The party against whom the testimony is now offered must have had the opportunity and similar motive to develop the testimony of the declarant when the testimony was given (see Illustration 11-8).

Illustration 11-8 _____

Where the prosecution establishes that a witness is apparently mentally incapable of testifying, owing to heavy drug use, as to the events previously recounted in testimony, the prior testimony given under oath and subjected to cross-examination in a previous trial of the same defendant is admissible under Rule 804(b)(1). *Thomas v. Cardwell,* 626 F.2d 1375, 1384-86 (9th Cir. 1980).

It does not matter if different attorneys were involved when the former testimony was given. What is important is that the party who now faces having the testimony used against him or her should have had the chance to develop the testimony while the declarant was under oath. The issues must be similar enough that the questioning of the declarant was motivated by reasons similar to those in the current litigation. Motive means opportunity; if an attorney chose not to explore and develop the former testimony because of tactical reasons, the hearsay evidence is admissible under the exception.

As depositions are conducted with the deponent under oath, they qualify for admission under Rule 804(b)(1), along with testimony at court hearings and earlier trials.

Dying Declarations

The second hearsay exception under Rule 804 is for a dying declaration, and this exception can be used in all civil cases. In criminal cases, though, the exception can be used only in prosecutions for homicide. The declarant had to have believed death was imminent at the time the statement was made. It does not matter whether the declarant actually died; the reasonable belief that death might soon occur is enough. The statement falls within the exception as long as it relates to the cause of death, such as the name of the person responsible.

The paralegal needs to research state law regarding dying declarations, because in some states dying declarations can be used in all criminal prosecutions, not just homicides.

Statement against Interest

The third exception to the hearsay rule under Rule 804 deals with statements by a declarant that are against the declarant's monetary or property interests because the statements could subject the declarant to civil or criminal liability. The statements might also qualify under the exception if they negate a declarant's claim against someone else. Reliability is predicated on the belief the harmful statement would not have been made if the declarant did not believe it to be true. The proponent must establish the declarant knew the statement was contrary to the declarant's interests when the statement was made. Whether the declarant was correct in the belief does not matter; the belief of the declarant when the statement was made is what controls.

If a criminal defendant offers the statement of an unavailable declarant that exculpates the defendant, it is admissible only if the defendant can also provide corroborating circumstances to indicate the exculpatory statement is trustworthy. Without this safeguard, defendants could encourage perjury by procuring a witness to testify to an exculpatory statement by an out-of-court declarant. So a statement against penal interest requires the added requirement of a foundation demonstrating the reliability of the statement.

Personal or Family History

The fourth exception, Rule 804(b)(4), applies where a declarant is unavailable and a witness is ready to testify to what the declarant said about (1) the declarant's own personal or family history or (2) the personal or family history of a family member or intimate associate.

Forfeiture by Wrongdoing

Finally, the most recent addition to the Rule 804 exceptions is Rule 804(b)(6). If any party, including the government, wrongfully keeps the declarant from testifying as a witness, then a statement offered against the wrongdoing party is admissible as an exception under Rule 804.

CATCH-ALL PROVISION

Rule 807 is a *catch-all provision* allowing an argument that hearsay evidence should be admissible even though it is not covered by the enumerated exceptions in either Rule 803 or Rule 804. Until December 1997, Rule 807 was a part of both Rules 803 and 804. In order to facilitate additions to those rules, the residual provisions were transferred to a new Rule 807.

If the paralegal identifies hearsay evidence for which no exception applies, Rule 807 may be the avenue to admissibility. However, the proponent of the evidence must notify opposing counsel of the intent to utilize Rule 807, and the notice must include the name and address of the declarant. The notice must be provided to the opponent in enough time to allow the opponent to prepare for argument before the judge in the event the opponent chooses to contest the hearsay evidence.

Rule 807. Residual Exception

A statement not specifically covered by Rule 803 or 804 but having equivalent circumstantial guarantees of trustworthiness, is not excluded by the hearsay rule, if the court determines that (A) the statement is offered as evidence of a material fact; (B) the statement is more probative on the point for which it is offered than any other evidence which the proponent can procure through reasonable efforts; and (C) the general purposes of these rules and the interests of justice will best be served by admission of the statement into evidence. However, a statement may not be admitted under this exception unless the proponent of it makes known to the adverse party sufficiently in advance of the trial or hearing to provide the adverse party with a fair opportunity to prepare to meet it, the proponent's intention to offer the statement and the particulars of it, including the name and address of the declarant.

To prepare the attorney for the hearing, the paralegal for the proponent should outline why the hearsay evidence should be considered an exception to the hearsay rule. The evidence must be shown to be trustworthy and offered to prove a material fact. See Illustration 11-9 for an example.

Illustration 11-9

Polls and surveys taken for litigation purposes might be admissible under Rule 807, assuming relevance, if certain conditions related to establishing trustworthiness are met.

Foundational requirements to establish reliability must show the poll was conducted in accordance with generally accepted survey principles, namely, that (1) a proper universe was examined, and a representative sample was chosen; (2) the person conducting the survey was an expert; and (3) the data was properly gathered and accurately reported, with the interviewers unaware of the purpose of the survey.

Objectivity is critical, so the poll or survey must be conducted independently of the attorneys involved in the litigation. *Pittsburgh Press Club v. United States*, 579 F.2d 751, 758 (3d Cir. 1978), discussing former Rule 803(24).

The evidence also has to be the only proof the proponent can reasonably procure to prove a matter. Finally, it must be shown the interests of justice will be served by admitting the evidence over the hearsay objection.

Rule 807 is meant for exceptional situations; it allows flexibility for those few times when fairness requires introduction of a statement that is otherwise hearsay. With this policy in mind, the paralegal needs to prepare a clear argument for admissibility of the hearsay evidence so the attorney can convince the judge to let the evidence in at trial. Of course, at the same time, the opponent will be arguing for its exclusion.

It should be noted that not all state evidence rules share the premise that there should be a catch-all provision. Some states reflect in their rules the policy that the exceptions should be limited to a list, without possibility of admitting other hearsay evidence. In this regard, not all states follow the federal lead.

In a criminal case, if a defendant convinces a witness not to appear or not to testify at trial, the prosecution can use an incriminating statement made by the witness during the criminal investigation against the defendant in court. Two conditions must be met, however. The statement must be otherwise admissible (for example, admissible under the co-conspirator exception), and it must have indicia of reliability (for example, made voluntarily and signed). If this foundation is established, then the statement is admissible under Rule 807 and is not a violation of the confrontation clause of the Constitution. The defendant is not allowed to profit from keeping a witness from testifying.

SUMMARY

Hearsay evidence can be excluded by the trial court judge when an appropriate objection is made by the opponent of the evidence. However, some hearsay evidence can assist the jury in its determination of the issues. Therefore, where the evidence is trustworthy, Rule 803 offers avenues of admissibility by means of exceptions to the hearsay rule, allowing the declarant to testify instead of the witness who is reporting the earlier statement by the declarant. Rule 801 defines certain testimony as non-hearsay despite the fact that it meets the hearsay definition, if it, as a matter of policy, is considered trustworthy.

Rule 804 recognizes that some hearsay evidence that fails to qualify for exception under Rule 803 may nevertheless be important to the determination of the matter being litigated, even though it is less trustworthy. Before the exceptions in Rule 804(b) can be utilized, the proponent must convince the trial court judge that (1) the declarant's testimony is not obtainable for presentation at trial and (2) the reason the declarant is unavailable is not because of action on the part of the proponent. Then each exception has its own further requirements.

The hearsay rule is sweeping in its definition, but it is shrunk by the numerous exceptions, not only listed in Rules 803 and 804 but also implied by the underlying policy embodied in Rule 807, which allows the possibility of more exceptions.

The paralegal must first identify whether evidence is subject to a hearsay objection and then determine whether an exception applies (see Figure 11-6).

Preparation before trial is critical when a piece of evidence is important as proof of a cause of action. Where a hearsay objection is anticipated, the argument against the objection should be prepared so the attorney can cogently argue the admissibility issue. Remember, when a hearsay objection is sustained, the jury does not hear the evidence.

FIGURE 11-6
Hearsay analysis determines whether evidence meets the hearsay definition, is subject to a hearsay objection, and qualifies for a hearsay exception.

FIGURE 11-6
Hearsay analysis determines whether evidence meets the hearsay definition, is subject to a hearsay objection, and qualifies for a hearsay exception.

HEARSAY ANALYSIS

HEARSAY DEFINITION:

(1) Witness testifies to what declarant said out of court

(2) Testimony is offered to prove the truth of its contents

AVOID HEARSAY OBJECTION:

(1) Rule 801(d): Non-hearsay Statements by Definition

    (A) Prior statement by witness

        • Inconsistent

        • Consistent

        • Identification

    (B) Statement (admission) by party-opponent

(2) Rule 803: 23 Exceptions

    Does not matter if declarant available to testify

(3) Rule 804: 5 Exceptions

    Declarant must be unavailable

    • Former testimony

    • Statement made under belief of impending death

    • Statement against interest

    • Statement of personal or family history

    • Forfeiture by wrongdoing

(4) Rule 807: Residual Exception

✔ CHECKPOINTS

❑ Exceptions to hearsay rule: availability of declarant immaterial

1. Present sense impression: statement about event is made soon after event.
2. Excited utterance: statement is made under stress of exciting event.
3. Mental, emotional, or physical condition:
   - Statement by declarant to anyone.
   - Statement contemporaneous with underlying condition.
   - Statement of intent to do something in the future (can include someone else's intent also).
4. Medical diagnosis or treatment:
   - Statements to medical professionals.
   - Statements on medical history.
   - Statements to non-treating doctor regarding person's condition or medical history.
5. Recorded recollection:
   - Record of event near time of occurrence.
   - No independent memory of event.
   - Record read to jury.
6. Business records:
   - Writing or data compilation.
   - Record of activities of a business.
   - Made in ordinary course of business.
   - "Business" includes wide variety of entities.

7. Absence of business record as proof of nonexistence.

8. Public records and reports:
   - Records and reports prepared by public officials.
   - Records and reports related to functions of public office or agency.

9. Vital statistics:
   - Obtained from public office with duty to compile.

10. Absence of public records as proof of nonexistence.

11. Religious organizations:
    - Personal or family history regularly kept by religious organization.

12. Certificates:
    - Memorializing marriage, baptism, and similar events.

13. Family records:
    - Not disputed by family members.

14. Property records:
    - Documents recorded in accordance with state law.

15. Statements related to property interests:
    - Unrecorded documents.

16. Ancient documents:
    - Documents that are 20 or more years old.
    - Maps, contracts, records, certificates, letters, newspaper articles, title documents are included.

17. Published compilations:
    - Prepared for use by public.
    - Market reports, telephone books, city directories, newspapers, actuarial material.

18. Learned treatises:
    - Written impartially by professionals.
    - Authoritative.
    - Read to jury.

- Substantive evidence or for cross-examination only.

19. Personal or family history:
    - Related to person's reputation in the community.
    - Birth, adoption, marriage, divorce, death, legitimacy, ancestry.

20. Boundaries or history related to land or general history.

21. Reputation as to character:
    - If otherwise admissible.

22. Previous convictions:
    - For use in subsequent civil or criminal cases as proof of essential facts.
    - Guilty pleas included.
    - Crime punishable by more than one year in prison or death.

23. Judgments:
    - Related to personal, family, or general history, or to property in community.

❏ Exceptions: declarant unavailable
1. Unavailable: testimony unobtainable at trial:
   - Privilege.
   - Refusal to testify.
   - Lack of memory.
   - Death or illness.
   - Unable to procure.

2. Exceptions:
   - Former testimony.
   - Dying declaration.
   - Statement against interest.
   - Statement of personal or family history.
   - Forfeiture by wrongdoing.

❏ Catch-all provision
1. Other exceptions possible.
2. Notice requirements.

⚖ APPLICATIONS

Application 11-1

James Hilyer was killed while working on a subway construction project in Washington, DC, when he was run over by a concrete mixer owned by Howat Concrete Co. In a wrongful death action against Howat, Howat claimed Mr. Hilyer was contributorily negligent and thus barred from recovery. The only evidence Howat presented to prove this defense was a statement by a fellow construction worker made to a police officer investigating the accident the evening the accident happened.

The trial court judge allowed the statement into evidence as substantive evidence of contributory negligence. On appeal, Mrs. Hilyer claimed the trial court judge made a mistake as a matter of law, because the statement was hearsay that did not come within any of the exemptions enumerated in Rule 803 of the Federal Rules of Evidence.

Hilyer v. Howat Concrete Co, Inc.
578 F.2d 422 (D.C. Cir. 1978)

I

The project on which the decedent had been working was at the corner of an intersection of two streets in downtown Washington, and it was necessary to place traffic barricades along the street between the traffic lanes and the worksite. The decedent and another worker, Howard Simms, had just placed a barricade on the street when a concrete mixer truck, making a right turn, hit the barricade and ran over the former.

The challenged testimony involves a statement made by Simms to a policeman, Officer Strother, who arrived at the scene soon after the accident occurred. Officer Strother's contemporaneous notes, as read at the trial, state:

> Howard Simms ... states ... Jim never looked at traffic set barricade down and backed into veh. #1 [the concrete mixer truck] which was making right turn.

R. 139, Tr. 139. Simms' remark that the decedent "backed into" the truck was of crucial importance at trial because it was the only evidence which directly substantiated appellee's defense of contributory negligence. However, less than three hours after the accident, Simms gave a written statement at police headquarters in which he indicated that he did not see the accident and only assumed that the decedent backed into the truck. Moreover, Simms testified (at both trials) that he had not seen the accident occur and did not remember talking with Officer Strother at the scene of the accident. Mem. Op. (Aug. 15, 1975) at 6, J.A. at 171; R. 139, Tr. 125–43.

At the trial which led to this appeal, Simms, called by appellee, testified that he "was so excited" at the time the police questioned him at the scene that he could not recall the questions asked of him. (R. 139, Tr. 127.) He also stated that he "didn't see exactly how the accident happened." (R. 139, Tr. 135.) At this point, appellee's counsel approached the bench and proposed to examine Simms concerning the oral statement made to Officer Strother. In response to an objection raised by appellant, appellee cited Rule 607 of the Federal Rules of Evidence, which allows a party to impeach his own witness. The court thereupon overruled appellant's objection and allowed the statement to be read to Simms, who, when asked whether he made the statement, replied, "Well, I was so upset, I wouldn't know exactly." (R. 139, Tr. 139.) Appellant's counsel did not request, and the court did not on its own give, an instruction to the jury limiting its consideration of the statement to an impeachment of Simms' testimony in court.

Appellee next called to the stand Officer Strother, who testified that he received a radio report of the accident at 6:47 p.m., arrived at the scene of the accident at 6:53 p.m., and interviewed Simms soon thereafter. Although Officer Strother estimated that the accident had occurred at 6:30 p.m. (R. 139, Tr. 158), this estimate appears to be too early, for it was established that the construction crew did not even arrive at the site until 6:30 (R. 137, Tr. 28). When asked to relate to the court his interview with Simms, Officer Strother testified as to Simms' statement from his present recollection, the court overruling appellant's timely objection that the statement was hearsay. (R. 139, Tr. 158–59.) Officer Strother further testified that he had requested Simms to repeat the statement, that he transcribed it verbatim into his notebook, and that Simms had immediately read that transcription and expressed his agreement with it. (R. 139, Tr. 159.) The notes were not themselves placed in evidence.

On cross-examination by appellant's counsel, Officer Strother at first stated that Simms had been excited at the time of the interview at the accident scene. Appellant's counsel then read to the officer portions of his testimony at the first trial—at which he repeatedly asserted that Simms had not appeared nervous. Upon further questioning, the officer admitted that his recollection of the events in question was not as good presently as it had been at the first trial. (R. 139, Tr. 183–85.)

II

We conclude that the statement given by Simms to Officer Strother at the scene of the accident was admissible not only to impeach Simms' later inconsistent testimony in court but also for the truth of the matter asserted, namely, that the decedent without regard to traffic conditions backed into the street and into the concrete mixer truck which ran over him. We first address the latter point.

Although the record does not disclose with precision under which hearsay exception the trial judge admitted the statement, we find no error in such admission because the statement was within the "excited utterance" exception stated in Rule 803.

The first two exceptions in Rule 803 read as follows:

1. Present sense impression. A statement describing or explaining an event or condition made while the declarant was perceiving the event or condition or immediately thereafter.

2. Excited utterance. A statement relating to a startling event or condition made while the declarant was under the stress of excitement caused by the event or condition.

The Federal Rules make clear that testimony qualifying under one exception is admissible even if not encompassed by the other. In the case at bar, the statement was admissible under the second of these exceptions. [FOOTNOTE: It is doubtful that Simms' statement to Officer Strother comes within the present sense impression exception. By our calculations, the statement could not have been made until at least fifteen minutes—and possibly up to forty-five minutes—after the accident. The accident took place soon after the construction crew arrived at the site at 6:30, and Officer Strother, who arrived at 6:53, interviewed two other witnesses before he spoke with Simms. The police officer remained at the scene of the accident for twenty-five minutes. (R. 139, Tr. 157–58.) This time span hardly qualifies as "immediately" after the accident as that term is used in Rule 803(1), particularly in view of the commentary on that Rule contained in the Advisory Committee Notes. This states that the "most significant practical difference [between 803(1) and 803(2)] will lie in the time lapse allowable between event and statement," and that 803(1) "recognizes that in many, if not most, instances, *precise contemporaneity* is impossible, 56 F.R.D. 187, 304 (1973) (emphasis added). The thrust of this commentary is that in a circumstance such as that before us, an out-of-court statement made at least fifteen minutes after the event it describes is not admissible unless the declarant was still in a state of excitement resulting from the event.]

The statement clearly meets one of the two prerequisites for admission as an excited utterance: it was "a statement relating to a startling event or condition." We conclude that it also met the second prerequisite: it was made while the declarant, Simms, was "under the stress or excitement cause [sic] by the event." The most damaging testimony relating to the latter issue was by Simms himself, as described heretofore. In addition to this testimony, Simms' lack of recall of his conversation with Officer Strother may also indicate that he was under stress at the time the officer spoke with him.

[W]e hold that the statement was properly admitted at the trial which led to this appeal, both for impeachment of Simms and for the truth of the matter asserted.

Affirmed.

Class Discussion Questions

1. Based on the facts enumerated by the appellate court, what was the time span between the accident and the statement made by Mr. Simms to Officer Strother?

2. With regard to the two hearsay exceptions described by the court, present sense impression and excited utterance, why was the time span significant?

3. What evidence was there that Mr. Simms was still excited when he gave his statement to Officer Strother?

4. If a hearsay statement does not qualify under one exception under Rule 803, does that preclude the use of another exception? Explain your answer.

Application 11-2

Mr. Tart suffered a heart attack shortly after completing a stress test conducted by the Life Extension Institute, a partnership of defendants Dr. John P. McGann and Dr. Ronald E. Costin. Mr. Tart filed a medical malpractice claim, but he lost at trial. On appeal, he alleged, among other things, that the trial court judge erred by excluding learned treatise evidence.

Tart v. McGann
697 F.2d 75 (2d Cir. 1982)

III.   LEARNED TREATISE EVIDENCE

Plaintiffs' second argument on appeal concerns the admissibility of so-called learned treatise evidence. During the course of the trial, plaintiffs attempted to bolster the testimony of their expert witness by introducing into evidence an article entitled "Maximal Exercise Testing." The article was written by Dr. Robert A. Bruce, who devised the Bruce-Protocol, which was used as the basis for the stress test taken by plaintiff William Tart. A stress test protocol is a set of directions that describes how a treadmill stress test should be conducted. It indicates, for example, the proper speed and incline of the treadmill at various stages of the test. The district court refused to allow plaintiffs to introduce the Bruce article into evidence as an exhibit or to quote from it on the direct examination of their expert.

The district court also severely restricted plaintiffs' use of learned treatise evidence on the cross-examination of defendants' expert. Plaintiffs sought to cross-examine defendants' expert by asking him whether he agreed with statements and figures contained in a booklet on exercise testing published by the American Heart Association. In particular, plaintiff wished to quote from a table on recommended target heart rates. Judge Palmieri refused to admit the table into evidence, and also refused to allow plaintiffs to quote from it. Judge Palmieri also instructed plaintiffs not to quote from the Bruce article, except to the extent it contradicted defendants' expert.

Judge Palmieri's evidentiary rulings on this issue evidently were based at least in part on a misunderstanding of the status of learned treatise evidence under the current Federal Rules. Judge Palmieri stated in explanation of his decision to prohibit use of the Bruce article as substantive evidence his belief that medical literature can only be used "as a cross-examination tool." But Rule 803(18) of the Federal Rules of Evidence provides as follows:

> The following are not excluded by the hearsay rule, even though the declarant is available as a witness:

> (18) Learned treatises. To the extent called to the attention of an expert witness upon cross-examination or relied upon by him in direct examination, statements contained in published treatises, periodicals, or pamphlets on a subject of history, medicine, or other science or art, established as a reliable authority by the testimony or admission of the witness or by other expert testimony or by judicial notice. If admitted, the statements may be read into evidence but may not be received as exhibits.

Thus, the Rule explicitly permits the admission of medical literature as substantive evidence "to the extent called to the attention of an expert witness upon cross-examination," as long as it is established that such literature is authoritative.

Prior to the enactment of Rule 803(18), learned treatises were generally usable only on cross-examination, and then only for impeachment purposes. See Weinstein, supra, Par. 803(18)[01]. Most commentators found the hearsay objections to learned treatise evidence unconvincing, and recommended that treatises be admitted as substantive evidence. Some commentators went so far as to suggest that treatises be admitted independently of an expert's testimony. Id. Par. 803(18)[02]. The Advisory committee rejected this position, noting that a treatise might be "misunderstood and misapplied without expert assistance and supervision." Fed.R.Evid. 803(18) advisory committee notes. Accordingly, the Rule permits the admission of learned treatises as substantive evidence, but only when "an expert is on the stand and available to explain and assist in the application of the treatise. ..." Id.

Nonetheless, it may not have been improper for Judge Palmieri to exclude the evidence at issue in this case. First, there was some dispute over the relevancy of the challenged evidence, particularly the chart on recommended target heart rates. Second, it does not appear that the evidence was properly proffered under Rule 803(18); the only rule explicitly referred to by plaintiffs was Rule 703, which deals with the bases of opinion testimony by experts. Cf. *Johnson v. Ellis & Sons Iron Works, Inc.*, supra, 609 F.2d 823 (refusal to admit safety code evidence not supportable on the basis that it was not properly proffered, because plaintiff did specifically not refer to Rule 803(18)). Finally, it appears that the substance of much of the disputed evidence was made available to the jury. Thus, the exclusion of the evidence at issue may have been harmless error. But see id., 609 F.2d at 823 (Direct quotation may be "more dramatic" and "more persuasive" than otherwise equivalent testimony). We need not decide whether exclusion of the evidence at issue was reversible error. We hold only that if on remand the disputed medical literature is shown to be relevant and authoritative, it may be read into evidence if properly proffered under Rule 803(18).

The judgment below is reversed and the case is remanded to the district court for further proceedings in accordance with this opinion.

Class Discussion Questions

1. Explain the difference between the use of learned treatises before and after enactment of Rule 803(18). Which position is followed by the evidence rules in your state?

2. Why should a trial court judge allow the appropriate witness to read the learned treatise to the jury?

3. Must the party proffering the learned treatise establish relevancy before the witness reads the document?

Application 11-3

O'Donnell v. Georgia Osteopathic Hospital, Inc.
748 F.2d 1543 (11th Cir. 1984)

Before RONEY and ANDERSON, Circuit Judges, and MORGAN, Senior Circuit Judge.

LEWIS R. MORGAN, Senior Circuit Judge:

Marjorie O'Donnell filed this suit pursuant to the Age Discrimination in Employment Act of 1967 (ADEA), 29 U.S.C.A. §§ 623, 626(c) (West 1975 & Supp.1984). She alleged that her employer, Georgia Osteopathic Hospital, d/b/a Doctor's Hospital (the Hospital), demoted her and later denied her a promotion because of her age and constructively discharged her when she complained to the Equal Employment Opportunity Commission. The trial jury rendered a special verdict that the Hospital had either discriminated against O'Donnell because of her age or retaliated against her because she filed a complaint with the EEOC, that O'Donnell had attempted to mitigate her damages, and that the Hospital moved alternatively for judgment *non obstante verdicto* or for a new trial. The district court denied both motions.

I. DENIAL OF THE MOTIONS FOR JNOV AND NEW TRIAL

A. Facts

The Hospital hired Ms. O'Donnell as a clerk-librarian in March 1972, at which time she was fifty years old. In 1974, the Hospital promoted her to secretary to the medical director. She still held this position in July 1980 when Dr. Stuart Harkness became director of medical affairs. On Dr. Harkness' first day at the hospital, Ms. O'Donnell informed him that she was scheduled to leave for vacation in three weeks. Dr. Harkness assigned her some typing which she completed before she left but which Dr. Harkness insisted at trial was replete with errors. Upon her return from her vacation, Ms. O'Donnell discovered that Dr. Harkness had hired Neysa Sharpless, a woman of thirty-four years, to be his secretary. Ms. O'Donnell's supervisors moved her to a new location where she now worked only for the volunteer services coordinator, the hospital chaplain, and the hospital social worker. From the evidence elicited at trial, the jury could reasonably have found that the work for these three persons occupied only a few hours of Ms. O'Donnell's workday. Ms. O'Donnell considered this move a demotion.

Ms. O'Donnell applied for a job as secretary to the hospital administrator, Rhea Keene, in October 1980. Mr. Keene did not interview her but hired Debbie Wunderle, a 29-year old woman. Ms. O'Donnell then filed an age discrimination complaint with the EEOC and later testified that her employment situation deteriorated further after she filed the complaint. She resigned in January 1981, but she labels this resignation a constructive discharge.

B. Evidentiary Issue

We must therefore first decide the admissibility of certain testimony that the Hospital claims the district court erroneously admitted.

Ms. Neysa Sharpless testified that Dr. Harkness told her of statements made by Mr. Jack Sartain, the executive director of the Hospital. [FOOTNOTE: Ms. Sharpless also related a conversation she had with administrator Rhea Keene. In October or November of 1980, after Ms. O'Donnell had been transferred, Keene told Ms. Sharpless that Ms. O'Donnell had applied for the vacant position of secretary to Mr. Keene. When Ms. Sharpless asked him if he would hire her, he simply laughed.] For example, after O'Donnell complained to the EEOC, Mr. Sartain told Dr. Harkness that "he would handle the Marge O'Donnell situation" but that he "was going to need Dr. Harkness' assistance and support around the charges being filed." Dr. Harkness further informed Ms. Sharpless that "Mr. Sartain had blown the situation in the way he had handled Marge O'Donnell, and that he [Mr. Sartain] would personally take care of getting rid of her." Ms. Sharpless also testified as follows:

> Dr. Harkness told me that I fit his needs as a secretary perfectly. I was young, I was attractive, I was personable, I had good communications skills, and he thought that I would be of great benefit to him in working interpersonally with the physicians on the staff, and that was very important to him. How I looked, how I behaved, and that I was a true reflection of medical affairs and all the work that he was doing there. So it was very important that I behave and I look a certain way.

The Hospital contends that the introduction of this testimony was error that requires remand for a new trial. To prevail on this issue, the Hospital must show (1) that the district court abused its discretion in erroneously admitting the testimony and (2) that the admission of the evidence affected the Hospital's substantial rights. See *Perry v. State Farm Fire & Casualty Co.*, 734 F.2d 1441, 1446 (11th Cir. 1984); *Dietz v. Consolidated Oil & Gas, Inc.*, 643 F.2d 1088, 1093 (5th Cir.) cert. denied, 454 U.S. 968, 102 S.Ct. 513, 70 L.Ed. 2d 386 (1981); *Rozier v. Ford Motor Co.*, 573 F.2d 1332, 1348–49 (5th Cir. 1978); Fed.R.Evid. 103(a). The testimony clearly may have influenced the jury's verdict. O'Donnell's counsel relied heavily upon it in his final argument to the jury. The district court also relied upon it to deny the Hospital's motion for new trial or JNOV. Thus, the admission of the testimony did affect the Hospital's substantial rights; if admission of the evidence was error, it was not harmless error. We must therefore determine if the district court abused its discretion in admitting the testimony. The Hospital argues that the testimony was irrelevant, inadmissible hearsay [FOOTNOTE: The district court admitted the testimony of Ms. Sharpless as consisting of admissions by a party-opponent. See Fed.R.Evid. 801(d). The Hospital objects to this characterization of the testimony because "the inferences which the plaintiff hoped the jury would draw from the statements could not have been drawn until a point after which they were made, i.e., at the time the plaintiff resigned. Moreover, the statements attributed to Sartain are double hearsay and therefore inadmissable." Appellant's brief at 31, n. 5. The Hospital has confused an admission by a party-opponent with a statement against interest. An admission must only be contrary to the trial position of the party against whom it is offered. A statement against interest, however, must be "*at the time of its making* so far contrary to the declarant's pecuniary or proprietary interest, or so far tended to subject him to civil or criminal liability, or to render invalid a claim by him against another, that a reasonable man in his position would not have made the statement unless he believed it to be true." *Id.* 804(b)(3) (emphasis added). The district court properly admitted the testimony as admissions by a party opponent. The objection of double hearsay also fails because both parts of the combined statement are admissions.

AFFIRMED IN PART, REVERSED IN PART, AND REMANDED.

Class Discussion Questions

1. Ms. Sharpless testified to statements made to her by Dr. Harkness. Explain why the statements are hearsay.

2. What was the nature of the double hearsay?

3. Why did the appellate court approve of the testimony of Ms. Sharpless in its entirety as an exception to the hearsay rule under Rule 801(d)?

4. According to the appellate court, how was the hospital confused with regard to the admissibility of the Sharpless testimony?

EXERCISES

1. Your firm represents a jewelry store that entered into a contract with a collection agency. The collection agency purchased the accounts receivable of the jewelry store and was supposed to collect the money owed by the jewelry store customers. Not long after the collection agency took over the accounts, the jewelry store started getting angry complaints from customers. You determine that the complaints were both verbal and in letters written to the jewelry store, and they are ongoing. A suit for breach of contract based on the mishandling of the accounts is filed on behalf of your client against the collection agency. The jewelry store claims it was damaged by the mishandling of the accounts, with the result of a serious loss of customer goodwill.

   a. If the store manager is called to the stand to testify to the angry phone calls of customers, and the letters are offered with more angry customer complaints, a hearsay objection will be made by the collection agency. Explain why the testimony of the manager and the letters are hearsay.

   b. Your supervising attorney tells you Rule 803(3) can be effectively argued to gain admission of this evidence because it relates to the claimed injury. Outline the argument for admissibility.

2. Your firm represents two police officers in a lawsuit brought by someone the officers had arrested. The plaintiff alleges a deprivation of his civil rights because the officers allegedly beat him during the course of an arrest. You have learned through discovery that the plaintiff intends to offer into evidence a statement by the treating physician at the hospital emergency room where the plaintiff was taken for treatment. The hospital record prepared by the treating physician reads, "Multiple contusions and hematoma, consistent with excessive force."

   a. Is the hospital record with the treating physician's statement hearsay if the doctor is not available to testify and only the record is offered?

   b. Prepare an argument that the entire statement, or some portion of it, is not admissible under Rule 803(4).

3. Survivors of a woman who died from toxic shock syndrome (TSS) are represented by your firm in a lawsuit against the manufacturer of tampons used by the woman immediately before she died as a result of bacterial infection.

   You have a copy of an epidemiological study conducted by the Centers for Disease Control (CDC), showing a correlation between tampon use and TSS. The manufacturer has filed a motion in limine challenging the admissibility of the CDC study, contending that the study is hearsay since neither the scientist who conducted the study nor the participants are going to testify. The manufacturer also contends the study is not trustworthy because it does not provide the opportunity of questioning the scientist who conducted the study with regard to statistical biases inherent in the study.

   Frame an argument for admissibility of the study under Rule 803(8)(C), including foundational requirements.

RULES REFERENCED IN THIS CHAPTER

Rule 803. Hearsay Exceptions: Availability of Declarant Immaterial

Rule 804. Hearsay Exceptions: Declarant Unavailable

Rule 807. Residual Exception

NOTES

[1] 145 U.S. 285 (1892).

[2] Anthony J. Bocchino and David A. Sorenshein. *A Practical Guide to Federal Evidence: Objections, Responses, Rules, and Practice Commentary,* 3rd ed.

Notre Dame, IN: National Institute for Trial Advocacy, 1993, p. 166.

[3] *In re Japanese Electronic Products Antitrust Litigation,* 723 F.2d 238, 289 (3d Cir. 1983).

Privileged Communications

PRIVILEGES AND FEDERAL COMMON LAW

The goal of a trial is to allow for the presentation of evidence to the jury so the jurors can make a fair determination of which party should prevail in the dispute. As we have seen throughout this book, the Rules of Evidence are the yardstick by which admissibility of evidence is judged. The trial court judge is the filter through which evidence offered by the parties must pass. Generally, the goal is to allow the jury to hear and see as much as possible, as long as the evidence relates to contested issues. Although the hearsay rule appears to stymie the admission of a large body of evidence, the exceptions in fact facilitate passage of much hearsay evidence through the filter of the judge to the jury.

There is no such reprieve for evidence that comes within the purview of a privileged communication. If the law recognizes a **privilege**, then the judge cannot allow the evidence to be heard or seen by the jury, no matter how important the evidence might be to a party's case. Generally, privilege involves the right to prevent disclosure of confidential information when it is communicated within certain favored relationships.

privilege A right enjoyed by a party when a communication is within a relationship that is recognized by the law as confidential, allowing the speaker to shield the communication from disclosure.

263

State rules generally list the privileges recognized in state courts. The Federal Rules of Evidence contain only one rule pertaining to privileges, and it refers the reader to **common law**, or case law.

Rule 501. General Rule

Except as otherwise required by the Constitution of the United States or provided by Act of Congress or in rules prescribed by the Supreme Court pursuant to statutory authority, the privilege of a witness, person, government, State, or political subdivision thereof shall be governed by the principles of the common law as they may be interpreted by the courts of the United States in the light of reason and experience. However, in civil actions and proceedings, with respect to an element of a claim or defense as to which State law supplies the rule of decision, the privilege of a witness, person, government, State, or political subdivision thereof shall be determined in accordance with State law.

History

Rule 501 differs from the original submission of the rules related to privileges in Article V. As originally proposed, Article V contained thirteen rules related to nonconstitutional privileges that were to apply in the federal courts. The only privileged communications protected under these rules were those between spouses, lawyers and clients, members of the clergy and those seeking spiritual advice, and patients and their psychotherapists, in addition to required reports, political votes, trade secrets, identity of informers, and secrets of state and other official information. Finally, a privilege was to be recognized if it was contained in some other act of Congress.

The proposed rules on privileges modified the existing common law and were submitted at the time of the Watergate scandal. In that political climate, the proposed government privileges made the rules very controversial (see Illustration 12-1).

Illustration 12-1

In 1974 the United States Supreme Court held that there is no blanket presidential privilege protecting the confidentiality of all communications related to the performance of the president's responsibilities in shaping policies and making decisions, when the administration of criminal justice is in the balance.

President Nixon and members of his administration had claimed the privilege to avoid responding to a subpoena duces tecum requiring the production of certain tapes and writings related to specific meetings between the president and his advisors.

The case was in the context of the Watergate scandal and resulted in the resignation of President Nixon when the incriminating tapes became public. The tapes produced revealed the President was involved in illegal activities against his Democrat opponents. *United States v. Nixon,* 418 U.S. 683 (1974).

common law A system of law that originated in England and was adopted in America, based on the decisions of judges, which generally are followed in settling subsequent similar disputes.

As adopted in its final form, Rule 501 recognizes the law of privileges as found in current case law but also allows for continued development through future court decisions. The rule is open-ended, whereas the original Article V was a finite list of privileged communications. On the other hand, in referring to privileges, the United States Supreme Court has stated that "these exceptions to the demand for every man's evidence are not lightly created nor expansively construed, for they are in derogation of the search for truth."[1] That is, the Court is reluctant to recognize new privileges, so any attempt to propose a new privilege must be carefully researched and argued.

Other rules in Article V dealt with the manner by which a privilege could be waived, such as voluntary disclosure, or not waived, such as wrongful involuntary disclosure. Also included were rules regarding inferences related to claims of privileges, as well as relevant jury instructions for situations involving privileged communications.

Rule 501 and State Rules

Rule 501 makes it clear privileges can be claimed by witnesses, natural persons, and government entities. In other words, a privilege belonging to a person or a unit of the government can be claimed by someone in a representative capacity. Thus, the witness may not necessarily be the party who holds the privilege. The privilege can be asserted by a non-witness or by the witness on behalf of the holder of the privilege. The person with the right to prevent disclosure of the communication is the holder of the privilege, but the other party to the communication (or the party's attorney) may claim that privilege on behalf of the holder of the privilege.

Under Rule 501, if a cause of action brought in federal court is based on a state right or defense, then the state's privilege law applies, not the privileges as found in federal common law. This fact demonstrates the need for the paralegal to fully understand the legal basis for the cause of action on which the litigation is brought—that is, whether it is grounded on state or federal law. State rules of evidence can apply in federal court in situations where the basis for the cause of action is state law and not federal law. An example is when a personal injury or products liability case is brought in federal court based on diversity jurisdiction but grounded in the law of the state where the incident occurred. If, however, substantive federal law applies to the cause of action, then Rule 501 and the federal privileges as found in the federal case law apply.

The expressed intent of the Advisory Committee is that where both state and federal privilege law apply, whichever rule allows admissibility should govern in federal court. This intent reflects the general preference for admission of relevant evidence.

PRIVILEGED COMMUNICATIONS

If a privileged relationship exists, the jurors will not hear testimony regarding communications between the parties in the privileged relationship. Privileged communications are found in federal cases in one of two ways. First, a federal court may apply the privilege law of the state in which the federal court sits. Second, the federal courts may create the law of privilege that may be applied differently in the thirteen circuits. Rule 501 leaves the law of privileges to common law, or judge-made law, as found in appellate court cases.

Generally, the federal courts recognize a privileged relationship protecting communications to exist between spouses, clients and their attorneys, and those who seek spiritual counseling and members of the clergy (see Illustration 12-2). Also protected by the privilege cloak are trade secrets, state secrets, and the identification of confidential informants. The United States Supreme Court has further recognized the confidential relationship between a patient and the patient's psychotherapist.[2]

Illustration 12-2 _____

The clergy privilege is limited to private communications and recognizes "the human need to disclose to a spiritual counselor, in total and absolute confidence, what are believed to be flawed acts or thoughts and to recognize priestly consolation and guidance in return." *United States v. Gordon,* 493 F.Supp. 822, 824 (N.D.N.Y. 1980).

Unprotected Communications

The types of relationships that are not protected are also important to know. Communications between patients and their doctors, and among family members, are not kept from the jury, because objections based on privilege find no support in federal case law (see Illustration 12-3).

Illustration 12-3 _____

The Second Circuit noted that "due regard for one's in-laws is a precept of ancient lineage" but nevertheless required the defendant to weather the storm of marital strife, because the court refused to recognize an in-laws privilege. The public's right to all testimony was deemed more important. *In re Grand Jury Subpoena Issued to Matthews,* 714 F.2d 223, 225 (2d Cir. 1983).
A parent-child privilege is likewise not recognized, especially where a parent might benefit from an adult child's criminal activity. *In re Erato,* 2 F.3d 11, 16 (2d Cir. 1993).

The accountant-client privilege is not recognized in federal cases, although many states recognize the relationship as privileged for certain purposes (see Illustration 12-4).

Illustration 12-4 _____

The Supreme Court held that there is no Fourth or Fifth Amendment protection against disclosure of information turned over to an accountant. Without finding constitutional compulsion for the privilege, the court did not find it wise to create one. *Couch v. United States,* 409 U.S. 322, 335 (1973).

The United States Supreme Court has declined to recognize a privilege against disclosure of academic peer review materials.[3] The Court has also limited the marital privilege, allowing the voluntary testimony of a spouse against a criminal defendant spouse.[4]

With regard to journalists and their confidential sources, the federal courts generally recognize a narrow privilege within the confines of the First Amendment, but this privilege must often yield in libel cases.[5] Finally, federal courts have narrowed the attorney-client privilege with a crime-fraud exception (see Illustration 12-5).

Illustration 12-5

Defendants owned companies that manufactured health food and skin care products and imported goods from Hong Kong and Asian nations. They were indicted for conspiracy, tax evasion, and other crimes related to their skimming almost $90 million in an import scam.

Attorneys for the defendants were subpoenaed to compel their testimony related to the defendants' scheme to evade taxes. The attorneys lacked any guilty knowledge about the criminal activities of the defendants, but that did not matter because the privilege belonged to the clients.

The misconduct of the clients was the element that resulted in the loss of the attorney-client privilege. The prosecutor offered enough evidence to establish reasonable cause to believe the defendants had used their attorneys in their tax evasion scheme.

Based on these facts, it was within the discretion of the trial court judge to allow the government to compel disclosures under the crime-fraud exception to the attorney privilege. *United States v. Chen,* 99 F.3d 1495, 1499, 1504 (9th Cir. 1996).

The law of privilege as it relates to businesses, particularly between in-house counsel and corporate management, is especially tricky, as the tendency of the decisions seems to be against finding a protected relationship. Although on its face this kind of situation appears to involve the attorney-client privilege, the courts in fact scrutinize the work of the attorney to determine if it is legitimately "lawyering" or simply corporate work that is not unique to an attorney.

Because Rule 501 is open-ended, the law of privileges continues to evolve, and the paralegal must carefully research the law relevant to the jurisdiction where the trial will take place. It should be determined whether state law applies in the federal trial. States have codified privileges, making identification of a privileged relationship easier under state rules of evidence (see Illustration 12-6).

Illustration 12-6

Often the claims of federal law and state law are presented in a single case. If there is a state rule that creates a privilege but no comparable federal rule is recognized, then the federal rule favoring admissibility governs.

An accountant-client privilege does not exist in federal cases pursuant to *Couch v. United States,* 409 U.S. 322 (1973), but some states recognize the privilege. Since there is a federal case governing the relationship, creating no privilege, then the federal case law governs rather than a state rule that would keep the evidence out. *Wm. T. Thompson Co. v. General Nutrition Corp., Inc.,* 671 F.2d 100, 104 (3d Cir. 1982).

Protected Communications

Once it is established a privilege exists under the relevant law, the next step is to determine who holds the privilege. Generally, the person seeking advice holds the privilege, which means it is the person seeking advice who can demand nondisclosure of communications made during the relationship. Another party can assert the privilege on behalf of the one who holds the privilege, but the holder of the privilege is the one who makes the decision on whether to claim the privilege.

For instance, clients of attorneys and those seeking counseling from members of clergy hold a privilege that can be claimed by the attorney or the member of clergy on behalf of the holder. But since the client and the person who seeks counseling hold the privilege, they can disregard the claim by the attorney or member of clergy and choose to testify to the communication that otherwise could have been kept from the jury. Furthermore, the holder of the privilege, by rejecting the privilege, also opens the door to the testimony of the attorney or the member of the clergy.

The attorney-client privilege and the privilege related to spousal communications are the most common ones faced by the paralegal, so they will be discussed in detail here.

Attorney-Client Privilege

The attorney-client privilege is the oldest of the privileges, grounded on the belief the privilege is necessary to protect candid communications between attorneys and their clients. If a client thought the attorney to whom the client was entrusting information could be called to testify with regard to that information, the client would not be forthcoming, and the attorney would be impeded in representing the client.

Generally, the attorney-client privilege protects communications between the attorney and the client as long as the communications are confidential and as long as the person is seeking the legal advice of the attorney.

With regard to confidentiality, it is imperative that discussions with a client be held in private, that is, under circumstances where there is a reasonable expectation of privacy. A confidential communication is one not intended to be disclosed to third parties other than (1) those to whom disclosure would be in furtherance of legal services to the client or (2) those who are necessary for the transmission of the communication. The presence of a third party who is not an employee of the attorney who is representing the client destroys the privilege. In this situation, the communication is not protected by the privilege, and any of the parties to the communication can be called to testify as to the content of the discussion.

Merely delivering papers, documents, or other physical objects to an attorney by the client will not shield the items, because these items are not considered communications. It is the communications themselves that are protected from disclosure, not evidence involved in a communication. The paralegal needs to research this issue when there is a question of whether an item is in fact a communication and not just underlying evidence.

A paralegal often is privy to confidential communications with clients, so it is critical that the paralegal respect the confidential relationship by not disclosing to others what transpires between the client and the attorney. Clients' cases must not be discussed in common areas of the law office where the conversations might be overheard. Neither should the paralegal ever discuss a client's case with someone outside the law office. Even though the courts recognize the privilege as being held by the client and thus waivable only by the client, it is unethical for the paralegal, attorney, or any employee of the law office to disclose information about a client, whether intentionally or negligently. When protected information is disclosed, the privilege likely will apply when it comes to testifying in court, but as a practical matter, the client's case may still be compromised.

The paralegal also needs to be cautious when two or more parties are clients. If those clients ever become involved in a lawsuit between or among themselves, there is no privilege as it relates to the communications they may have had as a group with the attorney who represented their collective interests. Although the privilege still attaches, in that a third party cannot claim the privilege is lost, those formerly friendly parties lose this protection if there is a dispute putting them at odds with each other.

Besides the need for confidentiality to determine the applicability of the attorney-client privilege, the person seeking legal advice must intend to receive the professional services of an attorney. In this regard, the person can then be characterized as a client. The client may be a private citizen, public officer, corporation, or any other organization or entity seeking legal advice. If the client is an entity, the person seeking the legal advice must be an employee who has the authority to secure legal advice on behalf of the entity. It must be within the scope of the employee's duties to seek legal advice on behalf of the entity.

If a person was posing as an attorney but was an imposter, or at least not licensed to practice law, the privilege still applies if it was reasonable for the client to believe the person was an attorney. In this analysis, remember it is the client who holds the privilege, not the attorney.

The client has the right to waive the privilege, like any holder of any of the recognized privileges. There is no such thing as partial waiver; all communications during the relationship are waived if there is a voluntary waiver of some of the communications. If there is a waiver by the holder of the privilege, then the client or the attorney can be compelled by the judge to testify.

Some matters constitute exceptions to the attorney-client privilege. If there is a dispute between the attorney and the client, giving rise to a malpractice claim by the client, then the communications between the client and the attorney are not privileged. If there is a fee dispute, the relevant communications are not privileged, either. Generally, the identity of a client is not privileged, but circumstances exist in which a claim of privilege by the attorney on behalf of a client might succeed. Illustration 12-7 offers an example.

Illustration 12-7 _____

In Florida an attorney cannot be forced to disclose the identity of a client if the disclosure would subject the client to criminal prosecution for criminal acts previously committed. In the case *Dean v. Dean,* 607 So. 2d 494 (Fla. 4th D.C.A. 1992), the victim could not compel the attorney to disclose the identity of the person who came to the attorney for advice on how to return the victim's property taken by the attorney's client.

A paralegal may also come across another situation where the privilege does not attach if the paralegal works for an attorney who handles probate cases. If there is a will contest, an attorney for a deceased client can testify to communications relating to the creation of the will that took place with the client prior to the client's death.

Marital Communications

Marital privileges can involve either testimonial privilege or confidential communications (see Figure 12-1).

The *testimonial privilege* applies to criminal, not civil, cases. If a spouse is on trial, the other spouse has the choice of testifying against the defendant spouse or of asserting the privilege and not testifying. Unlike the other privileges, the testimonial privilege as it applies in federal court does not allow a defendant spouse the sole discretion in determining whether the other spouse can testify. The witness spouse holds the privilege, not the defendant spouse. "The witness may be neither compelled to testify nor foreclosed from testifying."[6]

The testimonial privilege applies only to confidential communications between the spouses. If the communication does not fall within the definition of a confidential communication, then the testimonial privilege does not apply, and the witness spouse can testify to the extent any other witness could testify.

Confidential communications are protected from disclosure whether the case is civil or criminal. Both spouses hold the privilege, and either can assert the privilege, thus precluding the other spouse from testifying. As noted earlier, if a spouse is a criminal defendant, then the witness spouse holds the privilege as to the confidential communication.

Confidential communications can occur only between those who are married. This privilege does not apply to communications made during the marriage of people who are now divorced. The criteria for spousal confidential communications are similar to those for confidential communications between attorneys and clients. There must be an expectation of privacy, and the nature of the communication must be such that the communication would not have occurred between the parties but for the marital relationship. In other words, one spouse would not have told the other spouse about a matter but for the

FIGURE 12-1

Marital privileges can involve either testimonial privilege or confidential communications.

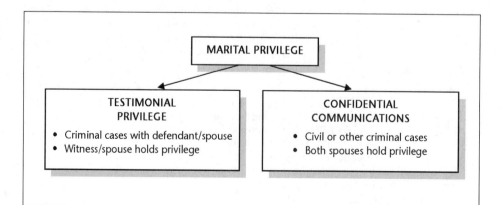

fact they were husband and wife. The social policy underlying the privilege is the desire to protect the marital relationship from unwarranted intrusion. This desire outweighs any loss of helpful evidence.

The social policy does not apply when the lawsuit is between spouses, or when the cases involve crimes against the testifying spouse or the spouse's children, such as incest, bigamy, and child abuse.

Application of the other privileges in federal courts should be thoroughly researched by the paralegal when it is apparent a privilege might attach to the testimony of a potential witness in a civil or criminal case. The underlying concerns and social policy issues are the same for the recognized privileges.

STATE PRIVILEGES

If a trial is in state court, the state rules and case law become the focus of attention. With regard to the marital privileges, some states still hold the traditional view that the defendant spouse in a criminal case holds the privilege and can keep the witness spouse from testifying (see Illustration 12-8).

Illustration 12-8

The concept that a spouse cannot testify for or against the other spouse has roots in medieval jurisprudence. An accused was not permitted to testify in his own behalf. Since a husband and wife were considered one person, and the wife had no legally recognizable existence, the husband was that one person. Therefore, what was inadmissible testimony from the husband was also inadmissible if the testimony was from the wife. *Trammel v. United States,* 445 U.S. 40, 44 (1980).

States differ with regard to communications between members of the clergy and those seeking spiritual counseling. Some states take the view the privilege belongs to the clergy members, and the clergy members alone can choose to assert the privilege or to waive it (see Illustration 12-9). But the majority view is that the privilege is held by the person seeking spiritual counseling, not the clergy member.

Illustration 12-9

The Supreme Court of New Jersey has held that the privilege belongs only to clergypersons, who may elect to assert or waive the privilege. No consent for waiver from the penitent is necessary. Furthermore, the penitent cannot waive the privilege and compel the member of clergy to testify. *State v. Szemple,* 135 N.J. 406, 423, 427, 64 A.2d 817, 825, 827 (1994).

In addition to these substantive differences with the federal common law of privilege, most states recognize more privileges than does federal common law.

CLAIMS INVOLVING PRIVILEGE

The law of privilege cannot be used as a sword and shield against another party. A party cannot proceed with a claim against another party asserting matters related to privileged communications while at the same time maintaining that evidence is protected from disclosure by a privilege. If the party bringing the action insists on asserting the privilege, the judge has the power to dismiss the claim against the defendant, because the plaintiff's assertion of the privilege keeps the defendant from defending against the claim.

CONSTITUTIONAL PRIVILEGES

Although not dealt with in this chapter, constitutional privileges also exist that might be applicable, such as the privilege against compulsory self-incrimination ("taking the Fifth"). These need to be kept in mind when researching the law of privileges.

SUMMARY

The paralegal must be familiar with both the federal law governing privileges and relevant state law on privileges. This is not an area of total uniformity between federal law and state law, or even among states.

Rule 501 is the only federal rule that applies to privileges. If a privileged communication is disclosed in conjunction with a confidential relationship, the court will defer to the policy reasons behind the privilege and protect the communication from forced disclosure. However, since the relationships that might lead to a privilege are not enumerated in the Federal Rules of Evidence, case law must be reviewed.

Generally, the federal courts recognize privileges involving attorneys and their clients, members of clergy and those seeking spiritual advice, spouses, trade secrets, state secrets, confidential informants, and psychotherapists and their patients.

On the other hand, most state evidence rules list the specific relationships that can give rise to a privilege. Although case law is also important, at least the rules are a point of reference from which to work.

The person with the right to prevent disclosure of a privilege is called the holder of the privilege. Someone else may claim the privilege on behalf of the holder of the privilege, but the holder of the privilege is the one whose decision it is to claim the privilege or not.

Other privileges exist that may be relevant, such as the constitutional privilege against compulsory self-incrimination. Privileges may be found in sources other than case law or rules, such as in statutes or other rules of the Supreme Court.

✓ CHECKPOINTS

❑ Privileges: elements
1. Protected relationship.
2. Confidential communication.
3. Right to prevent disclosure.

❑ Privileges: source
1. Case law.
2. Statutes.
3. Constitution.
4. Other Supreme Court rules.
5. State law.

❑ Privileges: application
1. Regarding a state issue in federal court, state law applies.
2. Regarding a conflict between federal and state law on privilege, the rule allowing admission of the evidence prevails.

❑ Federal privileges
1. Attorney-client communications.
2. Communications between clergy member and seeker of spiritual advice.
3. Marital communications.
   - Testimonial: criminal cases with defendant/spouse; witness/spouse holds privilege.
   - Confidential communication: civil or other criminal cases with both spouses holding privilege.
4. Trade secrets.
5. State secrets.
6. Confidential informants.
7. Psychotherapist-patient communications.

⚖ APPLICATIONS

Application 12-1

In the *Jaffee* case decided in 1996, the United States Supreme Court recognized a psychotherapist-patient privilege, resolving a conflict among the circuit courts of appeal. In reading the case, note especially the history of the law of privileges and the underlying social policies as they relate to the quest for justice through the trial process.

Justice Scalia, in his dissenting opinion (omitted here), denounced the expansion of the law of privilege as contrary to the "traditional judicial preference for the truth." Not only does he find the psychotherapist-patient privilege unnecessary, he states that its expansion to include licensed clinical social workers with medical doctors or licensed/certified psychologists is unwarranted and bad judicial policy. However, six of the justices joined Justice Stevens in his majority opinion.

Jaffee v. Redmond
518 U.S. 1 (1996)

JUSTICE STEVENS delivered the opinion of the Court.

After a traumatic incident in which she shot and killed a man, a police officer received extensive counseling from a licensed clinical social worker. The question we address is whether statements the officer made to her therapist during the counseling sessions are protected from compelled disclosure in federal civil action brought by the family of the deceased. Stated otherwise, the question is whether it is appropriate for federal courts to recognize a "psychotherapist privilege" under Rule 501 of the Federal Rules of Evidence.

I

Petitioner is the administrator of the estate of Ricky Allen. Respondents are Mary Lu Redmond, a former police officer, and the Village of Hoffman Estates, Illinois, her employer during the time that she served on the police force. Petitioner commenced this action against respondents after Redmond shot and killed Allen while on patrol duty.

On June 27, 1991, Redmond was the first officer to respond to a "fight in progress" call at an apartment complex. As she arrived at the scene, two of Allen's sisters ran toward her squad car, waving their arms and shouting that there had been a stabbing in one of the apartments. Redmond testified at trial that she relayed this information to her dispatcher and requested an ambulance. She then exited her car and walked toward the apartment building. Before Redmond reached the building, several men ran out, one waving a pipe. When the men ignored her order to get on the ground, Redmond drew her service revolver. Two other men then burst out of the building, one, Ricky Allen, chasing the other. According to Redmond, Allen was brandishing a butcher knife and disregarded her repeated commands to drop the weapon. Redmond shot Allen when she believed he was about to stab the man he was chasing. Allen died at the scene. Redmond testified that before other officers arrived to provide support, "people came pouring out of the buildings," App. 134, and a threatening confrontation between her and the crowd ensued.

Petitioner filed suit in Federal District Court alleging that Redmond had violated Allen's constitutional rights by using excessive force during the encounter at the apartment complex. The complaint sought damages under Rev. Stat. § 1979, 42 U.S.C. § 1983 and the Illinois wrongful death statute, Ill. Comp. Stat., ch. 740, § 180/1 *et seq.* (1994). At trial, petitioner presented testimony from members of Allen's family that conflicted with Redmond's version of the incident in several important respects. They testified, for example, that Redmond drew her gun before exiting her squad car and that Allen was unarmed when he emerged from the apartment building.

During pretrial discovery petitioner learned that after the shooting Redmond had participated in about 50 counseling sessions with Karen Beyer, a clinical social worker licensed by the State of Illinois and employed at that time by the Village of Hoffman Estates. Petitioner sought access to Beyer's notes concerning the sessions for use in cross-examining Redmond. Respondents vigorously resisted the discovery. They asserted that the contents of the conversations between Beyer and Redmond were protected against involuntary disclosure by a psychotherapist-patient privilege. The district judge rejected this argument. Neither Beyer nor Redmond, however, complied with his order to disclose the contents of Beyer's notes. At depositions and on the witness stand both either refused to answer certain questions or professed an inability to recall details of their conversations.

In his instructions at the end of the trial, the judge advised the jury that the refusal to turn over Beyer's notes had no "legal justification" and that the jury could therefore presume that the contents of the notes would have been unfavorable to respondents. The jury awarded petitioner $45,000 on the federal claim and $500,000 on her state-law claim.

The Court of Appeals for the Seventh Circuit reversed and remanded for a new trial. Addressing the issue for the first time, the court concluded that "reason and experience," the touchstones for acceptance of a privilege under Rule 501 of the Federal Rules of Evidence, compelled recognition of a psychotherapist-patient privilege. 51 F.3d 1346, 1355 (1995). "Reason tells us that psychotherapists and patients share a unique relationship, in which the ability to communicate freely without the fear of public disclosure is the key to successful treatment." *Id.,* at 1355–1356. As to experience, the court observed that all 50 States have adopted some form of the psychotherapist-patient privilege. *Id., at* 1356. The court attached particular significance to the fact that Illinois law expressly extends such a privilege to social workers like Karen Beyer. *Id., at* 1357. The court also noted that, with one exception, the federal decisions rejecting the privilege were more than five years old and that the "need and demand for counseling services has skyrocketed during the past several years." *Id., at* 1355–1356.

The Court of Appeals qualified its recognition of the privilege by stating that it would not apply if "in the interests of justice, the evidentiary need for the disclosure of the contents of a patient's counseling sessions outweighs that patient's privacy interests." *Id., at* 1357. Balancing those conflicting interests, the court observed, on the one hand, that the evidentiary need for the contents of the confidential conversations was diminished in this case because there were numerous eyewitnesses to the shooting, and, on the other hand, that Officer Redmond's privacy interests were substantial. [FOOTNOTE: Her ability, through counseling, to work out the pain and anguish undoubtedly caused by Allen's death in all probability depended to a great deal upon her trust and confidence in her counselor Karen Beyer. Officer Redmond, and all those placed in her most unfortunate circumstances, are entitled to be protected in their desire to seek counseling after mortally wounding another human being in the line of duty. An individual who is troubled as the result of her participation in a violent and tragic event, such as this, displays a most commendable respect for human life and is a person well-suited 'to protect and to serve. 51 F.3d at 1358.] *Id., at* 1358. Based on this assessment, the court concluded that the trial court had erred by refusing to afford protection to the confidential communications between Redmond and Beyer.

The United States courts of appeals do not uniformly agree that the federal courts should recognize a psychotherapist privilege under Rule 501. Because of the conflict among the courts of appeals and the importance of the question, we granted certiorari. 516 U.S. _____ (1995). We affirm.

II

Rule 501 of the Federal Rules of Evidence authorizes federal courts to define new privileges by interpreting "common law principles ... in the light of reason and experience." The authors of the Rule borrowed this phrase from our opinion in *Wolfe v. United States,* 291 U.S. 7, 12 (1934), which in turn referred to the oft-repeated observation that "the common law is not immutable but flexible, and by its own principles adapts itself to varying conditions." *Funk v. United States,* 290 U.S. 371, 383 (1933). See also *Hawkins v. United States,* 358 U.S. 74, 79 (1958) (changes in privileges may be "dictated by 'reason and experience' "). The Senate Report accompanying the 1975 adoption of the Rules indicates that Rule 501 "should be understood as reflecting the view that the recognition of a privilege based on a confidential relationship ... should be determined on a case-by-case basis." S. Rep. No. 93-1277, p. 13 (1974). [FOOTNOTE: In 1972 the Chief Justice transmitted to Congress proposed Rules of Evidence for United States Courts and Magistrates. 56 F.R.D. 183 (hereinafter Proposed Rules). The rules had been formulated by the Judicial Conference Advisory Committee on Rules of Evidence and approved by the Judicial Conference of the United States and by this Court. *Trammel v. United States,* 445 U.S. 40, 47 (1980). The proposed rules defined nine specific testimonial privileges, including a psychotherapist-patient privilege, and indicated that these were to be the exclusive privileges absent constitutional mandate, Act of Congress, or revision of the Rules. Proposed Rules 501–513, 56 F.R.D., at 230–261. Congress rejected this recommendation in favor of Rule 501's general mandate. *Trammel,* 445 U.S., at 47.] The Rule thus did not freeze the law governing the privileges of witnesses in federal trials at a particular point in our history, but rather directed federal courts to "continue the evolutionary development of testimonial privileges." *Trammel v. United States,* 445 U.S. 40, 47 (1980); see also *University of Pennsylvania v. EEOC,* 493 U.S. 182 (1990).

The common-law principles underlying the recognition of testimonial privileges can be stated simply. " 'For more than three centuries it has now been recognized as a fundamental maxim that the public ... has a right to every man's evidence. When we come to examine the various claims of exemption, we start with the primary assumption that there is a general duty to give what testimony one is capable of giving, and that any exemptions which may exist are distinctly exceptional, being so many derogations form a positive general rule.' " *United States v. Bryan,* 339 U.S. 323, 331 (1950) (quoting 8 J. Wigmore, Evidence § 2192, p. 64 (3d ed. 1940). [FOOTNOTE: The familiar expression "every man's evidence" was a well-known phrase as early as the mid-18th century. Both the Duke of Argyll and Lord Chancellor Hardwicke invoked the maxim during the May 25, 1742, debate in the House of Lords concerning a bill to grant immunity to witnesses who would give evidence against Sir Robert Walpole, first Earl of Oxford. 12 T. Hansard, Parliamentary History of England 643, 675, 693, 697 (1812). The bill was defeated soundly. *Id.,* at 711.] See also *United States v. Nixon,* 418 U.S. 683, 709 (1974). Exceptions from the general rule disfavoring testimonial privileges may be justified, however, by a " 'public good transcending the normally predominant principle of utilizing all rational means for ascertaining the truth.' " *Trammel,* 445 U.S., at 50 quoting *Elkins v. United States,* 364 U.S. 206, 234 (1960) (Frankfurter, J., dissenting).

Guided by these principles, the question we address today is whether a privilege protecting confidential communications between a psychotherapist and her patient "promotes sufficiently important interests to outweigh the need for probative evidence... ." 445 U.S., at 51. Both "reason and experience" persuade us that it does.

III

Like the spousal and attorney-client privileges, the psychotherapist-patient privilege is "rooted in the imperative need for confidence and trust." *Trammel,* 445 U.S., at 51. Treatment by a physician for physical ailments can often proceed successfully on the basis of a physical examination, objective information supplied by the patient, and the results of diagnostic tests. Effective psychotherapy, by contrast, depends upon an atmosphere of confidence and trust in which the patient is willing to make a frank and complete disclosure of facts, emotions, memories, and fears. Because of the sensitive nature of the problems for which individuals consult psychotherapists, disclosure of confidential communications made during counseling sessions may cause embarrassment or disgrace. For this reason, the mere possibility of disclosure may impede development of the confidential relationship necessary for successful treatment. [FOOTNOTE: See studies and authorities cited in the Brief for American Psychiatric Association et al. as *Amici Curiae* 14-17, and the Brief for American Psychological Association as *Amicus Curiae* 12-17.] As the Judicial Conference Advisory Committee observed in 1972 when it recommended that Congress recognize a psychotherapist privilege as part of the Proposed Federal Rules of Evidence, a psychiatrist's ability to help her patients

> "is completely dependent upon [the patient's] willingness and ability to talk freely. This makes it difficult if not impossible for [a psychiatrist] to function without being able to assure ... patients of confidentiality and, indeed, privileged communication. Where there may be exceptions to this general rule ... , there is wide agreement that confidentiality is a *sin qua non* for successful psychiatric treatment." Advisory Committee's Notes to Proposed Rules, 56 F.R.D 183, 242 (1972) (quoting Group for Advancement of Psychiatry, Report No. 45, Confidentiality and Privileged Communication in the Practice of Psychiatry 92 (June 1960)).

By protecting confidential communications between a psychotherapist and her patient from involuntary disclosure, the proposed privilege thus serves important private interests.

Our cases make clear that an asserted privilege must also "serv[e] public ends." *Upjohn Co. v. United States,* 449 U.S. 383 (1981). Thus, the purpose of the attorney-client privilege is to "encourage full and frank communication between attorneys and their clients and thereby promote broader public interests in the observance of law and administration of justice." *Ibid.* And the spousal [privilege, as modified in *Trammel,* is justified because it "furthers the important public interest in marital harmony," 445 U.S., at 53. See also *United States v. Nixon,* 418 U.S., at 705; *Wolfe v. United States,* 291 U.S., at 14. The psychotherapist privilege serves the public interest by facilitating the provision of appropriate treatment for individuals suffering the effects of a mental or emotional problem. The mental health of our citizenry, no less than its physical health, is a public good of transcendent importance. [FOOTNOTE: This case amply demonstrates the importance of allowing individuals to receive confidential counseling. Police officers engaged in the dangerous and difficult tasks associated with protecting the safety of our communities not only confront the risk of physical harm but also face stressful circumstances that may give rise to anxiety, depression, fear, or anger. The entire community may suffer if police officers are not able to receive effective counseling and treatment after traumatic incidents, either because trained officers leave the profession prematurely or because those in need of treatment remain on the job.]

In contrast to the significant public and private interests supporting recognition of the privilege, the likely evidentiary benefit that would result from the denial of the privilege is modest. If the privilege were rejected, confidential conversations between psychotherapists and their patients would surely be chilled, particularly when it is obvious that the circumstances that give rise to the need for treatment will probably result in litigation. Without a privilege, much of the desirable evidence to which litigants such as petitioner seek access—for example, admissions against interest by a party—is unlikely to come into being. This unspoken "evidence" will therefore serve no greater truth-seeking function than if it had been spoken and privileged.

That it is appropriate for the federal courts to recognize a psychotherapist privilege under Rule 501 is confirmed by the fact that all 50 States and the District of Columbia have enacted into law some form of psychotherapist privilege. We have previously observed that the policy decisions of the States bear on the question whether federal courts should recognize a new privilege or amend the coverage of an existing one. See *Trammel,* 445 U.S., at 48–50; *United States v. Gillock,* 445 U.S. 360, 368, n. 8 (1980). Because state legislatures are fully aware of the need to protect the integrity of the factfinding functions of their courts, the existence of a consensus among the States indicates that "reason and experience" support recognition of the privilege. In addition, given the importance of the patient's understanding that her communications with her therapist will not be publicly disclosed, any States's promise of confidentiality would have little value if the patient were aware that the privilege would not be honored in a federal court. Denial of the federal privilege therefore would frustrate the purposes of the state legislation that was enacted to foster these confidential communications.

It is of no consequence that recognition of the privilege in the vast majority of States is the product of legislative action rather than judicial decision. Although common-law rulings may once have been the primary source of new developments in federal privilege law, that is no longer the case. In *Funk v. United States,* 290 U.S. 371 (1933), we recognized that it is appropriate to treat a consistent body of policy determinations by state legislatures as reflecting both "reason" and "experience." *Id.,* at 376–381. That rule is properly respectful of the States and at the same time reflects the fact that once a state legislature has enacted a privilege there is no longer an opportunity for common-law creation of the protection. The history of the psychotherapist privilege illustrates the latter point. In 1972 the members of the Judicial Conference Advisory committee noted that the common law "had indicated a disposition to recognize a psychotherapist-patient privilege when legislatures began moving into the field." Proposed Rules, 56 F.R.D., at 242 (citation omitted). The present unanimous acceptance of the privilege shows that the state lawmakers moved quickly. That the privilege may have developed faster legislatively than it would have in the courts demonstrates only that the States rapidly recognized the wisdom of the rule as the field of psychotherapy developed. [FOOTNOTE: Petitioner acknowledges that all 50 state legislatures favor a psychotherapist privilege. She nevertheless discounts the relevance of the state privilege statutes by pointing to divergence among the States concerning the types of therapy relationships protected and the exceptions recognized. A small number of state statutes, for example, grant the privilege only to psychiatrists and psychologists, while most apply the protection more broadly. Compare Haw. Rules Evid. 504, 504.1 and N.D. Rule Evid. 503 (privilege extends to physicians and psychotherapists), with Ariz. Rev. Stat. Ann. § 32-3283 (1992) (privilege covers "behavioral health professional[s]"); Tex. Rule Civ. Evid. 501(a)(1) (privilege extends to persons "licensed or certified by the State of Texas in the diagnosis, evaluation or treatment of any mental or emotional disorder" or "involved in the treatment or examination of drug abusers"); Utah Rule Evid. 506 (privilege protects confidential communications made to marriage and family therapists, professional counselors, and psychiatric mental health nurse specialists). The range of exceptions recognized by the States is similarly varied. Compare Ark. Code Ann. § 17-46-107 (1987) (narrow exceptions); Haw. Rules Evid. 504, 504.1 (same), with Cal. Evid. Code Ann. §§ 1016–1027 (West 1995) (broad exceptions); R.I. Gen. Laws § 5-37.3–4 (1956) (same). These variations in the scope of the protection are too limited to undermine the force of the States' unanimous judgment that some form of psychotherapist privilege is appropriate.]

The uniform judgment of the States is reinforced by the fact that a psychotherapist privilege was among the nine specific privileges recommended by the Advisory Committee in its proposed privilege rules. In *United States v. Gillock,* 445 U.S. 360, 367–368 (1980), our holding that Rule 501 did not include a state legislative privilege relied, in part, on the fact that no such privilege was included in the Advisory Committee's draft. The reasoning in Gillock thus supports the opposite conclusion in this case. In rejecting the proposed draft that had specifically identified each privilege rule and substituting the present more open-ended Rule 501, the Senate Judiciary committee explicitly stated that its action "should not be understood as disapproving any recognition of a psychiatrist-patient ... privileg[e] contained in the [proposed] rules." S. Rep. No. 93-1277, at 13.

Because we agree with the judgment of the state legislatures and the Advisory Committee that a psychotherapist-patient privilege will serve a "public good transcending the normally predominant principle of utilizing all rational means for ascertaining truth," *Trammel,* 445 U.S., at 50, we hold that confidential communications between a licensed psychotherapist and her patient in the course of diagnosis or treatment are protected from compelled disclosure under rule 501 of the Federal Rules of Evidence. [FOOTNOTE: Like other testimonial privileges, the patient may of course waive the protection.]

IV

All agree that a psychotherapist privilege covers confidential communications made to license psychiatrists and psychologists. We have no hesitation in concluding in this case that the federal privilege should also extend to confidential communications made to licensed social workers in the course of psychotherapy. The reasons for recognizing a privilege for treatment by psychiatrists and psychologists apply with equal force to treatment by a clinical social worker such as Karen Beyer. Today, social workers provide a significant amount of mental health treatment. See, *e.g.,* U.S. Dept. of Health and Human Services, Center for Mental Health Services, Mental Health, United States, 1994 pp. 85–87, 107–114; Brief for National Association of Social Workers et al. as *Amici Curiae* 5-7 (citing authorities). Their clients often include the poor and those of modest means who could not afford the assistance of a psychiatrist or psychologist, id., at 6-7 (citing authorities), but whose counseling sessions serve the same public goals. Perhaps in recognition of these circumstances, the vast majority of States explicitly extend a testimonial privilege to licensed social workers. We therefore agree with the Court of Appeals that "[d]rawing a distinction between the counseling provided by costly psychotherapists and the counseling provided by more readily accessible social workers serves no discernible public purpose." 51 F.3d at 1358, n. 19.

We part company with the Court of Appeals on a separate point. We reject the balancing component of the privilege implemented by that court and a small number of States. Making the promise of confidentiality contingent upon a trial judge's later evaluation of the relative importance of the patient's interest in privacy and the evidentiary need for disclosure would eviscerate the effectiveness of the privilege. As we explained in *Upjohn,* if the purpose of the privilege is to be served, the participants in the confidential conversation "must be able to predict with some degree of certainty whether particular discussions will be protected. An uncertain privilege, or one which purports to be certain but results in widely varying applications by the courts, is little better than no privilege at all." 449 U.S., at 393.

These considerations are all that is necessary for decision of this case. A rule that authorizes the recognition of new privileges on a case-by-case basis makes it appropriate to define the details of new privileges in a like manner. Because this is the first case in which we have recognized a psychotherapist privilege, it is neither necessary nor feasible to delineate its full contours in a way that would "govern all conceivable future questions in this area." *Id.,* at 386. [FOOTNOTE: Although it would be premature to speculate about most future developments in the federal psychotherapist privilege, we do not doubt that there are situations in which the privilege must give way, for example, if a serious threat of harm to the patient or to others can be averted only by means of a disclosure by the therapist.]

V

The conversations between Officer Redmond and Karen Beyer and the notes taken during their counseling sessions are protected from compelled disclosure under Rule 501 of the Federal Rules of Evidence. The judgment of the Court of Appeals is affirmed.

It is so ordered.

Class Discussion Questions

1. For what purpose did Jaffee want the notes and testimony of Karen Beyer?
2. What happened at trial with regard to testimony about the counseling sessions between Beyer and Redmond?
3. What were the reasons that the Court gave to justify creation of the psychotherapist privilege?
4. Why did the Court include licensed clinical social workers within the privilege?

Application 12-2

United States v. Bolzer
556 F.2d 948 (9th Cir. 1977)

OPINION

JAMES M. CARTER, Circuit Judge:

This is an appeal by three defendants of their convictions by a jury for armed mail robbery, in violation of 18 U.S.C. §§ 1706 and 2114, and for conspiracy, in violation of 18 U.S.C. § 371.

Appellants argue that count one of the indictment for conspiracy should have been dismissed because of a fatal variance between the allegations in the indictment and the proof at trial. Appellant Thompson also objects to the introduction of testimony from his ex-wife. We find that appellants were not prejudiced by the variance and that the testimony of Thompson's ex-wife was properly introduced. We therefore affirm.

Facts

In May and June 1975, appellants met several times to plan a robbery of a United States Postal Service truck trailer at Livingston, Montana. On May 29, 1975, appellant LaRita Anne Bolzer purchased a shotgun for use in the robbery. Appellants Thompson and William Bolzer (LaRita's husband) conducted surveillance of the postal facility at Bozeman, Montana, allegedly to determine the custom and habits of the truck drivers on their routes. Thompson was a former postal employee and knew the details of the postal operation in the area.

On June 25, 1975, appellants robbed driver Donald Morrow using a sawed-off shotgun. They destroyed several mail pouches during the robbery, for which they were separately indicted. After the robbery, appellants removed coins, currency, and jewels valued at approximately $11,600, and disposed of the remainder of the mail in an abandoned well. Appellants went to Nevada to exchange the coins for currency, and deposited much of the money in their personal accounts. The remainder of the money was later found at a ranch owned by William Bolzer's father.

Appellants were indicted on three counts on May 12, 1976, and a consolidated trial began on July 6. The evidence showed that appellants conducted surveillance of the postal facility at Bozeman rather than the facility at Livingston, as had been charged in the indictment. As part of its case in chief, the government called Freida Fitzhugh, Thompson's ex-wife, to testify. She identified a pair of pants which were found in the bag containing some of the stolen mail as likely belonging to Thompson.

The jury returned its verdict on July 14. Thompson and William Bolzer were found guilty on all three counts. LaRita Bolzer was found guilty on counts one and two (conspiracy and robbery). Each was sentenced to five years of imprisonment with five years parole.

Testimony of Ex-Wife

Freida Fitzhugh, Thompson's ex-wife, was called as a witness to identify a pair of pants found in a well with much of the stolen mail. She testified that the style and size of the pants matched those of the kind Thompson wore and that the patches on the pants were the type she used. Thompson claims this testimony was received in violation of the privilege for confidential marital communications.

This claim is governed by Rule 501 of the Federal Rules of Evidence, which provides in relevant part:

> "Except as otherwise required by the Constitution of the United States or provided by Act of Congress or in rules prescribed by the Supreme Court pursuant to statutory authority, the privilege of a witness, person, government, State, or political subdivision thereof shall be governed by the principles of the common law as they may be interpreted by the courts of the United States in the light of reason and experience."

See also Fed.R.Crim.P. 26, as amended (1972). We therefore must turn to federal common law to decide Thompson's claim.

Federal courts recognize two distinct privileges arising out of the marital relationship. The first often called the "anti-marital facts" privilege, bars one spouse from testifying against the other. See *Hawkins v. United States,* 358 U.S. 74, 75–76, 79 S.Ct. 136, 3 L.Ed. 2d 125 (1958); *Bisno v. United States,* 299 F.2d 711, 721 (9 Cir.), cert. denied, 370 U.S. 952, 82 S.Ct. 1602, 8 L.Ed. 2d 818 (1962). This privilege does not survive the termination of the marriage and therefore does not apply in this case. See *United States v. Smith,* 533 F.2d 1077, 1079 (8 Cir. 1976); *United States v. Fisher,* 518 F.2d 836, 838 (2 Cir.), cert. denied, 423 U.S. 1033, 96 S.Ct. 565, 46 L.Ed. 2d 407 (1972).

The other privilege protects confidential marital communications. It bars testimony concerning intra-spousal, confidential expressions arising from the marital relationship. See *Blau v. United States,* 340 U.S. 332, 333, 71 S.Ct. 301, 95 L.Ed. 306 (1956); *United States v. Harper,* 450 F.2d 1032, 1045 (5 Cir. 1971). Unlike the "anti-marital facts" privilege, this privilege survives the termination of the marriage. *Pereira v. United States,* 347 U.S. 1, 6, 74 S.Ct. 358, 98 L.Ed. 435 (1954); *United States v. Lewis,* 140 U.S.App.D.C. 40, 433 F.2d 1146, 1150 (1970).

It is well established that this privilege applies only to utterances or expressions intended by one spouse to convey a message to the other. Fitzhugh's testimony related only her knowledge about and observations of Thompson's pants. No communications were involved at all. Accordingly, the testimony is not barred.

Conclusion

The judgment of the district court is AFFIRMED. Bond pending appeal is revoked forthwith.

Class Discussion Questions

1. Why was the testimonial privilege inapplicable in this case?
2. What was the testimony of Ms. Fitzhugh that Mr. Thompson argued was a confidential communication?
3. The court held that this testimony was not relaying communications, so it did not qualify as a confidential communication. If not a communication, what was it that she was relaying?

 EXERCISES

1. Locate the privileges found in your state evidence rules, and compare them with the recognized federal privileges.
2. Does your state recognize that the identity of a client may be privileged? If so, under what circumstances?
3. The criminal defense attorney that you work for represents a prisoner who is being tried for a murder. While he was in prison, the prisoner confessed to the murder to the prison chaplain. A security officer was present when the prisoner confessed to the chaplain. The prosecutor plans

to call the security officer to testify to the confession.

a. How will the prosecutor argue that the communication was not privileged?

b. What additional facts might counter the prosecutor's argument?

RULES REFERENCED IN THIS CHAPTER

Rule 501. General Rule

NOTES

[1] *United States v. Nixon,* 418 U.S. 683, 710 (1974).

[2] *Jaffee v. Redmond,* 518 U.S. 1 (1996).

[3] *University of Pennsylvania v. EEOC,* 493 U.S. 182 (1990).

[4] *Trammel v. United States,* 445 U.S. 40 (1980).

[5] *Miller v. Transamerican Press, Inc.,* 621 F.2d 721, 725 (5th Cir. 1980).

[6] *Trammel v. United States,* 445 U.S. 40 (1980).

FEDERAL RULES OF EVIDENCE*

Effective July 1, 1975
Including Amendments Effective December 1, 1997

Research Note

Rule requirements, case law applications, commentary, and references to treatises and law reviews are available in Wright, Graham and Gold, *Federal Practice and Procedure,* Volume 21 et seq.; in Graham, *Handbook of Federal Evidence,* 3d; and in Goode & Wellborn, *Courtroom Handbook on Federal Evidence.*

Use *WESTLAW*® to find cases citing a rule. In addition, use *WESTLAW* to search for specific terms or to update a rule; see the US–RULES, US–ORDERS and US–PL Scope Screens for further information.

Amendments to the Federal Rules of Evidence are published, as received, in the *Supreme Court Reporter, Federal Reporter 3d, Federal Supplement, Federal Rules Decisions* and *Bankruptcy Reporter* advance sheets.

TABLE OF RULES

ARTICLE I.   GENERAL PROVISIONS

RULE 101.   SCOPE

These rules govern proceedings in the courts of the United States and before the United States bankruptcy judges and United States magistrate judges, to the extent and with the exceptions stated in rule 1101.

[Amended March 2, 1987, effective October 1, 1987; April 25, 1988, effective November 1, 1988; April 22, 1993, effective December 1, 1993.]

RULE 102.   PURPOSE AND CONSTRUCTION

These rules shall be construed to secure fairness in administration, elimination of unjustifiable expense and delay, and promotion of growth and development of the law of evidence to the end that the truth may be ascertained and proceedings justly determined.

RULE 103.   RULINGS ON EVIDENCE

(a) Effect of Erroneous Ruling.   Error may not be predicated upon a ruling which admits or excludes evidence unless a substantial right of the party is affected, and

(1) *Objection.*   In case the ruling is one admitting evidence, a timely objection or motion to strike appears of record, stating the specific ground of objection, if the specific ground was not apparent from the context; or

(2) *Offer of Proof.*   In case the ruling is one excluding evidence, the substance of the evidence was made known to the court by offer or was apparent from the context within which questions were asked.

(b) Record of Offer and Ruling.   The court may add any other or further statement which shows the character of the evidence, the form in which it was offered, the objection made, and the ruling thereon. It may direct the making of an offer in question and answer form.

(c) Hearing of Jury.   In jury cases, proceedings shall be conducted, to the extent practicable, so as to prevent inadmissible evidence from being suggested to the jury by any means, such as making statements or offers of proof or asking questions in the hearing of the jury.

(d) Plain Error. Nothing in this rule precludes taking notice of plain errors affecting substantial rights although they were not brought to the attention of the court.

RULE 104. PRELIMINARY QUESTIONS

(a) Questions of Admissibility Generally. Preliminary questions concerning the qualification of a person to be a witness, the existence of a privilege, or the admissibility of evidence shall be determined by the court, subject to the provisions of subdivision (b). In making its determination it is not bound by the rules of evidence except those with respect to privileges.

(b) Relevancy Conditioned on Fact. When the relevancy of evidence depends upon the fulfillment of a condition of fact, the court shall admit it upon, or subject to, the introduction of evidence sufficient to support a finding of the fulfillment of the condition.

(c) Hearing of Jury. Hearings on the admissibility of confessions shall in all cases be conducted out of the hearing of the jury. Hearings on other preliminary matters shall be so conducted when the interests of justice require, or when an accused is a witness and so requests.

(d) Testimony by Accused. The accused does not, by testifying upon a preliminary matter, become subject to cross-examination as to other issues in the case.

(e) Weight and Credibility. This rule does not limit the right of a party to introduce before the jury evidence relevant to weight or credibility.

[Amended March 2, 1987, effective October 1, 1987.]

RULE 105. LIMITED ADMISSIBILITY

When evidence which is admissible as to one party or for one purpose but not admissible as to another party or for another purpose is admitted, the court, upon request, shall restrict the evidence to its proper scope and instruct the jury accordingly.

RULE 106. REMAINDER OF OR RELATED WRITINGS OR RECORDED STATEMENTS

When a writing or recorded statement or part thereof is introduced by a party, an adverse party may require the introduction at that time of any other part or any other writing or recorded statement which ought in fairness to be considered contemporaneously with it.

[Amended March 2, 1987, effective October 1, 1987.]

ARTICLE II. JUDICIAL NOTICE

RULE 201. JUDICIAL NOTICE OF ADJUDICATIVE FACTS

(a) Scope of Rule. This rule governs only judicial notice of adjudicative facts.

(b) Kinds of Facts. A judicially noticed fact must be one not subject to reasonable dispute in that it is either (1) generally known within the territorial jurisdiction of the trial court or (2) capable of accurate and ready determination by resort to sources whose accuracy cannot reasonably be questioned.

(c) When Discretionary. A court may take judicial notice, whether requested or not.

(d) When Mandatory. A court shall take judicial notice if requested by a party and supplied with the necessary information.

(e) Opportunity to Be Heard. A party is entitled upon timely request to an opportunity to be heard as to the propriety of taking judicial notice and the tenor of the matter noticed. In the absence of prior notification, the request may be made after judicial notice has been taken.

(f) Time of Taking Notice. Judicial notice may be taken at any stage of the proceeding.

(g) Instructing Jury. In a civil action or proceeding, the court shall instruct the jury to accept as conclusive any fact judicially noticed. In a criminal case, the court shall instruct the jury that it may, but is not required to, accept as conclusive any fact judicially noticed.

ARTICLE III. PRESUMPTIONS IN CIVIL ACTIONS AND PROCEEDINGS

RULE 301. PRESUMPTIONS IN GENERAL IN CIVIL ACTIONS AND PROCEEDINGS

In all civil actions and proceedings not otherwise provided for by Act of Congress or by these rules, a presumption imposes on the party against whom it is directed the burden of going forward with evidence to rebut or meet the presumption, but does not shift to such party the burden of proof in the sense of the risk of nonpersuasion, which remains throughout the trial upon the party on whom it was originally cast.

RULE 302. APPLICABILITY OF STATE LAW IN CIVIL ACTIONS AND PROCEEDINGS

In civil actions and proceedings, the effect of a presumption respecting a fact which is an element of a claim or defense as to which State law supplies the rule of decision is determined in accordance with State law.

ARTICLE IV. RELEVANCY AND ITS LIMITS

RULE 401. DEFINITION OF "RELEVANT EVIDENCE"

"Relevant evidence" means evidence having any tendency to make the existence of any fact that is of consequence to the determination of the action more probable or less probable than it would be without the evidence.

RULE 402. RELEVANT EVIDENCE GENERALLY ADMISSIBLE; IRRELEVANT EVIDENCE INADMISSIBLE

All relevant evidence is admissible, except as otherwise provided by the Constitution of the United States, by Act of Congress, by these rules, or by other rules prescribed by the Supreme Court pursuant to statutory authority. Evidence which is not relevant is not admissible.

RULE 403. EXCLUSION OF RELEVANT EVIDENCE ON GROUNDS OF PREJUDICE, CONFUSION, OR WASTE OF TIME

Although relevant, evidence may be excluded if its probative value is substantially outweighed by the danger of unfair prejudice, confusion of the issues, or misleading the jury, or by considerations of undue delay, waste of time, or needless presentation of cumulative evidence.

RULE 404. CHARACTER EVIDENCE NOT ADMISSIBLE TO PROVE CONDUCT; EXCEPTIONS; OTHER CRIMES

(a) **Character Evidence Generally.** Evidence of a person's character or a trait of character is not admissible for the purpose of proving action in conformity therewith on a particular occasion, except:

(1) *Character of Accused.* Evidence of a pertinent trait of character offered by an accused, or by the prosecution to rebut the same;

(2) *Character of Victim.* Evidence of a pertinent trait of character of the victim of the crime offered by an accused, or by the prosecution to rebut the same, or evidence of a character trait of peacefulness of the victim offered by the prosecution in a homicide case to rebut evidence that the victim was the first aggressor;

(3) *Character of Witness.* Evidence of the character of a witness, as provided in rules 607, 608, and 609.

(b) **Other Crimes, Wrongs, or Acts.** Evidence of other crimes, wrongs, or acts is not admissible to prove the character of a person in order to show action in conformity therewith. It may, however, be admissible for other purposes, such as proof of motive, opportunity, intent, preparation, plan, knowledge, identity, or absence of mistake or accident, provided that upon request by the accused, the prosecution in a criminal case shall provide reasonable notice in advance of trial, or during trial if the court excuses pretrial notice on good cause shown, of the general nature of any such evidence it intends to introduce at trial.

[Amended March 2, 1987, effective October 1, 1987; April 30, 1991, effective December 1, 1991.]

RULE 405. METHODS OF PROVING CHARACTER

(a) **Reputation or Opinion.** In all cases in which evidence of character or a trait of character of a person is admissible, proof may be made by testimony as to reputation or by testimony in the form of an opinion. On cross-examination, inquiry is allowable into relevant specific instances of conduct.

(b) **Specific Instances of Conduct.** In cases in which character or a trait of character of a person is an essential element of a charge, claim, or defense, proof may also be made of specific instances of that person's conduct.

[Amended March 2, 1987, effective October 1, 1987.]

RULE 406. HABIT; ROUTINE PRACTICE

Evidence of the habit of a person or of the routine practice of an organization, whether corroborated or not and regardless of the presence of eyewitnesses, is relevant to prove that the conduct of the person or organization on a particular occasion was in conformity with the habit or routine practice.

RULE 407. SUBSEQUENT REMEDIAL MEASURES

When, after an injury or harm allegedly caused by an event, measures are taken that, if taken previously, would have made the injury or harm less likely to occur, evidence of the subsequent measures is not admissible to prove negligence, culpable conduct, a defect in a product, a defect in a product's design, or a need for a warning or instruction. This rule does not require the exclusion of evidence of subsequent measures when offered for another purpose, such as proving ownership, control, or feasibility of precautionary measures, if controverted, or impeachment.

[Amended April 11, 1997, effective December 1, 1997.]

RULE 408.   COMPROMISE AND OFFERS TO COMPROMISE

Evidence of (1) furnishing or offering or promising to furnish, or (2) accepting or offering or promising to accept, a valuable consideration in compromising or attempting to compromise a claim which was disputed as to either validity or amount, is not admissible to prove liability for or invalidity of the claim or its amount. Evidence of conduct or statements made in compromise negotiations is likewise not admissible. This rule does not require the exclusion of any evidence otherwise discoverable merely because it is presented in the course of compromise negotiations. This rule also does not require exclusion when the evidence is offered for another purpose, such as proving bias or prejudice of a witness, negativing a contention of undue delay, or proving an effort to obstruct a criminal investigation or prosecution.

RULE 409.   PAYMENT OF MEDICAL AND SIMILAR EXPENSES

Evidence of furnishing or offering or promising to pay medical, hospital, or similar expenses occasioned by an injury is not admissible to prove liability for the injury.

RULE 410.   INADMISSIBILITY OF PLEAS, PLEA DISCUSSIONS, AND RELATED STATEMENTS

Except as otherwise provided in this rule, evidence of the following is not, in any civil or criminal proceeding, admissible against the defendant who made the plea or was a participant in the plea discussions:

(1)   a plea of guilty which was later withdrawn;

(2)   a plea of nolo contendere;

(3)   any statement made in the course of any proceedings under Rule 11 of the Federal Rules of Criminal Procedure or comparable state procedure regarding either of the foregoing pleas; or

(4)   any statement made in the course of plea discussions with an attorney for the prosecuting authority which do not result in a plea of guilty or which result in a plea of guilty later withdrawn.

However, such a statement is admissible (i) in any proceeding wherein another statement made in the course of the same plea or plea discussions has been introduced and the statement ought in fairness be considered contemporaneously with it, or (ii) in a criminal proceeding for perjury or false statement if the statement was made by the defendant under oath, on the record and in the presence of counsel.

[Amended by Pub.L. 94–149, § 1(9), December 12, 1975, 89 Stat. 805; amended April 30, 1979, effective December 1, 1980 (effective date pursuant to Pub.L. 96-42, July 31, 1979, 93 Stat. 326).]

RULE 411.   LIABILITY INSURANCE

Evidence that a person was or was not insured against liability is not admissible upon the issue whether the person acted negligently or otherwise wrongfully. This rule does not require the exclusion of evidence of insurance against liability when offered for another purpose, such as proof of agency, ownership, or control, or bias or prejudice of a witness.

[Amended March 2, 1987, effective October 1, 1987.]

RULE 412.   SEX OFFENSE CASES; RELEVANCE OF ALLEGED VICTIM'S PAST SEXUAL BEHAVIOR OR ALLEGED SEXUAL PREDISPOSITION

(a)   **Evidence Generally Inadmissible.**   The following evidence is not admissible in any civil or criminal proceeding involving alleged sexual misconduct except as provided in subdivisions (b) and (c):

(1)   Evidence offered to prove that any alleged victim engaged in other sexual behavior.

(2)   Evidence offered to prove any alleged victim's sexual predisposition.

(b)   **Exceptions.**

(1)   In a criminal case, the following evidence is admissible, if otherwise admissible under these rules:

(A)   evidence of specific instances of sexual behavior by the alleged victim offered to prove that a person other than the accused was the source of semen, injury or other physical evidence;

(B)   evidence of specific instances of sexual behavior by the alleged victim with respect to the person accused of the sexual misconduct offered by the accused to prove consent or by the prosecution; and

(C) evidence the exclusion of which would violate the constitutional rights of the defendant.

(2) In a civil case, evidence offered to prove the sexual behavior or sexual predisposition of any alleged victim is admissible if it is otherwise admissible under these rules and its probative value substantially outweighs the danger of harm to any victim and of unfair prejudice to any party. Evidence of an alleged victim's reputation is admissible only if it has been placed in controversy by the alleged victim.

(c) Procedure to Determine Admissibility.

(1) A party intending to offer evidence under subdivision (b) must—

(A) file a written motion at least 14 days before trial specifically describing the evidence and stating the purpose for which it is offered unless the court, for good cause, requires a different time for filing or permits filing during trial; and

(B) serve the motion on all parties and notify the alleged victim or, when appropriate, the alleged victim's guardian or representative.

(2) Before admitting evidence under this rule the court must conduct a hearing in camera and afford the victim and parties a right to attend and be heard. The motion, related papers, and the record of the hearing must be sealed and remain under seal unless the court orders otherwise.

[Adopted by Pub.L. 95–540, § 2(a), October 28, 1978, 92 Stat. 2046, applicable to trials that begin more than 30 days after October 28, 1978; amended by Pub.L. 100–690, Title VII, § 7046(a), November 18, 1988, 102 Stat. 4400; amended April 29, 1994, effective December 1, 1994; amended by Pub.L. 103–322, Title IV, § 40141(b), September 13, 1994, 108 Stat. 1919, effective December 1, 1994.]

RULE 413. EVIDENCE OF SIMILAR CRIMES IN SEXUAL ASSAULT CASES

(a) In a criminal case in which the defendant is accused of an offense of sexual assault, evidence of the defendant's commission of another offense or offenses of sexual assault is admissible, and may be considered for its bearing on any matter to which it is relevant.

(b) In a case in which the Government intends to offer evidence under this rule, the attorney for the Government shall disclose the evidence to the defendant, including statements of witnesses or a summary of the substance of any testimony that is expected to be offered, at least fifteen days before the scheduled date of

trial or at such later time as the court may allow for good cause.

(c) This rule shall not be construed to limit the admission or consideration of evidence under any other rule.

(d) For purposes of this rule and Rule 415, "offense of sexual assault" means a crime under Federal law or the law of a State (as defined in section 513 of title 18, United States Code) that involved—

(1) any conduct proscribed by chapter 109A of title 18, United States Code;

(2) contact, without consent, between any part of the defendant's body or an object and the genitals or anus of another person;

(3) contact, without consent, between the genitals or anus of the defendant and any part of another person's body;

(4) deriving sexual pleasure or gratification from the infliction of death, bodily injury, or physical pain on another person; or

(5) an attempt or conspiracy to engage in conduct described in paragraphs (1)–(4).

[Adopted by Pub.L. 103–322, Title XXXII, § 320935(a), September 13, 1994, 108 Stat. 2135, applicable to proceedings commenced on or after July 9, 1995, including all trials commenced on or after July 9, 1995 (Pub.L. 103–322, Title XXXII, § 320935(e), September 13, 1994, 108 Stat. 2137, as amended by Pub.L. 104–208, Div. A, Title I, § 101(a) [Title I, § 120], September 30, 1996, 110 Stat. 3009–25).]

RULE 414. EVIDENCE OF SIMILAR CRIMES IN CHILD MOLESTATION CASES

(a) In a criminal case in which the defendant is accused of an offense of child molestation, evidence of the defendant's commission of another offense or offenses of child molestation is admissible, and may be considered for its bearing on any matter to which it is relevant.

(b) In a case in which the Government intends to offer evidence under this rule, the attorney for the Government shall disclose the evidence to the defendant, including statements of witnesses or a summary of the substance of any testimony that is expected to be offered, at least fifteen days before the scheduled date of trial or at such later time as the court may allow for good cause.

(c) This rule shall not be construed to limit the admission or consideration of evidence under any other rule.

(d) For purposes of this rule and Rule 415, "child" means a person below the age of fourteen, and "offense of child molestation" means a crime under Federal law or the law of a State (as defined in section 513 of title 18, United States Code) that involved—

(1) any conduct proscribed by chapter 109A of title 18, United States Code, that was committed in relation to a child;

(2) any conduct proscribed by chapter 110 of title 18, United States Code;

(3) contact between any part of the defendant's body or an object and the genitals or anus of a child;

(4) contact between the genitals or anus of the defendant and any part of the body of a child;

(5) deriving sexual pleasure or gratification from the infliction of death, bodily injury, or physical pain on a child; or

(6) an attempt or conspiracy to engage in conduct described in paragraphs (1)–(5).

[Adopted by Pub.L. 103–322, Title XXXII, § 320935(a), September 13, 1994, 108 Stat. 2135, applicable to proceedings commenced on or after July 9, 1995, including all trials commenced on or after July 9, 1995 (Pub.L. 103–322, Title XXXII, § 320935(e), September 13, 1994, 108 Stat. 2137, as amended by Pub.L. 104–208, Div. A, Title I, § 101(a) [Title I, § 120], September 30, 1996, 110 Stat. 3009–25).]

RULE 415. EVIDENCE OF SIMILAR ACTS IN CIVIL CASES CONCERNING SEXUAL ASSAULT OR CHILD MOLESTATION

(a) In a civil case in which a claim for damages or other relief is predicated on a party's alleged commission of conduct constituting an offense of sexual assault or child molestation, evidence of that party's commission of another offense or offenses of sexual assault or child molestation is admissible and may be considered as provided in Rule 413 and Rule 414 of these rules.

(b) A party who intends to offer evidence under this Rule shall disclose the evidence to the party against whom it will be offered, including statements of witnesses or a summary of the substance of any testimony that is expected to be offered, at least fifteen days before the scheduled date of trial or at such later time as the court may allow for good cause.

(c) This rule shall not be construed to limit the admission or consideration of evidence under any other rule.

[Adopted by Pub.L. 103–322, Title XXXII, § 320935(a), September 13, 1994, 108 Stat. 2135, applicable to proceedings commenced on or after July 9, 1995, including all trials commenced on or after July 9, 1995 (Pub.L. 103–322, Title XXXII, § 320935(e), September 13, 1994, 108 Stat. 2137, as amended by Pub.L. 104–208, Div. A, Title I, § 101(a) [Title I, § 120], September 30, 1996, 110 Stat. 3009–25).]

ARTICLE V. PRIVILEGES

RULE 501. GENERAL RULE

Except as otherwise required by the Constitution of the United States or provided by Act of Congress or in rules prescribed by the Supreme Court pursuant to statutory authority, the privilege of a witness, person, government, State, or political subdivision thereof shall be governed by the principles of the common law as they may be interpreted by the courts of the United States in the light of reason and experience. However, in civil actions and proceedings, with respect to an element of a claim or defense as to which State law supplies the rule of decision, the privilege of a witness, person, government, State, or political subdivision thereof shall be determined in accordance with State law.

ARTICLE VI. WITNESSES

RULE 601. GENERAL RULE OF COMPETENCY

Every person is competent to be a witness except as otherwise provided in these rules. However, in civil actions and proceedings, with respect to an element of a claim or defense as to which State law supplies the rule of decision, the competency of a witness shall be determined in accordance with State law.

RULE 602. LACK OF PERSONAL KNOWLEDGE

A witness may not testify to a matter unless evidence is introduced sufficient to support a finding that the witness has personal knowledge of the matter. Evidence to prove personal knowledge may, but need not, consist of the witness' own testimony. This rule is subject to the provisions of rule 703, relating to opinion testimony by expert witnesses.

[Amended March 2, 1987, effective October 1, 1987; April 25, 1988, effective November 1, 1988.]

RULE 603. OATH OR AFFIRMATION

Before testifying, every witness shall be required to declare that the witness will testify truthfully, by oath or affirmation administered in a form calculated to awaken the witness' conscience and impress the witness' mind with the duty to do so.

[Amended March 2, 1987, effective October 1, 1987.]

RULE 604.   INTERPRETERS

An interpreter is subject to the provisions of these rules relating to qualification as an expert and the administration of an oath or affirmation to make a true translation.

[Amended March 2, 1987, effective October 1, 1987.]

RULE 605.   COMPETENCY OF JUDGE AS WITNESS

The judge presiding at the trial may not testify in that trial as a witness. No objection need be made in order to preserve the point.

RULE 606.   COMPETENCY OF JUROR AS WITNESS

(a)   At the Trial. A member of the jury may not testify as a witness before that jury in the trial of the case in which the juror is sitting. If the juror is called so to testify, the opposing party shall be afforded an opportunity to object out of the presence of the jury.

(b)   Inquiry Into Validity of Verdict or Indictment. Upon an inquiry into the validity of a verdict or indictment, a juror may not testify as to any matter or statement occurring during the course of the jury's deliberations or to the effect of anything upon that or any other juror's mind or emotions as influencing the juror to assent to or dissent from the verdict or indictment or concerning the juror's mental processes in connection therewith, except that a juror may testify on the question whether extraneous prejudicial information was improperly brought to the jury's attention or whether any outside influence was improperly brought to bear upon any juror. Nor may a juror's affidavit or evidence of any statement by the juror concerning a matter about which the juror would be precluded from testifying be received for these purposes.

[Amended by Pub.L. 94–149, § 1(10), December 12, 1975, 89 Stat. 805; amended March 2, 1987, effective October 1, 1987.]

RULE 607.   WHO MAY IMPEACH

The credibility of a witness may be attacked by any party, including the party calling the witness.

[Amended March 2, 1987, effective October 1, 1987.]

RULE 608.   EVIDENCE OF CHARACTER AND CONDUCT OF WITNESS

(a)   Opinion and Reputation Evidence of Character. The credibility of a witness may be attacked or supported by evidence in the form of opinion or reputation, but subject to these limitations: (1) the evidence may refer only to character for truthfulness or untruthfulness, and (2) evidence of truthful character is admissible only after the character of the witness for truthfulness has been attacked by opinion or reputation evidence or otherwise.

(b)   Specific Instances of Conduct. Specific instances of the conduct of a witness, for the purpose of attacking or supporting the witness' credibility, other than conviction of crime as provided in rule 609, may not be proved by extrinsic evidence. They may, however, in the discretion of the court, if probative of truthfulness or untruthfulness, be inquired into on cross-examination of the witness (1) concerning the witness' character for truthfulness or untruthfulness, or (2) concerning the character for truthfulness or untruthfulness of another witness as to which character the witness being cross-examined has testified.

The giving of testimony, whether by an accused or by any other witness, does not operate as a waiver of the accused's or the witness' privilege against self-incrimination when examined with respect to matters which relate only to credibility.

[Amended March 2, 1987, effective October 1, 1987; April 25, 1988, effective November 1, 1988.]

RULE 609.   IMPEACHMENT BY EVIDENCE OF CONVICTION OF CRIME

(a)   General Rule. For the purpose of attacking the credibility of a witness,

(1)   evidence that a witness other than an accused has been convicted of a crime shall be admitted, subject to Rule 403, if the crime was punishable by death or imprisonment in excess of one year under the law under which the witness was convicted, and evidence that an accused has been convicted of such a crime shall be admitted if the court determines that the probative value of admitting this evidence outweighs its prejudicial effect to the accused; and

(2)   evidence that any witness has been convicted of a crime shall be admitted if it involved dishonesty or false statement, regardless of the punishment.

(b)   Time Limit. Evidence of a conviction under this rule is not admissible if a period of more than ten years has elapsed since the date of the conviction or of the release of the witness from the confinement imposed for that conviction, whichever is the later date, unless the court determines, in the interests of justice, that the probative value of the conviction supported by specific facts and circumstances substantially outweighs its prejudicial effect. However, evidence of a conviction more than 10 years old as calculated herein, is not admissible unless the proponent gives to the adverse party sufficient advance written notice of intent to use such evidence to provide the adverse party with a fair opportunity to contest the use of such evidence.

(c) Effect of Pardon, Annulment, or Certificate of Rehabilitation. Evidence of a conviction is not admissible under this rule if (1) the conviction has been the subject of a pardon, annulment, certificate of rehabilitation, or other equivalent procedure based on a finding of the rehabilitation of the person convicted, and that person has not been convicted of a subsequent crime which was punishable by death or imprisonment in excess of one year, or (2) the conviction has been the subject of a pardon, annulment, or other equivalent procedure based on a finding of innocence.

(d) Juvenile Adjudications. Evidence of juvenile adjudications is generally not admissible under this rule. The court may, however, in a criminal case allow evidence of a juvenile adjudication of a witness other than the accused if conviction of the offense would be admissible to attack the credibility of an adult and the court is satisfied that admission in evidence is necessary for a fair determination of the issue of guilt or innocence.

(e) Pendency of Appeal. The pendency of an appeal therefrom does not render evidence of a conviction inadmissible. Evidence of the pendency of an appeal is admissible.

[Amended March 2, 1987, effective October 1, 1987; January 26, 1990, effective December 1, 1990.]

RULE 610. RELIGIOUS BELIEFS OR OPINIONS

Evidence of the beliefs or opinions of a witness on matters of religion is not admissible for the purpose of showing that by reason of their nature the witness' credibility is impaired or enhanced.

[Amended March 2, 1987, effective October 1, 1987.]

RULE 611. MODE AND ORDER OF INTERROGATION AND PRESENTATION

(a) Control by Court. The court shall exercise reasonable control over the mode and order of interrogating witnesses and presenting evidence so as to (1) make the interrogation and presentation effective for the ascertainment of the truth, (2) avoid needless consumption of time, and (3) protect witnesses from harassment or undue embarrassment.

(b) Scope of Cross-Examination. Cross-examination should be limited to the subject matter of the direct examination and matters affecting the credibility of the witness. The court may, in the exercise of discretion, permit inquiry into additional matters as if on direct examination.

(c) Leading Questions. Leading questions should not be used on the direct examination of a witness except as may be necessary to develop the witness' testimony. Ordinarily leading questions should be permitted on cross-examination. When a party calls a hostile witness, an adverse party, or a witness identified with an adverse party, interrogation may be by leading questions.

[Amended March 2, 1987, effective October 1, 1987.]

RULE 612. WRITING USED TO REFRESH MEMORY

Except as otherwise provided in criminal proceedings by section 3500 of title 18, United States Code, if a witness uses a writing to refresh memory for the purpose of testifying, either—

(1) while testifying, or

(2) before testifying, if the court in its discretion determines it is necessary in the interests of justice,

an adverse party is entitled to have the writing produced at the hearing, to inspect it, to cross-examine the witness thereon, and to introduce in evidence those portions which relate to the testimony of the witness. If it is claimed that the writing contains matters not related to the subject matter of the testimony the court shall examine the writing in camera, excise any portions not so related, and order delivery of the remainder to the party entitled thereto. Any portion withheld over objections shall be preserved and made available to the appellate court in the event of an appeal. If a writing is not produced or delivered pursuant to order under this rule, the court shall make any order justice requires, except that in criminal cases when the prosecution elects not to comply, the order shall be one striking the testimony or, if the court in its discretion determines that the interests of justice so require, declaring a mistrial.

[Amended March 2, 1987, effective October 1, 1987.]

RULE 613. PRIOR STATEMENTS OF WITNESSES

(a) Examining Witness Concerning Prior Statement. In examining a witness concerning a prior statement made by the witness, whether written or not, the statement need not be shown nor its contents disclosed to the witness at that time, but on request the same shall be shown or disclosed to opposing counsel.

(b) Extrinsic Evidence of Prior Inconsistent Statement of Witness. Extrinsic evidence of a prior inconsistent statement by a witness is not admissible unless the witness is afforded an opportunity to explain or deny the same and the opposite party is afforded an opportunity to interrogate the witness thereon, or the interests of justice otherwise require. This provision does not apply to admissions of a party-opponent as defined in rule 801(d)(2).

[Amended March 2, 1987, effective October 1, 1987; April 25, 1988, effective November 1, 1988.]

RULE 614.   CALLING AND INTERROGATION OF WITNESSES BY COURT

(a) Calling by Court. The court may, on its own motion or at the suggestion of a party, call witnesses, and all parties are entitled to cross-examine witnesses thus called.

(b) Interrogation by Court. The court may interrogate witnesses, whether called by itself or by a party.

(c) Objections. Objections to the calling of witnesses by the court or to interrogation by it may be made at the time or at the next available opportunity when the jury is not present.

RULE 615.   EXCLUSION OF WITNESSES

At the request of a party the court shall order witnesses excluded so that they cannot hear the testimony of other witnesses, and it may make the order of its own motion. This rule does not authorize exclusion of (1) a party who is a natural person, or (2) an officer or employee of a party which is not a natural person designated as its representative by its attorney, or (3) a person whose presence is shown by a party to be essential to the presentation of the party's cause.

[Amended March 2, 1987, effective October 1, 1987; April 25, 1988, effective November 1, 1988; amended by Pub.L. 100–690, Title VII, § 7075(a), November 18, 1988, 102 Stat. 4405 (although amendment by Pub.L. 100–690 could not be executed due to prior amendment by Court order which made the same change effective November 1, 1988).]

ARTICLE VII.   OPINIONS AND EXPERT TESTIMONY

RULE 701.   OPINION TESTIMONY BY LAY WITNESSES

If the witness is not testifying as an expert, the witness' testimony in the form of opinions or inferences is limited to those opinions or inferences which are (a) rationally based on the perception of the witness and (b) helpful to a clear understanding of the witness' testimony or the determination of a fact in issue.

[Amended March 2, 1987, effective October 1, 1987.]

RULE 702.   TESTIMONY BY EXPERTS

If scientific, technical, or other specialized knowledge will assist the trier of fact to understand the evidence or to determine a fact in issue, a witness qualified as an expert by knowledge, skill, experience, training, or education, may testify thereto in the form of an opinion or otherwise.

RULE 703.   BASES OF OPINION TESTIMONY BY EXPERTS

The facts or data in the particular case upon which an expert bases an opinion or inference may be those perceived by or made known to the expert at or before the hearing. If of a type reasonably relied upon by experts in the particular field in forming opinions or inferences upon the subject, the facts or data need not be admissible in evidence.

[Amended March 2, 1987, effective October 1, 1987.]

RULE 704.   OPINION ON ULTIMATE ISSUE

(a) Except as provided in subdivision (b), testimony in the form of an opinion or inference otherwise admissible is not objectionable because it embraces an ultimate issue to be decided by the trier of fact.

(b) No expert witness testifying with respect to the mental state or condition of a defendant in a criminal case may state an opinion or inference as to whether the defendant did or did not have the mental state or condition constituting an element of the crime charged or of a defense thereto. Such ultimate issues are matters for the trier of fact alone.

[Amended by Pub.L. 98–473, Title II, § 406, October 12, 1984, 98 Stat. 2067.]

RULE 705.   DISCLOSURE OF FACTS OR DATA UNDERLYING EXPERT OPINION

The expert may testify in terms of opinion or inference and give reasons therefor without first testifying to the underlying facts or data, unless the court requires otherwise. The expert may in any event be required to disclose the underlying facts or data on cross-examination.

[Amended March 2, 1987, effective October 1, 1987; April 22, 1993, effective December 1, 1993.]

RULE 706.   COURT APPOINTED EXPERTS

(a) **Appointment.** The court may on its own motion or on the motion of any party enter an order to show cause why expert witnesses should not be appointed, and may request the parties to submit nominations. The court may appoint any expert witnesses agreed upon by the parties, and may appoint expert witnesses of its own selection. An expert witness shall not be appointed by the court unless the witness consents to act. A witness so appointed shall be informed of the witness' duties by the court in writing, a copy of which shall be filed with the clerk, or at a conference in which the parties shall have opportunity to participate. A witness so appointed shall advise the parties of the witness' findings, if any; the witness' deposition may be taken by any party; and the witness may be called to testify by the court or any party. The witness shall be subject to cross-examination by each party, including a party calling the witness.

(b) **Compensation.** Expert witnesses so appointed are entitled to reasonable compensation in whatever sum the court may allow. The compensation thus fixed is payable from funds which may be provided by law in criminal cases and civil actions and proceedings involving just compensation under the fifth amendment. In other civil actions and proceedings the compensation shall be paid by the parties in such proportion and at such time as the court directs, and thereafter charged in like manner as other costs.

(c) **Disclosure of Appointment.** In the exercise of its discretion, the court may authorize disclosure to the jury of the fact that the court appointed the expert witness.

(d) **Parties' Experts of Own Selection.** Nothing in this rule limits the parties in calling expert witnesses of their own selection.

[Amended March 2, 1987, effective October 1, 1987.]

ARTICLE VIII.   HEARSAY

RULE 801.   DEFINITIONS

The following definitions apply under this article:

(a) **Statement.** A "statement" is (1) an oral or written assertion or (2) nonverbal conduct of a person, if it is intended by the person as an assertion.

(b) **Declarant.** A "declarant" is a person who makes a statement.

(c) **Hearsay.** "Hearsay" is a statement, other than one made by the declarant while testifying at the trial or hearing, offered in evidence to prove the truth of the matter asserted.

(d) **Statements Which Are Not Hearsay.** A statement is not hearsay if—

(1) *Prior Statement by Witness.* The declarant testifies at the trial or hearing and is subject to cross-examination concerning the statement, and the statement is (A) inconsistent with the declarant's testimony, and was given under oath subject to the penalty of perjury at a trial, hearing, or other proceeding, or in a deposition, or (B) consistent with the declarant's testimony and is offered to rebut an express or implied charge against the declarant of recent fabrication or improper influence or motive, or (C) one of identification of a person made after perceiving the person; or

(2) *Admission by Party-Opponent.* The statement is offered against a party and is (A) the party's own statement, in either an individual or a representative capacity or (B) a statement of which the party has manifested an adoption or belief in its truth, or (C) a statement by a person authorized by the party to make a statement concerning the subject, or (D) a statement by the party's agent or servant concerning a matter within the scope of the agency or employment, made during the existence of the relationship, or (E) a statement by a coconspirator of a party during the course and in furtherance of the conspiracy. The contents of the statement shall be considered but are not alone sufficient to establish the declarant's authority under subdivision (C), the agency or employment relationship and scope thereof under subdivision (D), or the existence of the conspiracy and the participation therein of the declarant and the party against whom the statement is offered under subdivision (E).

[Amended by Pub.L. 94–113, § 1, October 16, 1975, 89 Stat. 576; amended March 2, 1987, effective October 1, 1987; April 11, 1997, effective December 1, 1997.]

RULE 802.   HEARSAY RULE

Hearsay is not admissible except as provided by these rules or by other rules prescribed by the Supreme Court pursuant to statutory authority or by Act of Congress.

RULE 803.   HEARSAY EXCEPTIONS; AVAILABILITY OF DECLARANT IMMATERIAL

The following are not excluded by the hearsay rule, even though the declarant is available as a witness:

(1) **Present Sense Impression.** A statement describing or explaining an event or condition made while the declarant was perceiving the event or condition, or immediately thereafter.

(2) **Excited Utterance.** A statement relating to a startling event or condition made while the declarant was under the stress of excitement caused by the event or condition.

(3) **Then Existing Mental, Emotional, or Physical Condition.** A statement of the declarant's then existing state of mind, emotion, sensation, or physical condition (such as intent, plan, motive, design, mental feeling, pain, and bodily health), but not including a statement of memory or belief to prove the fact remembered or believed unless it relates to the execution, revocation, identification, or terms of declarant's will.

(4) **Statements for Purposes of Medical Diagnosis or Treatment.** Statements made for purposes of medical diagnosis or treatment and describing medical history, or past or present symptoms, pain, or sensations, or the inception or general character of the cause or external source thereof insofar as reasonably pertinent to diagnosis or treatment.

(5) **Recorded Recollection.** A memorandum or record concerning a matter about which a witness once had knowledge but now has insufficient recollection to enable the witness to testify fully and accurately, shown to have been made or adopted by the witness when the matter was fresh in the witness' memory and to reflect that knowledge correctly. If admitted, the memorandum or record may be read into evidence but may not itself be received as an exhibit unless offered by an adverse party.

(6) **Records of Regularly Conducted Activity.** A memorandum, report, record, or data compilation, in any form, of acts, events, conditions, opinions, or diagnoses, made at or near the time by, or from information transmitted by, a person with knowledge, if kept in the course of a regularly conducted business activity, and if it was the regular practice of that business activity to make the memorandum, report, record, or data compila-tion, all as shown by the testimony of the custodian or other qualified witness, unless the source of information or the method or circumstances of preparation indicate lack of trustworthiness. The term "business" as used in this paragraph includes business, institution, association, profession, occupation, and calling of every kind, whether or not conducted for profit.

(7) **Absence of Entry in Records Kept in Accordance With the Provisions of Paragraph (6).** Evidence that a matter is not included in the memoranda reports, records, or data compilations, in any form, kept in accordance with the provisions of paragraph (6), to prove the nonoccurrence or nonexistence of the matter, if the matter was of a kind of which a memorandum, report, record, or data compilation was regularly made and preserved, unless the sources of information or other circumstances indicate lack of trustworthiness.

(8) **Public Records and Reports.** Records, reports, statements, or data compilations, in any form, of public offices or agencies, setting forth (A) the activities of the office or agency, or (B) matters observed pursuant to duty imposed by law as to which matters there was a duty to report, excluding, however, in criminal cases matters observed by police officers and other law enforcement personnel, or (C) in civil actions and proceedings and against the Government in criminal cases, factual findings resulting from an investigation made pursuant to authority granted by law, unless the sources of information or other circumstances indicate lack of trustworthiness.

(9) **Records of Vital Statistics.** Records or data compilations, in any form, of births, fetal deaths, deaths, or marriages, if the report thereof was made to a public office pursuant to requirements of law.

(10) **Absence of Public Record or Entry.** To prove the absence of a record, report, statement, or data compilation, in any form, or the nonoccurrence or nonexistence of a matter of which a record, report, statement, or data compilation, in any form, was regularly made and preserved by a public office or agency, evidence in the form of a certification in accordance with rule 902, or testimony, that diligent search failed to disclose the record, report, statement, or data compilation, or entry.

(11) **Records of Religious Organizations.** Statements of births, marriages, divorces, deaths, legitimacy, ancestry, relationship by blood or marriage, or other similar facts of personal or family history, contained in a regularly kept record of a religious organization.

(12) Marriage, Baptismal, and Similar Certificates. Statements of fact contained in a certificate that the maker performed a marriage or other ceremony or administered a sacrament, made by a clergyman, public official, or other person authorized by the rules or practices of a religious organization or by law to perform the act certified, and purporting to have been issued at the time of the act or within a reasonable time thereafter.

(13) Family Records. Statements of fact concerning personal or family history contained in family Bibles, genealogies, charts, engravings on rings, inscriptions on family portraits, engravings on urns, crypts, or tombstones, or the like.

(14) Records of Documents Affecting an Interest in Property. The record of a document purporting to establish or affect an interest in property, as proof of the content of the original recorded document and its execution and delivery by each person by whom it purports to have been executed, if the record is a record of a public office and an applicable statute authorizes the recording of documents of that kind in that office.

(15) Statements in Documents Affecting an Interest in Property. A statement contained in a document purporting to establish or affect an interest in property if the matter stated was relevant to the purpose of the document, unless dealings with the property since the document was made have been inconsistent with the truth of the statement or the purport of the document.

(16) Statements in Ancient Documents. Statements in a document in existence twenty years or more the authenticity of which is established.

(17) Market Reports, Commercial Publications. Market quotations, tabulations, lists, directories, or other published compilations, generally used and relied upon by the public or by persons in particular occupations.

(18) Learned Treatises. To the extent called to the attention of an expert witness upon cross-examination or relied upon by the expert witness in direct examination, statements contained in published treatises, periodicals, or pamphlets on a subject of history, medicine, or other science or art, established as a reliable authority by the testimony or admission of the witness or by other expert testimony or by judicial notice. If admitted, the statements may be read into evidence but may not be received as exhibits.

(19) Reputation Concerning Personal or Family History. Reputation among members of a person's family by blood, adoption, or marriage, or among a person's associates, or in the community, concerning a person's birth,, adoption, marriage, divorce, death, legiti-

macy, relationship by blood, adoption, or marriage, ancestry, or other similar fact of personal or family history.

(20) Reputation Concerning Boundaries or General History. Reputation in a community, arising before the controversy, as to boundaries of or customs affecting lands in the community, and reputation as to events of general history important to the community or State or nation in which located.

(21) Reputation as to Character. Reputation of a person's character among associates or in the community.

(22) Judgment of Previous Conviction. Evidence of a final judgment, entered after a trial or upon a plea of guilty (but not upon a plea of nolo contendere), adjudging a person guilty of a crime punishable by death or imprisonment in excess of one year, to prove any fact essential to sustain the judgment, but not including, when offered by the Government in a criminal prosecution for purposes other than impeachment, judgments against persons other than the accused. The pendency of an appeal may be shown but does not affect admissibility.

(23) Judgment as to Personal, Family, or General History, or Boundaries. Judgments as proof of matters of personal, family or general history, or boundaries, essential to the judgment, if the same would be provable by evidence of reputation.

(24) [Transferred to Rule 807.]

[Amended by Pub.L. 94–149, § 1(11), December 12, 1975, 89 Stat. 805; amended March 2, 1987, effective October 1, 1987; April 11, 1997, effective December 1, 1997.]

RULE 804. HEARSAY EXCEPTIONS; DECLARANT UNAVAILABLE

(a) Definition of Unavailability. "Unavailability as a witness" includes situations in which the declarant—

(1) is exempted by ruling of the court on the ground of privilege from testifying concerning the subject matter of the declarant's statement; or

(2) persists in refusing to testify concerning the subject matter of the declarant's statement despite an order of the court to do so; or

(3) testifies to a lack of memory of the subject matter of the declarant's statement; or

(4) is unable to be present or to testify at the hearing because of death or then existing physical or mental illness or infirmity; or

(5) is absent from the hearing and the proponent of a statement has been unable to procure the declarant's attendance (or in the case of a hearsay exception under subdivision (b)(2), (3), or (4), the declarant's attendance or testimony) by process or other reasonable means.

A declarant is not unavailable as a witness if exemption, refusal, claim of lack of memory, inability, or absence is due to the procurement or wrongdoing of the proponent of a statement for the purpose of preventing the witness from attending or testifying.

(b) Hearsay Exceptions. The following are not excluded by the hearsay rule if the declarant is unavailable as a witness:

(1) *Former Testimony.* Testimony given as a witness at another hearing of the same or a different proceeding, or in a deposition taken in compliance with law in the course of the same or another proceeding, if the party against whom the testimony is now offered, or, in a civil action or proceeding, a predecessor in interest, had an opportunity and similar motive to develop the testimony by direct, cross, or redirect examination.

(2) *Statement Under Belief of Impending Death.* In a prosecution for homicide or in a civil action or proceeding, a statement made by a declarant while believing that the declarant's death was imminent, concerning the cause or circumstances of what the declarant believed to be impending death.

(3) *Statement Against Interest.* A statement which was at the time of its making so far contrary to the declarant's pecuniary or proprietary interest, or so far tended to subject the declarant to civil or criminal liability, or to render invalid a claim by the declarant against another, that a reasonable person in the declarant's position would not have made the statement unless believing it to be true. A statement tending to expose the declarant to criminal liability and offered to exculpate the accused is not admissible unless corroborating circumstances clearly indicate the trustworthiness of the statement.

(4) *Statement of Personal or Family History.*

(A) A statement concerning the declarant's own birth, adoption, marriage, divorce, legitimacy, relationship by blood, adoption, or marriage, ancestry, or other similar fact of personal or family history, even though declarant had no means of acquiring personal knowledge of the matter stated; or

(B) a statement concerning the foregoing matters, and death also, of another person, if the declarant was related to the other by blood, adoption, or marriage or was so intimately associated with the other's family as to be likely to have accurate information concerning the matter declared.

(5) *[Transferred to Rule 807.]*

(6) *Forfeiture by Wrongdoing.* A statement offered against a party that has engaged or acquiesced in wrongdoing that was intended to, and did, procure the unavailability of the declarant as a witness.

[Amended by Pub.L. 94–149, § 1(12) and (13), December 12, 1975, 89 Stat. 806; amended March 2, 1987, effective October 1, 1987; amended by Pub.L. 100–690, Title VII, § 7075(b), November 18, 1988, 102 Stat. 4405; amended April 11, 1997, effective December 1, 1997.]

RULE 805. HEARSAY WITHIN HEARSAY

Hearsay included within hearsay is not excluded under the hearsay rule if each part of the combined statements conforms with an exception to the hearsay rule provided in these rules.

RULE 806. ATTACKING AND SUPPORTING CREDIBILITY OF DECLARANT

When a hearsay statement, or a statement defined in Rule 801(d)(2)(C), (D), or (E), has been admitted in evidence, the credibility of the declarant may be attacked, and if attacked may be supported, by any evidence which would be admissible for those purposes if declarant had testified as a witness. Evidence of a statement or conduct by the declarant at any time, inconsistent with the declarant's hearsay statement, is not subject to any requirement that the declarant may have been afforded an opportunity to deny or explain. If the party against whom a hearsay statement has been admitted calls the declarant as a witness, the party is entitled to examine the declarant on the statement as if under cross-examination.

[Amended March 2, 1987, effective October 1, 1987; April 11, 1997, effective December 1, 1997.]

RULE 807. RESIDUAL EXCEPTION

A statement not specifically covered by Rule 803 or 804 but having equivalent circumstantial guarantees of trustworthiness, is not excluded by the hearsay rule, if the court determines that (A) the statement is offered as evidence of a material fact; (B) the statement is more probative on the point for which it is offered than any other evidence which the proponent can procure through reasonable efforts; and (C) the general purposes of these rules and the interests of justice will best be served by admission of the statement into evidence. However, a statement may not be admitted under this exception unless the proponent of it makes known to the adverse party sufficiently in advance of the trial or hearing to provide the adverse party with a fair opportunity to prepare to meet it, the proponent's intention to offer the statement and the particulars of it, including the name and address of the declarant.

[Adopted April 11, 1997, effective December 1, 1997.]

ARTICLE IX.   AUTHENTICATION AND IDENTIFICATION

RULE 901.   REQUIREMENT OF AUTHENTICATION OR IDENTIFICATION

(a) **General Provision.** The requirement of authentication or identification as a condition precedent to admissibility is satisfied by evidence sufficient to support a finding that the matter in question is what its proponent claims.

(b) **Illustrations.** By way of illustration only, and not by way of limitation, the following are examples of authentication or identification conforming with the requirements of this rule:

(1) *Testimony of Witness With Knowledge.* Testimony that a matter is what it is claimed to be.

(2) *Nonexpert Opinion on Handwriting.* Nonexpert opinion as to the genuineness of handwriting, based upon familiarity not acquired for purposes of the litigation.

(3) *Comparison by Trier or Expert Witness.* Comparison by the trier of fact or by expert witnesses with specimens which have been authenticated.

(4) *Distinctive Characteristics and the Like.* Appearance, contents, substance, internal patterns, or other distinctive characteristics, taken in conjunction with circumstances.

(5) *Voice Identification.* Identification of a voice, whether heard firsthand or through mechanical or electronic transmission or recording, by opinion based upon hearing the voice at any time under circumstances connecting it with the alleged speaker.

(6) *Telephone Conversations.* Telephone conversations, by evidence that a call was made to the number assigned at the time by the telephone company to a particular person or business, if (A) in the case of a person, circumstances, including self-identification, show the person answering to be the one called, or (B) in the case of a business, the call was made to a place of business and the conversation related to business reasonably transacted over the telephone.

(7) *Public Records or Reports.* Evidence that a writing authorized by law to be recorded or filed and in fact recorded or filed in a public office, or a purported public record, report, statement, or data compilation, in any form, is from the public office where items of this nature are kept.

(8) *Ancient Documents or Data Compilation.* Evidence that a document or data compilation, in any form, (A) is in such condition as to create no suspicion concerning its authenticity, (B) was in a place where it, if authentic, would likely be, and (C) has been in existence 20 years or more at the time it is offered.

(9) *Process or System.* Evidence describing a process or system used to produce a result and showing that the process or system produces an accurate result.

(10) *Methods Provided by Statute or Rule.* Any method of authentication or identification provided by Act of Congress or by other rules prescribed by the Supreme Court pursuant to statutory authority.

RULE 902.   SELF–AUTHENTICATION

Extrinsic evidence of authenticity as a condition precedent to admissibility is not required with respect to the following:

(1) **Domestic Public Documents Under Seal.** A document bearing a seal purporting to be that of the United States, or of any State, district, Commonwealth, territory, or insular possession thereof, or the Panama Canal Zone, or the Trust Territory of the Pacific Islands, or of a political subdivision, department, officer, or agency thereof, and a signature purporting to be an attestation or execution.

(2) **Domestic Public Documents Not Under Seal.** A document purporting to bear the signature in the official capacity of an officer or employee of any entity included in paragraph (1) hereof, having no seal, if a public officer having a seal and having official duties in the district or political subdivision of the officer or employee certifies under seal that the signer has the official capacity and that the signature is genuine.

(3) **Foreign Public Documents.** A document purporting to be executed or attested in an official capacity by a person authorized by the laws of a foreign country to make the execution or attestation, and

accompanied by a final certification as to the genuineness of the signature and official position (A) of the executing or attesting person, or (B) of any foreign official whose certificate of genuineness of signature and official position relates to the execution or attestation or is in a chain of certificates of genuineness of signature and official position relating to the execution or attestation. A final certification may be made by a secretary of an embassy or legation, consul general, consul, vice consul, or consular agent of the United States, or a diplomatic or consular official of the foreign country assigned or accredited to the United States. If reasonable opportunity has been given to all parties to investigate the authenticity and accuracy of official documents, the court may, for good cause shown, order that they be treated as presumptively authentic without final certification or permit them to be evidenced by an attested summary with or without final certification.

(4) Certified Copies of Public Records. A copy of an official record or report or entry therein, or of a document authorized by law to be recorded or filed and actually recorded or filed in a public office, including data compilations in any form, certified as correct by the custodian or other person authorized to make the certification, by certificate complying with paragraph (1), (2), or (3) of this rule or complying with any Act of Congress or rule prescribed by the Supreme Court pursuant to statutory authority.

(5) Official Publications. Books, pamphlets, or other publications purporting to be issued by public authority.

(6) Newspapers and Periodicals. Printed materials purporting to be newspapers or periodicals.

(7) Trade Inscriptions and the Like. Inscriptions, signs, tags, or labels purporting to have been affixed in the course of business and indicating ownership, control, or origin.

(8) Acknowledged Documents. Documents accompanied by a certificate of acknowledgment executed in the manner provided by law by a notary public or other officer authorized by law to take acknowledgments.

(9) Commercial Paper and Related Documents. Commercial paper, signatures thereon, and documents relating thereto to the extent provided by general commercial law.

(10) Presumptions Under Acts of Congress. Any signature, document, or other matter declared by Act of Congress to be presumptively or prima facie genuine or authentic.

[Amended March 2, 1987, effective October 1, 1987; April 25, 1988, effective November 1, 1988.]

RULE 903. SUBSCRIBING WITNESS' TESTIMONY UNNECESSARY

The testimony of a subscribing witness is not necessary to authenticate a writing unless required by the laws of the jurisdiction whose laws govern the validity of the writing.

ARTICLE X.   CONTENTS OF WRITINGS, RECORDINGS, AND PHOTOGRAPHS

RULE 1001. DEFINITIONS

For purposes of this article the following definitions are applicable:

(1) Writings and Recordings. "Writings" and "recordings" consist of letters, words, or numbers, or their equivalent, set down by handwriting, typewriting, printing, photostating, photographing, magnetic impulse, mechanical or electronic recording, or other form of data compilation.

(2) Photographs. "Photographs" include still photographs, X-ray films, video tapes, and motion pictures.

(3) Original. An "original" of a writing or recording is the writing or recording itself or any counterpart intended to have the same effect by a person executing or issuing it. An "original" of a photograph includes the negative or any print therefrom. If data are stored in a computer or similar device, any printout or other output readable by sight, shown to reflect the data accurately, is an "original".

(4) Duplicate. A "duplicate" is a counterpart produced by the same impression as the original, or from the same matrix, or by means of photography, including enlargements and miniatures, or by mechanical or electronic re-recording, or by chemical reproduction, or by other equivalent techniques which accurately reproduces the original.

RULE 1002. REQUIREMENT OF ORIGINAL

To prove the content of a writing, recording, or photograph, the original writing, recording, or photograph is required, except as otherwise provided in these rules or by Act of Congress.

RULE 1003. ADMISSIBILITY OF DUPLICATES

A duplicate is admissible to the same extent as an original unless (1) a genuine question is raised as to the authenticity of the original or (2) in the circumstances it would be unfair to admit the duplicate in lieu of the original.

RULE 1004. ADMISSIBILITY OF OTHER EVIDENCE OF CONTENTS

The original is not required, and other evidence of the contents of a writing, recording, or photograph is admissible if—

(1) Originals Lost or Destroyed. All originals are lost or have been destroyed, unless the proponent lost or destroyed them in bad faith; or

(2) Original Not Obtainable. No original can be obtained by any available judicial process or procedure; or

(3) Original in Possession of Opponent. At a time when an original was under the control of the party against whom offered, that party was put on notice, by the pleadings or otherwise, that the contents would be a subject of proof at the hearing, and that party does not produce the original at the hearing; or

(4) Collateral Matters. The writing, recording, or photograph is not closely related to a controlling issue.

[Amended March 2, 1987, effective October 1, 1987.]

RULE 1005. PUBLIC RECORDS

The contents of an official record, or of a document authorized to be recorded or filed and actually recorded or filed, including data compilations in any form, if otherwise admissible, may be proved by copy, certified as correct in accordance with rule 902 or testified to be correct by a witness who has compared it with the original. If a copy which complies with the foregoing cannot be obtained by the exercise of reasonable diligence, then other evidence of the contents may be given.

RULE 1006. SUMMARIES

The contents of voluminous writings, recordings, or photographs which cannot conveniently be examined in court may be presented in the form of a chart, summary, or calculation. The originals, or duplicates, shall be made available for examination or copying, or both, by other parties at reasonable time and place. The court may order that they be produced in court.

RULE 1007. TESTIMONY OR WRITTEN ADMISSION OF PARTY

Contents of writings, recordings, or photographs may be proved by the testimony or deposition of the party against whom offered or by that party's written admission, without accounting for the nonproduction of the original.

[Amended March 2, 1987, effective October 1, 1987.]

RULE 1008. FUNCTIONS OF COURT AND JURY

When the admissibility of other evidence of contents of writings, recordings, or photographs under these rules depends upon the fulfillment of a condition of fact, the question whether the condition has been fulfilled is ordinarily for the court to determine in accordance with the provisions of rule 104. However, when an issue is raised (a) whether the asserted writing ever existed, or (b) whether another writing, recording, or photograph produced at the trial is the original, or (c) whether other evidence of contents correctly reflects the contents, the issue is for the trier of fact to determine as in the case of other issues of fact.

ARTICLE XI. MISCELLANEOUS RULES

RULE 1101. APPLICABILITY OF RULES

(a) Courts and Judges. These rules apply to the United States district courts, the District Court of Guam, the District Court of the Virgin Islands, the District Court for the Northern Mariana Islands, the United States courts of appeals, the United States Claims Court, and to United States bankruptcy judges and United States magistrate judges, in the actions, cases, and proceedings and to the extent hereinafter set forth. The terms "judge" and "court" in these rules include United States bankruptcy judges and United States magistrate judges.

(b) Proceedings Generally. These rules apply generally to civil actions and proceedings, including admiralty and maritime cases, to criminal cases and proceedings, to contempt proceedings except those in which the court may act summarily, and to proceedings and cases under title 11, United States Code.

(c) Rule of Privilege. The rule with respect to privileges applies at all stages of all actions, cases, and proceedings.

(d) Rules Inapplicable. The rules (other than with respect to privileges) do not apply in the following situations:

(1) *Preliminary Questions of Fact.* The determination of questions of fact preliminary to admissibility of evidence when the issue is to be determined by the court under rule 104.

(2) *Grand Jury.* Proceedings before grand juries.

(3) *Miscellaneous Proceedings.* Proceedings for extradition or rendition; preliminary examinations in criminal cases; sentencing, or granting or revoking probation; issuance of warrants for arrest, criminal summonses, and search warrants; and proceedings with respect to release on bail or otherwise.

(e) Rules Applicable in Part. In the following proceedings these rules apply to the extent that matters of evidence are not provided for in the statutes which govern procedure therein or in other rules prescribed by the Supreme Court pursuant to statutory authority: the trial of misdemeanors and other petty offenses before United States magistrate judges; review of agency actions when the facts are subject to trial de novo under section 706(2)(F) of title 5, United States Code; review of orders of the Secretary of Agriculture under section 2 of the Act entitled "An Act to authorize association of producers of agricultural products" approved February 18, 1922 (7 U.S.C. 292), and under sections 6 and 7(c) of the Perishable Agricultural Commodities Act, 1930 (7 U.S.C. 499f, 499g(c)); naturalization and revocation of naturalization under sections 310–318 of the Immigration and Nationality Act (8 U.S.C. 1421–1429); prize proceedings in admiralty under sections 7651–7681 of title 10, United States Code; review of orders of the Secretary of the Interior under section 2 of the Act entitled "An Act authorizing associations of producers of aquatic products" approved June 25, 1934 (15 U.S.C. 522); review of orders of petroleum control boards under section 5 of the Act entitled "An Act to regulate interstate and foreign commerce in petroleum and its products by prohibiting the shipment in such commerce of petroleum and its products produced in violation of State law, and for other purposes", approved February 22, 1935 (15 U.S.C. 715d); actions for fines, penalties, or forfeitures under part V of title IV of the Tariff Act of 1930 (19 U.S.C. 1581–1624), or under the Anti-Smuggling Act (19 U.S.C. 1701–1711); criminal libel for condemnation, exclusion of imports, or other proceedings under the Federal Food, Drug, and Cosmetic Act (21 U.S.C. 301–392); disputes between seamen under sections 4079, 4080, and 4081 of the Revised Statutes (22 U.S.C. 256–258); habeas corpus under sections 2241–2254 of title 28, United States Code; motions to vacate, set aside or correct sentence under section 2255 of title 28, United States Code; actions for penalties for refusal to transport destitute seamen under section 4578 of the Revised Statutes (46 U.S.C. 679);* actions against the United States under the Act entitled "An Act authorizing suits against the United States in admiralty for damage caused by and salvage service rendered to public vessels belonging to the United States, and for other purposes", approved March 3, 1925 (46 U.S.C. 781–790), as implemented by section 7730 of title 10, United States Code.

* Law Revision Counsel Note: Repealed and reenacted as 46 U.S.C. 11104(b)-(d) by Pub.L. 98–89, §§ 1, 2(a), 4(b), August 26, 1983, 97 Stat. 500.

[Amended by Pub.L. 94–149, § 1(14), December 12, 1975, 89 Stat. 806; Pub.L. 95–598, Title II, § 251, November 6, 1978, 92 Stat. 2673, effective October 1, 1979; Pub.L. 97–164, Title I, § 142, April 2, 1982, 96 Stat. 45, effective October 1, 1982; amended March 2, 1987, effective October 1, 1987; April 25, 1988, effective November 1, 1988; amended by Pub.L. 100–690, Title VII, § 7075(c)(1), November 18, 1988, 102 Stat. 4405 (although amendment by Pub.L. 100-690 could not be executed due to prior amendment by Court order which made the same change effective November 1, 1988; amended April 22, 1993, effective December 1, 1993.]

RULE 1102. AMENDMENTS

Amendments to the Federal Rules of Evidence may be made as provided in section 2072 of title 28 of the United States Code.

[Amended April 30, 1991, effective December 1, 1991.]

RULE 1103. TITLE

These rules may be known and cited as the Federal Rules of Evidence.

INDEX TO FEDERAL RULES OF EVIDENCE

GLOSSARY

acceptance In contract law, the consent to the terms of an offer.

acknowledged documents Documents signed in the presence of a notary public, where the signing party declares the act of signing as the party's own, and the notary public attaches a formal statement acknowledging the party's act.

actus reus The criminal act.

adjudicative facts Facts related to proving a cause of action.

adversarial system The system of resolving legal conflicts where each party is represented by an attorney who argues the client's position by presenting evidence with the intent to establish the legal rights of the client.

agent Someone authorized to act on behalf of another.

appellant The party who brings the matter to the reviewing court. At common law, the appellant was known as the *plaintiff in error*.

appellee The party who argues to the reviewing court against setting aside a judgment. At common law, the appellee was known as the *defendant in error*.

assumption of risk Knowingly and purposefully exposing oneself to harm; a defense to allegations of negligence.

attestation clause A written statement acknowledging the witnessing of the signing of a document as well as the signing of the statement.

authenticated specimen A writing opposing parties agree is in fact written by a particular person; usually done by stipulation.

authentication The introduction of evidence that proves a document or object is what it appears to be.

beyond a reasonable doubt Standard of proof in criminal cases that requires a high degree of quantity and quality of evidence to support a conviction.

briefs Written arguments prepared for an appeal, outlining the facts and legal arguments that are the basis for the appeal.

burden of going forward with the evidence Requirement that a party produce evidence on an issue or risk losing on that issue.

burden of persuasion Requirement that a party offer enough evidence to convince a jury the party should prevail.

burden of production Requirement that a party offer evidence to support a claim or defense.

burden of proof Includes the requirement that a party present evidence to support allegations or defenses (*burden of production*) as well as the need to provide enough evidence to convince the jury one party should prevail over the other (*burden of persuasion*).

burglary An unlawful entry coupled with the intent to commit a specific crime once inside the structure or vehicle.

capacity In contract law, the mental ability to enter into a contract.

case-in-chief The main body of evidence offered by a party; does not include rebuttal evidence.

certified copy Officially approved document.

chain of custody The written record that establishes the location of physical evidence from the time it is collected until the time it is offered as evidence at trial.

character Consistent behavior that reflects a person's disposition or nature.

circumstantial evidence Testimony or other evidence that requires the trier of fact to draw an inference in order to establish a fact.

civil action Cases involving persons or entities who desire to enforce a private right or to redress a private wrong.

clear and convincing evidence Standard of proof in some civil cases where the outcome involves social policy issues; requires a higher degree of quality evidence than *preponderance of the evidence.*

closing arguments After both sides have completed their cases, each side summarizes the evidence presented at trial and argues to the jury why the party should prevail based on the evidence and applicable law.

common law A system of law that originated in England and was adopted in America, based on the decisions of judges, which generally are followed in settling subsequent similar disputes.

competent witness A person legally qualified to testify at trial.

conditionally admit The judge decides to allow evidence to be used by the jury, subject to later evidence confirming its relevance.

conditional relevance Evidence not directly tied to a claim, charge, or defense is relevant only if subsequent testimony or tangible evidence ties the evidence to the claim, charge, or defense.

consideration In contract law, something of value given in return for a performance or promise to perform.

conspiracy A plan with an illegal purpose.

contract An agreement between parties where the law recognizes a duty and gives a remedy for a breach of duty.

copy Reproduction of an original that is an imitation and may not be exactly the same as the original.

credibility Trustworthiness.

criminal homicide The intentional killing of a person without legal justification, or the accidental killing of a person as a consequence of reckless or grossly negligent conduct.

cross-examination Questioning of an opposing party's witness during a trial.

declarant A person who makes a statement.

defamation False statements, made in writing or verbally, that injure a person's reputation, property, or business.

defendant In a civil case, the person or entity disputing the action initiated by a plaintiff. In a criminal case, it is the party who is the accused.

defenses Issues raised by a defendant that, if proven, preclude the plaintiff in a civil case from recovery, or the government in a criminal case from obtaining a conviction.

demonstrative evidence An object or thing that assists the jury's understanding of testimony.

detrimental evidence Proof in a case that harms the opponent's position.

direct evidence Testimony or physical objects offered by a party that allow a jury to conclude that a fact has been established without having to use inference.

direct examination Questioning of a witness by the party who called the witness to the stand to testify at trial.

directed verdict The judge tells the jury how to decide a case, or the judge makes the decision for the jury because a party has not met the burden of production.

discovery The pretrial process where the parties to litigation learn about information held by the opponent, which includes disclosure of facts, documents, and related matters. Discovery is governed by rules of procedure.

documentary evidence A document that has legal effect and is offered at a legal proceeding.

duplicate Reproduction of an original that is exactly the same as the original.

evidence Various forms of proof submitted to a trier of fact in court in order to support a party's claims or defenses in a lawsuit.

exhibit Something tangible used or offered into evidence at trial, in a deposition, or at a hearing.

exclusion Keeping witnesses out of the courtroom during a trial.

exculpatory evidence Evidence that tends to prove someone is free from blame.

expert witness A witness who possesses special knowledge, training, or experience and whose testimony at trial includes an opinion.

gift Property or money transferred without payment or expectation of benefit.

grand jury A group of people selected according to law to investigate and inform on crimes committed within its jurisdiction. The grand jury has the power to accuse persons of crimes (indict) when there is sufficient evidence to warrant holding a person for trial.

greater weight of the evidence Phrase used in some states instead of *preponderance of the evidence* to mean the same thing.

habit A person's regular response to a repeated specific situation.

harmless error A mistake as to a matter of law made by the judge at trial but that did not sufficiently prejudice the appellant to warrant a modification of the court's decision.

hearsay A statement by a witness of what someone else said out of court, offered as evidence of the truth of the statement.

hostile witness A witness who shows so much hostility to the calling party that the witness can be treated as if called by the opposing party.

impeach Demonstrate a witness is not telling the truth.

implied assertion Inference from a statement.

in camera In the judge's chambers, with spectators excluded from the hearing.

judgment A judicial determination of the rights of the parties before the court.

judgment of acquittal In a criminal case, the term sometimes used to describe a directed verdict when the government fails to present enough evidence to support its case against a defendant.

judicial notice The judge recognizes the existence of a fact without a party offering evidence to prove the fact, based on common knowledge or by reference to an indisputable source.

laying a foundation Presenting preliminary evidence needed to make other, more important evidence, relevant.

lay witness A nonprofessional witness whose testimony at trial includes an opinion.

leading questions Questions that suggest an answer; usually allowed only on cross-examination of a witness.

legal relevance Relevant evidence that does not violate a specific rule or law.

legally operative words Words that have significance as part of a transaction.

legislative facts Facts that are related to policy and legal reasoning and have wider application than to the proof of a particular cause of action.

libel Statements that are false and publically communicated, injuring a person's reputation, property, or business.

limiting instruction Direction by the judge to the jury on how it should use evidence in deciding a case.

logical relevance Evidence that relates to proving a cause of action and tends to prove an issue in a case.

manifest facts Facts that can be easily verified in an indisputable source.

matters of fact Also called *questions of fact,* these are the occurrence or nonoccurrence of an event, as determined by a trier of fact.

matters of law Also called *questions of law,* these are the disputed legal contentions raised by the parties during the litigation process, as determined by the judge.

mens rea The mental state necessary to the commission of a crime.

motion A request by a party to the judge for a ruling in favor of the moving party.

motion for directed verdict A request to the court for a verdict without consideration by a jury because the plaintiff fails to present a *prima facie* case or the defendant fails to present a necessary defense.

motion for judgment of acquittal A request by a defendant in a criminal case for the court to direct a verdict of not guilty without consideration by the jury, based on the failure of the prosecutor to prove every element of the charge.

motion in limine A request for a court order, often before trial, to exclude reference at trial to anticipated evidence because the evidence allegedly violates a rule of law or a rule of evidence or procedure.

negligence Failure to exercise the degree of care that a reasonable person would exercise under the same circumstances.

nolo contendere A plea of no contest by a defendant in a criminal case where the defendant does not admit guilt but agrees to some punishment.

notorious facts Facts that are common knowledge in the community where a court sits.

objection A procedure where a party asserts that the opponent's evidence is improper and that the judge should not allow the jury to have the evidence.

offer In contract law, where a party manifests a willingness to enter into a bargain with the intent of securing the assent of another party.

offer of proof A procedure where evidence is presented at trial outside the hearing of the jury in order to establish for the record the nature of the evidence the judge has ruled as inadmissible.

opening statement Explanation by attorneys, usually at the beginning of a trial, based on evidence that will be offered, of their version of what happened between the parties and how they think the law should be applied to the case.

opinion What a witness thinks about a person, based on the witness's knowledge of the person's character.

ordeal A ritual where disputes were settled with a person being subjected to some peril as a test, with the outcome regarded as the consequence of divine intervention.

order A direction or command issued by a judge on a matter related to a lawsuit.

original Not copied or derived.

per se In and of itself.

petit jury Trial jury, which determines matters of fact in civil and criminal cases and renders a verdict.

plain error A mistake as to a matter of law by the trial court judge that substantially affects the rights of the appellant and, even though it was not objected to at trial, warrants a reversal of a verdict; also called *fundamental error.*

plaintiff The person or entity initiating a civil action.

preliminary questions Matters that must be determined before certain evidence is admissible.

preponderance of the evidence Standard of proof in most civil cases that requires enough evidence to tip the scales in favor of one of the parties.

presumption An allowable conclusion based on proof of underlying facts.

pretrial conference A meeting with the trial judge and the parties to a lawsuit before the trial begins. Its purpose is to define the matters at issue and in need of resolution at trial.

prima facie **case** A party presents enough evidence to meet the legal requirements of a cause of action, so the party can prevail unless the opposing party contradicts the evidence or presents a cogent defense.

privilege A right enjoyed by a party when a communication is within a relationship that is recognized by the law as confidential, allowing the speaker to shield the communication from disclosure.

pro se A person handles the person's own case in court without an attorney.

quid pro quo The exchange of one valuable thing for another.

real evidence An object produced at trial for inspection by the jury.

rebuttal evidence Proof offered by a party to contradict evidence offered by the opposing party.

redirect examination Questioning of a witness by the party calling the witness after the witness has been cross-examined.

remand To send a case back to the court below for action consistent with the appellate court's opinion.

remedy In a civil action, that which redresses a wrong or enforces a right.

representative capacity Standing in the place of someone else.

reputation What people in a community think about a person.

reversible error A mistake made by a judge as to a matter of law that substantially affects the rights of one of the parties during trial.

routine practice A business's regular response to a repeated specific situation.

Rule 104(a) determination The deciding by a judge of preliminary questions using underlying facts to decide whether evidence will be heard by the jury.

Rule 403 balancing test Is the evidence more prejudicial than probative—that is, more unfair than helpful to the jury in its determination of a case?

sequestration of witnesses Keeping witnesses out of the courtroom during trial.

sidebar A conference at the bench with a court reporter present, with the parties arguing a evidentiary matter outside the hearing of the jury.

standard of proof The measure of proof required to prevail in a case.

sua sponte The judge acts on his or her own, without the parties making a request.

substantive evidence Evidence used as proof of facts.

tangible evidence Nontestimonial evidence that can be touched or perceived by the senses; real evidence.

testimonial evidence Statements by witnesses under oath at a legal proceeding.

transcript An official written copy of legal proceedings, usually prepared by a court reporter.

trial process The actions taken to prepare for trial, and the trial itself, for the purpose of determining and enforcing legal rights of the opposing parties.

trier of fact In a trial, the person or group of persons with the responsibility of deciding which party should prevail; the jury in a jury trial and the judge in a nonjury trial.

verbal acts Words that have legal significance as part of a transaction.

verdict The opinion of the trier of fact as to who should prevail at trial.

voir dire The questioning of prospective jurors to determine if they are suitable to decide a case.

weight of the evidence The more convincing evidence offered at trial, as determined by the jury.

witness A person who takes an oath and whose testimony is evidence.